AXEL MADSEN

HENRY HOLT AND COMPANY
NEW YORK

CHANEL

CHANEL

A Woman of Her Own

Library of Congress Cataloging-in-Publication Data
Madsen, Axel.
Chanel : a woman of her own / Axel Madsen.—1st ed.
p. cm.
Includes bibliographical references.
ISBN 0-8050-0961-2
1. Chanel, Coco, 1883–1971. 2. Women costume designers—France—Biography.
3. Costume designers—France—Biography. I. Title.
TT505.C45M33   1990   89-24692
746.9′2′092—dc20   CIP
[B]

Henry Holt books are available at special discounts
for bulk purchases for sales promotions, premiums,
fund-raising, or educational use. Special editions
or book excerpts can also be created to specification.
For details contact: Special Sales Director, Henry Holt and Company, Inc.,
115 West 18th Street, New York, New York 10011.

First Edition

BOOK DESIGN BY CLAIRE M. NAYLON

Printed in the United States of America
Recognizing the importance of preserving the written word, Henry Holt and Company,
Inc., by policy, prints all of its first editions on acid-free paper. ∞

1   3   5   7   9   10   8   6   4   2

Grateful acknowledgment is made for permission to reprint from the following:
L'Allure de Chanel, by Paul Morand, copyright © 1976 by Hermann
Les Années Chanel, by Pierre Galante, copyright © 1972 by Mercure de France
Chanel, by Edmonde Charles-Roux, copyright © 1975 by Alfred A. Knopf, Inc.
Chanel solitaire, by Claude Baillén, copyright © 1971 by Editions Gallimard
Coco Chanel, by Marcel Haedrich, copyright © 1987 by Belfond
"L'Homme de la nuit," by Pierre Reverdy, copyright © 1949, reprinted with
permission of Mercure de France
Misia: The Life of Misia Sert, by Arthur Gold and Robert Fizdale, copyright © 1979 by
Arthur Gold and Robert Fizdale, reprinted with permission of Alfred A. Knopf, Inc.

*"I've a right to think," said Alice, for
she was beginning to feel a little worried.
"Just as much right," said the Duchess, "as pigs have to fly."*

—Lewis Carroll

Contents

ONE

TWO

THREE

FOUR

List of Illustrations

Acknowledgments

I could not thank all the people who took time to help me prepare this biography—and not all would want their names to appear. Let me thank at least:

In Paris and Cannes: Jacques Chazot, Thomas Quinn Curtis, Raymond Duparc, Alain LeGrignou, Leon Levine, François Mironnet, Sophie de Vilmorin, and, for an overview and sense of history, Yvonne Deslandres.

In Geneva, Zurich, and Munich: Jeanne-Marie Herter, Gjoko Ruzic, and Peter Gehrig.

In New York: Channa Taub, Horst, Alain Wertheimer, Suzanne Semilof, Debra Sherline, and the staff at Condé Nast's in-house library.

In Chicago and Los Angeles: Jane Jordan Browne, Margot Greenberg, and Michael Hargraves.

One

1

A FAMILY
TO DISAVOW

S he made up things.

   Gabrielle Chanel—Coco to a few intimates and a hundred million women—came from nothing. She reinvented her childhood, describing nasty aunts who pulled her ears and humiliated her. After she became rich, she paid off her brothers to pretend they didn't exist.

She was the illegitimate daughter of itinerant market traders. Her mother died when she was twelve, her father disappeared, and she was brought up a charity ward in a nuns' orphanage. Deep in her veins ran the fear of being discovered a bastard. Although her parents married shortly after she was born, she could never live with the truth and spent her adult years perpetually revising her life story. She went to her grave as Gabrielle Chasnel because to correct legally the misspelled name on her birth certificate would reveal that she was born in a poorhouse hospice.

Throughout her life she would make up an interesting, if not consistent, romance about her own existence with a good deal of color and detail. She made her wastrel father into a refined horse trader, denied she had brothers and sisters, and pretended not to remember people she had known intimately as well as benefactors and clients who had been the backbone of her early success. The fabrications—possibilities, really, in her own mind—sustained her self-esteem, and she defended her stories with noble desperation. Her name came to mean emancipation and casual feminine allure, but when she became famous and everything was known about her—her income, love affairs, tastes, successes, and sorrows—she kept telling lies.

She spent a lifetime breaking with people who knew those odds and ends of her story that did not coincide with the legend she wanted to create. She distorted and exaggerated to her friends, to the reporters who interviewed her, and to the writers she asked to help prepare her memoirs. At one point in her life, Chanel engaged Louise de Vilmorin, the author of elegantly witty and mannered novels, to write her life story. However, when she read Vilmorin's notes of their previous conversation, Coco exclaimed, "But this is a novel!"

When in old age a young woman suggested she see a psychiatrist, Chanel looked dismayed—"I, who never told the truth to my priest?"

Her father was Albert Chanel, a twenty-seven-year-old trader in wine, bonnets, buttons, overalls, and kitchen aprons; her mother was nineteen-year-old Jeanne Devolle. Albert was not around that August 19, 1883, when Gabrielle was born in the poorhouse in Saumur, a garrison and market town on the Loire River. The birth was recorded the next afternoon. Two employees of the hospice went to city hall and declared a child of feminine gender had been born the previous afternoon at four, to Albert Chanel and Jeanne Devolle, "a married couple." No papers were presented.

It was not the first time hospice employees had done this, and deputy mayor François Poitou dutifully wrote it all down in his big round handwriting. No one knew how to spell Chanel, so Poitou improvised and the family name was recorded with an *s*, Chasnel. The two hospice employees were illiterates. The last line of the registration said they had not signed the certificate because, in the standard phrase, they *declare not to know how.*

Gabrielle was not Jeanne Devolle's first child. When Jeanne was seventeen, Albert had visited her native village of Courpière just long enough to father her first child, Julie.

Albert's family came from Ponteils, a village in the dark hills of the Cévennes, where, across from the church, they had been tavernkeepers from father to son since the mid-eighteenth century. The Chanel name appears often in the village records, since the tavernkeeper did witness duty at baptisms, weddings, and burials, strolling across the village square to scrawl the six letters of his name at the bottom of documents. Henri-Adrien, Albert's father, was the first of the Chanels to become a wayfaring peddler.

It is not known why Henri-Adrien did not become a tavernkeeper like his father before him, but we do know that at twenty-two he left Ponteils, unskilled and penniless, and after eight months of looking for work found a job as a laborer at a silkworm farm. The farmer had a sixteen-year-old daughter, Virginie Fournier. Henri-Adrien seduced her, and when her pregnancy could no longer be hidden, married her in the presence of his parents, who came down from the hills to stand by their boy. Once the couple had married, the Fourniers threw out their daughter and the author of her misfortune.

With his child bride, Henri-Adrien took to the road, to become a fairground and marketplace hawker. Albert was born in Nîmes, at the poorhouse hospice, in 1856. His father was "traveling." Three hospital employees registered the infant's birth. The family name was written Charnet.

Henri-Adrien returned to Nîmes just long enough to pick up his wife and newborn son before he and his family set off on the road again. Albert's siblings, like Albert himself, were born wherever the family happened to be laying over, always at the public hospital. As the years passed, Henri-Adrien and Virginie continued on the road but took to spending the winters in Clermont-Ferrand, the bustling capital of the ancient province of Auvergne.

Like his father, Albert left home and took to the road; in 1881 he stopped off in the village of Courpière. He rented a room from Marin Devolle and, perhaps to impress his landlord about his intention to stay, went to the town hall and had himself put on the electoral list.

As family lore had it, Albert could charm the birds from the trees. He knew how to prattle with village girls, and he cast his spell over them all—especially his landlord's sister, Jeanne Devolle. She and Marin had lost their mother when they were children, their father when they were in their teens. Though Marin and Jeanne Devolle were orphans, they were far from destitute. Marin had inherited his father's carpenter shop; Jeanne was going to be a seamstress like her mother. One night Albert arranged a rendezvous with her. In January 1882, he vanished, leaving Jeanne pregnant.

Eventually, Marin tracked down Albert's family in Clermont-Ferrand, and from them learned that Albert was in a town called Aubenas. Nine months pregnant, Jeanne set out alone for Aubenas, almost two hundred kilometers down the Allier Valley and across the Cévennes. She found Albert in the local tavern. He had a room at the tavern and transacted his business there. There, Julie was born on September 11, 1882. Business was bad, Albert told Jeanne. At her insistence, he agreed to recognize the child but refused to get married. Yet he must have consented to pretend they were married, for Julie Chanel was declared the child of a wedded couple.

It was Albert's ambition to be a wine merchant. Together, Albert and Jeanne headed to Saumur, the garrison town way up in the wine district in the Loire Valley. In Saumur they found a garret in the ramshackle part of town a few minutes from the Place de la Bilange, the better of Saumur's two open markets where the local gentry did its shopping. Before Julie was three months old, Jeanne was pregnant again.

In Coco Chanel's own retelling of the circumstances of her birth, her coming into the world in Saumur's hospice was the result of a misunderstanding. "My father wasn't there. The poor woman who was my mother was on her way to join him. I won't tell this somber story because it's terribly boring, but my mother suddenly felt faint. With the fashion of the day it was hard to see that the woman was going to have a baby, so some very nice people brought her home with them.

"'I have to find my husband,' my mother said.

"'You will leave tomorrow,' they told her.

"They called a doctor, who said, 'This lady isn't sick; she's having a baby.'

"Angrily, these charming people tossed my mother out in the street. She was taken to the hospital where I was born. At hospitals, they christen you right away. They gave me the name of the nun who took care of my mother. Her name was Gabrielle Bonheur."

Gabrielle Chanel offered a different version of the event to André-Louis Dubois, a fabric wholesaler who would remain a lifelong friend. She said her mother went into labor while en route to Saumur and that she had given birth to her in a train compartment.

Because the name had been chosen by the hospital and not by her family, she would disavow Gabrielle on many occasions.

Julie was two and Gabrielle a year old when Albert Chanel and Eugénie Jeanne Devolle got married on November 17, 1884. Their prenuptial agreement stipulated that besides a 5,000-franc dowry*, Jeanne was bringing to the marriage furniture and personal objects valued at 500 francs, and that both she and Albert willed their joint assets to whoever survived the other. In marrying Jeanne, Albert legalized his paternity and the girls' names were recorded in the *livret de famille*, the handbook issued to every couple for registration of births and deaths.

Marriage did not change life. Jeanne was soon pregnant again. With his family in tow, Albert remained a migrant market merchant. His territory was the markets and fairs of the Massif Central, the Auvergne region of mountains and limestone plateaus and deep gorges in south central France. Albert preferred market towns lucky enough to lie in the path of the railway because such centers saw commerce flourish and industry spring up.

Issoire was one such town, and it was located close to the region both Albert and Jeanne knew best. Surrounded by rich countryside, Issoire was on the Paris-Lyon-Méditerranée railway line, forty-eight kilometers south of Clermont-Ferrand. A big central market was held every day in the shadow of the twelfth-century St. Austremoine Church.

Albert left his family in a one-room house he found in Issoire's Rue du Perrier while he made sorties to other towns or villages that fanned out from the railhead.

The Chanels moved several times but always lived in poor dwellings in Issoire's damp, narrow streets along a towpath where a few horses pulled barges to the last river mill still in service. In more vibrant parts of France, the industrial revolution was making steam churn engines and gas light up streets and houses. The neighborhoods where the Chanels lived belonged to the dying crafts—ropemakers, nailsmiths, potters and hemp weavers and chandlers. Albert bought his millinery stock from the hatters in their street.

A boy, Alphonse, was born March 15, 1885. Albert continued his errant life. Gabrielle would tell of a mistress her father had who bore him a son of about her own age, a half brother she never met. There is no evidence that Jeanne knew about her husband's womanizing and his swagger, but the family lore depicted him as always embroidering on his fortune, claiming his family owned land and vineyards.

---

*The turn-of-the-century dollar was worth five period francs, meaning Jeanne Devolle's $1,000 dowry equals $14,750 in 1990 currency. (Source: Federal Reserve Bank)

Jeanne suffered from a condition that took her breath away and racked her with attacks of suffocation. Eternally pregnant, often on the move, she grew thin and sunken-eyed. When her uncle Augustin saw her, her sallow looks and interminable coughs reminded him of the disease that had carried off her mother, his sister Gilberte. Maybe Jeanne should return to live in Courpière. The air was pure there.

In 1887, Jeanne gave birth to a girl. The family was on the road again, and the baby was born in Saintes, the market town where Cognac's famous brandy was traded. Jeanne and Albert, or somebody at the hospice, named her Antoinette. She was to be Gabrielle's favorite sister.

Jeanne's health deteriorated, and she decided to return to her hometown, with her four kids and, for a time, her husband. They lived in her uncle Augustin's house. Albert was soon off again.

The time in Courpière was the best years in the children's marginal childhoods. Jeanne was never sure Albert would return, so she continued to go "on the road" with him. She entrusted the children to the care of her abundant family, and, in rain or shine, rode with her husband in the buggy and stood behind her own stand at a hundred town markets.

Julie grew up slow-witted and afraid of everything. Gabrielle preferred playing with her brother Alphonse. But she often played alone. Among Gabrielle's earliest memories was playing in an old churchyard with graves full of weeds. She thought of the cemetery as a secret garden and of herself as the queen and defender of its subterranean inhabitants. "I told myself that the dead are not really dead as long as people think about them." To Carmen Tessier, a *France-Soir* gossip columnist, she said she had *her* tombs, *her* dead, that her family tried to lure her away from the cemetery by telling her that none of her next-of-kin was buried there. "That didn't bother me. I brought flowers, and forks and spoons and whatever else I could steal at home, and spread out my loot around the graves. One day, my family discovered the stuff that was missing. They locked everything up and since I could no longer bring things to my dead, I forgot about them."

In other retellings, she brought her rag dolls to the churchyard and talked to her dead. Her own explanation for her childhood need to confide in the dead was that she was unloved. "Because I lived with people who were insensitive, I wanted to be sure that I was loved. I liked to talk to myself and I didn't do what I was told. That, no doubt, comes from the fact that the first beings to whom I opened my heart were dead people."

When she was an old woman, living alone and convinced that the people who surrounded her were only out for her money, journalists caught her in cemeteries talking to the dead.

In 1889 when Julie was seven, Gabrielle six, Alphonse four, and Antoinette two, their mother gave birth to another boy at the tavern in Guéret, a market town northeast of Limoges. They called him Lucien.

By the time Gabrielle was eleven, the life on the road, poverty, and constant pregnancies—another son named Augustin for Jeanne's uncle in Courpière died in infancy—had ruined Jeanne's health. She was in Brive-la-Gaillarde, a market town halfway between Clermont-Ferrand and Bordeaux, when she fainted from shortness of breath and high fever. She was not well enough to leave the freezing room she was left in. One winter morning in February 1895, she was found dead. Her husband was "traveling." She was thirty-two.

2

ORPHANS, FOUNDLINGS, AND ILLEGITIMATES

A lbert Chanel disappeared for good. Julie, Gabrielle, and Antoinette spent the better part of the next six years at an orphanage at Aubazine near Brive-la-Gaillarde. No one in the family would take Alphonse and little Lucien either, and the boys were "placed" in a farm household, to become unpaid child labor from the age of eight.

Of the periods of Chanel's life, the years at Aubazine, the orphanage run by the sisters of the Congregation of the Sacred Heart of Mary, were to remain the most obscure. The word *orphanage* would never cross her lips, and when it came to writing her memoirs, she talked only of being thrown into a new life with several aunts and unnamed first cousins of her mother. A shortage of men, which she did not explain, had left all the aunts old maids. In her descriptions the aunts had neither names nor physical traits, but they were always dressed in black or gray, had dry hands, cold eyes, and black shawls wrapped over their chests. The "aunts," she would insist, did not like her. "People have said I cried when I was at my aunts' because they called me Gabrielle. I wasn't easy to handle."

To author-diplomat Paul Morand she described what happened when her father dropped her off at her aunts. "My aunts had already had dinner; we had not," she would say. "They were surprised that people who had traveled all day had not had anything to eat. That disturbed their program and their frugality, but they finally overcame their stark provincial rigidity and regretfully said, 'We will make you two soft-boiled eggs.' " Continuing her story in the third person, she said, "The little Coco guessed their loathing and feels hurt. She's dying of hunger, but at the sight of the eggs, she shook her head, and loudly said she didn't like eggs, that she hates them when in reality she loves soft-boiled eggs. After this first contact she needed to say no to everything that was offered to her, to the aunts, to everything that surrounds her, to a new life."

Gabrielle sometimes turned the loveless years with the "aunts" into inner strength: "I've been ungrateful toward the odious aunts. I owe them everything. A child in revolt becomes a person with armor and strength. It's the kisses, caresses, teachers and vitamins that kill children and turn them into unhappy or sickly adults. It's the mean and nasty aunts who create winners, and give them inferiority complexes, although in my case the result was a superiority complex. Under nastiness looms strength, under pride a taste for success and a passion for grandeur." In interpreting Chanel's accounts of her life with the aunts, more than one of her would-be biographers mentally substituted "nuns" for "aunts."

To confuse matters there *was* one aunt who took an interest in her—her father's sister, Louise Costier. Louise had been the first of the Chanels to marry a man who worked in an office. Paul Costier was a railway employee in Clermont-Ferrand, the central switching yard of the new Paris-Lyon-Méditerranée railroad. Gabrielle, along with her family, attended Louise's wedding.

By the time Gabrielle's mother died, Uncle Paul had been promoted to stationmaster and he and Louise were living in Varennes-sur-Allier, the midway station on the Vichy-to-Moulins line. Varennes was not much of a town, though the yellow brick station did serve to bolster the importance of Uncle Paul.

Paul and Louise had no children, but he believed that for a woman to work was a disgrace. To busy herself, Louise sewed and made hats for herself. Paul vetoed the idea of her orphaned nieces and nephews coming to live with them.

It was Grandma Virginie who placed the girls at Aubazine. Virginie had once taken in washing from the nuns in Moulins and a mother superior told her to contact the orphanage in Aubazine.

Gabrielle would assert that her father came to see her after one year, lied to her, and told her he'd come back and take her away from the "aunts," that they would be a family again and have a house together. In reality she never saw him again. She would claim she bore no grudge against him, saying she knew she could expect nothing from him. To hold her head high, however, she told classmates her father was seeking his fortune in America and would come and fetch her when he was rich.

To be a waif humiliated her. The century of Dickens and Zola, so cruel toward orphans, foundlings, cripples, and illegitimates, was drawing to a close, but the full weight of public opprobrium still crushed destitute children. The orphanage sheltered two kinds of orphans, girls who had next-of-kin who could pay something, and girls with indigent relatives or totally bereft of family. At Aubazine, Gabrielle insisted she had a father, that he was sending money. But along with the other destitute children, the Chanel girls slept in an unheated dormitory and had their meals at separate tables.

Late in life, when Coco Chanel told people she was six, not eleven, when her mother died, when she dropped Julie and the brothers from her story and turned her father into a not-yet-thirty-year-old widower, her attitude toward him and what had happened to her was equivocal. "He had a chance to remake his life, and he got himself a new family," she would say. "Why should he worry about his two daughters? He knew they were in good hands and that they were being given an education. He didn't give a damn. He had other kids. I would have done the same thing. I don't think that before thirty anyone can stay faithful to things like that."

She hated to hear her relatives refer to her mother as "Poor Jeanne." The Devolles were all consumptive and none of them lived to be forty, she would say, though it is likely that the condition her mother died of was not consumption, with all its romantic connotations. When Gabrielle was twenty and upset about someone's death, a friend of hers would remember her snapping, "Don't tell me what I'm feeling. Since my earliest childhood I've been certain that they've taken everything away from me, that I'm dead. I knew that when I was twelve. You *can* die more than once in your life."

Aubazine was a bleak place. Perched on a plateau high above the Corrèze River and surrounded by wooded hills, the orphanage, with its steep-
pitched roof, high walls, and enclosed courtyard, stood between the
former abbey and the ruins of a medieval cloister. Church and convent
had been built in the golden age of monasteries by Etienne d'Aubazine,
or Etienne of Limousin. This twelfth-century monk, a coarser St. Francis
of Assisi, was revered as part hermit, part madman. With a handful of
barefoot, unwashed, and mendicant wanderers, Etienne added stone to
stone until a monastery stood on the edge of the Corrèze overlooking the
gorges of the Coiroux. With vows of silence and solitude, the monks lived
out their lives in sackcloth. The penitent Etienne found himself unworthy
of anything but the most repellent tasks, such as carrying away his brothers' excrement and cleaning the cesspool. He saw to it, however, that a
cloister for women was built deep in one of the Coiroux gorges, and an
earthy saying had it that "Whoever has daughter at Coiroux has son-in-
law in Aubazine." This less than reverent adage, however, did not figure
in the *Life of Etienne d'Aubazine* that, with the approval of the bishop of
nearby Tulle, was read during the orphans' walks and at mealtimes.

Free, compulsory, secular education was the cornerstone of the restored French Republic of 1870. The tradition of hostility between church
and republic led to the disbanding of Jesuits in 1880, and to the law of
October 30, 1886, that abolished all distinctively religious teaching. In
boys' schools, members of religious communities were displaced within
five years, but in girls' schools the *religieuses* were allowed to remain until
death or resignation. Aubazine was very much an institution in transition
during the years Gabrielle spent there. The fifteen-member teaching staff
was about evenly divided between older nuns and younger lay teachers.
Yet it was still a world of naked stone and black and white.

Before the government reforms, the only secondary education open
for girls had been in convents and in a few expensive private schools.
Now, the government mandated that girls spend five years in school; for
boys, seven years were compulsory. Semisecularized orphanages like Aubazine did not strive to teach a great deal but rather to teach a few things
well. Lessons were taught by rote—whether it was the three R's, the
names of France's eighty-six *départements*, or the kings of France since
Dagobert.

Aubazine was no Cluny or Cîteaux, Burgundian monastic communities of Romanesque beauty; it was only mass and volume of rock. The orphans wore white blouses, washed and washed again, and black skirts. The corridors and walls were whitewashed, the doors to the dormitories, where once the penitent monks had slept, were painted black. School was taught six days a week, and evenings were filled with household tasks. The girls were not bent over dainty needlepoint but were taught to hem sheets and knit baby clothes, and those who were awkward, clumsy, and untalented with their hands were reproved. Sunday mornings were spent at Mass, but on sunny Sunday afternoons, one of the teachers would take the girls on a hike to the summit of the Coiroux.

Gabrielle would never refer to the years behind the high walls at Aubazine. When she was in her eighties, she told Claude Baillén, a young woman psychiatrist who became a friend and after Chanel's death wrote a book about her, that there were no mirrors at the "aunts'," that to reach a tiny looking glass she had to climb up on pieces of furniture.

Gabrielle never spoke ill of convent orders. After the initial shock of being left at Aubazine, she might have found a vague affection for the place and the women who had given her sanctuary. As Edmonde Charles-Roux, a French *Vogue* editor who wrote a biography of Chanel, speculated, "Whenever she began yearning for austerity, for the ultimate in cleanliness, for faces scrubbed with yellow soap; or waxed nostalgic for all things white, simple, and clean, for linen piled in high cupboards, white-washed walls, . . . one had to understand that she was speaking in a secret code, and that every word she uttered meant only one word, Aubazine."

Every Christmas she received five francs from Grandpa Henri-Adrien. She loved menthol drops and bought a box for one franc. The remaining four francs went into her piggy bank. She was furious when she was told to contribute the contents of her bank to hungry children in China.

As Chanel later described herself, she was a fierce little thing, pretty and restless. She knew she was different from the others and felt herself a victim of injustice. She said no to everything, because people either irritated or wounded her, because she wanted to be loved. She both detested and adored the nuns, hated them because she was sure they believed love was a luxury and childhood a sin, loved them for their well-stocked orderliness. She hated to kneel, to bow her head, to submit. She pretended not to understand a word of catechism.

"I was a pest, a thief, someone who listens at doors," she would tell

Morand with ferocious candor in 1946. "Today, like back then, arrogance is in everything I do. It is in my gestures, the harshness of my voice, in the glow of my gaze, in my sinewy, tormented face, in my whole person."

The girls spent the school holidays with their grandparents. Henri-Adrien and Virginie had given up tramping from fair to fair and were living in Moulins; on market days they had their stall at the covered *halles.* What Gabrielle liked best about visiting Henri-Adrien and Virginie was being with Adrienne, their youngest daughter, Gabrielle's aunt, who was Gabrielle's age. When Gabrielle came to visit, she and Adrienne were inseparable. They looked like sisters and let people believe they were. They had in common an innate sense of elegance. They shared a garret bedroom and talked all night, rivals and best friends. Adrienne, who was growing up to be a great beauty, was serene, hopeful, and possessed of a trust in life that was painfully lacking in her niece. Gabrielle was resourceful and creative, dizzy with longing for the future. She was convinced life was *something else.*

As for Gabrielle's real sisters, it seemed fate had cast them in inferior roles. Julie was passive and her mental abilities below average; Antoinette frail and insecure. Both knew they could not compete with the dazzling Gabrielle and Adrienne. Adrienne's old parents doted on her, and she was also the favorite of Louise, her sister who was nineteen years her senior. In many ways, Louise and her stationmaster husband were the true epicenter of the family. Varennes-sur-Allier was only twenty-five kilometers from Moulins and the railway supplied the Costiers with a house surrounded by a plot of land that Louise turned into a bountiful garden. Paul was warming up to his in-laws to the point that he allowed them to use the perquisite of a stationmaster—to have his family travel free in second class (during a period when trains still had a third class).

It was Louise who got the brothers off the farms when they were thirteen, and with the grandparents' help, placed Alphonse and Lucien in apprenticeship with market retailers in Moulins. They would have their father's and grandfather's trade. Alphonse would one day tell his children, "I was put on the road at thirteen."

Louise inspired the girls. The orphanage had taught Gabrielle to sew, dutifully; Louise showed her how to do it with imagination. Louise knew not only how to sew straight pleats and make fringes, but also how to embellish a blouse, how to use remnants for collars. In the stationmaster's kitchen, aunt, young sister, and niece stitched elegant tablecloths and sheets. Louise made trips to Vichy, the fashionable resort town fifteen kilometers south of Varennes, to choose her hats. When she came home from her shopping expeditions, she summoned Gabrielle and Adrienne to show them her newest bonnet, which she would trim with notions of her own.

When Gabrielle visited Aunt Louise and Uncle Paul, she read the novels of Gyp and of Pierre Decourcelle, romances that were serialized in provincial newspapers, and in modest households often cut out, assembled, and passed around. Under the pseudonym Gyp, Sybille de Mirabeau, Countess of Martel, wrote amusing and clever society novels whose heroines were young women with a flair for being bold yet graceful, free yet modest. Decourcelle's pop fiction described in lush detail what his heroines wore—mauve dresses over white petticoats were a favorite—often set off in interiors of upholstered splendor. Gabrielle would remember the description of a purple dress worn by the female protagonist in a Decourcelle novel that inspired her to ask for permission to have a dress made for herself. Whether this took place at her grandmother's or at Louise's she didn't say, but the seamstress was told to make a robe according to Gabrielle's wishes.

In retelling the story to Morand, Gabrielle wondered whether repressed narcissism or glamorized conceit was what motivated the local seamstress. The woman rarely spoke, but she knew how to make the most amazing clothes and dressed herself in extraordinary gowns with trains that she held above the ground with a kind of drapery or sugar pincers in the form of a hand. Gabrielle thought the imitation hand was the height of refinement and vowed she would one day have a gown with a train. The dress the seamstress made for Gabrielle was mauve and gave her airs. "It had a high neck with flying ribbons and matching slip, purple, and underneath a ruffle. I was perhaps fifteen or sixteen, although I looked twelve. I chose a clinging linen, not that I had anything to mold or underline."

Gabrielle decided to make her debut one Sunday morning. She got dressed and appeared at the top of the stairs. Without quite looking, grandmother or aunt told her to hurry downstairs or she would be late for mass. When the women realized what the girl had done, Gabrielle was ordered out of the outfit and into proper clothes. The drama ended in tears, with the dress being returned to the seamstress, who was told she would never again work for the household.

"The woman was angry at me, but I told her again that my aunts had agreed to everything," Gabrielle would recall. After that, Gabrielle was afraid of running into the seamstress in the street.

There was to be a later version of the story. In the 1970s, Chanel told her young admirer Baillén that the famous mauve dress was a communion gift from her father in America, that the quilted and laced robe was obviously more appropriate for a prostitute than an adolescent convent girl.

Though she knew the Decourcelle romances were forbidden at Aubazine, Gabrielle took them back with her to the orphanage and hid them in the attic. The huge loft became her library. Since the "books" were assembled newspaper clippings, she slipped pages into her notebooks and, in a creative writing test, copied entire excerpts. That proved her undoing. After the teacher read her essay, Gabrielle had to own up to her confidential collection of women's romances.

She turned seventeen in 1900, and began her last year at Aubazine. After eighteen, the nuns kept only those girls who aspired to the novitiate.

When she came to Varennes that summer, Adrienne was there. The normally cheerful Adrienne was in a despondent mood. The notary in town wanted to marry her. She didn't like him. He was old.

A county fair came to town, with fairground booths, organ grinders, and merry-go-round. A candy seller hired Gabrielle and Adrienne to tend his stand on a percentage basis while he took his wife to the hospital. The two girls were popular, the stock of bonbons and caramel fudge soon sold out. When they counted their earnings, they realized they had enough money to take the train to Paris. Adrienne had someone to see in Paris, someone who would save her from the old notary.

They sneaked out of Uncle Paul's house at night, got to Moulins, where no one at the station knew them. Adrienne was in charge of the money and bought two second-class tickets. Once on the train, Gabrielle said, "Let's travel first class."

The conductor was not amused when he found them in a first-class compartment with second-class tickets. On top of the surcharge, the conductor added a fine.

Gabrielle would never forget the conductor who left them practically penniless. When interviewers asked what happened once she and Adrienne got to Paris and how they got back, she changed the subject, saying only that friends of the family lodged them. Adrienne would remember that after a few days they obediently returned to Varennes, that she didn't have to marry the notary, and that Gabrielle didn't return to the orphanage.

3

COCO

With Julie and Gabrielle too old to return to Aubazine, their grandmother found, with the help of the nuns, an institution in Moulins suitable for them, and, a year later, Antoinette joined them there. The Notre Dame *pensionnat* was a finishing school for young ladies, an establishment where future wives of officers and gentlemen were taught how to run a household. Since Grandma Virginie could not pay the tuition, the Chanel girls were taken in as charity cases, who would work for their keep by taking part in the "downstairs" duties.

"Nobody can live with low horizons," Gabrielle would say late in life. "A narrow outlook will choke you. All I had when I left my Auvergne was a summer dress in glossy, wiry, black woolen fabric with cotton warp and, for winter a suit in Scottish tweed and a sheepskin, but my mind was full of fabulations.

"You have no idea what damages provincial attics can cause to young minds. I had one teacher, a dud of an author of maudlin novels, Decourcelle."

Whatever fantasies and longings she had, she kept them to herself. She might fantasize herself the lady in white in Decourcelle's *Ace of Clubs*, but in the company of strangers, she learned to be a model of poise and reticence. People described her eyes as ebony black. She preferred to think of them as sable, spangled with gold and with glints of purple and green. Her neck was extraordinarily long, her silhouette slim, and she sensed that men, however fleetingly she came in contact with them, were interested in her.

Young girls never went out alone, especially not young women left in the care of teaching nuns. But as the escapade to Paris showed, Gabrielle and her aunt knew how to land on their feet, emancipated, in a sense, by their poverty.

The outings that the nuns at Notre Dame permitted were few. When they did occur, they were dedicated to Catholic piety and the girls were well chaperoned. Moulins had a rich Protestant past. A hundred years after it reached its height of splendor under Pierre de Bourbon and his cunning wife, Anne of France, an act of justice and religious tolerance was issued in the town in 1566. When Gabrielle attended Notre Dame, however, its Roman Catholic bishop was bringing pomp and circumstance back to Catholic observances.

Monsignor de Dreux-Brézé's high mass was invested with greater ecclesiastic pageantry and lasted longer than any other in France. Every Sunday the school attended—nuns and paying young ladies sitting in center pews near the children of army officers, the charity cases sitting in side aisles. With young Catholics from other parishes, the Notre Dame girls, the youngest dressed as angels and all carrying tall, unlit tapers, marched in the annual Corpus Christi procession. The processions halted at various wayside crucifixes and at temporary altars set up outside some of the military garrisons. The year Gabrielle took part, cavalry officers planted tapers in the barrels of their guns and stood in frozen attention with crossed sabers.

The Moulins chamber of commerce liked to stress the town's cabinet and furniture manufacturing, millinery, and vinegar production, and to mention the cathedral and the fourteenth-century square tower, part of the ancient castle of the dukes of Bourbon. The fact was, however, that Moulins was dedicated to the martial arts.

France's defeat in the Franco-Prussian War in 1870 and the controversy of the Dreyfus Affair in the 1890s had resulted in a sharp alignment of political and social forces, with conservative nationalists on one side and left-wing antimilitarists on the other. While the country remained deeply divided over whether Captain Alfred Dreyfus was guilty—he would not be completely exonerated until 1906—the armed forces drew their support from the traditional right and the Church. The military might be popular in garrison towns like Moulins, but to many Frenchmen the armed forces appeared as a state within the state led by a caste of career officers unwilling to accept modern ideas. Led by the Socialist Jean Jaurès, progressives in the National Assembly had reduced the draft from five to three years in 1899. Jaurès and his followers, who wanted to replace France's garrison army with a Swiss-style home reserve, still considered the period of service to be too long.

Moulins was home to several regiments, but the Tenth Light Horse overshadowed all the others. Bluebloods served in the 10e Chasseurs. A list of its members read like a roll call at Versailles before the Revolution. Its colonels were named d'Estremont de Maucroix, de Chabot, du Garreau de la Mécherie, Renaudeau d'Arc; its captains Verdé de l'Isle, Marin de Montmarin, Anisson du Péron, de Gaullin des Bordes, des Courtils de Montchal; and its lieutenants Doublet de Persan, de Vincens de Cauzans. The bearers of the regimental ensign were de Ponton d'Amécourt and de la Bourdonnaye.

The Light Horse was based at Quartier Villars on the left bank of the Allier, facing the old town and its narrow medieval streets. As the British Light Brigade had done in its celebrated charge during the Crimean War, the Tenth had covered itself with suicidal glory during the Franco-Prussian war. The French were losing the Battle of Froeschwiller in Alsace on August 6, 1870, when the cuirassed cavalry of the Tenth executed a diversionary counterattack at the village of Reichshoffen.

The men of the Tenth frequently came to town in their scarlet breeches with their peaked caps raked over one ear for an evening of entertainment in one of the music halls, where lady singers belted out patriotic and bawdy songs. Inevitably the men asked for "Les Cuirassiers de Reichshoffen":

> *See, back there, like a lighting of steel*
> *Those squadrons passing in the haze*
> *They will die and, to save the army,*
> *   Give the blood of the last cuirassier.*
>
> *They were told, "France must be saved.*
> *"The future depends on you.*
> *"Keep the memory of Waterloo.*
> *"Like them, we must win or die."*
> *The evening breeze makes the horses' manes stand,*
> *the armor quiver, and, in their rat holes, the Ger-*
> *   mans tremble.*
> *   See, back there, etc.*

Cafés-concerts—*caf'concs* in Parisian argot—were at the height of their turn-of-the-century popularity. Caf'concs were cafés where small orchestras entertained in the evening and, on Sundays and holidays, gave *matinées musicales* in the afternoon. There were no cover charges, and in garrison towns like Moulins the better cafés-concerts advertised their entertainment as being supported "by collection only." By announcing that a hat would be passed around, management tried to attract officers, and to avoid having the establishment labeled a *beuglant*. From the verb *beugler* ("to bellow" and, by extension, "to bawl out a song"), a *beuglant* denoted a low-class music hall where soldiers bawled along in boozy merriment.

During her year at Notre Dame, nineteen-year-old Gabrielle was allowed to travel to Vichy, apparently to see her ailing grandfather. It was the first time in her life that she was entirely on her own. By train Vichy was only an hour south of Moulins—past Uncle Paul's Varennes station—but in every other way the elegant resort was another world. Gabrielle found Vichy enchanting.

The town with its profusion of hotels was separated from the Allier River by gardens. When she wasn't with Grandpa Henri-Adrien at the spa where he was under treatment, she took walks along the river in the Parc Napoléon, and listened to the orchestra at the bandstand in the shade of the chestnut and sycamore trees in the Parc des Sources. At night the park was illuminated, and hotels, restaurants, and elegant stores in the adjoining streets were thronged with people. She peeked into the Grand Casino, where touring Parisian cabaret acts were playing, and one afternoon sat at La Restauration, the outdoor café where people taking the cures mingled.

There were hot and cold springs. Sufferers of kidney, gallbladder, and other digestive ailments or of migraines and rheumatic disorders sat in pools of hot mineral water from the Grande Grille, Chomel, and Lucas springs, while those nursing alcoholic excess merely drank copiously from the cold Parc and Célestin fountains. That most of the *curistes* were elderly disappointed Gabrielle, but she was fascinated by everything else, from the splendid appointments at the mineral wells to the many foreigners speaking languages she had never heard. Vichy offered its visitors more than cures. Besides the Grand Casino, there were the Eden Theater, where operettas were performed twice a day, and the Alcazar and the Elysée Palace with their variety shows, and for outdoor recreation golf, horse racing, and regattas on the Allier.

By the time Gabrielle turned twenty she had discovered there was more
to Moulins than the Notre Dame boarding school. The town had more
tailors and pastry shops than any other town of 22,000—tailor shops
where the young bloods were fitted for uniforms and had their officers'
stripes sewn on, and *pâtisseries* where visiting mothers, sisters, fiancées,
and cousins embraced their heroes. Moulins was a town of martial concerts on public squares, a town where colonels' wives held open houses
on the first and the third Wednesdays of the month. During the racing
season, Moulins became the rallying point of the horsey set. It was at the
nearby stables at Champfeu that Frontin and Little Duke, winners of the
Paris Grand Prix, had been foaled. To rival Vichy, Moulins possessed one
elegant caf'conc. Situated on a green across from the railway station, La
Rotonde was an octagonal, cast-iron pavilion where an orchestra and
visiting comedy acts and cantatrices performed every evening. It was the
officers' café, and sedate enough, at least during matinees, for single ladies
to enjoy tea on the terrace.

Julie had left Notre Dame and was helping her grandparents, who were
still working the markets. At the recommendation of the mother superior,
Gabrielle was allowed to join Adrienne as shop assistant to a respectable
couple who owned a lingerie and hosiery shop. The proprietor was Henri
Desboutin, but the busy boutique kept the name of its original owner and
was known as the House of Grampayre. Gabrielle and Adrienne lodged
with their employers and shared a third-floor attic room.

The House of Grampayre was at the bottom of the short Rue de
l'Horloge, so named because it afforded a view of the clock on the
Jacquemart tower. In the Middle Ages the twice-burned and twice-restored
tower had been a symbol of Moulins's civic liberties. Like the Campanile
in Venice, it marked the time with mechanical figures popping out of the
belfry every quarter hour. Father Jacquemart and his wife Jacquette
chimed the hours, while their children, Jacquelin and Jacqueline, rang
out the half and quarter hours.

The Desboutins preferred to hire girls recommended by the nuns. For
one, they sewed like angels. Gabrielle was especially adroit with needle
and thread. She also waited on the ladies who came in for trousseaux
and layettes, scarves, skirts, embroideries, mourning crêpe, feather boas,

neckwear, lining fabrics, and sewing needs. However, she did not share her employers' enthusiasm for the disdainful ladies who patronized the House of Grampayre. Desboutin liked to recite the names of the blue-blooded clients when no one was in the store. Le Riau, Pomay, Rochefort, and Fourchaud were the châteaux surrounding Moulins. Two of the four castles were turned into stables—a shame, of course—but the owners *were* of the Bourbon-Parma family. There were the Palice family at the Château de Palice, the Bussets at the Château Busset high up in the Bourbonnais hills, where a hundred of the mineral springs that fed the Vichy baths originated.

Gabrielle would conveniently forget the year and a half at the House of Grampayre. Instead, she would invent pastures owned by her "aunts," grazing grounds with short grass unsuited for dairy cows but appreciated by horses. The aunts, she would say, rented out the grasslands to the army and from the age of sixteen she grabbed foraging cavalry horses by their manes and swung up on them to ride bareback. Shy as a fawn, she watched strapping officers come on inspection tours, handsome hussars and *chasseurs* dressed in sky-blue jackets with black frogs and loops, and with fur-lined coats thrown over the shoulders.

"They drove up in a smartly harnessed open phaeton carriage," she would say. "They determined a horse's age by looking in its mouth, caressed its fetlock joint to see if it had been exposed to fire, slapped the flanks. The horses belonged to the army, of course, and I was always afraid they'd take away my favorite mounts. In fact, they didn't pick my favorites because when these horses were grazing and unshod, I had rid-den them so hard that their feet were affected. I can still see the officer come into the kitchen to warm his hands on the fire and say, 'Those horses have hooves like cows, the soles are lost, the frogs [the elastic, horny substance in the middle of a horse's sole] rotten.' I didn't dare look at him, but he had guessed it and when the aunts turned their backs to us, he whispered, 'So, you gallop them without shoes, eh, you little wretch.' "

Fashionable lieutenants came into her life, not to inspect horses at her aunts' farm, but to have their breeches altered in a tailor's shop where she worked to make a little extra money. The summer she turned twenty-one, Gabrielle took a room in the threadbare part of Moulins. It was all she could afford. Adrienne hesitated, but after her sister Louise approved, she, too, moved away from the shop to stay with Gabrielle.

Word got around that women wishing their wardrobes altered could come to the demoiselles Chanel's place in Rue du Pont Guinguet. Some customers preferred to consult the Chanel girls directly, without going through the Desboutins. Occasionally, Gabrielle was picked up and driven to a château to do the final fittings of a dress.

On Sunday mornings, Gabrielle worked in the tailor shop. At the height of the 1904 racing seasons, six lieutenants, all as concerned about their sartorial splendor as about their equestrian glory, came in one Sunday for last-minute alterations. One stood cap in hand, another in his shirttails, when they caught sight of the tailor's pretty assistants busy with needle and thread in the next room. One was fair, the other dark and beguiling.

One of the men twirled his mustache, another stood at the door to the workroom and smiled seductively, but the enchanting twosome never lifted their eyes from their work. A third asked the tailor questions and was told the girls worked in a lady's dress shop. Later that afternoon, the lieutenants asked Gabrielle and Adrienne to come and watch the jumping competition. The next invitation was for sherbets. The pastry shop was called La Tentation.

When the officers invited one of the Chanel "sisters," both showed up. Sometimes they even brought Antoinette, now going on sixteen. People called them the Three Graces.

The lieutenants took them to La Rotonde to hear the lady "attractions" belt out their repertoire. In this era before electronic amplification, a headliner needed a sonorous voice to be heard over the din of the evening's gaiety, and the stamina to sing, to the accompaniment of a piano player, from 8:00 P.M. to midnight. The singer had no backup choir, but had behind her on the stage a row of seated *poseuses*, debutante singers striking a pose and, during intermissions, taking turns filling in popular refrains. Girls were hired by the month—"dismissible after two weeks," according to most caf'conc house rules, and had to appear in evening dress. If a *poseuse* was no good she faced a volley of cherry pits from the audience. If she sounded promising, she could graduate to become a "starlette" or an "attraction."

It is not known whether the Chanel girls boasted to their dates that they could sing as well as any of the *poseuses* or whether their admirers

egged them on. In any case, Gabrielle, who was more brazen than her
aunt, soon got her chance. Perhaps with a wink from the lieutenants, the
director of La Rotonde recruited her. Her voice was of less than stage
quality, but with her Tenth regiment claque in the house, she held her
own. With her rendition of a popular dirge about a Parisian young lady
who lost her dog at the Trocadéro amusement park across from the Eiffel
Tower, she gained her nickname:

> I've lost my poor Coco.
> Coco, my lovable dog,
>   Lost him, close to the Trocadéro.
> He's far away, if he's still running.
>   I admit my biggest regret is that the more my
>   man cheated me,
> the more Coco remained faithful.
>   (Refrain) You didn't happen to see my Coco?
>   Coco near the Trocadéro.
>   Co at the Tro
>   Co at the Tro
>   Coco at the Trocadéro.
> Who has seen Coco?
> Oh, Coco,
> Who has seen Coco?

Since Adrienne's voice was the kind that invited cherry pits, the management soon delegated her to pass the collection plate. "For the artists,
ladies and gentlemen." Despite her small voice, Gabrielle put her heart
and gumption into it, and her appearance became a routine. In another
account of how she came by her nickname, it was said that she was
greeted with barnyard noises when she broke into a timid *cocorico*, (the
French version of "cock-a-doodle-doo") in a rusty voice that had little of
the strutting rooster's passion. The flushed faces in the audience shouted
"Coco! Coco!" In yet another version, the only cabaret songs she knew
besides "Qui qu'a vu Coco?" was "Ko ko ri ko," the latter the title song
of a revue by the playwright Robert de Flers that had been a smash hit
at the Scala caf'conc in Paris in 1897. Both songs had Coco in the refrain,
and to the audience at La Rotonde Gabrielle became "la petite Coco."

4

BALSAN

Who among the barrack rakes deflowered her? The question was not one she would answer directly, but over the years she came to intimate that Etienne Balsan was her first lover. Marie-Jeanne Viel, a journalist who grew up in Moulins a few years after the Chanel sisters, would remember whispered rumors of a very young Coco Chanel risking prison over an abortion, and Marcel Haedrich, the most persistent of the Chanel biographers, would suggest that Balsan was the seducer who had enough manners to help find a solution to an unwanted pregnancy. "Could such a mishap be at the origin of the somewhat bizarre and complex liaison of Coco and Etienne?" Haedrich would ask.

Abortion would not be legal in France in Coco Chanel's lifetime, and her infertility—there would come a time when she desperately tried to have a child—might well point to a botched abortion in her youth. She was tough as nails and had only to recall her mother's fate to act. And if her mother's example was too distant, Julie was repeating the curse; she had got herself knocked up by a fairground vendor. The father had recognized the baby boy but was in no mood to marry Julie.

Etienne Balsan had spent the better part of his military service in Algeria with the Chasseurs d'Afrique regiment. A bet had won him a promotion to the Tenth Light Horse for the last months of his tour of duty. Etienne was the youngest of three brothers of a family whose fortune was made in textiles. Over the previous hundred years a succession of dynamic Balsans had built up the business in Châteauroux, an old wool center in the middle of France. To double their chances, they had all married girls with substantial dowries.

As a boy, Etienne had been sent by his parents to a boarding school in England, where, besides learning English, he had contracted a passion for horses. His parents died shortly after the eighteen-year-old Etienne returned to Châteauroux, and he immediately told the family lawyer he had no intention of following his brothers, Jacques and Robert, into textiles. With his part of the fortune, he intended to buy a horse farm and concentrate on raising thoroughbreds. The brothers persuaded him to postpone this plan until after he had finished his army service.

Jacques and Robert Balsan continued in the textile trade and, over the next decade, greatly expanded the family business and influence. They became defense contractors delivering the dyed fabrics used for uniforms during World War I. Jacques became an aviator and in 1914 flew over enemy lines to discover a German troop buildup that showed an offensive was imminent. Had he been an ordinary flier, he would have reported to his squadron chief, who would have alerted his superiors at headquarters. Jacques, as his nephew François Balsan would remember, instead had his chauffeur take him to the Ministry of War in Paris. Such was the clout of the Balsans.

Unlike his respectable older brothers, Etienne was a bit of a rogue. Jacques married Aimée Seillière de Laborde, and Robert wed Thérèse de Chabaud la Tour, but Etienne was interested in the kind of women one did not invite to the Château du Parc in Châteauroux or the Parisian family town house in Rue de La Baume. Yet Etienne had a knack for talking himself out of trouble. Algiers was hot and boring, and while on guard duty at the governor's palace one afternoon, he had dropped his rifle and fallen asleep. When a passing civilian dressed him down, the rudely awakened Etienne talked back. The civilian, unfortunately, proved to be the governor himself, and the derelict soldier spent time in the stockade before he was detailed to the worst fatigue duties. At this time, the regiment's horses came down with an unfamiliar disease of the skin. In the face of veterinarian puzzlement and impotence, Etienne extorted from an officer the promise of promotion to a regiment based back in France if he could cure the horses. The vets laughed. Etienne applied a prescription he had learned in England, healed the horses, and got himself transferred to Moulins.

Etienne was twenty-four, Gabrielle twenty-one when they met, probably in one of Moulins's caf'concs. On one of their first dates he explained that once out of the army, he would breed horses. The army used a lot of horses and he could supply them, but his real ambition was to raise thoroughbreds. He was impressed when Gabrielle said she was born in Saumur. Her birthplace, he explained, was where one would find Captain Georges Blacque-Blair, France's most famous military horseman.

Coco and Etienne liked what they saw in each other. That Etienne would be more interested in a spirited *chanteuse* than in a dutiful daughter of the Châteauroux bourgeoisie was characteristic. (François Balsan, Etienne's nephew, would recall growing up with stories of his uncle's nonconformist life-style—anything to shock the family.) Though Etienne was neither tall nor particularly striking, Gabrielle found him more real and natural than the blue-blooded swells of the Tenth. He told her about a property near Compiègne he was thinking of buying. By train it was less than an hour and a half from Paris, on the edge of the Compiègne forest. It would be ideal for horse breeding.

Life for a young lady could not be all horses, and social distractions beckoned at Maud's. Together with Adrienne, Gabrielle was coming under the heady sway of Maud Mazuel, a woman of some style who in the garrison town was something of an institution as matchmaker and fashion trendsetter, life of the party and chaperon.

An invitation to tea at Maud's was cherished by everybody, from pale and intense young officers striking Nietzschean poses to neighboring gentlewomen dropping in for a whiff of gossip and divine chocolate cake. Maud was a stout woman of undistinguished origins but vast social appetites, who made it possible for young women to move about under respectable protection, for women to see suitors without arousing suspicious families, and for the local gentry to discuss horses, fashion, the hunting season, and the new Beaujolais.

On summer afternoons, tea and cake were served in Maud's garden. The hostess talked fashion with the ladies, racing statistics with the horse breeders, all the while arranging meetings in chaises longues under the trees. It was understood that if love blossomed as a result of a meeting at Maud's, the couple would not forget what they owed their hostess and would express their appreciation with a couple of hundred-franc notes tucked into a discreet envelope.

Maud invited Gabrielle and Adrienne to her teas and found Adrienne especially appealing. At twenty-one, Adrienne was prettier than ever, with a softness Gabrielle did not possess. Adrienne lit up Maud's afternoons, and the hostess introduced her young discovery to bachelors who were older and richer than the gentlemen officers of the Tenth Light Horse. She also invited Adrienne to live with her and made her understand that if she, the daughter of an old itinerant vendor couple, dreamed of being accepted in society, she could wish for no better guarantor of her respectability than her protector and friend Maud.

Gabrielle had other ideas.

Moulins was a dead end, she told Adrienne. Instead of being social climbers at Maud's, they should get out of Moulins. Gabrielle was tough, wiry, and ready to take chances. Adrienne and she should try for the brass ring together. If they could be a success at La Rotonde, why not in Vichy? All right, so Adrienne had not become a *poseuse* right away, but she was attractive and singing was something one could take lessons to learn.

Did Gabrielle see herself as another Yvette Guilbert, the Montmartre songstress who had progressed from backroom sewing to the floodlights of Paris and now was the subject of posters designed by Henri de Toulouse-Lautrec? It is hard to say how serious Gabrielle was about a career in vaudeville. In various retellings of her life story, she skipped the vaudeville experience and went conveniently from the aunts' equine stockfarming to Etienne's horse-breeding venture. Still, Adrienne let herself be persuaded to go with Gabrielle to Vichy. Before they left they stitched together a new wardrobe and made new hats for themselves.

The "season" at Vichy was highlighted by an orgy of musical events from oom-pah-pah performances to light, variety, and classical concerts. Orchestras played at the park bandstands and spas during the mornings. In the afternoon, the music emanated from the caf'concs, while at night the Grand Casino, the Eden Theater, the Alcazar, and the Elysée Palace featured lyrical opera, vaudeville, and variety shows. Coco decided to try for auditions at all four and to start at the top—the Grand Casino, where only noted artists, touring Parisian headliners, performed. The two young women had themselves photographed in the park. In the first known photograph of Coco, she and her aunt stand in all their homemade *belle époque* splendor, Gabrielle looking severely into the camera, her aunt smiling at her. The squared shoulders, big belt, and neat shirtwaist of

Coco's dress, with its shoulder and skirt embroidery as the only embellishment, have been seen as the genesis of the Chanel style. More than one fashion writer has contrasted the two girls' dresses and marveled at the romantic frilly scarf that attenuated the severity of Gabrielle's clothes, compared with Adrienne's high collar, which, despite her smile, gives her a more laced-up look. Some have seen the beginnings of the horsewoman, others a tentative homage to military fashion in the cavalry braid on Coco's shoulders and a hint of the feminizing of masculine fashions to come.

Gabrielle's auditions were less than promising. She had presence and a certain acid charm but not much of a voice. A house pianist transposed variety hits for her, and taught her the rudiments of stage dancing. Her chance, he told her, was to become a *gommeuse*, theater argot for a costumed *poseuse* who accompanied her singing with a bit of cakewalk twists and twirls. A *gommeuse* performed in a sequined dress and showed a lot of cleavage and legs. Coco rented a stage costume that the pianist found less than risqué. Besides being stiff and nearly inaudible, he declared, her bones stuck out. Why didn't she add some ruffles to her décolleté? The trick, he said when they began to rehearse, was the way she turned her hips.

Etienne Balsan came to Vichy. He was out of the army and invited Gabrielle to the races. The sporting club and *hippodrome* were across from the Parc Napoléon on the far side of the Allier River, and in talking to Morand forty years later Coco could still remember the racetrack, the jockeys on their mounts being led to the starting post by lads in silk jerseys.

Etienne had bought his dream property. It was called, rather pompously, Royallieu, although it had never belonged to a king. Sometime in the twelfth century, after King Philippe le Bel stopped over, the fortified castle had been given its name. A queen had turned it into an abbey, which had been demoted to a priory. Etienne had bought the property from a racetrack trainer.

"God, are you lucky to have racehorses," Coco would remember telling Balsan.

Etienne asked if she would like to come and see them train.

She said yes.

It was without regrets that she left Vichy. Adrienne had given up and returned to Moulins, taking up Maud on her invitation to share her house.

Even if Etienne didn't exactly sweep Gabrielle off her feet—he already had a live-in mistress at Royallieu, she learned—she was happy to escape the shabbiness of her past and the certain mediocrity that awaited her kind in the provinces. Anything to escape her mother's—and Julie's—fate as unwed mother and common-law wife of a market hustler. As an orphan without a dowry, she couldn't expect to attract honorable young men looking for a wife, but she was pretty enough to aspire to that other solution that penniless young women aimed for—to find a protector.

5

GOLD DIGGERS AND CLAUDINES

The *belle époque* had a number of euphemisms to designate the categories of the vast underclass of kept women. These ranged from the *grande horizontale* or *croqueuse de diamants* (literally, "diamond scruncher"), who destroyed fortunes and reputations and fascinated the gossip columns, through the *irrégulière*, the near-permanent mistress who for family reasons a gentleman could not marry, down through the *demimondaine*, the *cocotte*, the one-hundred-franc "little woman," to the bordello inmate and street tart.

Balsan's live-in companion was a slightly over-the-hill gold digger who had salted away the diamonds dukes and monarchs had thrown at her feet. Emilienne d'Alençon was a famous social amazon who captivated with her appraising, mocking dark eyes, her round cheeks, pert nose, and perverse little ruby mouth. At thirty-three, she was living on her past glories. To Etienne, she was something of a tourist attraction.

Together with Caroline Otéro—universally known as la Belle Otéro—Liane de Pougy, Léonide Leblanc, Cora Pearl (real name Eliza Crouch), and Alphonsine Plessis (the model for Alexandre Dumas's *La Dame aux Camélias*), Emilienne belonged to the caste of grand courtesans. A photo shows her glancing frankly at the camera, with a sensuous mouth and round face under a veil and with her trademark man's tie wing collar and pearl tie clip and white carnation in her buttonhole.

Her most celebrated liaison was with the king of Belgium; her most lucrative her affair with Jacques d'Uzès.

"I am going grouse hunting in Scotland so come with us," Leopold II wrote her. "You'll call yourself the Countess of Songeon, and I'll introduce you to my cousin Edward." The cousin was King Edward VII, to whom Emilienne was alleged to have said that only Frenchmen, provided they came from the upper classes, knew how to make love.

Jacques d'Uzès was the son of the formidable Duchesse Anne d'Uzès, a horsewoman, poetess, novelist, sculptor, yachtswoman, feminist, and the first woman in France to hold a license to drive the newfangled motor carriages. When her son became infatuated with d'Alençon—and Emilienne was seen wearing the Uzès family jewels—the duchess packed her son off to the Congo. Unfortunately, the young man died of enteric fever in Kabinka in the Sudan in 1893.

Born Emilienne André, the daughter of a Parisian concierge couple, she had graduated from white rabbit tamer in a summer circus at fifteen to cheeky seductress with nouveau riche appetites and literary aspirations. In 1981, when Karen Black played her in the movie *Chanel Solitaire*, the screenplay gave her the line, "And when I read one of my poems, even Marcel Proust applauded." In reality it was the poet Raoul Ponchon who chanted her glory in bawdy verse, and Proust who lifted the story of her affair with young Jacques d'Uzès and put it into *Remembrance of Things Past*. Emilienne became the character Rachel, the woman who snared family jewels from Robert de Saint-Loup and caused his banishment to Tunisia. Unlike the hapless d'Uzès, however, Saint-Loup gets to marry Swann's daughter. Like Etienne, Emilienne loved to offend the sensibilities of the *bourgeoisie*. When Etienne was thrown from a horse and transported to the Balsan family residence in Châteauroux with a fractured leg, she had the impudence to show up, brush the servants aside, and dash to his bedside.

What Balsan, Emilienne, and their friends thought of Coco was no mystery. Etienne banished virtuous spouses and intimidating dowagers from Royallieu. The aristocratic sportsmen, turf stars, and thoroughbred owners he did invite appreciated being able to show up with companions who were not their wives. The ladies who came to Royallieu were women of independent means, actresses like the up-and-coming Gabrielle Dorziat, and other unconventional females. Balsan and his friends were there to have fun, to ride to hounds, and to throw parties. When Balsan brought Coco home with him from Vichy, everybody assumed this unusual girl with her sharp tongue and lovely profile was a new distraction for him.

"Claudines" and a taste for unripe femininity (*fruits verts* was the expression) were fashionable. Claudine mirrors, Claudine lotions, and Claudine hats all had their inspiration in Sidonie Gabrielle Colette's semiautobiographical romances. In swift, frank, tender, and witty prose, Colette wrote about adolescent femininity, about nostalgia and the cult of youth and regret, and about the unchecked life of the instincts. Her forty-six-year-old husband, Henry Gauthier-Villars, had the gift for publicity and published her books under his own pseudonym, Willy. Colette was not the only ghostwriter he used, but marrying her when she was twenty was his biggest coup. Willy dressed his wife and the singular eighteen-year-old songstress-actress Polaire, who played Claudine onstage, in identical clothes, cut their hair the same way, and let the rumor spread they were living *à trois*. Parisians gasped when, flanked by his feline "twins" in similar short suits, the beefy, walrus-mustached Willy entered the Palais de Glace in tails and top hat, with his shirtfront hidden by an immense, loosely tied bow.

Emilienne told Coco the details of the scandalous separation of Willy and Colette. Colette had left her husband for the Marquise de Belbeuf, known as Missy. Even blasé Parisians, who had applauded the two women when, at private parties, they performed lesbian pantomimes, were shocked when Colette and Missy made their debut at the Moulin Rouge cabaret in something they called *Rêve d'Egypte*. What added zest to the premiere was that Willy was in the audience, applauding wildly at the last curtain before police closed down the show.

Colette divorced the imposing boulevardier in 1906 and became a music hall entertainer until she took up writing again in 1919. Gabrielle would not meet her until they were both famous. They became friends in the 1920s when both bought villas on the Riviera. Colette would teach Chanel to eat ice-cold melon with Riesling on the rocks, and would write a masterful short portrait of her; Coco would shelter the writer during the darkest days of World War II.

In image and taste the Claudine phenomenon introduced the idea of a new type of woman, younger and freer in style and morals, a woman who knew a lot more than Victorian strictures assumed she knew, a woman who in fashion would soon dethrone the rustle of lace and silk and huge millinery constructs that passed for hats.

Imperceptibly, the diamond scrunchers were beginning to fade. *Le Figaro* continued to describe in minute detail what la Belle Otéro, Liane de Pougy, and Emilienne were wearing at the races, and sons of leading families still fought over who should have the honor of ruining himself over which *grande horizontale*—Henri Meilhac, coauthor with Jacques Offenbach of *La Vie Parisienne*, paid 80,000 francs to see Liane naked.* But the new woman was being portrayed in literature, plays, caf'conc refrains, and on the canvases of Henri Matisse and Kees van Dongen. Her allure was obvious. Her education was often summary, but she had a quick sense of humor and her diffuse moral sense was based on personal integrity. She was often the mistress of ambitious young men and was also to be found in artistic milieux.

Gabrielle was a Claudine. Although not consciously aware of the "new woman," she expressed her youthful, slightly defiant femininity in the only way she knew how—in her clothes. If *cocottes* overdressed, she made sure she looked like a schoolgirl. If ladies at the grandstand at Longchamp came in feather hats and skirts that swept the grass, she was at the racetrack in strict tailor-made and boater. If Dorziat came to the stables dressed in bias-cut to ride sidesaddle, Gabrielle swung onto her horse wearing riding britches.

The horsey set was not in on the latest depictions of womanhood, nor on the new talk of women's rights. Feminism was making inroads in France. The Chamber of Deputies turned down giving women the right to vote in 1901 and again in 1906; never'heless, Marguerite Durand and Sarah Monod scored two parliamentary successes. The new "seat law" authorized shopgirls to sit down when there were no clients to serve, and the Emile Loubet Law allowed women to become lawyers.

Balsan initiated Gabrielle in the sport of kings at the Longchamp racetrack in the Bois de Boulogne. She would one day be a thoroughbred owner herself, but she would never forget her introduction in 1907, the grandstand and its view of the vast field of green, the Eiffel Tower soaring off to the east, the woods to the left of the track, the owners, the regulars, the *beau monde* pouring into the infield, the members' enclosures, the Panoramique restaurant, and the owners joining their trainers, jockeys, and horses on the sculptured grass of the paddock under the chestnut trees before each race.

*Nearly $160,000 in 1990 currency.

Closer to Royallieu was Chantilly with its picture-book *hippodrome* next to the castle; in the Chantilly woods and downs each morning, a hundred trainers put thoroughbreds through the paces for eight hundred owners. Gabrielle was also taken to the races at Maisons-Laffitte, Saint-Cloud, Tremblay, and Enghien. She learned that the "season" moved from Longchamp in the spring to Chantilly in June, Deauville on the Normandy coast in August, then back to Longchamp for the fall, capped by the Prix de l'Arc de Triomphe on the first Sunday in October.

Royallieu, which was just over an hour from Paris by train, was an ivy-covered manor in the heart of France's horse country. The three-story residence was surrounded by a handsome park with century-old oaks and chestnuts. Stables, paddocks, and grazing lands stretched toward the nearest neighbor, the Royallieu barracks, and the property was only a few hundred meters from the 15,000-hectare Compiègne forest.

An unwritten law of the turf world proclaimed that, in order to aspire to the highest destiny, a purebred had to have been trained in the Compiègne region. Trainers originally brought from England had formed veritable dynasties of Carters, Cunningtons, and Bartholomews; Chantilly and Maisons-Laffitte were like English villages. The stag hunt was the biggest event. Hunters rode off dressed in gray-blue coats, red velvet waistcoat, and white breeches. Gamekeepers beat the woods, while carriages, piled high with spectators, nannies, and governesses with the hunters' offspring, drove out to picnic areas assigned by officers of the Fifth Dragoons at Compiègne.

If asked what they did *do* all day, Etienne and his friends would no doubt answer with Elisabeth de Gramont that horses and racing were their own universe, "a world whose anxieties and ecstasies fill a life, and the seven days of the week—Mondays at Saint-Cloud, Tuesdays at Enghien, Wednesdays at Tremblay, Thursdays at Auteuil, Fridays at Maisons-Laffitte, Saturdays at Vincennes, and Sundays at Longchamp." Gramont was the daughter of Antoine de Gramont, Duc de Guiche, the owner of a prized stable, and the half sister of Armand de Gramont, a fixture in the most glittering Parisian society (and whom Proust would turn into Saint-Loup in *Remembrance of Things Past*). She was observant of both worlds and noted that "if the sportsman despises the intellectual, the loathing is mutual. However, when the intellectual witnesses a particular stable's triumph, this immediate and visible glory tends to make him envious."

Balsan and his friends mingled with the grandstand crowds of top-hatted hedonists and parasoled demimondaines, the corseted, sidesaddled baronesses and racy *nouveaux riches* that Proust wrote about. At the paddocks and the weighing-in, they mixed with the owners and the breeders—Jacques de Brémond, who had sent his two-year-old *Garde Feu* to England to win the Golden Cup at Ascot, Edouard de Roth-schild, Henri de Foy, Maurice de Gheest, and Joseph Lieux, who was believed to train his horses in railway cars since there wasn't a race where his colors were not entered. Gabrielle admired the thorough-breds and the little jockeys in satin shirts, carrying their big saddles to the scales. From the grandstands at Longchamp and Auteuil in the Bois de Boulogne, she watched the races and thought of the lengthening band of horses and riders coming around toward the stretch as an ele-gant arabesque. Around her, grand ladies skirted grand courtesans—the former often picking up fashion tips from the latter. Still, the crowd from Royallieu respected social taboos. Henri de Foy might party with Suzanne Orlandi at Royallieu, but at the races his sister-in-law, Anita de Foy, would no more speak to Suzanne than would Henri's wife. For Anita and Henri's brother Max, it was Suzanne who had "debauched" dear Henri.

Emilienne did not feel threatened by Balsan's new conquest, and Coco was smart enough to know she was no match for the live-in odalisque. That men might find her youth, defiant black stare, and feisty repartee as enticing as Emilienne's full-bodied experience and come-hither titters never occurred to Gabrielle. Besides, Emilienne smelled nice.

Coco's sense of smell was exceptional and throughout her life her memories were olfactory. Nothing turned her stomach more than people who stank. Coco would never forget the agreeable bouquet that emanated from Emilienne's person.

Gabrielle would say she was never in love with Balsan. The claim led more than one of the intimate friends of her more mature years to believe that she had been indebted to him, that his arranging, and no doubt paying for, an abortion linked the two, that he might actually have found her to be overly clinging but that he hesitated to be too brutal in getting rid of her. By coming to Royallieu she made a decision to depend on him, and she would sometimes admit that she "owed" Balsan a lot.

Coco was twenty-two when she went to live at his estate. To dramatize the six years she spent with Balsan, she would say she had lied to him about her age, that when he had found out that she was sixteen and not twenty, as she had told him, he was afraid police might discover him harboring a minor. Another time she would say that because she was underage Balsan refused to introduce her to Emilienne, apparently for fear the notorious *cocotte* would denounce both Etienne and her to the police.

"I just didn't know anything," she would say on one occasion. "I understood in the broadest sense, but I had to teach myself. The boys with whom I was living didn't want me to change. They played with me, and had a great time. They had found a person who was straightforward. They were wealthy men who had no idea who this girl was who came into their lives."

Etienne's affair with Emilienne was short-lived, and it was apparently with some glee that he told his brothers he had dropped her. His brothers—and society women with daughters to marry—considered him a hero not only for having escaped the famous "diamond scruncher" without dropping the family fortune, but for turning the tables on her. In reality, Emilienne was less lethal than her reputation. Her fortune made, she was turning to writing and was quite frankly out to enjoy life. The life-style at Royallieu had suited her perfectly.

Etienne had no parents to look askance at the company he kept, and his lack of snobbery was not all for show. If anyone knew more about horses than he, the circle was immediately enlarged to include the equestrian expert. Maurice Caillaut, a beefy man of modest background, rode to hounds with Balsan's bluebloods because of his unerring eye for fast yearlings.

Nothing daunted Gabrielle. She tackled her riding lessons in rain or shine. Her endurance was in direct proportion to the size of her ambition: she wanted to surprise people. She was fearless on horseback, and Etienne himself taught her how to manage a horse in training. When he was busy elsewhere, she spent her days with trainers, jockeys, grooms, and stable lads.

Coco would try to forget the years with Etienne, and, once she became rich and famous, deny them. Jealousy, she would say on a number of occasions, was alien to her, and we can only speculate about her feelings as outsider and second-stringer. The way she dressed gives a hint of her defenses. No voluptuous crinolines, no pagoda hips, no lace, no sable wrap, row of pearls, or hat of vulture quills two feet tall for her. She dressed in tailor-made frocks, mannish high collar and tie, and with a boater and hatpin holding her luxuriant long hair in place—a kind of reverse elegance. For riding to hounds she could transform herself into a stern and stately sidesaddle rider, her hair in a pigtail under a bowler hat, but at an age when lady bicyclists in bloomers were arrested for indecent exposure, she dared show up for cross-country rides in jodhpurs, cut from a stable groom's pattern. When she was in her eighties, she would explain in earthy stable terms the correct posture for females wanting to ride astride. A woman must imagine herself with a pair of balls. "Under no circumstances," she warned, "can you put an ounce of weight on them."

The role she assigned to herself was that of buddy, chum, and side-kick. Etienne was surprised by her capacity for languishing in bed. "She would lie in bed until noon, drinking coffee and milk and reading cheap novels," he would recall thirty years later. If an outing was planned, however, she was the first to be up and ready. Did the boys want to ride through the Compiègne forest? She'd slip into her jodhpurs and tear after them. François Balsan would remember talk of his uncle's liaison with Coco Chanel, but the family recollections would have it that the future fashion designer took her meals in the "office," and at least on one occasion, when a friend of Balsan's arrived with his wife, was not invited to the "upstairs" dinner.

She tried to please Etienne. Their relationship was not conventional; nor were they. Each had tried to flee provincial rectitude. Etienne was the only man who cared enough about her to make an effort, to help her discover a new world. She tried to please by being different, by being unlike any of the real ladies who visited, by telling the boys she found these women disagreeable and the demimondaines fanciful and ravishing. The cocottes looked like the heroines of the novels of her adolescence.

There is no doubt that there were moments when her situation was trying. She was far away from her grandparents, from her aunt Louise, from Adrienne. She was with people who, whether conspicuously or furtively, looked down on her. Etienne never tried to have her accepted by society. Perhaps he knew it could not be done; she was out of her depth in intimidating drawing rooms. To compensate, she ridiculed the real ladies they met at racecourses.

"You find her pretty?" she asked Etienne after they passed a ravishing lady at a grandstand.

"But Coco, she's the daughter of the Marquess of . . ."

"She looks dowdy, tacky."

In reality she was intimidated. She was observant and quick to admire aristocratic women's behavior, their "ravishing duplicity, their stylish manners, and pointed, ever-vigilant insolence," as she would tell Morand. Only they knew how to enter a room at the right moment. Only they knew when to leave. She never went to Paris with Balsan and Emilienne. The name Chanel would one day stand for the essence of Parisian chic, but in her mid-twenties Coco still did not know Paris.

True love and good fortune, meanwhile, seemed to have smiled on Adrienne. Letters from the less bold, less defiant young aunt announced she had fallen in love with an ardent suitor she had met at Maud's. He was young and handsome with a funny mustache and a winning smile. They had traveled to Vichy, where she had granted him her favors. His name was Maurice Edouard Armand Ferréol, Baron de Gay de Nexon.

There was a picture of Adrienne and her swain in an open carriage in Vichy. Adrienne sat gloriously dressed, with a feathered hat and a small dog in her lap. Maurice closed his eyes, unfortunately, the instant the photographer snapped the picture, but he looked blissful enough. His family was another matter.

The scion of the Limoges nobility, Maurice was the son of Baron and Baroness de Nexon, squire and châtelaine of the Nexon château in the Haute-Vienne *département* less than fifty kilometers from Aubazine. His mother, née Hainguerlot, burst into tears at the news that her son wanted to marry a shopgirl. His father threatened to disinherit Maurice. It was totally out of the question that the family would allow him to marry a seamstress. But Maurice and Adrienne were in love. They would wait.

With Adrienne in Vichy, Coco had to find friends among the Royallieu crowd. In 1908, she met a vivacious young actress who visited Royallieu with Etienne's best friend, Count Léon de Laborde. Two years her junior, Gabrielle Dorziat had just made her stage debut. She was to have a lifelong career in the theater, acting in plays by Paul Bourget and Jean Cocteau, in Molière and Giraudoux with Louis Jouvet and, after 1930, become one of the French cinema's *grandes dames*. In 1908, however, she was a lively if plain young woman with a round face, a mischievous laugh, and great presence. Coco was a little afraid of her, and when they first met had a third person introduce her, but they soon became friends.

Coco was no more confident when it came to visiting femmes fatales. Count de Laborde asked her if she wanted to meet Pauline de Saint-Sauveur, a much-talked-about concubine.

"No, thank you, those women scare me," Coco answered.

Laborde insisted, and Coco agreed to take tea with Pauline.

"So, how did you find her?" the racy Leon asked afterward.

"Awful."

"What do you mean, awful?"

"Awful. She looks nasty and cruel; she isn't clean and uses rice powder in her hair to cover up her odors. And why so much hair?"

Laborde laughed and told everybody how Coco found the notorious beauty atrocious. In retrospect, Gabrielle would admit that Pauline, with her face made up like an actress and her flinty profile, impressed her. "I've got to admit they taught me a few, those people."

It was hard for Coco to get used to a society in which no one ever worked. She was quick, however, to learn the rules of the game, the class separations that everybody tacitly respected, the principal names of the 1,200 families that made up the Parisian *beau monde*, the old clans and new nobility into which one could accede only by marriage.

"The rich young men were coveted by a bunch of women who wanted them as lovers for themselves or as husbands for their daughters," she would say. "I didn't know anything. I thought all men were the same, and I couldn't see what was so special about these fellows."

She was assertive. Once her superior riding skills made their mark, Etienne took pride in showing her off. Valéry Ollivier, a brilliant horseman of the time, would remember Coco at Royallieu. "She was a pretty little thing, not striking but with an expressive, lovely face. She was fearless on horseback and that impressed us. Otherwise, you'd never have guessed she would become Coco Chanel. To us, she was Etienne Balsan's little friend."

6

ROYALLIEU

If the officers of the Tenth Light Horse were the first to discover Gabrielle—and give her a nickname—a famous courtesan and a star of the racetracks were the first to launch her creations in society.

Etienne Balsan's breakup with Emilienne d'Alençon and her conquest of Alec Carter, a famous jockey, did not prevent the former mistress and her new lover from coming to Royallieu. On the contrary, Etienne welcomed the publicity the turf press, racing forms, and gossip columns poured on the new twosome, and the ribald aura that, by refraction, the liaison bestowed on the master of Royallieu. Coco was noted because she was *seen* with them, and because Alec's fantastic winning streak as a jockey had made him a celebrity. Because Emilienne followed him to the races wearing one of Coco's straw boaters, absurdly simple but, as worn by Emilienne, chic, Coco garnered special attention.

Alec was a charmer and Emilienne was not the only woman to pursue the diminutive jockey, who by 1907 was called "Carter, the unbeatable." Four years younger than Coco, he was a small man, but his manners were princely and the members of the Jockey Club thought him the very incarnation of the equestrian arts. When he died during the opening skirmishes of World War I, Emilienne remembered him in a love poem:

> *Back then, he slept on my arm, softly. Behind the*
> *eyelids I saw his eyes.*

When he died, did he assume that familiar pose?
Perhaps his eyes, without a gaze, are open.

Surviving snapshots of Coco's years at Royallieu show her at the stables, taking part in Etienne's pranks, sitting on the terrace and partici-
pating in the morning ritual of newspaper reading. She was photographed
with Baron Henri de Foy and his dogs, at the mews with Léon de Laborde
and Etienne.

As one of his practical jokes, Etienne asked the ladies to dress up for
the Compiègne races, and then the entire Royallieu party rode into town
on donkeys. On one such excursion, the group lined up for a photographer. Maurice Caillaut, the breeder who knew how to pick winning yearlings, was there, with Eddy Forchemer, Suzanne Orlandi, Baron Henri de
Foy, Coco, and Etienne. Under huge black velvet hats, all three ladies
were dressed in appropriate sidesaddle attire, but Coco set herself apart.
The necks of Eddy and Suzanne were swathed in starched ruffs; Gabrielle
sported a masculine bow tie. One of her little idiosyncrasies was to "borrow" haberdashery items from men.

But there were other, less cheerful photographs, pictures often showing
her squinting at the camera with smiles that are not quite smiles, and
expressions of aloof disinterest and even disdain. There was a lot she had
to swallow.

Balsan's gentlemen friends might be exquisitely mannered and defer-
ential when they were with their mothers and wives, but they saw no
reason to put on gloves in the company of women of inferior station.
Coco's title as the host's "little friend" gave her stature and protected her
from the crudest advances, but the men were often brutally insensitive, if
not downright caddish, in her presence.

When she was in her seventies, she would talk freely about Balsan,
and about efforts by his brothers to make her Etienne's wife. "Etienne
Balsan didn't care about beauty," she told *Marie-Claire* magazine. "He
liked older women, loved the *cocottes*, scandalized his family. The family
was actually happy to see him with me. His brother Jacques came to see
me and told me the dirtiest stories about Etienne. He wanted me to marry
Etienne. I said, 'I don't love him.' He said, 'That doesn't matter.' I
thought to myself, what a terrible old monster. Jacques was ten years
older than Etienne."

Jacques Balsan tried again a year later. Coco found his proposal both
obnoxious and funny.

He got angry. "You'll end up in the dumps. What will happen to you?"

"I don't know and I don't care. I want to work."

"Work! You don't know anything."

"But since all the women want to know how I dress . . ."

What the lady friends of Balsan's visitors really wanted to know was where she bought her hats.

Parisians were discovering Matisse and the flaming landscapes of the Fauves painters, the shock of Picasso's *Demoiselles d'Avignon*, the tone poems of Claude Debussy, but horses—and practical jokes—were what counted at Royallieu. The morning and evening newspapers from Paris were devoured for the racing results, not for the significance of the National Assembly vote that toppled the administration of Georges Clemenceau or the granting of the vote to women in Denmark. A photo taken at Royallieu shows the morning ritual on the terrace, Coco looking dreamily up from a newspaper in her lap, Lucien Henraux reading *Le Journal* while Gabrielle Dorziat scans the new illustrated daily *Excelsior*. All the papers featured at least one page of racing news, and competition demanded that all the papers report as breathlessly as *Le Figaro* on the leading *cocottes'* newest toilettes.

Léon de Laborde was one of the first of the Royallieu set to own an automobile. His chauffeur-driven red coupé had carriage work by Charron, but its radiator demanded constant refilling.

"I had never been in an automobile," Gabrielle would remember. "I found them terribly ugly. I said, 'What a horror, there are not even any horses.' And the coachman sits up front. I was afraid he'd fall off." She quickly learned to borrow Léon's car and chauffeur, however.

The traveling to and from the races was done mostly by train and Balsan and his friends merely skirted Paris, changing trains at the Gare de l'Est. On the way back, the men recapitulated the day's most exciting "pony" or played cards until the train chugged into Compiègne. The young women in the group talked clothes and hats.

Adrienne and Maurice went to Paris with Maud Mazuel, and Gabrielle went to see them. Her aunt was deliciously happy; her "fiancé" appeared to be a gentleman, and Maud hovered protectively over the couple. They took Gabrielle to see the sixty-four-year-old Sarah Bernhardt in *La Dame aux Camélias*. The story of the beautiful courtesan who scorns a wealthy count for her penniless lover and, to save her true love's life, returns to a life of frivolity only to be reunited with Armand on her deathbed made Adrienne sigh in ecstasy and Maud admit she was deeply moved. On various occasions, Coco would say she wept so loudly that night that people behind them hissed, or that she had found the divine Bernhardt hopelessly grotesque.

The City of Lights was dedicated to pleasure and dissipation. It had more than twenty major theaters offering evening shows and, on Sundays and Thursdays, matinees. The *beau monde* went to the Opéra on Mondays and the Comédie-Française on Tuesdays. Orchestra seats were usually reserved for men, but at the Théâtre Français women were admitted at the *parterre* (without hats) while at the Opéra Comique the best seats required evening gowns. Maurice de Nexon wanted Gabrielle to come with them to see Edmond Rostand's smash hit *L'Aiglon*, but she didn't join them. During her years with Balsan, *La Dame aux Camélias* remained the only play she saw. Adrienne and her nobleman lived discreetly in Vichy while he waited for his parents to give in and let him marry the woman he loved. For appearances—and because Adrienne had a big heart—Antoinette lived with them. Gabrielle's youngest sister was twenty-one and more beautiful than ever. Fresh from the convent in Moulins, the tall, willowy Antoinette, with her soft face and big almond eyes, was also trying show business in Vichy. While she trained and waited for engagements, Adrienne looked after her and slipped her some of the pocket money Maurice dispensed.

Adrienne stayed in contact with the family, with Louise and Paul Costier in Varennes, with Gabrielle and Antoinette's brothers. Alphonse had become a traveling salesman in newspaper subscriptions—life on the road was in the blood. After making a silkworker named Madeleine Boursarie pregnant, Alphonse had married this woman and, together with their little son, was living in a hamlet near Aubenas, where thirty years earlier the teenage Jeanne Devolle had found Albert Chanel in the local tavern and Julie had been born. The gentle Lucien had stuck with Alphonse and become a subscription jobber as well. In 1907, however, he had decided to try for a career in the army. He lasted one year in the infantry and, instead of joining Alphonse again, made up his mind to look for their father. As the various members of the Chanel clan knew, Albert was supposed to be living in Normandy, selling his wares near Quimper, the old pottery and stoneware capital.

Lucien tracked down the long-lost father in 1909. Albert was not embarrassed to be found living with a woman who was considerably younger than he and drank as heartily. Albert welcomed his son, invited him to stay with them, and promptly disappeared. From the lady friend, Lucien learned that the old man was living in Quimper, where no one knew him, because he had had a run-in with the gendarmes. Without waiting for his father's return, Lucien went back to Varennes, where he set himself up as a market trader selling shoes.

Gabrielle turned twenty-five in August 1908. She didn't want to become like the other women, forever dependent on men, on their appetites, their whims, their money. What would happen to her when Etienne found another Emilienne d'Alençon? The question of her future gnawed at her.

Etienne was reading *L'Excelsior* on the terrace one morning when she wondered out loud what would happen to her.

He looked up and said, "Why, aren't you all right here?"

As the months passed, her question became more insistent. His answer remained the same.

One day, she said, "I can't earn my living riding horses. I think I'd like to work."

She told him about her hats.

She had a way with ribbons and lace, brims and bands that added chic and charm to the simplest boater. At the racetracks, where enormous, florid bonnets were de rigueur, she was a sensation wearing one of her own confections. Lately, several of Etienne's lady friends had asked her to fix up their hats. He might not have noticed, but Emilienne had sported one of her creations at Longchamp.

Etienne let her talk. Women usually asked him for silly frippery, clothes and jewels. Nobody had ever asked him to bankroll a millinery store. Besides, his horses already cost him enough.

As long as he could tease her, he was ready to indulge her.

She persisted. He gave in, halfway, suggesting she might open a boutique in Compiègne. She said Paris or nothing. He told her Paris was full of milliners.

There were all kinds of practical questions to consider. Etienne had been invited to visit Argentina, South America's equestrian center. He wanted to go, and didn't mind letting her have his Parisian bachelor apartment on Boulevard Malesherbes for a while. But if Coco went into business, she would need to set up something legal. She would need a line of credit for her suppliers. Should he guarantee her credit, cosign for her? Should he keep it in his own name or, as he had always done with women, just fork over the money? He disliked the various choices, and decided the next time she'd ask he would offer her the use of the apartment. In the meantime, why didn't she come with him to Pau for the fox hunt he had been invited to attend. They would be staying at the thirteenth-century château in Pau, the ancient capital of Béarn and Gascony. It was going to be fun.

She had never seen the Pyrenees. She said yes, never guessing that on the horse trails below the snowcapped mountains she would find the love of her life.

7

BOY CAPEL

His name was Arthur Capel, but everybody called him "Boy." Years later, she would remember it all, the soft drizzle, the horses, his casual manner and soft eyes. With revisions and embellishments, she would tell the various authors she tried to charm into ghostwriting her autobiography the story of how she met the only man she ever loved.

By the most extravagant account, Boy Capel and she had galloped off from the others and found themselves riding through iridescent green meadows with the snowcapped Pyrenees towering above the oaks and rushing streams. It had been a marvelous week, the fox hunt, the rusty glow of red costumes in the rain, and the purebreds—Morgans and saddle horses, stallions, hunters, and Arabians. She had never known that winter was so mild in southwestern France.

They had stopped to let their horses rest. "And you and Etienne?" he suddenly asked.

The question surprised her. She looked across at him, flustered for a second. Maybe the English *were* funny. "Why do you ask?"

His green eyes met hers. "Etienne told me last night I was trying to seduce you."

"And what was your answer?"

He smiled. "I said, 'What do you want, Etienne? You're neglecting her.' "

Arthur Capel, polo player and ladykiller. Gabrielle liked the way he smelled of leather, horses, forest, and saddle soap; she liked his easygoing ways. He was handsome, with his darkish skin, straight brown hair, and striking green eyes. Etienne judged people according to the depth of their equestrian knowledge. Boy Capel's passion was people. He was so engaging that men and women revealed their hidden cravings and ardor to him.

The two riders were drenched when they saw the château with its squat castle keep and crenellated battlements.

Late that night, when Boy and Etienne were sipping a last cognac in front of a fire in the candlelit manor hall, Gabrielle joined them. Boy poured her a glass.

The brandy, the embers in the grate, and the candlelight that cast shadows on their faces invited intimate conversation. Gabrielle talked about her wish to change her life. It was not the first time she had told Etienne about her aspirations, but it was the first time a third person was present, the first time a man agreed with her, the first time she analyzed and explained. All the lady friends of Etienne's turf companions loved her ways with hats. Women constantly asked her to smarten up their hats.

Turning out hats was a pastime, not a profession, Etienne said. He had said that before.

Boy Capel took her side. Standing with his back to the fire and swirling his snifter, he said he thought it was a great idea. Etienne looked surprised.

Why shouldn't she want to do things? Boy said.

Etienne was not convinced she could earn a living whipping up hats. Paris was full of milliners. But if she wanted to have a go at it, all right. She could borrow the apartment on Boulevard Malesherbes.

She would recall how, the next day, she discovered Boy Capel was returning to Paris. She went to his room.

"You are leaving?" she asked.

"Unfortunately, yes."

"At what time?"

She scribbled a note to Etienne. It said, "I am leaving with Boy Capel. Forgive me, but I love him."

Louise de Vilmorin was one of the half-dozen writers to whom the mature Chanel told the story of how, without a suitcase, she had gone to the railway station in Pau to wait for Boy Capel to show up for his train. Vilmorin was a woman of verbal spark and an intricate love life. She wanted to be sure she understood it right.

"Are you telling me that you were not at all convinced he wanted you?" she interrupted. "What did he say when he saw you on the platform?"

"He opened his arms." Gabrielle smiled.

In retelling how Chanel described the embrace, Vilmorin could not help adding, "Coco could easily have taken the time to close a suitcase. She knew very well the time of the evening train. There was only one."

Gabrielle was twenty-seven when she fell in love with Arthur Capel. To her, Boy Capel was someone solid, someone who assumed she had a mind and asked what she thought. To him, she was a singular beauty. Slim, straight, and with an aristocratic head on a long, graceful neck, she looked like a Gainsborough duchess in profile. Yet full face, with her mocking raven eyes, generous mouth, charming dimple and knowing presence, she was an alluring street urchin.

During the week in the Pyrenees he had come to appreciate her acid charm, her spontaneity and sharp tongue. She was energetic, frank, and witty, yet just beneath her deceptively accessible and limpid demeanor there was something severe. She loved what was beautiful and detested what was merely pretty. Her taste was nervy and she divined the phony, the contrived, the spurious in people. That she was Etienne's mistress somehow added to her stature in Boy's eyes. Etienne's persistent reminders that he would be going to Argentina for an extended visit practically invited Boy to attempt her conquest.

What Gabrielle would discover in Boy was his irrepressible appetite for accelerated living, a taste for elegance, success, and adventurous women. His skepticism matched hers, his determination also. He had inherited interests in Newcastle coal and was hard at work doubling his fortune. The British turf aristocracy found him both eccentric and vaguely comical because he actually enjoyed working and making money.

In London, Capel lived in Cheyne Walk, Chelsea. In Paris, he had a smart apartment in Avenue Gabriel, a discreet, tree-lined street running parallel to the Champs Elysées between the Place de la Concorde and the presidential Elysée Palace. When their train pulled into the Gare d'Orléans the next morning, Boy and Gabrielle took a taxi to Avenue Gabriel. They were meant for each other.

Chanel's French biographers would surround Arthur Capel with an aura of mystery and hint that he might have been the illegitimate son of a Frenchman who had died shortly before Boy finished school, that he might have had some Jewish blood. Some said he was the son, allegedly, of one of the Pereire brothers, the financiers of French railroads. But, in fact, he was the son of Arthur Joseph and Flora Capel. He had three sisters, one of whom would marry Herman Alfred Stern, the second Baron of Michelham.

Wealthy Catholic families were coming into their own in Edwardian England—the Capels' money was made in coal mining—and the energetic young Arthur allowed himself only one diversion from business, and that was to excel on the polo grounds. A year older than Gabrielle, Boy had spent his adolescence in boarding schools—at first Beaumont, a Jesuit school for the sons of Catholic gentlemen, then Downside, an equally fashionable institution run by Benedictines in Somerset. He spoke French fluently, and if he was trying to add to the family fortune instead of spending it, no one in Paris held it against him. Etienne and the rest of the French horsey set were awed by his reputation as a polo player—and a ladies' man. Boy Capel was an intimate of Armand de Gramont, the dashing Duc de Guiche.

"To me, he was my brother, my father, my whole family," Gabrielle would say of Boy. But until the millinery success and Boy's money—or bank credit—allowed her to open her little store, a certain ambivalence persisted. Boy was not as wealthy as Etienne, and Coco depended on her former lover's generosity to continue selling hats in the Boulevard Malesherbes apartment. More than one friend would wonder about the exact relationship of the three. Biographer Marcel Haedrich would suggest the two men might have shared her. "For a while, probably; not officially," Haedrich wrote. "Balsan was not the jealous kind. What counted for him was first of all the horses. For the rest, long live life! There is probably a basis of truth in the Balsan version of how Coco went from Balsan to Capel."

Besides demeaning Coco, such speculation takes no account of her dramatic break with Etienne after six years, her showing up at the Pau railway station without knowing if Boy would want her. Regardless of what the two men's feelings were, it is not in character, from what we know of Coco's upbringing and her fear of being taken for a kept woman, to imagine her sleeping in turn with Boy and Etienne until the two decided who should pick up the tab—and her.

What we do know is that after Etienne came back from Argentina, Boy and Gabrielle went to Royallieu. It was the first time Coco had seen her former lover since Pau.

Etienne pretended everything was forgotten. He handed her a gift he had brought back from South America—a bag of lemons. When she opened the bag they were rotten.

"So where are you with your Englishman?" Etienne asked when they were alone.

"I am . . . where men and women generally are."

"That's perfect. Continue."

Behind the spare phrases were tears and strife. "This dialogue doesn't replicate a very complicated situation," she would tell her author friend Paul Morand thirty-five years later. "Today, everything is easy. Relationships are lived in a hurry; like everything else. Boy was English. He didn't quite understand; things became complicated. He was very honorable. I took him away from his friends; they hated me." On another occasion she said that Etienne no longer loved her, but "like men in general, he began to love me again when he realized that I loved someone else."

The two men had their own gentlemanly talk.

"You like her?" Etienne asked.

"Indeed, yes," said Boy.

"She's yours, my dear fellow."

In Etienne's recollections, their conversation took place before he left for Argentina, and the delicate question of who should finance her millinery shop came up.

"If you're interested in her, my dear fellow, she's yours," Etienne said.

"I'm not sure I can afford . . ."

"I won't mind helping. Since she wants to get into fashion, she can use my apartment but that's all."

Later, Etienne told Coco that Boy used too much brilliantine, that Boy ruined people's chair backs with the goo he put in his hair.

Gabrielle and Etienne remained friends, and to the end of her life she would wear an amethyst ring he had given her on a chain around her neck. Together with Boy, she occasionally joined the Balsan house parties at Royallieu. One Sunday, they, Etienne, and Count Léon de Laborde decided to play a prank on the guests. They engaged Gabrielle Dorziat and Jeanne Léry, an actress recently abandoned by Russia's Grand Duke Boris after a long liaison, to improvise a country wedding. They also engaged someone to photograph the proceedings.

Gabrielle was in charge of the disguises. Jeanne and Etienne dressed up as groom and bride, Etienne in tails and top hat, the actress in white with a bouquet of mandarin oranges. Boy became the mother-in-law in gray twill and one of Gabrielle's hats, Laborde a squealing baby, Dorziat a village bridesmaid. Coco dressed up as the best man. She had bought the parts of her costume in the boys' department at the Samaritaine.

The beginning of her life's work was in this tomboy creation, in the feminizing of masculine fashions.

Success came almost at once. While Boy tended to his business in London and Paris, Gabrielle sold hats in Etienne's apartment on Boulevard Malesherbes, a bourgeois thoroughfare running from the Madeleine Church through the Eighth and Seventeenth arrondissements peopled with an eclectic mix of old money and *nouveaux riches.*

She bought simple, flat-topped strawhats and boaters by the dozen in the Galerie Lafayette department store and trimmed them herself. Her first clients were Etienne's former mistresses. These women in turn brought their friends, charmed by the nervy little Chanel hats. What Gabrielle came up with was often absurdly simple, and many of her buyers thought of her creations as a new form of eccentricity, creations with little airs of defiance that made conversation.

Gabrielle and Boy lived in insouciant bliss in Avenue Gabriel that winter. They invited few people—society did not call on bachelors and their live-in mistresses. Instead, they went out a lot. They dined at Maxim's, the Café de Paris, and at the Pré Catelan restaurant in the Bois de Boulogne.

Governments in France might succeed each other at a dizzy pace and the Boulanger and Dreyfus affairs make tempers flare, but life and opportunities coursed richly along the grand boulevards with their confident architecture, smart shops, celebrated fashions, and cosmopolitan nightlife. Boy worked and Gabrielle was engrossed in her business. She had never suspected what it was to live with a man who was busier making his fortune than squandering it. The handmaiden of progress, Boy declaimed, was commerce.

Boy showed her a Paris where English lords and Russian grand dukes played. For a while she was fascinated by high society. If the time with Etienne had schooled her about the habits and tastes of the wealthy— and allowed her to ride some of France's best horses—living with Boy exposed her to social nuance, caste, and family scandals, "all the things," as she would put it, "that Parisians know but isn't really written anywhere. Since I was too proud to ask, I remained unaware. I lied all the time, too, because I didn't want to be taken for a country bumpkin."

When Boy caught her at it, she said she was just rearranging truth a bit.

Of the men in Coco Chanel's legendary life, Boy Capel was the only one about whom she almost told the truth, the only one she liked to talk about. In the various retellings she made herself into an eighteen-year-old ugly duckling, silly and inexperienced but certain of his love.

"We were made for each other," she would say late in life. "That he was there and that he loved me, and that he knew I loved him was all that mattered."

She called him the one man she could never forget. She liked to tell of her own naïveté, timidity, and little revolts, to underline his ardent nature and strong personality, and how women were attracted to him. On an impulse, she made him cancel a gala at the Deauville Casino and have dinner with her alone. Once when they went out together, he made her wear a white ballroom dress, a dress that clashed with her timidity and made people stare. She saw women size her up and swoon in front of him.

"All the women ran after him," she would remember. "I wasn't jealous. I said, 'It's curious, women can't take their eyes off you.' He answered, 'It's you they're looking at, silly.' "

She wasn't naïve enough to believe that, and told him to go out with his lady friends. He did. "They didn't understand and told him, 'Get rid of that woman.' With his innate gift for honesty, he answered, 'No. I need her.' "

Another time she asked to be introduced to them. "They're so pretty," she said. "Why don't they ever come here?"

"Because . . . because you're not one of them. You're like no one else. Besides, when we get married . . ."

"I'm not pretty."

"No, you're not, but I know no one more beautiful than you."

8

RUE CAMBON

Boy advanced the money that permitted Coco to rent commercial space in the street that would be associated with her name for the next eighty years—Rue Cambon. Situated in the heart of the tradespeoples' First Arrondissement, the narrow street ran parallel to the stately Rue Royale and the Rue Castiglione–Place Vendôme–Rue de la Paix continuation of elegant boutiques, the Hotel Ritz, and the Ministry of Justice. Rue Cambon was a short street beginning at Rue de Rivoli, crossing Rue St. Honoré, and ending at Boulevard de la Madeleine. Its renowned tenants included Voisin's, patronized by gourmets from all over the world, the Ritz bar, and, at the Rue de Rivoli corner, Smith's English Tea Room. The Hotel Ritz, whose noble main entrance was at 15 Place Vendôme, had a convenient back entrance on the Rue Cambon.

Elisabeth de Gramont would throw an intriguing light on the origins of the House of Chanel, saying the initiative behind the boutique was Capel's and that the motivation was to give Coco something to do. Elisabeth knew Boy through her half brother Armand de la Guiche, and in her memoirs would describe how Boy broke away from a group of solemn men one evening and came to sit next to her. "Are you happy?" he asked her in English, a question she took as a hint of intimate conversation to follow.

Boy told her he was very attached to Coco, but that he was terribly busy. Coco's inactivity irritated him and he was trying to find something for her to do. "You have no idea how idleness can hang heavy on certain women, especially when they are intelligent, and Coco is intelligent," he told Gramont. "You've got family, relatives, social obligations. She's got nothing. When she's through polishing her nails, the time between two and eight P.M. is a void. Of course, I don't like her to linger. We don't always realize how important schedules are in people's emotional lives. We speak of the heart. It's not that difficult to attune two hearts, but to synchronize two watches! I set her up in a little millinery shop, but it's not going too well. However, she's energetic; she has the qualities of a businesswoman."

Coco rented a mezzanine at number 21, on the west side of Rue Cambon. She brought pretty things from the apartment and hired a young woman as her assistant. She told Boy, "I'll know that I love you when I don't need you anymore."

She needed him. She knew little about business. She was shocked when he told her one night as they went for dinner that the reason the bank allowed overdrafts on her business account was that he had deposited securities to back her up. She felt humiliated, threw her handbag in his face, and stalked off under a torrential downpour. He ran after her. When he caught up with her, she was in tears, and both were soaked. Sixty years later she would still remember the unobtrusive solicitude with which Boy had propped up her business venture. "I was convinced I was making money, that I was becoming rich."

The next day she let her assistant know that she was not there to have fun. "I'm here to make a fortune. Henceforth, nobody spends a centime without my permission."

When she told Boy, he said, "You're proud and conceited. You will be hurt in life."

She hated advice, not because she was stubborn but, on the contrary, because she was easy to persuade. She was beginning to believe that people only handed out advice that was good for them. In her conversations with Morand in 1946, Coco would claim that she hated the selling of her hats—the need to flatter clients. A lady showed up who, when Coco asked if she could be of assistance, said, "I just came to have a look at *you.*"

After that when a client asked to see her, she tried to hide in the back room.

"You go out," she told the assistant.

"But it's you she wants to see, Mademoiselle."

Coco stayed in the back room, afraid the lady would find her stupid, provincial.

The client insisted. "But where's the little person I've heard so much about?"

The assistant came to the back and whispered, "Come out."

"I can't. If she finds the hat too expensive, I know I'll give it away."

Coco was also shrewdly aware that to be too available destroyed some of her allure, that by making herself scarce she increased people's curiosity about her. Later, when famous, she made up a proverb for herself: "A client seen is a client lost." She sensed that many women who felt bewildered by a surfeit of choice, actually liked to be *told* what was right for them, and she knew how to surround herself with competent salespeople.

Among her first clients was Countess de Gontaut-Biron, the daughter of the United States ambassador to Germany, one of many American heiresses to marry into penurious European aristocracy. Antoine de Gontaut-Biron had spent a fortune recklessly on the Deauville racecourse.

Imperceptibly, Coco's clientele changed. The turf society women were replaced by society women in general, women who were clients of the Worth and Doucet fashion houses. Boy sensed she needed technical assistance, someone trained in the workrooms of one of the Rue de la Paix or Rue Royale milliners. Coco managed to hire away Lucienne Rebaté and two of her best assistants from the famous Maison Lewis boutique. Rebaté was three years younger than Coco, but she had been through the rigors of apprenticeship, climbing from errand girl to second fitter. Several actresses and society women already swore by her. What made Rebaté decide to join Chanel Modes, she said, was that Coco was more fun than the owners of the Lewis establishment.

Chanel's increasingly fervent patrons encouraged her to enlarge her field. Knitted shirts of the kind Boy wore playing polo were added, along with sweaters and blazers. Prematurely, as it turned out. Fashion still demanded frills à la Doucet and "Turkish" notes from Paul Poiret, the newest fashion tyrant.

The years 1911 and 1912 were the happiest times in Gabrielle's life. Her hats were seen publicly when Dorziat got the leading role in an adaptation of Guy de Maupassant's *Bel-Ami*. Her wardrobe was by Jacques Doucet, the most famous couturier in the Rue de la Paix. But

Gabrielle persuaded the actress to wear her hats in the play. She designed two strawhats with wide brims turned up on one side without plumes or trimmings, that worked wonderfully with Dorziat's stage costumes. A photograph of Dorziat in a Chanel hat appeared in the May 1912 issue of the *Journal des Modes*.

In the spring of 1913, Adrienne and her Baron Maurice de Nexon had moved to Paris, bringing with them Antoinette. Forever the fiancé with honorable intentions, Maurice was resigned to the fact that his parents would never allow him to marry Adrienne, that all he could hope for was to outlive them. The lovers found an apartment at 8 Avenue Parc Monceau, and Adrienne came often to visit Gabrielle's shop. Antoinette came to work.

It was Adrienne's idea. Antoinette had grown into an attractive young woman of twenty-five. She had little of Gabrielle's talent, but she had much of her audacity and charm. She also possessed the family virtues of being uncomplaining and a hard worker. Coco allowed herself to be persuaded.

Perhaps it was the death of their sister Julie that led Gabrielle to agree to "protect" her younger sister. For Gabrielle and Antoinette, the death was a sharp reminder of where they came from, of their mother's short, brutal life. Little is known of the circumstances of Julie's death or the fate of her common-law husband, but she left behind a young son, André Palasse.

Gabrielle had never known this nephew, but with Boy's help she assumed responsibility for little André. They sent the six-year-old orphan to Beaumont, the boarding school that Boy had attended. Late in life, Coco would say that Boy thought of André as his son. During school holidays when, on walks with Coco, André saw coal barges on the Seine, he shouted, "Look, they're ours."

"No, they're Boy's barges."

"But since you're going to marry him. He told me."

Boy and Coco were a tony couple. People came to see them. Success and the appearance of marriage made a difference, and Coco discovered she had talents for interior decorating. She transformed the Avenue Gabriel apartment. The first time she saw a so-called Coromandel screen from China, she was overwhelmed. She had never seen anything so beautiful. The screens were made of wooden panels finished with a coat of lacquer through which designs—landscapes, figures, flowers, and lucky emblems—were incised and filled with various thick, opaque watercolors. Coromandel screens had nothing to do with India. They simply acquired the name because they had been shipped to Europe via Madras, on the Coromandel coast of India.

Boy and Coco bought Coromandel screens because, she said, you could take them with you and reconstitute your intimate surroundings anywhere. She had the rugs dyed the color of raw wool because it reminded her of mud floors. She also chose furnishings in natural colors until her furniture dealer cried for mercy.

"Try draping things in white satin," she suggested.

The living room looked like a snow scene. She put white flowers in tall vases and rearranged the Coromandel screens.

"God, how beautifully you live!" exclaimed Henry Bernstein, the dramatist whose hectic plays amused a generation of boulevard theatergoers, when he and his wife, Antoinette, came for dinner.

To please Boy, Coco got dressed every night, knowing full well a moment would usually come when he'd say, "Why go out?" Thirty years later, she would say, "He loved me in the setting I had made and I, well, part of me is a harem woman who adjusts very well to this kind of reclusion."

Boy knew people who were not members of the turf aristocracy and their courtesans. He knew painters, writers, and people from the stage. Gabrielle liked them because, in the company of artists, her status as Boy's mistress went unnoticed. She didn't approve of their unconventional living, but she could at least be herself.

Isadora Duncan's performances at the Gaieté Lyrique made Gabrielle want to dance. Boy encouraged her and she began taking lessons from Elise Toulemon, an extravagant personage who, under the name Caryathis, was a specialist in character dance and developed choreographic concoctions for Erik Satie's *Belle excentrique* and Maurice Ravel's *Mother Goose*.

Caryathis's studio was way up on Montmartre in Rue Lamarck, and Gabrielle climbed up to the Butte almost every day for her morning lessons.

Caryathis was frank. Gabrielle was not gifted, the dancer decided after several months. Gabrielle faced the fact. She had no talent for singing and no talent for dancing. To keep fit, however, she continued to attend Caryathis's classes.

Both Boy and Coco were absorbed in their respective accomplishments. Hers were immediate and tangible. His were long-term and promised great wealth.

In Paris, Boy began to associate with a statesman twice his age. Georges Clemenceau was a man with a long career behind him as a doctor, a teacher, a politician, and a newspaper publisher. He became the mayor of the Eighteenth Arrondissement in 1870 and, for twenty years, a member of the National Assembly.

What the seventy-one-year-old Clemenceau saw in the handsome coal-mine owner turned shipowner was a young man with fresh ideas. Boy was an Englishman—but he was also an entrepreneur full of simple solutions and practical advice. Clemenceau was gutsy, instinctual, while Capel was far more aesthetic, cerebral, and studied. Aristocratic friends of Capel, however, advised Boy to keep his distance from the old senator.

Coco wanted to know what Boy and Clemenceau had in common.

He told her the old man believed war was coming. As a member of the senate committee for foreign affairs and the army, Clemenceau could not be in a better position for surveying European fluctuations and for sensing Germany's political aims or for inquiring into the French forces' readiness. And Clemenceau was haunted by the fear that France might be caught unprepared.

"Still, what has that to do with you?" she asked.

Boy was convinced that in a war the nation controlling the sea lanes would ultimately win.

To get his message across that Germany meant war, Clemenceau founded a daily paper, *L'Homme libre*, with himself as editor.

In May, when Boy was traveling, Caryathis invited Coco to the first-night opening of the Ballets Russes' *The Rite of Spring* at the new Théâtre des Champs Elysées. Caryathis was herself the guest of her new German admirer, Herr von Recklinghausen. To appease her current lover, Charles Dullin, an influential actor and theater director, she asked Coco to be Dullin's "date" for the evening.

Sergei Diaghilev's ballet company had been the sensation the year before, performing Igor Stravinsky's *Firebird*. Parisians had been in ecstasy watching Vaslav Nijinsky and Tamara Karsavina express the legendary savagery and surging dreams of the Slavic soul, and expectations were high when Von Recklinghausen and his party made their way to their seats.

The May 13, 1913, date had been chosen by the superstitious Diaghilev and free tickets given out to avant-garde admirers in the hope that the recipients' enthusiasm for the new would countervail the anticipated shock of the bejeweled public in the stalls and boxes who expected to see the Russians perform elegant gymnastics in ballet.

The new ballet was no spring of soft clouds and daffodils but a pagan fertility rite exploding with primitive violence and primordial urges. Stravinsky's dissonant rhythms and violent and percussive sounds combined with the Dionysian dancing by Nijinsky and the barbaric splendor of Léon Bakst's sets provoked a riot. The smart audience was interspersed with Diaghilev's aesthetic crowd. The latter applauded novelty simply to show their contempt for the people in the boxes. Insults and bravos rained down on Stravinsky, sitting in the fifth row.

Gabriel Astruc, the theater director, restored some kind of order by letting the house lights go up. A lady slapped the face of a man in a neighboring box; Maurice Ravel spat out crushing remarks at those who insulted the work. Somebody called him a dirty Jew. The carnal frolic resumed in a shudder of insults, howls, and hoots, and ended in a climax that showed a maiden frenziedly dance herself to death to renew the life of the soil. At the last curtain, Countess Renée de Pourtalès, her tiara askew, declared that nobody had dared to make a fool of her before. Gabrielle was stunned—by the audacity on the stage and the behavior of the audience.

Intuitive, aware, and quick to pick up on trends and manners, Coco was beginning to see a place for herself in fashion. Paris had always had a reputation for luxurious elegance. To work in the fashion trade meant to know how to divert and astonish a rich and discriminating clientele with invention and skill. It meant to be able both to create and to assimilate what one creates.

She couldn't draw or make sketches, but she could tell what was right or wrong with one glance at a client trying on one of her hats. She immediately knew what needed to be changed, what had to be worked on. Her talent was in her hands and eyes. She absorbed flaws almost physically.

She was also learning that a certain kind of assertiveness paid, that there was nothing people loved more than to be surprised. By the spring of 1913, the benefits generated by the Rue Cambon boutique were such that Boy no longer needed to secure her bank credit. Pride had its good side, she told Morand nearly forty years later. But the day Boy was able to withdraw his securities from her bank account she had the impression her youth was over.

9

FIRST SUCCESS

~~~~~~

It all came together in Deauville, the fashionable English Channel resort, during the summer of 1913, when Boy rented the loveliest suite at the Normandy Hotel. With Boy's money, Coco opened a shop in the smartest street, added turtleneck sweaters to her stock of hats, and showed herself at the polo club in an open-necked shirt. Everything conspired in her favor: her fresh charm, fashion instinct, and her association with the renowned polo player. Bertha Capel came over and Boy introduced Coco to his sister. Bertha, who was thirty and unmarried, would remember the twenty-eight-year-old Coco Chanel as slender, dark, and looking ten years younger than her age.

Deauville was a cosmopolitan resort in a rural setting, a wealthy, ebullient seaside town dedicated to horses, baccarat, and boutiques to be enjoyed by monied Parisians and Londoners. Surrounded by chalky cliffs and hills of granite, by Normandy pasturelands and apple orchards, Deauville was a town built in neo-Norman style, of brick and stone façades overlaid with timber beams. The town was launched as a summer resort in 1862 when Charles, Duke of Morny, the illegitimate half brother of Louis Napoleon Bonaparte and the tycoon of mid-nineteenth-century industry, built a racetrack.

To spend the summer by the bracing English Channel was a privilege of the leisure classes; the common people worked year-round (a mandatory two-week vacation would not become law in France until 1936). Like Bournemouth and Brighton across the Channel, Deauville had enormous hotels and splendid villas that catered to notables and *nouveaux riches*, arbiters of elegance, sportsmen, "diamond scrunchers," and women from the theater.

The vogue for bathing had not yet caught on. A few plucky souls, including Coco, ventured in demure costumes into the surf, but in general the sea was there to be looked at. Instead, one strolled along the jetty, in frock or printed dress, and watched the sailboats. A vacation was spent serenely and decorously. Mornings were given over to walking along the pier, afternoons to visiting acquaintances in residence, taking tea at the polo club, or making appearances at the races. Evenings provided elegant dinners, strolls along the promenade, conversation in wicker chairs on the verandas of private residences hidden behind their parks, games at the Casino. On sunny afternoons, ladies wore white and twirled parasols.

Boy had a pair of East Indians on his polo team. Gabrielle thought the two Indians, with their ebony eyes and turbans, were the handsomest men she had ever seen. Boy told her about Hinduism.

Gabrielle never had any deep religious feelings, and insofar as she had any beliefs they were largely those of Boy. In Paris, Boy took her to meet Isabelle Mallet, a theosophist who, with Boy and many Buddhists, believed in mystical insights into the divine. He read to her aloud from the Bhagavad Gita, the philosophical poem in which Prince Arjuna asks Khrishna, the most charming and human of Vishnu's incarnations, a number of questions. Late in life when she heard that J. Robert Oppenheimer had also read the Bhagavad Gita, Coco wanted to meet the physicist, not to ask him about the quantum theory but to ask why he helped invent the atom bomb. Religion vaguely troubled her, but if she was pressed she talked of her respect for the inexplicable, for what humans can never know. "Nothing dies, not even a grain of sand," she said when she was in her eighties. "I like very much whatever it is that makes sure nothing ever disappears."

Coco's boutique was located on the thoroughfare named after the family of Coco's first aristocratic client—Rue Gontaut-Biron. Strategically situated in the beautiful people's path between the gabled Normandy Hotel, the Casino, and the beach, the store was on the sunny side of the street. Coco added a huge white awning. For the first time she put her name on a storefront. Big black letters on the awning spelled Gabrielle Chanel. She had all kinds of ideas, and hired two local girls.

Antoinette stayed in Paris to help run the Rue Cambon boutique, but

Adrienne and Maurice came to Deauville, bringing with them Maud Mazuel. The former matchmaker and trendsetter from Moulins was no longer giving Adrienne the benefit of her connection; on the contrary, Adrienne was hoping to find a husband for Maud. Adrienne and Gabrielle had themselves photographed in front of the store, Adrienne looking older and more demure in black hat and shoes, veil and fur-trimmed coat, Coco energetic and sporty in her white hat and shoes, with her hands in the pockets of her oversized knit jacket. On the beach Maurice sat stoically between Maud and Adrienne for a snapshot with their dogs.

Antoinette Bernstein, who together with her playwright husband had visited Boy and Coco's apartment in Paris, was one of the first society ladies to be charmed by the clothes at Chanel's boutique. "I'm not quite sure when I met Chanel for the first time," Bernstein would say in 1970, "but she was a young woman, not yet thirty, and physically absolutely charming. It was the time of Deauville's revival, and I loved to see what was in her boutique. Then, in Paris, I went again."

The step from millinery novelty to full-fledged couture design was a big one but not impossible. During the Gay Nineties, Madame Paquin had been the first woman to achieve a top position in fashion. Her real name was Jeanne Becker, and she was a woman of obscure Levantine origins who designed for the queens of Belgium, Spain, and Portugal and the queens of the *cocottes*. With her banker husband, she founded her house in 1892 and was an immediate success. The House of Paquin was the first Parisian couture enterprise to expand abroad, opening a subsidiary in London in 1898, followed by branches in Buenos Aires, Madrid, and New York. For the 1900 Universal Exhibition, Madame Paquin had a beautifully dressed wax figure of herself on display. She was the first designer to create publicity for herself, sending ten models wearing identical dresses to the races at Longchamp.

Two other women had made their mark during the first decade of the century. Madeleine Vionnet and Jeanne Lanvin had started at the bottom and opened modest houses. Vionnet was a sorceress with a pair of scissors. She began sewing at the age of eleven, was apprenticed to Kate Reilly in London, and worked in fashion houses in Paris until she opened her boutique in Rue de Rivoli in 1912. She invented the bias cut as a dressmaking technique, and her success in the 1920s would allow her to purchase a town house on Avenue Montaigne, thereby making that cross-avenue to the Champs Elysées a new couture street. Like Coco, she did not know how to draw and created all her fashions by draping on a wooden dummy. "I never did fashion, I did harmonies, things that were pretty together," she would say.

Lanvin's love of Botticelli, stained-glass windows—her famous *bleu Lanvin* was derived from the heavenly blue of medieval church glass—Impressionist paintings, and embroidery was reflected in her romantic and slightly theatrical clothes. A tiny woman, she was orphaned young and widowed young. She dressed her only daughter, Marie-Blanche, so exquisitely that mothers of the girl's classmates asked Lanvin to make dresses for their daughters. When Jeanne was twenty-three, she rented a loft at 22 Rue Faubourg St. Honoré and, with nothing more than three months' credit from her suppliers, set herself up in business. Her clientele was youthful and elegant, and the romantic styles for which she would become known in 1915 continued in popularity throughout the 1920s. The House of Lanvin grew in the twin image of mother and daughter, and Lanvin's inspiration remained Marie-Blanche, who became the Comtesse de Polignac.

Both Lanvin and Vionnet lived and worked in the tradition of the carriage trade. They catered to a clientele of exceptional taste and refrained from ostentatious advertising of themselves. "One did not talk to one's tradespeople when I started," Coco would say in a parody of the nasal snarl of the Parisian upper class. "One did not recognize them if one ran into them at the races and one certainly didn't invite them to dinner." She, of course, would change all that.

The powers that be were men—the owners of two older houses and a dazzling couturier who, with the exception of one delirious decade, was always magnificently out of step.

Fashion news had become current events in the 1840s with the appearance of ladies' journals, but there were few top fashion figures until the rise in 1860 of Charles Frederick Worth, whose sons and grandsons continued his house. Worth was the first to use live models, including his wife. Their son Gaston was a man of exquisite taste. He had wanted to be a painter, and when he took over from his father, his coloring was dominated by soft pastels. He knew how to use the large-patterned Lyons silks with a precision that enhanced the sweeping lines of a garment. By 1900, the House of Worth had branches in all the major European capitals, dressed most of the courts of Europe, and was known for the dignity and splendor of its designs.

Jacques Doucet, whose grandfather had opened a men's shop in Rue de la Paix in 1824, branched into women's dresses in 1871, with immediate success, and lived long enough to be a wealthy patron of Paul Cézanne, Picasso, Matisse, and Georges Braque, whose canvases he bought when the artists were unknown. Picasso's shattering *Demoiselles d'Avignon* hung in his hallway, and Henri Douanier Rousseau's *Snake Charmer*, which he willed to the Louvre, graced his studio. Doucet created both the stage and the street wardrobes for leading actresses; his fashion was sumptuous, elegant, and safe.

Women who wanted to defy and be noticed were dressed by Paul Poiret, the first conscious artist of dress. A native Parisian, Poiret was a sharp-tongued bon vivant and influential artist who was fleeced out of his despotic dressmaking business by bankers. He outlived his financial ruin by nearly twenty years to earn a living as a painter and a sometime stage and movie decorator, exhibiting his poverty as he had once vaunted his wealth.

After his first, easy success with straight dresses that fell in graceful folds to women's feet, Poiret created a simplified form of fashion and caught the updraft of the era, exemplified by the emancipation of women and the intense interest in modern art. He was inspired by Diaghilev's Ballets Russes and its electrifying fantasies and, by the time Coco was adding beachwear to her line, he had *le tout Paris* dressed like Asiatic princesses in the vivid colors of van Dongen, Matisse, André Derain, and Raoul Dufy. He forbade his clients to wear corsets, and on travels, had his models wear uniforms with a *P* embroidered in their hats.

His clients included Caryathis, Sarah Bernhardt, Isadora Duncan, and the Ballets Russes star Ida Rubinstein. He attended opening nights in capes and flannel evening clothes, and, in summer, affected white. Bearded, dark-skinned, and chubby, Poiret trod the Parisian avenues during the summer in the Indian silk bush jacket of a visiting lion hunter. In the history of fashion, Poiret and Coco Chanel belong to different ages. Yet Coco was only four years younger than the megalomaniacal and inconsistent fashion dictator.

What Coco invented that summer was a fashion whose time had come—sports clothes. Her millinery had been a reaction against the *belle époque* fruit bowls that passed for hats. Her idea was to do the same for the rest of a woman's attire. Her instinct told her that to pare down to function and logic was to rejuvenate. Poiret was making the corset and high collars old-fashioned and cleaning up the lines of the feminine silhouette, but he compensated with an orgy of feathers, colors, and dizzying pleats and folds. Chanel would no doubt have failed had she decided to go up against his beguiling excesses, the flowing understatements of Vionnet and Lanvin, or the secure rectitude of Worth and Doucet. Deauville was different. The holiday spirit allowed for a certain temerity, a certain license. Coco Chanel's masterstroke was to start with casual summer clothes.

She created her first originals—loose, informal clothing requiring no corset. She took a fancy to turtleneck sweaters worn by English sailors in port, and sold several of them in her store. Fashion historians would attribute her lasting success to the internationalism of her personal style, and her realization that she had to be at the right spot at the right time. Her choice of knits and flannels, fabrics more readily associated with English schoolboys and sports haberdashery than with ladies' fashion, would be cited as evidence that her look "has everything to do with elegance but is based on elements alien to elegance—comfort, ease, and common sense." In 1913, knits were considered unsuitable and too limp and lifeless for anything but underwear, flannel too working class or masculine, to be stylish for women. She made jersey chic with her simple gray and navy dresses that were quite unlike anything women had worn before. It would all look elementary in retrospect, but at the time nothing guaranteed that a demanding patrician clientele would accept the notion that natural casualness underscored femininity, that a secure woman could afford *not* to accentuate her charms.

Her own description of her debut was as that of a seamstress, not a designer. "I cut the front of an old jersey so I wouldn't have to pull it over my head," she would say in 1960. With her thumbs and index finger she showed her interviewer how she had added a ribbon, a collar, and a knot. "People asked me, 'Where did you find that dress?' I said, 'If you like it, I'll sell it to you.' 'How much?' I said I will have to find out. I sold ten dresses like that. My dear, my fortune is built on that old jersey that I'd put on because it was cold in Deauville."

She turned thirty on July 19. On the beach she had herself photographed, full-face and in profile, modeling her subversive sports clothes. Over a flouncy blouse and ankle-length skirt she was wearing an oversized cardigan with too-long, pushed-up sleeves, huge pockets, and belt and button.

"Everybody wanted to meet me," she would remember. "I became something of a celebrity, and there, too, I started a fashion—couturiers as stars. Before my time that didn't exist. No one knew anything of a remarkable man like Jacques Doucet, what he did for painters. People ignored him because he was a dressmaker. His clients wouldn't salute him if they happened to meet him in the street."

Chanel was already enough of a celebrity to be caricatured in the newspapers. *Le Figaro's* cartoonist Sem caught Boy Capel and Chanel with his racy pen. The satirist, whose caricatures could launch careers, depicted Boy as a centaur at full gallop abducting Coco, one of her toques high on his polo mallet and a hatbox swinging behind her.

Boy and Coco also caught the fancy of Paul Morand, a young diplomat—man of letters who wrote a successful novel depicting their story. A friend of Proust and Jean Cocteau, Morand was a Parisian who had entered the diplomatic corps and just been named attaché to the French embassy in London. It would be another ten years before Morand wrote *Lewis et Irène,* a story of a couple lucky in business and unfortunate in love, but the tone, the evocation of quickly made fortunes and of the two characters' joshing bliss dated from that summer. "They didn't see anybody," Morand wrote of their beginning together. "Irène didn't really like people." In 1923, Morand would dedicate *Fermé la Nuit,* his first big success as a novelist, to Coco Chanel.

Yet the bliss Morand saw in Boy and Gabrielle's relationship was not absolute. Boy was gone a lot. There were rumors of new feminine conquests. Lady Aimée Michelham, the wife of the wealthy art collector and horse breeder Lord Herbert Michelham, was mentioned. Gabrielle, however, chose to believe business was the only reason for Boy's travels. When she found out the gossip was true, she pretended it was just a dirty habit. "All his business activities didn't prevent him from being unfaithful to me," she would recall. "Not that it mattered. I was sure he loved only me. Let him sleep with these ladies. I found that dirty, a bit disgusting, but I didn't care."

By New Year's 1914, she was convinced Boy believed his career could be capped with an aristocratic marriage. She knew how to hide her bitterness, how to live for the moment, how not to ask herself *why* he wandered. He called her his sole confidante and said he would always come back to her.

She couldn't bring herself to force the issue. He was everything she wanted.

10

WAR

Crowned heads confidently ruled most of Europe during the early summer of 1914. Queen Victoria had died in 1901, but her dream of giving birth to a close-knit royal family occupying the continent's thrones had come true. She had left behind fifteen children and grandchildren who either ruled or married the men who ruled Russia, Germany, Greece, Romania, Spain, Norway, and assorted smaller states. Her eldest son, Edward VII, a shrewd, polished man of the world who enjoyed pomp and luxury, gaiety and self-indulgence, was the king of England.

In France the republic had in one generation raised the country to a position of world influence. Overseas the French had acquired a bountiful empire in Africa and Southeast Asia. Paris itself glittered as the epicenter of stylish living and art. Paul Poiret was the newest fashion star—and dictator—but below him were Worth, Doucet, and Paquin, and below Lanvin and Vionnet was an entire luxury trade based on centuries of expert craftsmanship. In the decorative arts René Lalique was the master jeweler of Art Nouveau, that new style sweeping the world with plant and animal motifs and sinuous flowing lines found in furniture, posters, books—even in entire houses. The avant-garde was without borders. From Paris to Moscow, from Florence to London, Prague to New York, theories of form and content, art and society, present and past clashed and united, argued and cross-pollinated in cubism, *futurismo*, vorticism, *Blaue Reiter*, and ashcan. Richard Wagner's *Parsifal* was performed at the Paris Opéra, and the musical scene ranged from French and Russian composers like Debussy, Ravel, and Stravinsky to the big Germans, Gustav Mahler and Arnold Schönberg. The theater had absorbed the Scandinavians Ibsen and Strindberg. Bernard Shaw was writing *Pygmalion* and Luigi Pirandello his first big plays. Marcel Proust was publishing *Du Côté de chez Swann*, André Gide *Les Caves du Vatican* and Colette *L'Entrave*. James Joyce was writing *Ulysses* and Thomas Mann *Tonio Kröger*.

Nationalism, however, was tearing at the European fabric. The Germany of Kaiser Wilhelm II felt as confident as England and France, but the Austrian Empire was an assortment of subordinate peoples in whom nationalist fervor grew ever fiercer. The aging emperor Franz Joseph was autocratic and resistant to the encroachment of democracy, and his empire was an uneasy compromise of German and Hungarian gentry and a variety of increasingly restless Slavic minorities.

Clemenceau took an impassioned part in the national defense debate. Convinced that Germany meant war, he worried that France was unprepared. A month after Germany had increased the size of its army in July 1913, he was instrumental in imposing a three-year term of conscript service for French draftees. The three-year service, which still left France with a standing army inferior in number to Germany's, was unpopular. A general election in the spring of 1914 returned an imposing majority of leftists campaigning for a return to the two-year draft.

Gabrielle had no sense of politics. To make her aware of current events, Boy took her to watch a session of the National Assembly. He had his entrées at the British embassy and it was at the spectators' row reserved for His Majesty's diplomats that Coco was to be introduced to parliamentary democracy. As Boy and she sat down, a young deputy took the floor and tore into Clemenceau. The orator's tone was biting, the words rude. After a while Coco could take no more.

Rising to her feet, she shouted, "Shame on you! To insult the savior of the country like that!"

Heads were turned. The sergeant at arms came huffing. Five minutes later, Coco and Boy were out on the street heatedly discussing parliamentary decorum.

On June 28, Archduke Franz Ferdinand, heir to the Austrian throne, was murdered in Sarajevo. For Coco, however, the summer chased away all war jitters. The Deauville season had never looked more promising.

The crowds reached a record, and an exceptional heat wave in July filled the boutique in Rue Gontaut-Biron with customers looking for loose, casual clothes. The baroness Diane ("Kitty") de Rothschild visited the boutique, bringing with her Cécile Sorel, the leading actress and clotheshorse of the Paris theater. The baroness, Coco learned, had decided she was going to destroy Paul Poiret. The couturier was ferocious when it came to protecting his models, and the way the story was told, a retinue of Kitty's young male admirers had not only followed her into the Poiret dressing salon where she stripped to a "tea gown" for easier fittings but had made ribald remarks to Poiret's young employees. Poiret had ordered the young men, if not Madame de Rothschild herself, from his premises. She had sworn revenge.

The baroness now pronounced Coco Chanel not only a milliner of talent but a personality. In her wake came the young Anglo-French Princess Bab de Faucigny-Lucinge, Princess Pracomtal, and Pauline de Saint-Sauveur, a young lady so taken with the Chanel millinery that she decided to buy hats no longer from anyone else.

The headlines grew ominous. A month after the murder in Sarajevo, Austria-Hungary declared war on Serbia, whose appeal to its ally and protector led Russia to order a partial mobilization. The same day, an imperial council in Berlin declared war on Russia, and, as a corollary, against France, although hoping to bargain for Britain's neutrality. While the chancelleries of Europe argued at cross-purposes, the military tide swept everybody away. On July 31, Russia ordered a general mobilization, and Germany, taking the same steps, demanded that St. Petersburg revoke its call-up within twelve hours. Berlin sent an ultimatum to Paris demanding to know within eighteen hours whether France would remain neutral. At noon on August 1, a state of war existed between Russia and Germany. The French government told Berlin it would act "in accordance with its interests" and, the same day, ordered a general mobilization.

The mobilization order emptied Deauville. On August 3, when Germany formally declared war on France, Coco was almost certain the Kaiser was doing it just to spite her.

Communications were difficult, but from Paris Boy telegraphed to tell Coco not to close the shop. The next day the question of what Great Britain would do was settled when Germany invaded Belgium, whose neutrality Britain, along with France, had guaranteed. The British government demanded that the Germans respect Belgian neutrality and so notify London by midnight August 4. When the ultimatum ran out, Great Britain declared war on Germany.

The main German blow came on the front where French generals had said it couldn't happen—through Belgium. By the third week of August, the main force of the German army was sweeping across the Franco-Belgian border. Between its advancing columns and Paris there was very little to stop it. Under intense pressure, French and British forces retreated. By the end of August, when Boy had been mobilized, Deauville filled up again, this time with frightened Parisian women without husbands, coachmen, and all other male servants.

German officers had the Eiffel Tower in their field glasses. Coco found out that Boy was with the staff of Sir John French, the commander of the five British divisions on the Marne. Boy's long years in France and his fluency in French gave him the instant rank of lieutenant.

Coco learned that the Germans had occupied Royallieu. A letter from Alphonse announced that both he and Lucien were in the army. Alphonse was a mechanic repairing the newfangled tanks the war introduced. Lucien was in the infantry. Coco wanted Adrienne and Antoinette to join her. Adrienne did not know where on the front her beloved Maurice was and refused to leave Paris. Antoinette came to Deauville, telling Gabrielle how the streets of Paris were the scene of patriotic bombast, pranks, fear, and uneasiness, how shops and theaters were closed, newspapers reduced to one sheet, and people ran around aimlessly with suitcases.

The German advance wavered before Paris and on August 30, General Alexander von Kluck turned his army southeast, passing to the east of Paris instead of surrounding the city. The Allies rallied, and fresh forces, transported to the front in six hundred Paris taxicabs, struck the flank of von Kluck's army. The Battle of the Marne saw Compiègne retaken— and the Royallieu barracks behind Etienne Balsan's garden transformed into a frontline hospital. In mid-September, however, the Germans dug in and a French assault was checked.

In Deauville, the women in flight said they had lost everything, which was not quite true. They still had money to buy a new wardrobe in which to do voluntary work at the hospital. Chanel was the only shop open, and her sporty clothes were just right for physical activities—oversized, hip-length knit jackets and straight linen skirts, sailor's blouses with open collars and hats devoid of decoration.

Elisabeth de Gramont was an early patron of the Gabrielle Chanel boutique on Rue Contaut-Biron. She would remember how crowded the shop
was and how quickly the Deauville wardrobes became somber, how the
summery satins disappeared, "and how mothers who had twenty-year-
old sons had a distinctive expression when they read the 'posters'—one
didn't say 'communiqués' yet."

Gabrielle needed help and summoned Adrienne. Her aunt didn't want
to leave Paris before learning the fate of Maurice. Coco told her there
was nothing like work to take the mind off waiting. Adrienne came to
Deauville.

From his seat in the senate and in *L'Homme libre*, Clemenceau denounced the shirkers. He demanded technical efficiency, attacked red
tape, insufficient munitions factories, and badly run hospitals. Echoing
Boy Capel's prewar hunch that superior efficiency and technology would
win the war, he railed against all who failed to realize this was a conflict
of supplies and organization.

Clemenceau's plain speaking meant *L'Homme libre* suffered in the
hands of military censors. In mid-September, the newspaper was suppressed, only to reappear two days later as *L'Homme enchaîné* (chained
man). News dispatches were mutilated, but Clemenceau was winning
many of the daily skirmishes with the censors. In the senate, he agitated
for more guns, munitions, and soldiers, for better use of available man-
power, and for a better-equipped and better-organized medical service.

Gabrielle wanted to be closer to Boy, and in December, as the front
stabilized and the country settled into the war, Adrienne, Antoinette, and
she followed the returning aristocracy and actresses to Paris. A saleswoman was left in charge of the Deauville boutique.

Again the war favored Coco.

Fashion in clothes and much else was turned upside down as the war
changed the way of life, attitudes, society, politics, and people themselves.
No war had ever involved so many civilians. Restrictions on women's
social activities lessened. Upper-class ladies, lacking servants, could no
longer entertain. With the exception of boys and old men, Paris was a
city without a male population. War widows were beginning to outnum-

ber war brides, and the patriotic ardor of the war's first months was giving way to sullen gloom. Amid references to hard times and reduced incomes, fashion magazines tried to be upbeat with articles headlined "Paris Makes a Brave Show in Spite of Guns" and "Paris Lifts Ever so Little the Ban on Gaiety" (British *Vogue*, January 1916).

Crinolines, pagoda hips, and tapered hems gave way to sports clothes and jerseys. Shortages of material supposedly led to shorter dresses, while shortages of metal helped bring an end to stays and "tight-lacing." The war was held responsible for new narrow skirts and, because of coal rationing, for an insatiable appetite for fur. Women were seen wearing hats of vulture quills, calf-length dresses under tunics nearly touching the ground, the whole attire swathed with a tempest of monkey-fur bands. By lucky chance, Chanel Modes was at the back entrance to the Ritz, the favorite meeting place for society ladies because it was heated and, it was insinuated, because Allied officers stayed there. "The Hotel Ritz was, if not cheerful, at least filled with a variety of people who liked to rub shoulders in the best-heated interior in Paris," said Elisabeth de Gramont.

Adrienne had reassuring news about Maurice, but she was called to Varennes to bury her parents, Gabrielle and Antoinette's grandparents. First seventy-five-year-old Virginie, then eighty-one-year-old Henri-Adrien had died. It was almost sixty years since Henri-Adrien and his child bride had taken to the road. Adrienne buried them together in Vichy.

Staring death in the face made men at the front want to cleanse their consciences. Alphonse wrote that there was a second woman in his life, a woman named Jeanne Causse, who had just borne him a son. The trouble was that he had never told Jeanne he was married. The Causses were a respectable family, and when Jeanne's pregnancy could no longer be hidden, she had run away. She had given birth to a boy she named Yvan in a hospice in Nîmes. If Alphonse came back alive, he would set things straight. He would divorce Madeleine and marry Jeanne Causse.

Coco sent a monthly money order to Mademoiselle Causse. During a furlough Alphonse made her pregnant again. When a daughter was born, she was named Gabrielle, in gratitude for the monthly allowance.

Boy commuted between Paris and London on mysterious missions. His coal mines and his ships worked flat out to supply the Allied fleet. He was making millions. If anyone knew anything about coal it was Lieutenant Arthur Capel. He was detached from Sir French's general staff and appointed to a hastily set-up Allied War Coal Commission. Increasingly, the appointment served merely as a "cover," because Boy was becoming a discreet go-between and emissary for two men biding their time— Clemenceau and David Lloyd George.

The senator was the stentorian hawk, the white-maned conscience of France striving to create an indomitable "will to win." He made trip after trip to the front. He harried government departments. As the war dragged on in the mud of the Marne, essentially at a stalemate, weariness and pacifism began to appear. In public, Clemenceau fulminated against draft dodgers and profiteers; in private he knew morale at the front was sagging, resources were nearly at an end, and no solution—military or political—was in sight.

In London, Lloyd George knew it even better. As munitions minister in the cabinet of Prime Minister Herbert Asquith, he was a staunch advocate of an increased war effort. Boy Capel became a friend.

Paris was tired and drab. The lack of demand for costly gowns, perfumes, furs, and jewels led to the loss of jobs for many women who worked. The munitions factories took up the slack, and the first women appeared wearing pants and dungarees because the clothes went with the job: making bombs, driving locomotives, delivering mail. Tired of rolling bandages, society ladies began to entertain again, prudently under the guise of charity work. The new British *Vogue* carried features on the Citroën munitions factory, on an eyewitness account of a night with a convoy, on the new ambulances, but the magazine gave more space to the charity matinees that combined worthy war work with society spectaculars. Lady Duff Gordon was photographed as "the personification of the mystery and power of Russia" at the Ten Allies Costume Ball, Fay Compton as a rose, and Viola Tree as a "tall bramble" at the *Our Day* matinee.

The theaters reopened, but the government banned jewels and evening dress at the Opéra, the Odéon, and the Comédie Française. Although the government might appeal to the public not to buy new dresses, the House of Doucet nevertheless advertised an irresistible evening wrap of rose panne velvet with skunk trim and tassel. The outbreak of the war had caught Poiret on a fashion tour of Germany. With his models, he presented himself to the French consul in Cologne and caught a last train to the border. Since then he had designed a new greatcoat for the army, and was putting together a fabulous collection to open his New York branch at 1239 Broadway.

Lanvin, Worth, and Paquin pioneered a new chemise dress, cut loose and full, belted under the bosom, calling it "comfortable, graceful, and economical." Diet and exercise were recommended for the new shape.

Coco also sold slimness. "I let go of the waistline and came up with a new silhouette," she would remember. "To get into it, and with the war's connivance, all my clients lost weight, to 'become skinny like Coco.' Wearing Coco Chanel clothes makes you look young, they said." She cut her gorgeous long hair—in stages, until she looked like a young boy. Her clients loved it.

Elisabeth de Gramont observed Coco and sensed that the striking, dark, thirty-two-year-old Chanel represented the future. "If her little hat shop was not much to talk about, the boutique where, between tea and apéritifs, society clients came to gossip, never stopped working," wrote the countess, who was one of the most elegant women in Paris. (Madeleine Vionnet said that if she wanted to tell if a dress was right she had only to try it on de Gramont.) "It was here, overhearing the flutter of conversations, that Coco Chanel realized that after the war these ladies would need sports frocks."

Boy was also thinking of the time when the murderous assault on sanity would be over. His presence in the wings of power made him want to write a book. When asked what the title would be, he said, "Reflections on Victory." In preparation for the writing, he was reading Napoleon and Bismarck, Plutarch and Balzac. The reading he preferred above all others was the *Memoirs* of the Renaissance statesman Maximilien, the Duke of Sully.

The summer of 1915 gave Boy a respite. To get away from it all, if only for a few days, he took Gabrielle with him to Biarritz, that other Atlantic seaside playground tucked against the towering Pyrenees and the Spanish border. The Pau-to-Paris express had stopped there that night ten years before when they had first become lovers.

A steady stream of faithful Latin clientele from across the border of neutral Spain gave Biarritz an eerie peacetime feeling. Once the favorite holiday resort of royalty, Biarritz was a pleasure capital for those not at war. There was dancing till dawn at the Miramar and the Hôtel du Palais, and there were automobiles, sleek, noiseless, high-powered machines with foreign license plates. A photo would survive of Boy and Coco on the beach, with a wicker basket of sausage, fruit, and wine on a towel. They were invited out by Constant Say, the heir to a sugar-refining fortune, and his opera-singer friend, Marthe Davelli, who had just made a brilliant debut at the Opéra Comique and, with the help of her sugar baron, was building an extravagant villa in nearby St.-Jean-de-Luz.

Davelli looked strikingly like Coco. The two women had the same wide mouth, big eyes, and long neck, and for the fun of it accentuated their resemblance by imitating each other's short hairstyle. Davelli was the life of any party.

Boy and Coco played golf with a pair of aging authors in white slacks, blazers, and strawhats—Edmond Rostand and Pierre Decourcelle. Coco had missed Rostand's *L'Aiglon* but had since seen *Cyrano de Bergerac*. On the green, she told Decourcelle of the mauve dress she had copied from a description in one of his mystery romances, and how her grandmother and Aunt Louise had ordered the outfit returned to the seamstress.

"Ah, monsieur, you cost me a sad day," she told the novelist, "actually sad weeks and difficult months."

Late in life, she would call Decourcelle a mushy author of trashy bathos, but the only real educator of her adolescent years. "After all the novels I read, nothing ever surprised me in life."

Boy and Coco dined in prewar splendor and both had the same idea— to repeat the Deauville coup.

They knew how to take risks and how to move fast. Boy would advance the initial capital, and before he returned to Paris, he had money wired to her. From the widow of Count Tristan de L'Hermite, they rented the Villa Larralde on Rue Gardères across from the Casino. Coco ordered Adrienne and Antoinette to join her. Adrienne refused. Maurice was about to receive a furlough and she was to spend a few days with him. She would come later. Antoinette arrived with a convoy of Rue Cambon seamstresses. Others were hired locally. On July 15, 1915, Coco opened not just a shop but Biarritz's first fashion house. The town had never seen anything like it.

Chanel hired Marie-Louise Deray, a twenty-one-year-old with some experience in couture. Before long she had sixty girls sewing under her.

"We worked with jersey, a fabric that no one had dared use before to make dresses," she would recall forty years later. "The 'diagonals' went every which way and we had to start over again several times. Mademoiselle was demanding. If a fitting went wrong she exploded. She loved to pester people. I cried a lot, believe me. She was tough, unrelenting with the staff. But what she came up with was sensational, both chic and exceedingly simple, so different from Poiret and Madeleine Vionnet."

And so different from the prewar fashion. *Harper's Bazaar* in far-off America was the first magazine to publish a picture of a Chanel creation. The dress had neither collar nor bodice, but was worn with a deep V-cut in front under a masculine-styled waistcoat. The garment had no puffing in the sleeves, no Poiret "kimono" effect, and it was worn with a large hat decorated not with ribbon but with a twist of fur. "Chanel's charming chemise dress," read the caption.

Coco shuttled between Rue Cambon and Rue Gardères, and tried to ship personnel back and forth between Paris and Biarritz. Provincial families were not eager to have their daughters go to Paris. Coco pleaded. Mothers were adamant. There were dangers in the capital—the war, zeppelin attacks, soldiers on the loose. Coco talked about the need for everybody to sacrifice. The mothers yielded.

Textiles were hard to come by. Boy helped her get tweeds and *homespuns* from Scotland. Jacques and Robert Balsan, who had once tried to make her marry their kid brother, helped her obtain broadcloth and put her in contact with silk manufacturers in Lyon.

"She chose everything herself—lace, accessories, colors," Deray would recall. "Of all the pastels that the dyeing factories in Lyon and Scotland could come up with for silk and wool, she always knew how to get the most beautiful ones. Our workrooms were an enchantment of colors, a rainbow."

If Chanel and her staff worked a great deal with machine-knit jersey, it was because Jean Rodier, an important fabric manufacturer, offered Chanel a huge stock of it. Echoing the story of how newspaper magnate Jean Prouvost started his fortune by printing his newspapers on a glazed paper that a wholesaler was stuck with, Gabrielle would say Rodier gave her a huge discount on the raw, natural-colored machine-knit because he feared he couldn't find a buyer.

Did fabric lead Chanel to style, supply to inspiration?

In one version of how she started with Rodier's jersey, she said that the wartime demand for an austere wardrobe led her to put in a large order for Rodier's jersey. Before the war, men had found the machine knit too scratchy for underwear, and Rodier could not imagine women buying couture dresses made in the fabric. He refused to go into production and told Chanel to try it out first. She was furious, but she created elegant frock coats in his jersey and proved him wrong. In another version, Rodier was so anxious to sell his stock that he showed her swatches in twenty-five shades of gray. She told him to simplify. Clients, she was sure, would never be able to make up their minds.

The war changed everything for women. "Nice" girls nursed war casualties, drove ambulances, worked in canteens, while middle-class women typed government letters and working-class women drove trains and shoveled explosives in munitions factories. Fashion in clothes changed to suit wartime living. "Dressing on a war income" was a regular feature in the patriotic press, with a recommendation that women should slim down in order to use less fabric.

By upbringing, if not inclination, Gabrielle was trained to "make do." The orphanage and Aunt Louise had taught her to improvise with bits and pieces, to find ideas in what was handy, to work with what was available. She understood that the war demanded a fashion of rummage, of salvage, a fashion that was simple and functional, and could be made up with opportunities and remnants.

Most of Coco's Biarritz production went to Spain, where elegance was still permissible. And if her clothes were cut from Rodier's jersey there was no reason not to insist on fit and function. Members of the Madrid royalty ordered by the dozen.

Coco never went to the workrooms. After choosing the fabrics, she called in Deray, the first of her *premières*, and told her what she wanted. She didn't always know the technical terms and, to compensate, spoke in a snappy, wounding voice. Misunderstandings and scenes were frequent, but, as Deray would remember, there was method to the madness. "We did lovely things. In jersey, of course, but also in cotton. The straight tunic, with a large tied bow low over the hips, became fashionable."

When Deray was asked what Mademoiselle herself was wearing, the *première* would say, "Big loose jerseys that were as simple as a boarding-school girl's frock, and extraordinarily chic. You had to see her arrive at noon, getting out of her Rolls—she very quickly got a Rolls, a chauffeur, and a footman. She looked like a queen."

Coco would claim she never cared about money, but after closing, Deray saw her at the till counting bank notes. It was incredible. They sold dresses at 7,000 francs each.*

Boy came down whenever he could. Coco was anxious to join him in Paris and worked to convince her sister to stay in Biarritz with full power in running the boutique. But Antoinette was beginning to rebel; she was twenty-eight and feared she would be a spinster forever. Gabrielle tried to cajole her. Antoinette would not have to do fittings—Deray could do that. "All you have to do is run the salons and greet the customers."

Antoinette gave in.

By early 1916, the combined staff of Paris, Deauville, and Biarritz totaled three hundred.

*The franc lost value throughout the war and through the following decades. The dollar, which fetched five francs in 1905, bought twenty-six francs by 1921, and, after the 1926 French financial crisis, fifty francs. The dollar itself started to skid after the Wall Street crash of 1929 and especially through inflation in the 1940s and 1970s. The Wharton School of Econometrics estimates a 1990 dollar is worth about one-sixth of its 1928 equivalent. Thus someone who paid 7,000 francs for a Chanel couture dress in 1915 paid some $350 period dollars, or $2,100 in today's money.

11

MISIA AND
DISTRACTIONS

~~~~~~

Misia, the divine Misia.

"We love people only for their faults," Gabrielle said of the plain-looking, insufferably snobbish, meddling tyrant of Parisian society. To Paul Morand, who also got to know Misia during the war, Gabrielle would say that her best friend "gave me ample and numerous reasons for loving her. Misia only connects with what she doesn't understand. Actually, she understands almost everything. To her I've remained a mystery, which explains the fidelity to me that she has so often denied." Less cattily, Coco once admitted that listening to Misia made her feel intelligent.

It was in May 1917 that Gabrielle met the remarkable woman whose influence she, in turn, would deny. The occasion was a dinner at Cécile Sorel's on Quai Voltaire. The actress was at the height of her glory, and besides Misia and Coco, Morand was present, together with his boss, Philippe Berthelot, the deputy director for political affairs at the Quai d'Orsay, and his wife, Hélène. Charity galas were as popular in Rome as in London and Paris, and Misia was just back from Rome, where, together with Picasso and Cocteau, she had been involved in getting a new production off the ground for Sergei Diaghilev. The Ballets Russes had had only one wartime season in Paris, and to keep the company alive, Diaghilev had sent the troupe on a tour of the United States and provincial Spain. Cocteau had in mind to do a *parade*, a ballet simulating the fairgrounds barkers' presentation of the attractions inside, and, in Rome, was writing a story that featured a Chinese conjurer, a precocious little

American girl, and a pair of acrobats, who would perform extracts from their acts. The music was by Erik Satie and Cocteau asked the composer to introduce real noises from everyday life—typewriter clatter, pistol shots, and ships' sirens—in his score. Picasso, who had fallen in love with Olga Koklova, one of the Ballets Russes stars, was painting the sets.

When Misia left the room for a moment, Berthelot whispered that she was a woman who aroused the genius in people, that her cruelty was subtle, her treacherousness devastating.

Coco said little that evening, but Misia observed her. "Despite the fact that she did not say a word, she radiated a charm I found irresistible," Misia would recall thirty years later. "She made me think of Madame du Barry. Therefore I arranged to sit next to her after dinner. During the exchange of banalities appropriate to a first meeting in a drawing room, I learned that she was called Mademoiselle Chanel and that she had a milliner's shop in Rue Cambon."

When they were ready to leave and Gabrielle was getting into a ravishing fur-trimmed red velvet coat, Misia couldn't help complimenting her. Gabrielle slipped out of the coat and hung it on Misia's shoulders, saying she would be happy to give it to her. "Obviously, I could not accept it, but her gesture had been so pretty that I found her totally bewitching and thought of nothing but her. The next day I couldn't wait to go to her store in Rue Cambon. In her shop one found sweaters, hats, all kinds of accessories. When I entered, two women were there, talking to her and calling her 'Coco.' I don't know why this nickname upset me, but my heart sank. I had the feeling my idol was being crushed. Why pin such a vulgar pet name on such an exceptional person?"

That evening, Misia and her longtime lover, the Spanish painter José-Maria Sert y Badia, were the guests of Gabrielle and Boy. "We found ourselves in the midst of innumerable Coromandel screens. Sert was scandalized by this 'love at first sight' of mine. I was not in the habit of being carried away like that and I must admit I was rather surprised that a woman I had met the night before could really fill such a place in my thoughts."

Jojo, as Misia called her lover, was a small, hairy man of vibrating energy who spoke French with an accent that delighted Gabrielle. Born to an immensely rich Catalan family, Sert was a sculptor of reliefs that graced the ballroom at New York's Waldorf-Astoria Hotel and the painter of elephantine murals (and future decorator of New York's Rockefeller

Center). "How very Spanish," remarked Degas on viewing one of Sert's huge frescoes in his Paris studio, "and in such a quiet street, too." Sert was fussy and loved to tell cruel and bizarre stories.

The first time Coco and Boy were invited to Misia and Jojo's apartment, they found the place so overcrowded they both thought Misia was dealing in antiques. Coco's sensitive nose smelled dirt under the accumulation of knickknacks, the aquarium, the displays of ships in bottles, the African art and glass-encased fans.

Eleven years older than Gabrielle—and three years senior to Jojo—Maria Sophie Olga Godebska Natanson Edwards was the granddaughter of the cellist Adrien-François Servais and the daughter of the sculptor Cyprien Godebski, whose statues graced the Casino in Monte Carlo and the presidential palace in Lima, Peru. High drama attended Misia's birth in St. Petersburg in 1872. Eugénie Servais had traveled to St. Petersburg in the dead of winter in pursuit of her recklessly unfaithful Cyprien when she died giving birth to Misia. The child's life was luxurious and loveless, but she was musically precocious and became an accomplished pianist, capable of later sight-reading scores for Diaghilev. She had Gabriel Fauré as her first piano teacher and sat on the knees of the aging Franz Liszt to play Beethoven. Her opinion was respected by Debussy, and Ravel dedicated a waltz to her.

When she was twenty-one, she married Thadée Natanson, the delightful and learned editor of the avant-garde *Revue Blanche.* The fortnightly magazine published Proust, Gide, Zola, Paul Claudel, and rich new talents, illustrating their works with paintings, sketches, and woodcuts of Bonnard, Vuillard, Toulouse-Lautrec, and Suzanne Valadon. The next thirteen years of Misia's life were spent in a charmed circle of painters, writers, and musicians, and her importance derived from the artists she knew and had modeled for—Toulouse-Lautrec, Renoir, Vuillard, and Bonnard in paint, Proust and Cocteau in prose. Misia had an acute sense of what was utterly new and flawless in the arts.

When Renoir did the first of two portraits of her he asked her to open her dress. "Why won't you let me see your breasts?" he asked. In her memoirs, she would regret not having let him see everything. "Nobody appreciated better than he the grain of a woman's skin." One of the portraits ended up in the Leningrad Museum, the other at the Barnes Foundation in Philadelphia.

She discovered Vincent van Gogh and offered his paintings to her friends for 200 francs.* They laughed and asked if they were to hang a van Gogh, which end was up. They were the same friends who put their fingers in their ears when she played Stravinsky for them.

Misia was a woman who went too far in her reactions and emotions, and had a way of concealing her *joie de vivre* behind a mask of ill-humor. She was fascinating, ruthless, vain, and quarrelsome—"very Slav," according to Valentine Gross Hugo, who painted her portrait. "A fishwife," according to fellow Pole Helena Rubinstein, who bought Jojo's house on Ile-St.-Louis in the 1930s. Proust, who found Misia and her entourage distasteful, delineated her in two less-than-appealing characters, Princess Yourbeletieff and Madame Verdurin in *Remembrance of Things Past.* Proust maintained she brought together friends of hers who didn't know each other for the pleasure of seeing them quarrel. Cocteau depicted her as the Princess in *Thomas the Imposter* and called her Aunt Brutus because she "stabbed" her friends. It was said she never read a book, and her correspondence seemed to support this conclusion, yet she knew Verlaine and was a friend of Mallarmé. In his play *Les Monstres Sacrés,* Cocteau made her say, "It's perfectly normal that extraordinary things happen to me. I'm an exceptional person. Oh, don't think I'm boasting. I mean to say that, unfortunately, I'm exceptional and that, unfortunately, I can't live by the rules. I must make my own."

Natanson pushed his wife into the arms of Alfred Edwards, a newspaper tycoon. Women of Misia's milieu usually avoided too-dazzling divorces, but in 1904 Misia flaunted the affair and divorce court drama. It was as Mrs. Edwards that she met Diaghilev.

The meeting was crucial for both of them. Diaghilev and Misia had much in common. They were both born in St. Petersburg in March 1872. Both had lost their mothers at birth and had seen their fathers remarry. Both had stepmothers who had encouraged their musical talents. Misia introduced Diaghilev to her favorite composers. Ravel's *Daphnis and Chloë* and Debussy's *Afternoon of a Faun* were Diaghilev's first pioneering ballets. Misia understood Stravinsky's music far better than Diaghilev, and the composer soon realized that she was Diaghilev's chief musical adviser.

The marriage to Edwards ended when the tycoon transferred his passion to a stunning demimondaine. After humiliations and scandal verging on farce, a divorce was arranged in 1909. On the rebound, she met Sert.

*About $200 in 1990 currency.

She was thirty-six and for the first time melted in sexual pleasure. "Without Misia," Sert would say, "I would die stupid."

Arthur Capel went from one success to another. His book came out in London to reviews that made him something of a literary celebrity. To his *Reflections on Victory*, he had added the subtitle *A Project for the Federation of Governments*, and in 135 crisp pages suggested the British Empire and its allies form a federation, invite neutral nations to join, "and eventually include those of our enemies who really desire peace." To suggest a formula for peace while the war was entering its fourth year was perhaps even more daring than calling the extermination of Germany both "impossible and unthinkable." The *Times Literary Supplement* noted the author's special stress on something better than the balance of power, but its reviewer commented that the book would "gain in cogency if more attention were paid to the practical working out of the proposed scheme."

In December 1916, when simultaneous offensives on all fronts had misfired, the French army was demoralized, the Russian forces were ready to rebel against the czar, and Germany's submarines were terrorizing the seas, Lloyd George became prime minister. By ensuring that a steady supply of guns and shells reached the western front, Lloyd George had become a hero of the press but made many political enemies. Exhaustion spread through the Allies' ranks. In Britain, the House of Lords demanded a truce while troubles broke out in Ireland. A neutralist movement was growing in Italy; strikes plagued the home front in France; and in Russia the monk Grigory Rasputin, whose ascendancy over the czar had reached pathological proportions, was assassinated.

The air war intensified in March 1917, but it was Germany's unrestricted submarine warfare that brought the United States into the war on the Allied side a month later. The collapse of Russia and Vladimir Lenin's decision to seek an armistice with Germany, however, spread dissension among the Allies, dissatisfaction with the conduct of the war, and a tendency to discuss the taboo subject—peace by negotiation. Allied misfortunes gave Clemenceau his chance. An October offensive by the Axis forces in Italy led to the Allied disaster at Caporetto and had German-Austrian armies on the outskirts of Venice. The German commander, General Erich von Ludendorff, did not have the means to exploit the success. The event, however, forced Lloyd George to agree to more coordination in the conduct of the war and the creation of an Inter-Allied Military Committee headquartered in Versailles. A month later, French president Raymond Poincaré asked Clemenceau to form a government.

Boy was one of the first to see Clemenceau when the "Tiger," as the frontline soldiers called Clemenceau, formed his government. As prime minister, Clemenceau knew how large a task he faced. Morale at the front was bad, and at home even worse; resources were meager, and no end to the war was in sight. France was bent on absolute victory, Clemenceau thundered, and would accept no half measures. Those who spoke of wavering or yielding would be silenced; anyone who was an obstruction to victory would be ruthlessly removed. Arthur Capel & Co., Ltd., had difficulty finding freighters not already requisitioned by the British government, but Boy offered Clemenceau to put what ships he could find at the service of France and, despite the U-boat attacks, to continue to keep French factories supplied with coal. The Tiger accepted. Over the next months, Boy was the private go-between for the two leaders, moving from merely important circles to governing circles as he was seen dashing into 10 Downing Street and his chauffeured car was waved into the courtyard of the Elysée Palace.

The war entered its fourth and bloodiest year. The Germanic alliance was weaker in numbers but directed by a single commander, Ludendorff; the Allies were stronger in number but with too many heads. Owing to their own excessive losses, diffusion of effort, and the collapse of Russia, the Allies were faced with the grim fact that the numerical balance had been reversed, and months would elapse before the troops from the United States arrived to tilt the scales once more in their favor. In November, a Supreme War Council was formed. Headquartered in Versailles, it was made up of the principal ministers of the Allies and military representatives. Boy Capel was appointed political secretary to the British delegation. To Gabrielle it meant he would spend more time in France.

In Russia, the appalling hardships suffered by millions of soldiers, ill-supplied and poorly commanded, the grotesque bureaucratic muddle, and inertia had combined to create an explosive situation, especially in Petrograd. Progressives in the Duma, the legislative assembly, warned of impending revolution and denounced Czar Nicholas's absolutism. Tens of thousands of starving workers were on the streets, regiments mutinied, and by March 1, 1917, the 170,000 men of the Petrograd garrison refused orders and began shooting their officers. Michael Rodzianko, the president of the Duma, telegraphed the czar that the city was in anarchy.

Diaghilev and the Ballets Russes were in Rome when the czar dismissed the Duma. Its members refused to disperse and instead formed a provisional government with the lawyer Alexander Kerensky as its leader. Rodzianko headed a list of signatories, which included Maxim Gorky and the Ballets Russes' electrifying stage designer Léon Bakst, urging Diaghilev to return to Russia and become Minister of the Fine Arts. Diaghilev hesitated, but for the opening night in Rome substituted the "Song of the Volga Boatmen" for the old czarist hymn.

In Paris, Misia was bedridden with a cold, but Paul Morand, who was visiting, caught her excitement. "Misia speaks with enthusiasm of the Russian revolution, which she sees as a vast ballet," he noted in his diary. "She says that Bakst finds his brother-in-law is Minister of War. Diaghilev is related to Rodzianko. All the group headed by Gorky, Argutinsky, Benois, Bakst are coming into power. In Rome Stravinsky has been commissioned to write the national anthem on the theme of the 'Song of the Volga Boatmen.'"

Knowing she was altering their relationship, Gabrielle reimbursed Boy Capel, and bought the Biarritz villa outright for 300,000 francs cash.* Her declaration of independence seems to have made Boy experience a novel sentiment: jealousy. Coco was dynamic and much admired. At Misia's dinners, she was introduced to Pablo Picasso and his Russian wife, Olga, to Igor Stravinsky, who preferred to leave his wife in Switzerland, to Cocteau, and to Raymond Radiguet, whose clever poetry scandalized *le tout Paris.* Coco acquired the manners of the social elite, but since she still felt less than secure among the artistic lions of Misia's entourage, she accepted—for a time—her new friend's tutelage. Her aunt Adrienne was less impressed. While Adrienne was still only the mistress of Maurice de Nexon, she felt sufficiently superior to Misia for Coco to remember Adrienne's remarks after first meeting Misia:

"I had tea with your Polishwoman," Adrienne told Gabrielle.

"My Polishwoman?"

"Yes, the lady who wears satin shoes in the morning. I don't like her. She's too prying, tried to make me tell everything about you. I told her, 'Madame, are you taking me for a private investigation agency?' You've got some funny friends."

*Circa $600,000 in 1990 currency.

Coco in bobbed hair and Boy were at the May 18 premiere of *Parade*. Diaghilev wanted to show that the Russian ballet could renew itself. Besides the typewriter clatter, pistol shots, and steamship hoots, Satie had written a score with hints of ragtime and satire. Picasso's curtain, a naïve depiction of a nineteenth-century fairground, gave no hint of the cubist novelties that its raising revealed. Much applause and a few whistles greeted the torero, harlequin, turbaned Negro, Chinese conjuror, and Little American Girl. The French barker, in top hat and starched shirtfront, carried a background of Paris chestnut trees around with him, and the American barker was a Buffalo Bill with a Manhattan skyscraper on his shoulder and a huge megaphone.

Coco admitted she didn't understand the "Cubist ballet." "It was too new, and it scared me," she would recall. "I asked myself, Is this beautiful?"

She appeared alone at Cécile Sorel's dinner for the *Parade* troupe and met Picasso. "He was nasty then, but he fascinated me. He watched you like a hawk ready to swoop down on its prey. He scared me. When he came into a room and I didn't see him yet, I knew he was there and that he was watching me."

Both Boy and Coco were becoming rich. During the bleak winter of 1917–18, a ton of coal rose in price to 300 francs in Paris. To keep warm, society ladies chose furs, and the status symbol of the moment was leopard skin. For women who could not afford leopard, fur trimmings appeared on hats, hems, muffs, and veils. British *Vogue* cautioned its readers "not to inquire too closely into the origins of some of the strange skins which have been cut into strips or folded into collars to trim many of the smartest frocks." It is not known where Gabrielle got her pelts, but the Chanel boutique's fur-trimmed jersey costumes were making her a fortune.

Boy was increasingly distracted. The Ludendorff attack was a disaster for the British army—300,000 casualties, ending with the Chemin des Dames battle. But Coco sensed he was also becoming evasive. When she asked him if anything was wrong, he said he didn't want to lose her. She was ready for the truth, she said. He told her he was engaged to marry another woman.

12

SPURNED

~~~~~~

He had met the daughter of Lord Ribblesdale while visiting the front line at Arras. Diana Lister Wyndham was an ambulance driver, doing Red Cross duty under the Duchess of Sutherland. Cynicism had not yet reached Marchioness of Londonderry's Women's Service Legion. "Noble and well-mannered ladies are no more leaving their hospitals than soldiers their trenches," wrote Elisabeth de Gramont, "even if, little by little, the sons of the *grande bourgeoisie* have learned to take cover." Diana was one of the titled ladies in the ambulance corps, a delicate and beautiful young woman of twenty-five who had become a widow right after she was married. First her husband, then her brother had been killed in battle.

Gabrielle could only feel betrayed. She and Boy had been together nearly eight years. They had sacrificed depth for reach, and they had been successful. Yet there were things she could not give him—a brilliant marriage, conventionality, aristocratic connections. She would never say what her reaction was to Boy's announcement. In her dialogues with Paul Morand in 1946, she talked of Boy as a singular human being whose mellow, cheerful authority and ironic severity both charmed and conquered people, as a cultivated man, who beyond his polo-player dandyism and business agility possessed a deep inner life that touched on the otherworldly and religious thought.

"We were in love, we could have gotten married," she would tell several of the writers of her life story. One of them, Marcel Haedrich, emphasized the conditional of the phrase, "We *could* have gotten married."

Coco could understand Boy's secret dream of effacing the lurking rumors of his bastard antecedents by marrying into the aristocracy. Diana was the youngest daughter of that fourteenth Baron Edward Ribblesdale whose portrait by John Singer Sargent illuminated the Tate gallery and whose munificence was notorious because he had given his mistress, Rosa Lewis, the Cavendish Hotel in London's Jermyn Street when he tired of her.

Friends of Coco who met Diana found the young widow to be a sweet-tempered and candid person. In talking to Pierre Galante forty years later, Antoinette Bernstein would suggest that it was Gabrielle who, in an overwrought defiance, suggested Boy marry Diana. "Boy was a very captivating man with a lot of women in his life," Bernstein would say. "Chanel knew that and she also knew—she was an intelligent woman—that he probably would never marry her. Chanel knew the insignificance of the young woman, and no doubt thought she could keep her hold on Boy. Which is of course not exactly what happened."

A turn for the worse on the western front forced Boy to postpone any thought of marriage. A new offensive by General Ludendorff cut a railway line to Paris and threatened to drive a wedge between the British and French on the northern front. While General Douglas Haig's Sixth British Army bore the brunt of fighting, General Philippe Pétain threw everybody under his command in the twenty-kilometer break. Clemenceau went to the front, creeping within 300 meters of the enemy positions, haranguing Australian troops in English and agreeing to Haig's suggestion that Ferdinand Foch be named generalissimo of the Allied armies. Compiègne was bombarded and Paris threatened once more. At the Supreme War Council headquarters in Versailles all leaves, including Captain Capel's wedding furlough, were canceled.

Boy's engagement didn't prevent him and Coco from living together or being seen together, at least by Henri and Antoinette Bernstein and by Misia, José Sert, and their friends. Still, Coco was looking for a place of her own, and in the early months of 1918, Misia told her about a beautiful apartment vacated by a friend who had fled Paris. Coco jumped at the opportunity. The owner had decamped with such dispatch that he had left behind a huge Buddha statue and a closetful of kimonos. When the window curtains were opened, they revealed a beautiful view of the Seine and the Trocadéro across the river.

Misia also recommended a butler and his wife. Joseph Leclerc was a domestic of Chekhovian demeanor who had been in her service since 1912. As Misia planned to finally marry Jojo Sert, she thought it expedient to change servants. Monsieur Joseph, as everyone called him, and his parlor-maid wife, Marie, came with a twelve-year-old daughter, Suzanne. The Leclercs were to stay in Coco's service for fifteen years and Suzanne grew up in the household.

Coco spent time redoing the apartment. Boy came by every day; his duties as secretary to the delegation kept him in Paris. Big Bertha, Germany's new long-range cannon, shelled the outskirts of Paris; on a night of particularly heavy bombardment the guests at the Ritz were told to assemble in the lobby and descend to the basement. The next day several ladies slipped across the Place Vendôme to Chanel's in search of nocturnal attire that would allow them to go downstairs in something other than nightgowns. Coco managed to locate a shipment of men's pajamas, and sold them out in one afternoon. Wartime uncertainty permitted much improvised living.

The collapse of Bulgaria, Germany's Balkan ally, convinced Ludendorff that it was necessary to sue for peace. In September, when the French started a general offensive, the new American forces attacked in the Meuse-Argonne, and a Belgian-British attack opened in Flanders, the German supreme command lost its nerve—only for a matter of days, but that was sufficient and recovery too late. On September 29, Germany made the abrupt decision to appeal for an armistice.

In October, Captain Arthur Capel married Diana Lister Wyndham. There was no notice in the society pages, perhaps because the war was in its last throes. The wedding was celebrated at the private chapel at Beaufort Castle, Major General Simon Fraser's Invernesshire mansion in the heart of Scotland. Sir Simon, the fourteenth baron of Lovat, was Diana's brother-in-law. No firsthand accounts survive of Gabrielle's reaction to Boy's marriage.

The war ended on November 11 in an armistice, signed in Marshal Foch's sleeping car on a railway in the Compiègne forest, where Coco and Balsan's merry friends had ridden so many times before the war. Eight and a half million men had died, including 1.3 million Frenchmen and 900,000 British Empire soldiers, hundred of thousands crippled, amputees, *mutilés de guerre*. Coco's brothers and many of her friends, including Etienne Balsan, were among the survivors.

Coco marked the outbreak of peace—and her solitary status—by renting a villa in the suburban hills of St. Cloud. She chose the house for the fragrant garden, for the view of Paris, and because Henri and Antoinette Bernstein lived close by. She was seen at victory celebrations with Eduardo Matinez de Hoz, a wealthy Argentine and man-about-town. Paul Morand came to Rue Cambon for nightly têtes-à-tête. He found her to be "very alone, very timid, and very much watched over by Misia."

By summer, she was back in Rue Cambon, when chiefs of state, envoys, and emissaries arrived for the peace conference. Paris might be grimy and war-weary, but there were embassy receptions and the delegates' wives could not pass up the occasion to renew their wardrobes. Together with Lanvin and the Rue de la Paix couture house of Martial et Armand, Chanel did a roaring business both in formal wear and sports clothes.

With the war over and men back from the front, marriage was in the air. Both Gabrielle's and Boy's sisters were wed, Antoinette foolishly, Bertha Capel cunningly.

Oscar Fleming was a Canadian airman, a twenty-three-year-old Royal Air Force volunteer who came to Paris to celebrate the victory. The eldest son of a Windsor, Ontario, lawyer, he was whooping it up in the company of men infinitely wealthier than he. When he and Antoinette became engaged he was careful not to mention that he had ten brothers and sisters and that his father was anything but rich. Antoinette was thirty-two and ready to believe that life with Oscar would be one of chic transatlantic shuttles. She imagined herself the ambassadress of Parisian elegance in Canada.

Oscar and Antoinette were married on the first anniversary of the armistice, November 11, 1919. Gabrielle created the wedding gown and Antoinette's witnesses were Arthur Capel and Adrienne's ever-faithful Maurice de Nexon. The newlyweds sailed for Canada with a chambermaid and seventeen trunks.

Captain Capel was more than a witness at his sister's marriage to Herman Stern, the son of Lord and Lady Michelham. Boy was the chief architect of a scheme that left Bertha married in name only, and independently wealthy for life.

In late December, the less-than-robust Lord Herbert Michelham caught a chill that turned into pneumonia. His lordship was the son of the late banker, Baron de Stern—the title was a Portuguese creation—and although he and his wife, Aimée Geraldine, had squandered a good part of the $100-million fortune,* there was still a lot of money that the Stern family thought they, and not the flighty Aimée, should inherit. During one of Aimée's absences from the Michelham town house, members of the Stern clan managed to gain the sick man's ear. A new will that effectively took his fortune away from Lady Michelham, leaving her with no more than the contents of various houses and a fixed income, was drawn up and witnessed. The existence of this new will was kept secret. Through the influence of one of the new executors, Boy was made a coexecutor of the secret will.

Since Boy was close to Aimée, indeed was rumored to have been her lover, he told her of the new will. Her ladyship wasted no time persuading physicians and lawyers that her dying husband wished to make a codicil. Nodding to a lawyer's obligingly drafted codicil, Herbert Michelham in effect reversed the new will and named his wife as executor of the entire fortune until the sons, Herman and Jack, reached the age of thirty.

Aimée made Bertha a proposition she could not refuse—marry the slightly dotty and underdeveloped eighteen-year-old Herman and she would have no cause to regret it. The final amount Bertha agreed to was a sum that would generate a yearly income for her of $125,000,† free of all present and future taxes. Only two strings were attached: no children, and no scandals. By depriving the retarded Herman of legitimate offspring, Aimée made sure Jack, the son fathered by her lover Jeff Cohn, would carry on the Michelham title. Bertha accepted.

Boy flew his sister and Herman to London, where he had arranged for the ceremony to take place by special license the following afternoon at All Saints Church, Knightsbridge. Herman was excited at the chance of a ride in an airplane, and on January 4, 1919, he and Bertha were married. Lord Michelham died three days after the wedding.

Boy had other successful ventures during the first month of peace. On December 12, the House of Lords had upheld a Court of Appeals judgment in Capel's favor in a contract dispute over a freighter lease. The S.S. *Quito* had been leased to Arthur Capel & Co., Ltd, in 1915, when

*Circa $850 million in 1990 currency.
†About $700,000 in 1990 money.

the government had requisitioned the freighter. After three months in dry dock, however, the government decided not to use the vessel and released it to its owners. When Capel heard they were selling the *Quito*, he demanded that they honor the original charter and lease the steamer to him. The owners refused, claiming the lease was no longer valid. In upholding the lower court judgment, the lord chief justices awarded Arthur Capel & Co., Ltd, £15,344 in damages. A month later, Boy was awarded a civil Commander of the British Empire (CBE) honor for his work as political assistant secretary to the British section of the Supreme War Council in Versailles.

Paris was shabby and sad in victory—nearly a million and a half Frenchmen were dead. "Never again," proclaimed the politicians. The northern third of France was in ruins, the nation's treasury empty, and the war debts piled so high that they were almost beyond counting. Imperceptibly, however, Paris began to revive. Attracted by its beauty, its charm, its civilities, its balmy air of freedom, its appreciation of the arts and of artists, and the life of the mind, students, painters, writers, designers flocked from the four corners of the world.

There was racing at Longchamp, and the season started up again. Paul Morand took Gabrielle to the Gaya nightclub, where a pianist and a black saxophonist played syncopated music. The bar became fashionable when the Prince of Wales, on a quick visit to Paris, showed up in the company of Arthur Rubinstein and Princess Violette Murat. When the Gaya moved to Rue Boissy d'Anglas and was renamed Le Boeuf sur le Toit (literally "the ox on the roof") after a Brazilian hit song, it became the gathering place of both high society and the avant-garde, a world less interested in art, writing, and music than in the sheer celebrity of artists, writers, and musicians. "Chic" talent, renown, beauty, and vice superseded landed titles here, and enthroned Coco Chanel along with Derain, Picasso, Rubinstein, Satie, and Etienne de Beaumont. With Cocteau leading the parade, opium, sexual ambiguity, and campy parody soon became topics of the day.

Demobilized, Poiret opened up his salon again, and with it a nightclub, L'Oasis. Coco, who had eight workrooms at the end of the war, moved her *maison* from number 21 to a six-story building at 31 Rue Cambon. For four years, women had driven streetcars, turned out munitions, sewn uniforms, and, more important, learned to administer, make decisions, earn livings, enjoy careers, and practice independence without quite calling it that.

Coco had created functional chic. She had taken the wartime fabrics, especially jersey, and molded everything to her own taste. The Chanel silhouette stayed close to the lines of the uncorseted figure, making the bouffant skirts of Lanvin look old-fashioned, and the follies of Poiret too theatrical. Vionnet made dresses that were works of art, but Chanel was more commercial. "Everything she does makes news—the first quilted coat, the narrow crêpe de chine dress inside a cage of tulle, and the suntan which she cultivates," wrote *Vogue.*

In October, Captain Edward Molyneux, an Irishman who had served his apprenticeship at Lucille in London and had the financial backing of a British press lord, opened a new house in Rue de la Paix. He showed glamorous black evening dresses and hats with ostrich feathers. Together with Lanvin, however, Chanel was beginning to find a large market between sportswear and formal afternoon dressing. Summer weekends included motoring, swimming, sailing, and tennis, and the fashion magazines told readers that their suitcases were not complete without a plain yet chic traveling suit of wool jersey with a tailored blouse, day frocks, sports dresses, and low-heeled shoes. Chanel's simple "poor look" was expensive, but it made the wearer look young and casual, and she was not afraid of telling her clients and the fashion press what was passé. Dresses with flounces and laces were out, along with tulle veils, Coco declared. Referring to the smart little motorcars Albert Dion and Bouton & Trepardoux were marketing, she said, "How can such women even get into a Dion-Bouton when a Rolls-Royce is barely large enough for them?"

The 1919 summer afternoon uniform was a dress in organdy or silk, the essential accessory a parasol. The styles were an eclectic mix favoring "sack" dresses with V necks. All evening dresses were fringed for dancing, with ostrich, steel beads, velvet ribbons, or tassels of silk. Women were no longer content to choose clothes from sketches or wooden mannequins—"They want to see how the clothes will move," wrote *Vogue.* For the first time couturier collections were presented on live models.

The reckless twenties were a rich cocktail of society and the avant-garde, of verve, jazz, the automobile, Hollywood, and the headlong pursuit of freedom. If wearing Chanel fashions said something, it was, Look, I'm young and I'm pretty. And I'm not sure I'm prudish, priggish, or straight-laced. The statement was not proclaimed in window displays at 31 Rue

Cambon, but divined as being part of the exquisite forces that accelerated the revolution in manners and morals. Paris fashion extended its influence and territory as newspapers, magazines, and movie newsreels energetically reported its gospel of style and chic.

Coco's sister heard of all the excitement in faraway Canada. Lovely Antoinette, who had been there to help when Coco started out and had run the booming Deauville and Biarritz stores, was not the first war bride to be disappointed by what she found in her husband's homeland. If Windsor, Ontario, was not exactly the sticks, its elders in general, and the Fleming family in particular, seemed to be living by bygone strictures.

Antoinette had married a penniless student, she realized, and she had been relegated to the depths of intolerant provincialism. Custom still frowned upon women smoking on the street or in the office, and in the evangelical hinterlands the old taboo died hard. Because Antoinette smoked in public and one of the Fleming daughters had been found smoking in the toilet, the pater familias took a dim view of the French daughter-in-law.

Antoinette poured out her misery in letters to her sisters. Coco and Adrienne wrote back, urging Antoinette to make herself useful. Gabrielle appointed her sister North American agent for Chanel fashions and, when Oscar was sent to Toronto to study law, Antoinette extracted from her trunks part of her costly trousseau and went across the Charles River to sell the dresses to Detroit department stores.

The next letter from Antoinette begged her sister for a ticket back to France. But by return mail, Gabrielle told Antoinette to give it another chance.

Automobiles were the new postwar craze. Fast cars had a tremendous romantic allure, the appeal of speed, powerful machinery, and status symbol rolled into one. Auto races started up again, often with wartime aviators, such as the American flying ace Edward Rickenbacker, seeking new thrills behind the wheels. Paul Morand got himself a Bugatti and enjoyed taking off at dawn for a hair-raising spin to Le Mans. Boy bought a fast convertible and came to Paris—without Diana.

He was rich, married, and living in a world of elegance, power, and privilege. But it was not enough. He wanted Coco, too. He stayed with her in her St. Cloud hideaway. As Antoinette Bernstein would put it, "Boy came regularly to see her, but only to tell her how unhappy he was. He wished he could have his former bachelor existence back again, the existence in which Gabrielle had been his lodestar. With her he had freed himself from prejudices. She mocked him and the landed nobility he tried to embrace by marrying Diana."

His wife was pregnant, he told Coco. He was driving down to Cannes to spend Christmas with her and his sister, Lady Michelham. Also, he was going to look for an appropriate Riviera winter residence.

It was in the middle of the night of December 22–23 when Léon de Laborde rang the bell on Gabrielle's door in suburban St. Cloud. Nobody answered, but he kept ringing. His ringing, hammering on the door, and shouting finally produced Joseph.

The butler hesitated to admit him, but when Léon told him his news, Joseph led him in and ran upstairs.

Gabrielle came downstairs, in white pajamas and with her short hair tousled—"the silhouette of an adolescent, a youth in satin," Laborde would recall. Boy had had an accident, he told her. It had happened on the road from St. Raphael to Cannes. Gabrielle's gaze made him lose his nerve, and he stammered something about a very serious injury.

"There is no need for that, sir," Joseph interrupted, "Mademoiselle has understood."

The details were sketchy, Laborde continued. A tire on Boy's car had burst, causing the automobile to overturn. Boy had been killed in the fiery blaze that resulted.

Joseph hurried away to make tea. Coco's face was a grimace of agony, but not a tear showed. After a while she disappeared upstairs only to return, fully dressed, an overnight bag in her hand.

Outside, Joseph held Laborde's car door. Gabrielle got in. It was dawn when they were off on the 1,000-kilometer drive to Cannes.

Under the headline "English Motorist Killed in France," the Christmas Eve edition of the London *Times* said, "Lord Rosslyn, telegraphing last night from St. Raphael, stated that Captain Arthur Capel, who was killed in an automobile accident on Monday, is being buried today at 2:30 P.M. at Fréjus with full military honours." A Reuters telegram from Nice stated that Captain Capel had been killed owing to one of the tires of his car bursting, and that his chauffeur, named Mansfield, had been injured. Captain Capel was traveling from Paris to Cannes. The next day the *New York Times* carried the following news item:

BRITISH DIPLOMAT KILLED

Arthur Capel, Friend of Lloyd George, Victim of Motor Accident

NICE, Dec. 24—Arthur Capel, who during the war was Political Secretary to the Inter-Allied War Committee, was killed last night in an automobile accident while he was on his way from Paris to Monte Carlo. A tire on his car blew out, ditching the machine. Mr. Capel was a close friend of Premier Lloyd George.

Laborde and Gabrielle reached the Riviera late Christmas Day. From Cannes to Nice, all the big hotels were full for the holidays. It was the first season the British were back en masse, and everyone was celebrating the first year of peace and the dawn of the new decade. Laborde wanted to rest, but Coco refused to stop. He drove on to Monte Carlo, arriving at the Casino late at night. He wanted to find Lady Michelham and Bertha. Going from reception desk to reception desk, he tracked down Boy's sister and phoned her suite.

Bertha had a suite of rooms and could put up both of them. But if it was to see Boy one last time, they had come too late. Because of the holidays the funeral had taken place the day before. In any case, the casket had been closed because Boy had been burned beyond recognition. The *Times*'s funeral notice spoke of Boy's death as being "a great blow" to his many friends. "He was probably one of the best-known Englishmen living in France, where he had important coal interests. During the war he did excellent work, both officially and unofficially, and was a great favourite of M. Clemenceau. He was a thorough sportsman, and at the same time a lover of books."

Coco came upstairs. Despite Bertha's entreaties, she refused the bed she was offered and spent the rest of the night in a chaise longue. In the morning, she told Bertha she wanted to go to the scene of the accident, alone.

Aimée Michelham's chauffeur drove Gabrielle to the spot where the wreck of Boy's car was still on the shoulder. Bertha would never forget the driver's account. He parked a little past the crash site, he reported. The lady got out, walked back to the wreckage, and like a blind person, touched it with her hands. After that she sat on the kilometer stone, turned her back to the road, and cried. He had kept at a discreet distance, and watched her terrible grief.

Two

13

GRIEF

There was nothing to explain. The only man she ever had really loved had died. His death erased any need to delve into the deeper meaning of their relationship, any need to scrutinize why she felt stranded and alone, why he had married someone else. Fate had taken him away from her. In death he was hers.

"I lost everything when I lost Capel," she would tell Paul Morand twenty-five years later. "He left in me a void that the years have not fulfilled. I had the impression that he protected me from beyond the grave." Six months later, one of the Indians who had played on Boy's polo team came to see her. "I have a message for you, miss, a message you already know, from a person who lives in bliss in a world where nothing can any longer reach him. Accept the message I am bringing you, a message whose meaning you no doubt understand." The message was a secret that no one in the world besides Capel and she could have known.

Diana would marry a third time, becoming the Countess of Westmoreland and later a Chanel client. It was Coco who felt she was the widow.

Back in Paris, her grief assumed alarming forms. She ordered Joseph and Marie to do up her bedroom in black—black sheets, black curtains, and drapes on the walls. She spent only a few minutes, however, in this mausoleum. "Quick, Joseph, get me out of this tomb and tell Marie to make me up a bed somewhere else," she told the butler. She was too sane, too much a Chanel from the earth of blackest Auvergne, to give in to overemotional self-dramatization.

In February 1920, the London *Times* published the last will and testament of "Arthur Capel, of Boulevard Malesherbes, Paris, and of Cheyne Walk, Chelsea, S.W., lately liaison officer at the Versailles Conference." One hundred words, written in his own hand, apportioned his enormous fortune of £700,000.* The executors in Britain were Lord Ribblesdale and Lord Lovat; in France, Armand de Gramont. With the exception of a few bequests, including £20,000 to each of his sisters Henriette and Edith (Bertha was left out, presumably because her marriage to Lord Michelham had set her up for life) and £40,000† to "Gabrielle Chanel, of Quai de Tokio, Paris," his property went to "my wife Diana for life, and then for our child."

In March, Coco gave up the rented St. Cloud villa, and in Garches, a nearby luxury suburb, bought a house of her own. She took Joseph, Marie, and their little daughter with her, as well as two little terriers, Pita and Poppée, she doted on. They were Boy's last present. The imposing *art nouveau* villa in Rue Alphonse de Neuville, a quiet residential street, was a half-timbered, slate-roofed house. Gabrielle's immediate neighbors were Henri and Antoinette Bernstein. A notorious charmer of actresses in his plays, Henri was often absent. Antoinette pretended not to notice and was happy with the couple's three-year-old daughter. Gabrielle was photographed taking walks with the child.

Diana Capel gave birth to a girl she named June.

News from Canada was disconcerting. A few months earlier, Coco had recommended a nineteen-year-old Argentine, returning to Buenos Aires via Canada and the United States, to the Flemings. Now, her brother-in-law wrote a confusing, tragicomical tale of Antoinette running off with the young Argentine. The Flemings had opened their house to the young man, who apparently had impressed Antoinette more than anyone else in the house. When he left for Buenos Aires, Antoinette had left with him.

A month later, Coco learned that her younger sister had died in Buenos Aires from complications of the Spanish flu, the septic influenza epidemic that swept Europe and the rest of the world killing twenty-seven million

---

*An amount equal to $3.5 million in 1919 dollars, or about $21 million in 1990 currency.
†The equivalent of $1.2 million in 1990 money.

people—twice as many as the war itself. First Julie, now Antoinette. Of Jeanne Devolle and Alphonse Chanel's daughters, Gabrielle was now the only survivor.

The brothers had come back from the war unscathed, and Coco now showered largess on them. While Lucien, still a bachelor, returned to Clermont-Ferrand and his shoe stall, Alphonse settled down with Jeanne Causse, to whom Coco had sent a monthly stipend throughout the war, in Valleraugue, a village at the bottom of a deep valley in the southern part of the Cévennes. In a fit of wartime remorse—and because fathers had certain advantages over bachelor soldiers when it came to furloughs—he had recognized Yvan and little Gabrielle as his children. Jeanne bore him another daughter, Antoinette, in 1919, but in peacetime Alphonse proved unwilling to marry the mother of his three children.

Gabrielle sent money to Alphonse every month, but her brother was also quick to take advantage of privileges accorded to war veterans. The government created a monopoly on tobacco and, on applications for retail licenses, gave preference to veterans. When Valleraugue's only licensee was evicted, Alphonse managed to pull the right strings to take over the license and to open a *tabac*, the traditional combination tobacco/stamp outlet and bistro.

Misia thought Gabrielle was on the edge of a breakdown, and to cheer up her friend she invited her to come with her and Jojo to a *bal costumé*. Paris was trying to dance away the memories of the war, but there was also a great artistic resurgence. Practically everything of importance that was written, painted, or composed in the first dizzy years of peace was done in Paris, the city where, as Gertrude Stein told the onrushing Americans, "the twentieth century is."

Stateless Russian princesses were selling their jewels, Americans were coming with new money, and in every town house, grand hotel, and nightclub everybody tangoed and one-stepped at cocktails, fancy dress balls, and dinners. In the morning, at five o'clock tea, and all night, people danced, not to the romantic violin but to the barbaric saxophone. To its passionate crooning and wailing, fox-trotting couples moved glued to each other, body to body, cheek to cheek, in a syncopated embrace. In London, the Prince of Wales kept a band playing for an hour and a half without a break while he Charlestoned with Penelope Dudley Ward.

Neither Misia nor Sert had been invited to the fancy-dress dance given by Mr. and Mrs. Ferdinand Blumenthal, a couple that Misia described as "terribly rich and terribly snobby." Misia, however, convinced Jojo and Coco that they should crash the party, Sert dressed as a black woman and making his entrance grinding a street organ. The Blumenthals were not amused when the trio showed up at their *bal masqué*, and the three were actually booted out by the hosts' valets. The incident did, however, lead to Misia and Jojo's being invited to devise ideas for Count and Countess de Beaumont's upcoming costume ball.

Etienne and Edith de Beaumont were the only members of the aristocracy to dare fall in love with the avant-garde. Etienne was an aristocrat of exquisite manners, taste, and flair, frivolously obsessed with perpetual youth, his homosexual inclinations sublimated in his patronage of attractive artists. A balletomane, he had been introduced to Diaghilev by Misia before the war. Edith was a ravishing woman with short hair à la Jeanne d'Arc, more cultivated, more serious, wealthier, and older than her husband. An affection that many found strange united the Beaumonts; the countess had had several unsuccessful pregnancies and they were thought of as a close couple. They entertained lavishly in their palatial town house in the Rue Duroc. Etienne liked to dress up and give splendid balls; the countess consented to lead a public life, even to pose as the Virgin opposite Cocteau's Annunciation angel in the poet's first photo montage, but left to herself she read and translated Greek poetry.

The Beaumonts were the patrons of the newest avant-garde, the surrealists, and asked Sert to decorate their ballroom for the great soirée. Misia dragged Coco along to a planning session, where count and countess listened to her suggestions about the costumes.

Gabrielle was beginning her conquest of society. Paul Morand talked of her "definitely becoming a personality" and Jean Cocteau claimed she was to couture what Picasso was to painting, so it was with consternation that Misia realized her friend had not been invited to the ball. In a huff, Misia decided that she would not go either.

"I know perfectly well that in those days society would never dream of inviting its 'tradespeople,' and the latter never allow themselves to recognize you or greet you outside your home," Misia would recall. "No doubt the Count de Beaumont had acted instinctively in sending an invitation to me only. But Mademoiselle Chanel was *my* friend. I was profoundly offended by her exclusion, by the fact that an exception could not be made."

It would be only two years before Chanel's name grew so luminous that the Beaumonts begged her to be their guest at their parties. She went because their invitation opened doors to the uppermost social stratosphere, yet she would never forget the slight. "All those bluebloods," she told Marie Laurencin, the painter, "they turned their noses up at me, but I'll have them groveling at my feet." Laurencin would add that Coco began affecting the silky manners of society women, ridiculing these women while envying them.

Gabrielle also began living at the Ritz Hotel on the Place Vendôme. She had no intention of giving up the villa in Garches, but on certain weeknights she found it too boring to be chauffeured to the suburbs.

In May 1921, Chanel met Igor Stravinsky. Misia introduced her to the composer, who had spent the war years in Switzerland with his wife, Catherine Nossenko, and their two daughters. The triumph of the Bolsheviks had left him without a Russian income and the Stravinsky family without passports. He had decided to opt for French citizenship and with Catherine and the girls was to spend the summer in Carantec, a fishing village near the tip of Brittany.

With his slicked-down blond hair, bad teeth, myopic eyes, and thick lips, Stravinsky was still an impressive figure. He gave himself the airs of a fop, showing up in black jacket, blue shirt and blue collar, mustard-colored pants, and yellow shoes. When he mentioned that friends of his had been unable to find an apartment for him and his family in Paris, Coco invited them to stay in her villa.

To make some money, Stravinsky had agreed to collaborate with Diaghilev and the Ballets Russes—as stateless as he—and was putting the finishing touches on *Pulcinella*. Diaghilev and Picasso had seen puppet shows in Naples in 1917 and were building the ballet around some themes by Pergolesi and a *commedia del l'arte* style. The sets were by Picasso and the choreography by Léonide Massine, Diaghilev's new lover and star of the company since Nijinsky had left in 1916. In September, Stravinsky accepted Coco's offer to stay in Garches.

Pulcinella was first performed at the Opéra on May 15. Picasso had designed a Neapolitan street scene in cubist style and painted blue, gray, dark brown, and white houses framing a view of the bay, Vesuvius, and the full moon. Paris was enraptured.

Gabrielle spent the month of June in Biarritz, where her boutique in Rue Gardères was booming. The clientele was largely foreign—Spanish, Argentine, British, American, Egyptian, and people from other countries with strong currencies. A novelty was the influx of Russian grand dukes, Romanovs, who, the saying went, were "being kept by women and drinking to forget the Revolution." More immediately, Coco met her lookalike from 1915, Marthe Davelli, and her friend from the Royallieu days, Gabrielle Dorziat. Both were enormously successful, Davelli as a soprano performing in *Madame Butterfly* and *Carmen*, Dorziat as an actress of the stage and that newest craze, the movies.

The three women were the center of attraction. On the beach, Davelli was one of the first women to try sunbathing. Coco invented a black taffeta bathing costume for her. The swimsuit covered most of the thighs and the décolleté was modest, but Coco insisted that her friend wear a body stocking underneath.

Davelli introduced Coco to Grand Duke Dmitri Pavlovich and wasted little time telling Coco that the handsome first cousin of the late czar was her lover. The tall duke looked nothing like a murderer, yet it was he who, together with Prince Yusupov, had assassinated Rasputin in 1916 in the hope of saving the monarchy from itself.

Fame as an opera star had not diminished Davelli's taste for partying. Whatever the hour of the night, she had a way of rounding up some nightclub pianist and saxophone player, and continuing the party until the wee hours. At the end of one such all-night revel, she noticed the bachelor duke was showing more than polite interest in Coco.

"If you're interested you can have him," the soprano is alleged to have said to Coco. "He really is a little expensive for me."

Misia finally persuaded José Sert to marry her. The wedding took place August 2, 1921, in the hideous but chic St. Roch church in the Faubourg St. Honoré. The twice-married, twice-divorced bride was forty-eight, the bachelor groom forty-five. Marcel Proust sent his congratulations.

Gabrielle had never been to Italy, and in August, when Misia insisted that she join Sert and her on their honeymoon, she said yes. In Misia's memoirs, the invitation was something of a gesture of charity, to make Coco forget the noninvitation to the Beaumont party. "Sert and I brought her to Venice, where I was giving a huge dinner in order to introduce my new friend to the upper crust, and I invited Princess de Poix, Count and Countess de Volpi, the Prince of Greece, in fact all the high society." In Coco's recollection, Misia and Sert forced her to come with them. Still, the trip was to remain something of an epic journey, and it was during this summer of 1921 that Gabrielle was introduced to more than a handful of crowned heads.

The Sert honeymoon was to be a rather grand Mediterranean cruise aboard a private yacht with landings in various ports for excursions in rented automobiles to Renaissance sites. They sailed the Adriatic first and went to Venice, where Misia met Diaghilev to discuss fund-raising for the ballet company's first complete postwar season. The Bolshevik triumph had left the ensemble exiled and in financial tatters. Diaghilev, however, was convinced a revival of Stravinsky's *The Rite of Spring*, perhaps with the new *Pulcinella* as an added attraction, could become his box office bread-and-butter in a Paris theater. When the newlyweds and Gabrielle arrived on the Lido in Venice, they found Diaghilev lunching with the young Grand Duchess Maria Pavlovna, the widow of the late czar's uncle, the Grand Duke Vladimir. Before the Revolution, the Grand Duchess had received Diaghilev in her salon in St. Petersburg, and her late husband had been among his first backers, but now neither the impresario nor the Grand Duchess had a penny to his or her name. The Serts and Chanel joined the luncheon.

It was the first time Coco met the divine Sergei. Misia introduced her effusively, but true to habit Gabrielle let the Serts and Diaghilev hold forth. As Diaghilev plunged into the reasons for reviving *Le Sacre du printemps*, he soon forgot about this Mademoiselle Chanel. He still had the 1913 sets and costumes, he said. The only difficulty was the great expense of the huge orchestra that Stravinsky's score demanded.

At forty-eight, Diaghilev was a plump, double-chinned nobleman of unusual appearance. He had a large head that seemed too large for even his massive body, dark impressive eyes, a small, neat mustache, and a streak of white through his dark hair that earned him the nickname "Chinchilla." His hands were covered with rings, his tie held in place with a huge black pearl. Even now, crushed by debt, he lived at the best hotels in a flurry of impossible telegrams, gastronomic feasts, promises of new heights, and threats of suicide, and, with lordly cunning, played dancers and creditors against each other. He had an ineffable gift for charming money out of wealthy patricians and *nouveaux riches* to finance his unerring taste in the arts. He could kiss a lady's hand in such a way that she felt *she* was curtsying to a monarch.

Cruel jokes had accompanied the arrival in France of the Grand Duchess Maria Pavlovna. She would have to be put up, the mordant Comtesse Adhéaume de Chevigné sniffed, waited on, and provided for for the rest of her life. Gabrielle said nothing of having met Grand Duke Dmitri in Biarritz.

Over the next few days, while Misia and Diaghilev talked fund-raising, Sert showed Gabrielle the sights. She had to agree with Misia that when one was around Sert everybody else seemed bland.

"He was an ideal traveling companion, always in a good mood and always a guide full of baroque and prodigious erudition," she would remember. "Like his dizzy pictorial fantasies, each fragment of his knowledge balanced on another. This fat monkey, with his dyed beard, his hump in the back, his huge tortoiseshell glasses, simply loved everything that was colossal. He slept in black pajamas, never washed, and, even naked, was so hairy he seemed to be wearing a fur coat. He wasn't even indecent. He was hairy all over except on the head.

"He took me through museums like a wild animal would take you through his territory, explaining everything, happy to teach. He found me to possess an innate taste that he thought superior to science. We made huge, one hundred kilometer detours in order to look for some *osteria*, where you have birds wrapped in vine leaves. In his youth, he had traveled through Italy, on foot, on a donkey, and, in any case, assured us, he remembered the place very well. He folded out maps. Finally, the inn could not be found.

"'Tosh (that's what he called Misia), we were wrong; we should have turned right. Let's go back.' We got lost again. So we bought a pig, put it on the car, and had it roasted during a roadside halt. He loved his own mistakes; loved what was improvised. An instinctive ostentation made this temperate man, accompanied by two women who ate little, order rare wines and dishes that made our table look like a painting by Veronese."

When the trio got to Rome, the ladies were ready to spend the evening at the Grand Hotel. Sert, however, insisted Rome had to be seen by moonlight and dragged Misia and Coco to the Coliseum, where he enchanted them with descriptions of imaginary parties he'd give in the city's ruins, "the city's skeleton," as he called it. Watching Gabrielle closely, he added, "Architecture is the bone structure of a city. Everything is in the bone structure. A face without bones will not last. You, for example, Mashemoiselle, you will look pretty dead."

A few weeks later, Diaghilev was in his suite at the Hôtel Continental in the Rue Castiglione, the elegant street parallel to Rue Cambon, when he was told a Mademoiselle Chanel was asking for him. His ballet company was on a provincial tour of England, three nights in Bournemouth, one night each in Nottingham, Sheffield, and Leeds, and two weeks in Liverpool, yet he still didn't have the funds to produce *The Rite of Spring*. He could not remember any Mademoiselle Chanel, but with a shrug went to meet her. When he saw the slim, elegant dark-haired woman in the lobby, he recognized Misia's friend. What followed has been described differently in several accounts.

Coco told him she had thought a lot about the *Rite* and would like to help—on the condition that no one would find out. "By that she meant Misia," Misia's biographers Arthur Gold and Robert Fizdale would write. "She had barely left before Diaghilev ran to a telephone to tell Misia what he had in his pocket, because Chanel had given him a check for a very high amount. It was Chanel's first gesture as Misia's rival; a gesture combining calculation and social advancement." In her conversations with Paul Morand, Coco would put it a little differently. Diaghilev had run to see Princess Edmond de Polignac, the formidable American-born Winaretta Singer of the sewing machine fortune, and to Nancy Cunard, the steamship heiress, to explain he needed a thousand pounds that same evening or the curtain wouldn't go up. "He clasps his hands, the diabetes has him in sweat. 'I've been to the Princess. She gave me seventy-five thousand francs!' 'She's a grand American lady,' I said, 'I'm only a French *couturière*, here's two hundred thousand.'"

Boris Kochno, who would play a large part in Diaghilev's career in the 1920s, also put Coco's gift at 200,000 francs. Richard Buckle, Diaghilev's biographer, put the amount Coco wrote out at 300,000 francs.*

*Until the mid-1920s devaluation of the French currency, the franc stood at twelve to the dollar. Thus, 300,000 francs was the equivalent of $25,000 in 1920 dollars, or $140,000 in 1990 money.

The Stravinskys were still at the villa and Coco stayed at the Ritz. In Misia's shadow, she watched some of the ballet rehearsals. Nobody knew her, and she was hardly ever introduced to anyone. In *The Rite of Spring* revival, Massine and Lydia Sokolova—an English dancer whose real name was Hilda Munnings—would dance the parts that Nijinsky and Tamara Karsavina had performed at the uproarious May 22, 1913, premiere.

If the refugee composer had no passport and therefore could not travel outside France, Gabrielle could. In December 1920, she was in London, meeting Stravinsky's friend and admirer Gerald Tyrwhitt, fourteenth Lord Berners. The peer was a composer, painter, writer, and intimate of London's Bright Young Things. During the war, he had been an official at the British embassy in Rome and had managed to get Stravinsky to Italy. On December 7, 1920, Tyrwhitt wrote Stravinsky from his residence in Half Moon Street, London, that although it had been "a century" since they had last seen each other, he had kept himself informed of Stravinsky's whereabouts, "recently through Mlle Chanel, who was here the other day."

With *Pulcinella* and *The Three-Cornered Hat* as warm-ups, the ballet company opened its 1921 Paris winter season at the Théâtre des Champs Elysées on December 15 with *The Rite of Spring*. Coco loved *Le Tricorne*. The music by Manuel da Falla, the spare sets by Picasso, and Massine's performance as the governor trying to seduce Karsavina as the miller's wife enchanted her more than the Stravinsky revival she was financing. For the *Rite*, Massine added new, difficult passages for Sokolova. At the last curtain, Igor Stravinsky leaped onto the stage and, before an applauding audience, kissed the hand of the twenty-four-year-old Sokolova.

With the Serts and Picasso, Gabrielle was at the big supper party that followed at the Hôtel Continental. Diaghilev sat at one end of a long table, Stravinsky at the other, with the guests, the company's staff, and the principal dancers in between. Massine got drunk and burned Picasso's hand with a cigarette, and, under Diaghilev's jealous scowl, flirted with Sokolova and Vera Clark, another British import rechristened Vera Savina by the master.

There was to be no record of how Coco finished the night. She and Stravinsky were already lovers.

14

STRAVINSKY

The portrait Coco would draw of Stravinsky was acidulated and less than flattering. He was so Russian, she would tell Paul Morand, that when he pressed his ardor on her and she reminded him he was married and asked what his wife would say, he answered, "She knows that I love you. To whom, if not her, would I confide a thing as great as this?"

Misia Sert picked up the scent of the tryst. "What are you up to, you two? I hear Igor is walking your dog. Tell me."

First two hundred thousand francs to Diaghilev, now an affair with Stravinsky. Coco was not quite the ambitious young ingenue trying to depose a tempestuous star onstage and in bed, but Misia took it that way.

The affair was furtive, distracted, and carried out with less than total abandon. Coco was vulnerable, still not over the loss of Boy, and for Stravinsky it was a difficult time. Going on forty, the composer was emotionally at a loss, uprooted, stateless, and unsure of his future. Her business success was a further complication.

The name Coco Chanel was on all lips, and the Chanel fashion was becoming the essence of the new decade. On the eve of the war Gabrielle had made jersey chic in simple gray and navy dresses that were quite unlike anything women had worn before. Now she was on the verge of her biggest triumphs.

Misia was seen, cruelly, as the patroness of the artists who had buried the nineteenth century, Coco the incarnation of the new era. Always a woman with an instinct for what was just about to happen, Coco sensed that a break with the world before 1914 was coming, that young people longed for a clean slate, longed to be everything their elders were not. The virtual destruction of an entire generation increased the distance between the old and the young, between the official and the unofficial.

Prewar mores no longer held sway. Emilienne d'Alençon and the magnificent *horizontales* were a vanishing breed. Powdered women in their forties clung to pre-1914 traditions—and Poiret's vaporous glamour—but sports and physical activity firmed the feminine ideal, sunbathing changed skin tones, the taste for faster living modified elegance, as discriminating languor gave way to litheness and affected primness yielded to energetic directness. Serpentine slimness replaced Rubenesque fullness, and the new feminine ideal was "flexible and tubular, like a section of boa constrictor," as Aldous Huxley described the New Woman in *Antic Hay*. Said the Marquis Boni de Castellane, the most extravagant Parisian dandy and a friend of Misia, "Women no longer exist; all that's left are the boys created by Chanel."

Chanel was all the feminine postwar aspirations rolled into a snowballing success story. She typified womanhood in the decade in which everything seemed possible: A woman might earn her own living, choose who to love, and live according to her own precepts. With her sharp eye for taste, she invented very expensive clothes that were ideal for tomboyish girls. The younger set, those who had come of age during the war, loved it. They went modern and defined the word *chic*. It was chic to be dressed by Coco Chanel. It was chic to dance the tango, to be seen at the Boeuf sur le Toit nightclub, to smoke opium, to attend surrealist demonstrations, and to admire whatever Jean Cocteau wrote.

For 1921, Coco was putting women into sweaters and short pleated skirts with dropped waistlines, cloche hats, and bandeaux for a willowy silhouette that Paris would call the *garçonne* look, London and New York the *flapper*. *La Garçonne* was the name of a 1921 bestseller, a "scandalous" novel that told the story of a young woman who rejects family hypocrisy in favor of earning her own living (the scandal saw its author, Victor Marguerite, stripped of his *légion d'honneur*).

Chanel was later quoted as saying that she alone created the flapper. Women had for some time shortened their skirts and thrown away tassels and trains, laces and loops, but she was the first to make clothes for the young. Until the 1920s, youth was a preparatory step, not life itself.

The Chanel hemlines were nine inches above the ground in 1920, and although it was freely predicted that skirts would come down again, her lines climbed a few shocking inches higher. "The straight line is her medium," cooed the British *Vogue*. Starting in 1920, *Femina* and *Minerva*, a pair of tony Parisian fashion magazines, filled their pages with Chanel models and told their readers, "Chanel is making us forget yesterday's woman, teaching us to walk naturally, by snipping a lock here, the flounces of a dress there." Flappers wore thin dresses, short-sleeved and occasionally sleeveless; some of the wilder young things rolled their stockings below their knees, revealing to shocked eyes a fleeting glimpse of shinbones and kneecaps. In Deauville, Biarritz, on the racetracks, in the ballrooms, and at Maxim's, society women imitated the brisk step and quick breath of the young.

Chanel was the pied piper who led women away from complicated, uncomfortable clothes to a bone-simple, uncluttered, and casual look that eventually became synonymous with her name. By the end of the decade, *Vogue* would be able to say that the most important designers to emerge from the 1920s "were the two most involved with new movements in other fields—Chanel, whose circle included Picasso, Cocteau, and Stravinsky, and the new Schiaparelli, whose friends were the surrealists."

Paul Poiret called her style *"misérabilisme de luxe."* The grand rival had made a spectacular comeback in 1919, but he was never quite able to translate his prewar inspirations into clothes that the new generation found acceptable. He regretted the new look he had himself helped create, but reopened a palatial house at the Rond Point des Champs Elysées, where the zodiac painted on the foyer ceiling indicated the stars at the moment of his birth. He gave splendid garden parties—recorded on canvas by van Dongen—and designed clothes into which he was able to bully many of his clients for a while. Still, Poiret was never accepted as a social equal to the ladies he dressed. Chic, however, enthroned Chanel.

Gabrielle answered Poiret's multicolored splendor with her famous "little black dress." Women had worn black only as a sign of bereavement; Chanel made it a fashionable color women might wear anytime. In one version of how she invented the little black dress, she was at a gala opening at the Opéra when, during the intermission, she leaned over the railing of her box and watched the women in vibrant Poiret fringes of beads and feathers. The sight gave her the idea of her enduring little black dress. In another retelling it was the death of Boy Capel that made her say, "I'm going to put the whole world in mourning for him."

Time and again Coco came up with just the thing women wanted, and her name came to mean the total look, from sailor hat to beige-and-black sling-back shoes. Her flair was instinctive. Everything she invented was terribly sensible. Her travel coats were comfortable, with big pockets, her hats could be folded in a suitcase, and her buttons were there to fasten dresses, not to be decorative.

She demanded slimness, the slender body she maintained herself. "Cut my head off, and you still think you're looking at the body of an adolescent," she snapped. The quintessential 1920s woman—slim, sophisticated, streamlined, and modern—didn't so much demand a fashion that was "boyish" as one that was *youthful.* As young women began to lead more independent lives, *they* became the trendsetters. The postwar disillusionment with the "old" who had sent the young off to die also contributed to the apotheosis of youth.

Chanel and Poiret were not the only Paris fashion houses, but the traditional Paquin, Vionnet, and the male designers Jean Patou and Lucien Lelong were obliged to adapt the uniform of short skirts, dropped waists, and simplicity demanded by the lives and tastes of the 1920s woman. And it was not only the way women dressed that changed. The arts and, in their wake, textiles, color schemes, architecture, and interior design were entering their most inventive period.

A young writer who knew how to rub shoulders with the rich and the chic as well as the fashionable people in the avant-garde drew a picture of Coco Chanel in the cusp of her first big triumphs. "Coco Chanel created a feminine personage of a kind Paris had not known before," wrote Maurice Sachs, Cocteau's sometime secretary and an astute chronicler of the 1920s scene. Sachs lived by his wits, writing clever pieces in little magazines and sponging off people, including Chanel. His verbal portrait of Coco was eloquent: "What surprised you when you first met her was how small she was. She was very slim; the line of thick black hair was low, her eyebrows met over the nose and when she laughed her eyes were hard and sparkling. She was almost always wearing the same thing—simple, black clothes. She put her hands in her pockets and began to speak. The flow of her words was extraordinarily fast, rushing forward, but she laid out clearly what she had in mind. She had none of the circumlocution and fabricated asides that so often make women halt at incidéntal subjects and never reach the target of their conversation.

"Two distinct qualities surfaced in her, I believe, her deep peasant roots and her femininity. In the company of brilliant men she was attentive as if, standing in the fields of her childhood, she were waiting for the wind to change and carry to her ears familiar sounds that she could identify. Her womanhood made her emulate (a mark of profound femininity) and use what pleased her in others."

Stravinsky's marriage was not a happy one and it was not the first time he had been unfaithful to Catherine. He had married his first cousin in 1906 and the couple had two daughters. Milene and Ludmila were two rather sickly little girls—Ludmila would die of tuberculosis in 1938—but in an absent, offhanded way Stravinsky was a dutiful husband and father, and a devoted son, as well. He was in contact with Lenin's commissar for the arts, Anatoly Lunacharsky, seeking an exit visa for his mother— the permission for her to emigrate would come two years later.

Although Stravinsky was famous, earning a living as a composer was a high-wire act. His three ballet compositions for the Ballets Russes— *Firebird*, *Petrushka*, and *The Rite of Spring*—had catapulted him into the musical limelight, but working with Diaghilev was painful and, when it came to money, humiliating. Though the ballet company was facing a less than certain future, it still represented the best source of a somewhat stable income for Stravinsky, with a chance of big money should they come up with a seminal work like *The Rite*, increasingly seen as the most influential piece of twentieth-century music. Igor was therefore still working for "the master," rearranging Tchaikovsky's *Sleeping Beauty* and writing *Mavra*, a very "un-Russian" opera that dismayed many of his followers.

The presence of Catherine and the girls in Garches was awkward, and in May 1921, Stravinsky moved them to Biarritz. The Atlantic coast resort was chosen for its healthy climate and superior schools, but for the roaming husband, the arrangement conveniently entailed long periods of separation.

If Coco could subsidize a revival of *The Rite*, she could also amuse herself guaranteeing a Stravinsky concert. In order not to be too obvious about underwriting her lover's progress, and perhaps to disarm Misia, she had Ernest Ansermet, a Swiss conductor and one of Stravinsky's closest musician friends, make the arrangements for renting the Salle Gaveau.

Knowing Misia would somehow find out, Coco told Stravinsky he'd have to tell Misia.

Coco was not in love. The idea of separating pleasure from love was something new—for her and for 1920s women—something Misia was too old-fashioned to understand.

"I'm flabbergasted with sorrow," Misia sighed the next day. "When I think Stravinsky is accepting money from you!"

Coco had already heard her friend say, "When I think . . ." in regard to Coco's bankrolling Diaghilev. Misia was an incorrigible meddler, and now she became convinced Stravinsky would divorce his wife. Jojo got in on the melodrama and lured the composer to their Quai Voltaire apartment while Misia held Coco captive in the next room.

"Mossieur," Sert began in his inimitable accent, "Mr. Capel confided Mashemoiselle to me. There is only one word to describe a man like you, Mossieur. You are a shit!"

At the appropriate moment, Misia left Coco alone, came back, and announced Stravinsky was in the other room. "He wants to know if you will marry him."

The Serts loved everything that spelled amorous suffering, but Coco finally had enough and got hold of Ansermet. "It's silly," she told the conductor who had known Stravinsky for ten years. "The Serts are crazy. Everybody is talking about this now. Picasso is making jokes. Why doesn't Igor come back and we'll be friends."

A rather elegant way for a spurned lady to remember the story. Stravinsky, in fact, was head over heels in love, with Vera de Bosset, an actress and sometime dancer, the wife of the painter and Diaghilev's set designer Sergei Sudeikin. The two had met in February 1922 at a dinner Diaghilev was giving in a Montmartre restaurant. "He is moody today, so please be nice to him," Diaghilev had told Vera. The beautiful Vera had a deck of cards with her and told the composer's future, presumably highlighting the role of the queen of hearts.

Coco had never been the jealous type, even with Boy Capel. But a part of her, it seems, had died with him. There is no other way to reconcile her ardent love for him and the casualness with which she began pursuing and dropping other liaisons. "She's a pederast," Cocteau said of her, implying that her sexual appetites were virile and that she set out to conquer like a man. "I've squandered millions," she herself would say. "The richest men I knew are the ones that cost me the most."

She loved men. She could not stand the idea of not being loved in return, but hated being dependent on any man, falling prey to anyone. The company of a man was welcome, but not if his presence turned into an impediment. Any man who forced her to choose between him and her work was sure to be the loser.

Her obsession with her work made an impression on Valéry Ollivier, a friend from the Royallieu days, who, with Etienne Balsan, sometimes went to see her in the Rue Cambon: "We saw Coco, of course, and Pauline de Saint-Sauveur, who was in charge of perfumes, knickknacks, and scarves. In fact, we went mostly to see the models. We sat at the top of the stairs until lunch.

"Coco was full of personality but she wasn't much interested in us. She didn't care for what we were doing, or what we had to say. Her only interest was her work."

The "Slavic period," as she would later call it, was not over. Davelli had not been joking the previous summer when she told Gabrielle she could have the grand duke.

Dmitri came to Paris. Coco had dinner with him, and *à deux* found him to be elegant and brimming with charm. He was also full of stories and witty asides.

"I just bought a little blue Rolls, let's drive down to Monte Carlo," she told him.

"I only have fifteen thousand francs. . . ."*

"I'll match you. With thirty thousand we'll have enough to have fun for a week."

Misia got wind of it and, in Coco's recollections, sent a wire to Stravinsky in Spain, saying, COCO IS A LITTLE SEAMSTRESS WHO PREFERS GRAND DUKES TO ARTISTS. Diaghilev in turn wired Gabrielle to warn her about Stravinsky: DO NOT COME. HE WANTS TO KILL YOU.

Vera de Bosset, who would become the second Mrs. Stravinsky in 1940, and Robert Craft, Stravinsky's biographer, would make light of the Chanel affair, calling it "the bragging of her late-in-life memory of it." But a letter from the composer to Misia more than a decade later throws a cruder afterglow on the relationship.

*Fifteen thousand francs would be about $3,500 in 1990 currency.

February 6, 1933

Dear Misia.

I'm dreadfully sorry always to be asking you for something or bothering you with my petty affairs, but you know that Chanel has not sent us anything since the 1st and so we are without a radish to live on this month; therefore I ask you to be kind enough to mention it to her. . . .

I thank you in advance for all your kindness, which is so great that one easily gets into the habit of counting on it, and I embrace you thousands and thousands of times, very warmly,

Igor.

Chanel and Stravinsky would remain lifelong, if distant, friends. They would die the same year, she in a hotel room under an icon he had given her half a century earlier.

By spring of 1922, Dmitri was Gabrielle's lover. She gave him money and had him come with his "man," Piotr, to live with her in Garches. He gave her the Romanov pearls he had managed to save when he fled the Revolution. She made copies of them and launched the fashion of long strands of fake *or* real pearls. To be alone with him, she bought a property in the Landes, the isolated stretch of pineland coast between Bordeaux and Biarritz.

Eight years younger than Gabrielle, Dmitri was an eccentric spoiled brat. It is doubtful that Coco ever mentioned the hospice in Saumur where she was born, the orphanage in Aubazine, or her start in the *beuglant* in Moulins, but in their own way, Dmitri's beginnings were as troubled as hers. Dmitri was the son of Grand Duke Paul and Alexandra of Greece. His mother died giving birth to him, and, together with his elder sister Maria, he was brought up by energetic British nannies. He was raised strictly and became a timid child with only his sister for comfort. When he was eleven, he lost his father as well, for Grand Duke Paul was banished from St. Petersburg, having offended both Nicholas and Alexandra. (The forty-year-old widower had wanted to marry a divorcée. The czar feared other members of the imperial family would follow his bad example and live "in Paris with their semilegitimate and illegitimate wives.")

The czar's nephew—cousin to England's Prince Edward—was a tall and very handsome man. Coco fell for his green eyes, his long, elegant hands, and, in their intimacy, his shyness. For the summer of 1922, Coco rented a villa in Moulleau on the Bay of Arcachon, west of Bordeaux. The Atlantic thundered against the garden wall, and for two months she and Dmitri enjoyed the sun and the sea. A fishing boat took them out for a swim every morning. Afternoons were spent walking on the beach, evenings gambling at the Arcachon casino or having Monsieur Joseph and Piotr prepare oysters right out of the bay. Coco listened to the rest of Dmitri's story, how the czar had put an end to the brother and sister's devotion to each other by marrying Maria to the homosexual crown prince of Sweden, how Dmitri's banishment to Persia following Rasputin's murder saved his life in 1917, while the ruthless logic of the Soviet revolution resulted in his father being executed in a last roundup of Romanovs in 1919.

It was the longest vacation Coco ever allowed herself. They saw few people. Cocteau wrote teasing postcards about a theater project he was developing. A friend of his had just returned from Greece and given him one of those shepherd's crooks that end in a goat's horn. The shepherd's staff gave Cocteau the idea of updating one of the ancient Greek tragedies for the fall season. He chose Sophocles' *Antigone* because of its anti-establishment theme and its vindication of the unwritten law of conscience.

Charles Dullin, the erstwhile lover of Caryathis and Coco's "date" at the May 13, 1913, performance of *The Rite of Spring*, was the new director of L'Atelier theater high up on Montmartre. He agreed to produce Cocteau's "free adaptation" of *Antigone*. Arthur Honegger was going to write the score and Picasso had promised to do the sets, Cocteau purred over the telephone to Coco, "Why don't you do the costumes?"

In addition to directing, Dullin played Creon, the king and Antigone's uncle against whom she rebels. Genica Atanasiou, a Greek actress who spoke little French but had a gorgeous face under a crewcut hairdo, would play the title role. Her lover, Antonin Artaud, a theorist of avant-garde theater, was cast as Tiresias.

Coco agreed once she knew that Picasso would be associated with the production. She had a specialist knit a full-length coat in raw wool with Greek vase motifs in maroon and black.

Picasso took his time creating his violet-blue backdrop with its painted masks of men, women, and children of the "chorus" clustered around a grilled opening. Doric columns, marveled Cocteau, "emerged from his brush so suddenly, so surprisingly, against the backdrop that everybody applauded." Perhaps jealous of the raves that accompanied the painter's work, Coco one day asked whether the costumes she was creating were supposed to disappear with Antigone down the stage trap.

"It's silly to continue until I know," she shouted testily from the front row.

Cocteau got annoyed. "We're trying to rehearse the text right now."

"What text?"

"Sophocles exists!" he shouted.

Angrily, Coco got up on stage and grabbed hold of a thread in Antigone's coat. While the assistant who had knitted the coat broke into tears, Coco unraveled the work. At the December 22 premiere, Mademoiselle had a *mot* for the members of the press who gossiped about the unraveled-coat story. "It's funny, the theater," she began airily. "When, in the last minute, I threw my own coat over the actress's shoulders, well, that's what made the play!"

With the masks, which hid loudspeakers, representing the chorus, and the actors wearing painted faces, *Antigone* disconcerted. But people came to rave over the transformations that Cocteau, Picasso, and Chanel had wrought and the insolence and cleverness with which they treated antiquity. The play ran for a hundred performances.

Coco was inventing her personage. What captivated the public, however, was her fashion. Chanel's definition of style was clever and pertinent. "Fashion is not something that exists in dresses only; fashion is something in the air. It's the wind that blows in the new fashion; you feel it coming, you smell it. Fashion is in the sky, in the street, fashion has to do with ideas, the way we live, what is happening."

Society in the 1920s was large enough to be diverse and international, yet small enough for the prime figures to be well known. It was a clever, amusing, worldly set, and the fashion dictates were slavishly followed. Fashion, Cocteau observed, was not so much the whim of a few couturiers as a vestment. "Whether husband or lover hated the style, a woman followed it. She followed it even if *she* hated it. All women cut their hair short and wore the waist on the hips."

Not all women have the figure of a Venus, Chanel said, yet nothing should be hidden. To conceal was to accentuate. To her, the art of dressmaking was one of highlighting, of underscoring. She understood the old adage of the fashion business that if you cover one erogenous zone, you must uncover another. Long robes demand plunging necklines, diminished décolletés mean legs must be visible. Because the part of the body that is temptingly covered always excites the most interest, clothes that are supposed to be the triumph of modesty are often the most seductive.

Fashion magazines repeated her truisms: By raising the waist in front, a woman appears taller, lowering it in the back downplays a drooping derrière. A dress must be cut longer in the back because it has a tendency to creep up. A dress must move on a woman's body. All body movements, all articulation, begin in the back, meaning it is best to layer fabrics in the back. A dress should be cut in such a way that when the wearer moves it is too big and when she is immobile it adjusts itself.

Everything is in the shoulders. If a dress doesn't hang right, the front doesn't move; it is the back that is distorted. A hefty woman always has a narrow back, a slim person a large back. The back of clothes must be able to give, at least ten centimeters, so that one can bend over, play golf, put on shoes. A woman must therefore cross her arms when she has her measurements taken. A well-cut dress fits everybody, although no two women have the same measurements or have the shoulder at the same place.

Chanel believed the business of fashion was to be responsive to ever-changing interactions of people, events, creative minds, prevailing attitudes, and the ways in which it all rebounds.

Over the years, the House of Chanel has changed far less in the style of its clothes than in its style of doing business. The creative thrust of design in the 1990s is the big bang at the beginning of an immensely complicated machinery that coordinates the interests of textile and marketing, dress manufacturing, and brand-new recognition to a global consumer society. Haute couture is a straw in the wind, an exercise in public relations, a tonic for the designers who can afford it, and a haven for exceptional craftsmanship and last-of-a-kind artisans. The money is now in ready-to-wear, menswear divisions, mass merchandising, and in the licensing of logos to manufacturers of sunglasses, bed linens, penknives, and luggage. In the twenties, however, haute couture was a made-to-measure luxury trade still manageable by a sharp and energetic businesswoman like Chanel, whose core clientele was no more than two hundred wealthy women.

Coco spent most of her working days out of public view, with her intimate crew and models. From the beginning, she decided to make herself less than available in the salon, and it was the salesladies who dealt with the often difficult clients.

The *vendeuses*—all older and reassuring as hospital nurses—were the sales personnel. Assisted by the *habilleuses*, the saleswomen were usually former models who possessed sufficient ascendancy over very demanding clients to inspire immediate and lasting confidence. "They know how to listen standing up, and when to sit down," Coco once said of her saleswomen. "They are wonderful confidantes—a woman is always afraid of being blackmailed by her maid, but has total confidence in her *vendeuse*."

Chanel's clients rarely paid cash. Most charged their purchases to their private account, which was settled in monthly, and sometimes yearly, installments. Coco hated it but, like other tradespeople catering to the leisure classes, had to grin and bear it. In private, she sarcastically referred to her clientele of difficult duchesses, ministerial wives, and kept women as "the darlings," and told stories of their feverish demands that a gown they ordered at 2:00 P.M. be delivered to their homes for a ball that evening. Some darlings had the nerve to return the gown for credit the next day, saying they had changed their minds.

"To earn a living in the feminine trade you must know women," she said. "A darling has no shame, she is like a praying mantis." Coco told of widowed darlings who need clothes because the late husband "would hate to see me bored."

Never an early riser, Coco arrived at Rue Cambon at noon and, with the exception of a quick afternoon tea at *Fleurs*, in Rue St. Honoré, worked until seven or eight in the evening. The way Coco worked was to fashion a gown in *toiles*, the pattern sewn together in muslin. She believed there was nothing prettier than a well-made toile, all form, the idea executed in white muslin. To work in toiles allowed her to reserve her choice of fabric for a later stage. Department stores were given the toiles when they bought the rights to copy a dress.

Assisted by one of her *premières*, the heads of her workrooms who understood the Chanel style perfectly, knew what Mademoiselle, as she was always called, was aiming at, and later helped translate intentions into a first toiles draft, Coco explored her ideas with scissors and pins on the live models. *La pose*—the interminable standing that the model must do while effects are viewed and alterations suggested—could last for hours.

Her style tended toward classicism because she was not good at perpetual innovation. To compensate, she had her workrooms execute her creations with exquisite workmanship, and in luxurious, often striking fabrics.

Her sense of color was masterful, yet she let difficult, "risky" fabrics grow on her before using them. She avoided bizarre and whimsical fads. Very few women looked sublime in ridiculous clothes. Besides, she said, men watch a woman because she is beautiful, not because she is eccentric.

The actual making of Chanel's clothes was a cottage industry employing thousands of women. The work force was rigorously structured. The *premières*—short for *premières mains*, or "first hands"—laid down the law in the workrooms all the way down to the *arpètes*, the apprentices who, despite the education laws, had probably left school before twelve. The *arpètes* learned by "passing the magnet" to pick up needles from the floor three times a day, by sweeping up threads and swatches, fetching rolls of fabric, holding up cloth, getting coffee and cigarettes for the seamstresses. The success of the apprenticeship depended entirely on the seamstresses' goodwill and the girls' own willingness. They were paid very little or nothing at all since they were being trained. After a few years a determined and gifted *arpète* could graduate to *petite main*, the intermediate stage, where she could really learn the tricks of the trade and become *seconde*, and after several years perhaps *habilleuse*, or dressing assistant in the sales salon.

The métier was all in the hands. To have supple, fast hands meant an apprentice was destined to a career in haute couture. Fabric that created the right effect was said to "have hand." Coco's own instincts and professional knowledge were in her hands.

15

GLITTER
AND NO. 5

~~~~~~~~~~~~~~~~~~~~~~~~~~~~~~~~~~~~~

Coco turned forty in 1923 and celebrated the occasion by bringing out Chanel No. 5, the perfume that would become a classic, and by signing a long-term lease on the main-floor residence of Count Pillet-Will's town house in Faubourg St. Honoré. The garden ran all the way to the tree-lined Avenue Gabriel, where Boy and she had first become lovers.

She settled into the long chain of enormous rooms opening onto the garden, and asked Misia and Jojo Sert to decorate the residence. Monsieur Joseph was ordered to hire cooks, footmen, and kitchen maids. The first piece of fine furniture she acquired was a grand piano. Stravinsky, who visited as a friend, Diaghilev, Misia, and the pianist of the Ballets Russes—now the Ballets de Monaco—played on it at all hours until the count, living upstairs, complained. Money was the solution. Pillet-Will agreed to move out and rent her the entire town house.

Chanel had a great appetite for luxury, fine furniture. She covered all her *haute époque* chairs with beige-gray satin and her walls with pale *boiserie*, and scattered large square sofas all about her carpeted drawing rooms. She hired Maurice Sachs to fill the library with the books she should read. Cocteau's young friend—Sachs was turning twenty—knew where to find rare editions and Coco paid him 60,000 francs a month. Maurice had never seen so much money. He moved to a hotel, hired himself a secretary and a chauffeur, and spent wild nights out. The books he lined her library with were less than a first-class choice of incunabula,

out-of-print volumes, and first editions. But it was not until 1929 that
Coco dismissed him.

She held court, dispensed privilege and pensions to her artist friends,
and admitted to her table society people and artists and those who were
neither quite society nor quite artists but knew how to make money with
style. Picasso and Cocteau on occasion stayed at the garden apartment.

The move from the villa in Garches to 29 Rue du Faubourg also
coincided with the petering out of the affair with Dmitri. There were no
scenes, and late in life Coco would speak of the duke, and of other
Romanovs she had known, as big, handsome men of little substance.
"Those Grand Dukes were all the same—they looked marvelous but there
was nothing behind. Green eyes, fine hands and shoulders, peace-loving,
timorons. They drank so as not to be afraid . . . behind it all—nothing,
just vodka and the void." Dmitri was looking for a rich woman to support
him and Coco had no intention of being the one. Audrey Emery was
an American heiress who found him and his name and title sufficiently
alluring to marry. Audrey could afford him, too. She was one of three
sisters from Cleveland, heiresses to the Benjamin Moore paint fortune.

Coco's work habits were relentless and her creations followed each
other at a dizzying pace. Princess Marthe Bibesco, for whom Coco invented a wardrobe for aeroplane travel, would say Chanel knew how to
sell not only her own preferences and penchants but even her disapproval.
"Chanel is faster than anyone in fashion to air her criticism and objections. What's trendy now and what's no longer smart are the two absolutes of her power," wrote the princess. "Her eyes are alert, her
little head, her step are decisive. She doesn't talk much. If she did, it
would probably be to say, after the physicist Henri Poincaré, that one
must always be ready to leave behind one truth for a verity that's even
truer. 'She came from nothing,' her friends say. 'Her grandmother was
a shepherd, her mother from Auvergne.' Yes, but it's in Paris that
she made it."

To accommodate the nearly three thousand employees working for
her, the House of Chanel annexed 27, 29, and 31 Rue Cambon. The
boutique in Rue Gontaut-Biron in Deauville, where the elegant crowd
from Paris and London still spent the summer, was doing well. But to
compensate for the decline of Biarritz as a summer resort, she opened a
branch in Cannes, the rediscovered Mediterranean playground.

Her private quarters in Rue Cambon were open to only a few members of the staff, friends, and clients who impressed her. The third-floor secret lair was filled with bookcases, Louis XVI furniture, Coromandel screens, a fifth-century B.C. torso of Venus, life-sized black porcelain deer, and, in honor of her astrological sign, lions of various dimensions.

She gave marvelous parties in Rue du Faubourg St. Honoré and was a sought-after dinner guest. The Beaumonts not only invited her, but hired members of her staff to work on settings and costumes for their own fancy-dress parties.

Her Christmas 1922 party would stand out. Society-page chroniclers gasped at the expense and the guest list. "Unlike certain salons where the champagne is not exactly vintage, the caviar and champagne amassed at Mademoiselle Chanel's table are premium," Marie Laurencin would remember. "And there is more. The artists and authors invigorate the party with a liveliness that the aristocracy, always frozen in its arrogance and bigotry, is only now discovering."

Stravinsky was there and Cocteau brought "the six"—the modern composers Honegger, Erik Satie, Darius Milhaud, Francis Poulenc, Georges Auric, and the pretty twenty-nine-year-old Germaine Taillefer. Paul Morand and his Romanian heiress, Hélène Soutso, were there with Philippe and Hélène Berthelot. Léon-Paul Fargue, the poet, came late, announcing Maurice Ravel would be coming soon, too. Satie wanted Gabrielle to do the costumes for a musical. He stopped talking when Misia, apparently sniffing a plot, came closer. To Coco, the composer whispered, "There's the cat, let's hide our birds."

The parties kept her name in the society pages, and she was not averse to subsidizing her celebrity by giving away dresses to highly visible women, who, when asked by other *élégantes* for the name of the couturier of their sparkling clothes, would whisper, "Chanel." Occasionally, such generosity backfired. A few Parisians who accepted Coco's clothes showed their independence by criticizing her. Coco tried to turn *that* into a gossip item by saying she was giving away dresses, "so they'll say nasty things about me."

She had little regard for society people. "Their dishonesty is irresistible," she told Morand. "In Berlin, the duchess [she mentioned an Italian name] who accompanied me had a gorgeous fur coat delivered to the hotel just before we were checking out. I was in a sour mood that morning."

" 'I refuse to pay for that,' I said.

" 'Oh, there's nothing to pay,' her friend answered (because of course I had brought along her lover).

" 'How's that?'

" 'We leave without paying. Aurelia didn't give her name.' What that meant was of course to add a theft to my bill. I love Aurelia very much, she's a grand courtesan, a quarter century behind the times."

She became a friend of the aging Countess Laure de Chevigné, whose azure eyes, ruby hairpiece, arched nose, hoarse voice, birdlike profile, and mannerisms so enchanted Marcel Proust that he turned her into the Duchess de Guermantes. The dowager took little interest in writing, and was particularly uninterested in *A la Recherche du temps perdu*, which she pronounced intolerably tedious, but she loved to exchange gossip with Chanel. The countess knew all the upper-crust men Coco had met in her youth, from the Duc de Gramont to Jean de Laborde, and she knew the society women who were Coco's clients—from Princess Marthe de Bibesco and Baroness de Rothschild to Anna de Noailles and Hélène de Chimay.

Chevigné claimed that all she knew she had learned from her lovers. "My lover took me to the Louvre; one cannot spend the entire time . . . kissing. It was back when a lady wore a small veil to enter a bachelor's apartment. Today, they do it everywhere, in front of the servants. My children are all Adhéaume's; God, no bastards! My daughter has been learning since she was three. She's sixty now and doesn't know anything."

Raymond Radiguet was the youngest celebrity to come to dinner. The writer was the unsettling, exciting presence in Cocteau's life, and Radiguet, who lived in a world of debt, alcohol, insomnia, and dirty linen, was very much under the spell of Cocteau. In the spring of 1923, Radiguet turned in the manuscript of his first novel *Le Diable au corps* to Bernard Grasset, the publisher, and, with Cocteau traveled to England. When they returned, Radiguet was famous. His novel was an immediate *succès de scandale*, and newsreels showed Grasset, sitting nobly at his desk, signing the first check for 100,000 francs ever presented by a French publisher to a twenty-year-old author. The very first sentence shocked: "Those who are already resenting what I say must realize what the war was for so many young boys—a four-year vacation." The story of a youth's love for an older married woman whose husband is off fighting the war was written in ardent prose of great purity and was a brilliant pastiche of a classic.

Coco came to work every morning smelling of the lye soap that the "aunts" of her childhood had taught her to use. Her sense of smell was as acute as ever, and if there was one thing she hated it was the smell of female body odors. She loved perfume and adopted as her own the poet Paul Valéry's quip, "A woman who doesn't wear perfume has no future." She believed the droplets of "smell good" that a woman daubed behind an ear, in the hollow of a shoulder, on the back of the wrist were mandatory.

The history of perfume touches on medicine, mythology, religion— and so does the genesis of Chanel No. 5. Other couturiers, Paul Poiret in particular, had sensed that fashion and perfume had points in common that might lend themselves to a profitable association, but no one before Gabrielle had dared to move away from floral scents. Until 1920, a woman's choice was to adopt the smell of one flower or a few easily identified flowers. With the help of Ernest Beaux, the owner of a laboratory in Grasse and one of the first perfumers to suspect the importance of synthetic scents in the development of new fragrances, Gabrielle changed all that.

There is no evidence that Dmitri was the one who introduced Coco to Beaux, but Misia Sert and Paul Morand, among others, were to find it more than a coincidence that this perfume chemist was the son of a former employee of the czar's court and had spent most of his youth in St. Petersburg. It is possible that it was Colette who introduced Chanel to Beaux. Colette and Coco became friends during the summer of 1923. The writer had shed her second husband and, together with her young lover Maurice Goudeket, spent the summer season in Beauvallon, a fishing village not far from Nice and Cannes, finishing her masterpiece, the story of pubescent love called *Le Blé en herbe.*

Colette was ten years older than Gabrielle, but they had a lot in common. Both were country girls who had made it. Both were level-headed and shared an attitude toward their work that was practical and unassuming. Together, they toured the Côte d'Azur in Coco's chauffeured Rolls, stopping in sleepy villages in the hills above the Mediterranean to look at pottery, wicker baskets, and corkscrews with handles made of gnarled vine stock. Grasse, with its guided tours of perfume factories, was on their itinerary, and it is likely that the two women toured the Fragonard laboratory, named after the eighteenth-century painter who was Grasse's most illustrious son.

Beaux was skeptical when Chanel first suggested he develop a scent for her, but soon discovered she was fearless and willing to leave behind all known formulas. "I don't want hints of roses, of lilies of the valley," she told him, "I want a perfume that is composed. It's a paradox. On a woman, a *natural* flower scent smells *artificial*. Perhaps a natural perfume must be created artificially."

Misia Sert would claim she had something to do with the savant composition of the Chanel perfume. Renovations in a château in the Loire region had brought to light a manuscript entitled *Le Secret des Médicis* by René the Florentine, the inventor of a cologne that gave the aging Queen Marie of Médicis and Diane de Poitier the skin of a young girl. The manuscript included the formula for this tonic water, and without a moment's hesitation Misia promised the owner of the Renaissance manuscript 6,000 francs for the beauty recipe. She dashed to Rue Cambon, demanded to see Mademoiselle, and, once in Coco's private quarters, told her friend that the combination of the René the Florentine formula and the name Chanel could only guarantee a fortune for what she decided should be called Eau Chanel. "Together we studied the packaging, a solemn, ultra-simple, quasi-pharmaceutical bottle, but in the Chanel taste and wrapped in the elegance that she bestowed on everything."

Coco found Beaux and his test tubes mesmerizing. She was not the first couturier to express interest and demand a tour of the premises. As they talked and he showed her around, however, he realized her sense of smell was extraordinary. "When someone offers me a flower, I can smell the hands that picked them," she said. She was quick to learn to distinguish between essences. When she suggested startling combinations, he was totally won over.

She was back the next day, to sniff benzyl acetate, which derived from coal tar but smelled like jasmine, and to hear him explain how the colorless liquid could not be used instead of the flower extract, but how mixing the two would fortify the natural scent. Extracting perfume from the flowers of the Spanish jasmine was painstaking and expensive using the process known as *enfleurage*, by which the oils of petals were absorbed into specially purified animal fats and finally extracted with volatile solvents. By mixing benzyl acetate with jasmine extract the resulting perfume was unalterable—that is, a perfume that would not fade. Beaux was also one of the first in the industry to suspect the importance of aldehydes, a class of organic compounds that yield acids when oxidized and alcohols when reduced.

Chanel stayed in Grasse and spent long days in the lab. Her acute sense of smell identified jasmines, Bulgarian roses, musks from Indochina, magnolia.

"When the petals fall from the magnolia trees and begin to rot, you can smell the mushrooms," Beaux told her.

She sniffed. "That smells like leaf mold, of wet grass, something refreshing. It will help soften the scent of the tuberose."

At the end, Beaux whittled the choices down to seven or eight samples. She sniffed them one after the other, compared, lingered, and came back to the fifth specimen.

"That's what I expected," she said. "A perfume unlike any other ever made. A woman's perfume, redolent, evocative of woman."

When the first batch of L'Eau Chanel was ready, Gabrielle invited Beaux and a few friends to dinner at the most exquisite restaurant in Cannes. She planted an atomizer on the table and whenever an elegant lady passed by she gave the atomizer a squeeze. "The effect was amazing," Beaux would recall. "Whenever a woman passed by our table, she stopped and sniffed. We pretended we didn't notice, of course."

Nothing boosts perfume sales like a fable, and several legends would grow up around the naming of Chanel No. 5. It was Coco's birthday (but she was born on the nineteenth); five was her lucky number. To name a perfume after a numeral was shrewdly contrary and as different as the composition of her fragrance from the flower-based Nuit de Chine, Lucrèce Borgia, Mille et Une Nuits, and other evocative appellations. The House of Worth had its Dans la Nuit perfume, Callot had La Fille du Roi de Chine and Il Pleut des Baisers, Poiret conjured with Coeur en folie and Tais-toi mon Coeur, and Lelong played on his own name with Tout le Long. Coco's second brilliant idea was the square bottle, again so different from the cupid-shaped flasks and flower-etched flacons on the market.

Of more immediate concern to Beaux was that the sample she chose contained more than eighty ingredients. It would be expensive, he told her. Nothing was more expensive than jasmine.

"In that case, put even more jasmine in it," she said. "I want to make it the world's most expensive perfume."

She had long since learned that the secret of the carriage trade was not just to ask the rich for a lot of money. Now she knew the way to launch something was to make socialites believe they had something to do with the success of the product.

She returned to Paris with little sample bottles, which she graciously began offering to her best clients. Next, she had her salesgirls atomize the fitting rooms with the scent. When one of the clients came back for a fitting a few days later and asked how she could buy the perfume, Coco professed surprise. "Ah, the little vial I gave you the other day." She smiled. "My dear, I don't sell perfume. I found the little bottles almost by chance in Grasse, at a perfumer whose name I've forgotten. I thought it would be an original little gift for my friends."

The scene repeated itself as salesgirls kept vaporizing the fitting rooms and other "dear friends" who had been among the privileged to receive a little gift came back and recognized the sample perfume.

Coco bombarded Beaux with telegrams demanding that he accelerate the start-up of the production. With her clients she went to phase two of her campaign.

"You think I should have it made and sell it?" she asked. "You mean you really like *my* perfume?"

When Beaux announced he was in production, she had new lines for the clients. "Maybe you're right," or, "Yes, I followed your advice. I'll be getting the perfume you like so much."

A few weeks later, the first commercial production of L'Eau Chanel reached selected stores. "The success was beyond anything we could have imagined," Misia would remember. "It was like a winning lottery ticket. 'Why don't you actually start making perfume?' I told Coco. 'In view of the Eau Chanel, René the Florentine seems to me to be the hen laying the golden eggs.' "

Never someone to neglect the traditional avenues of commercial success, Coco asked Théophile Bader, the owner of the Galeries Lafayette, to carry her perfume. A man in his early sixties, Bader was a retailing success story. He had transformed the notions and novelty shop he opened in 1895 into the biggest department store in Paris, an emporium with 130 departments, including a ready-to-wear section where Parisian women who could not afford haute couture found trendy and often intrepid fashions. It was in the Galeries Lafayette that young Coco had bought the straw boaters she trimmed with ribbons and lace and turned into hats nobody at Longchamp had seen before.

Bader was interested in carrying Chanel No. 5 at the Galeries Lafayette, but said he would need quantities greater than what a "nose" like Beaux could produce in his research laboratory. Bader had two young friends, the brothers Pierre and Paul Wertheimer.

As Pierre Wertheimer would recall, Bader phoned him one day and said he wanted him to meet Chanel. "She's a *couturière*, she's got an idea; she wants to launch a perfume." To Chanel, Bader said, "You've come up with a perfume that I think deserves a much bigger market than to be sold in boutiques, even a boutique as distinguished as yours. I want you to meet Pierre Wertheimer, who has one of the most important factories in the country, and therefore, an important distribution network."

16

THE WERTHEIMERS

Coco Chanel met Pierre Wertheimer at the Longchamp racetrack. After Théophile Bader introduced them the dialogue was brief and to the point.

"You want to produce and distribute perfumes for me?" Coco asked.

"Why not? But if you want the perfume to be made under the name Chanel, we've got to incorporate."

The association of Gabrielle Chanel and Pierre Wertheimer, which was to last to the end of their lives, was chaotic and complex, full of jealousy, conflicts, violent arguments, hatred, antagonism, fear, and, under it all, a kind of lumbering respect. He was ruthless in business, while she had all the guile, cunning, and duplicity of the generations of Chanel market hawkers. Almost in the same breath, she would call him "that bandit who screwed me" and "that darling Pierre," conceding that when they fought he always sent her flowers the next day. By 1928, the Wertheimers had an in-house lawyer who dealt exclusively with the lawsuits instigated by that "bloody woman," as Pierre called her.

The brothers Pierre and Paul Wertheimer were intelligent, rich, and aggressive. They were the owners of Les Parfumeries Bourjois, France's largest cosmetics and fragrance company. Pierre, who would figure in the American fragrance sagas of Charles Revson and Estée Lauder, was a trim, handsome, charming man. He spent money on thoroughbreds, boats, and the fine arts. His ambition was to have one of his horses win the Epsom Derby—something he ultimately achieved. In matters of art, he was audacious enough to be one of the first to patronize Chaim Soutine. Paul remained more in the background.

The Wertheimers were Jewish. Like the Rothschilds, they traced their roots to medieval Germany, and, like the Rothschilds, they were thoroughly Gallicized. The family residence was near the Bois de Boulogne on Avenue de Neuilly, where a portrait of Ernest Wertheimer, a Balzacian figure in top hat, greeted visitors in the vestibule. It was Ernest who, in the 1870s, had bought into Bourjois, a theatrical makeup company, which had introduced dry rouge to women in 1890.

"Like so many truly rich people, they have always managed to obscure their control over things," Léon Lévine, a Parisian lawyer specializing in international law, would observe. "I remember the year I graduated from law school, the summer of 1936. After visiting relatives in Vilna, Poland, I traveled back to Paris through Berlin. I had bought a gramophone, and a Jewish family with whom I stayed at the Kurfurstendamm told me the place to buy records was at Israel's. We were at the height of the Nazi era, swastikas on every public building, and I asked my host if the Germans didn't mind buying their records at Israel's. 'Not at all,' I was told. 'It's a tradition. Besides, Israel's belongs to the Wertheimers.' "

Over the decades, the Wertheimer family would obscure its control over the Chanel empire. Alain Wertheimer, Pierre's grandson, who would be running the Chanel empire in 1990, refused all interviews and, as *Forbes* magazine learned when it did a cover story on the Chanel empire, was quick to threaten lawsuits. Chanel biographer and *Paris-Match* editor Pierre Galante would quote Gabrielle as rather flippantly telling Paul Wertheimer at their first meeting in 1924 that she was not interested in his enterprise, that besides contributing her business card, she would "be satisfied with ten percent of the capital. For the rest, I don't want to have to answer to anyone."

Did she mean she would kick in 10 percent of the capitalization of the new company, or that she would be satisfied with 10 percent of the benefits? Galante seems to think that Chanel wanted her association with the Wertheimers to be at arm's length, and that to keep control of her House of Chanel she would be satisfied with 10 percent of the perfume profits. Her lawyer, René de Chambrun, would become convinced that her fear of losing control over her fashion house made her sign away the perfume for 10 percent of the corporation. He would also discover that for merely introducing Chanel to Wertheimer, Théophile Bader received 20 percent of the partnership.

Chambrun, who would become Coco's counsel only in the early 1930s but would litigate specific paragraphs in the original agreement, could recite by heart the clause by which she ceded to Les Parfums Chanel, S.A., her rights to "all the perfumes currently sold under the name Chanel, the proprietary production formulas, methods and designs copyrighted by her, as well as the exclusive right of said company to make and sell under the name Chanel, all perfumes, beauty products, soaps, etc." To be sure, her new partners did not encroach on her fashion territory; the new company's rights to sell products under the name Chanel were restricted exclusively "to objects usually sold in the perfume business." To allay her fears of inferior perfume products being commercialized under her name, a special paragraph was inserted: "The Parfums Chanels can only sell top quality products. Given the fact that Mlle Chanel is the owner of a luxury article couture house, it is understood that the merchandising under her name of inferior perfume products could cause her serious prejudice." The Wertheimers' investment was substantial. Besides contributing the 90 percent of the new company's working capital, they agreed to distribute the Chanel perfumes.

The partners had such confidence in each other and in their venture that they used the same lawyer.

Gabrielle was the fashion spirit of the Reckless Twenties. For 1924, women dressed in ⚭, as the back-to-back, intertwined C's on the new perfume had it. Chanel's steel beads were the crowning touch of day clothes—an unbuttoned skirt to show gray crêpe pantalets—along with stiffly tied "aeroplane bows." For evening, Coco offered a low-slung chiffon with feather boas and scarves, or butterfly wings floating from the shoulders.

The competition was stiff. Within a block of Rue Cambon, a woman of means could gratify her wishes for radiance and luxury in the shops of dressmakers, milliners, jewelers, bootmakers, and perfumers whose names glittered in the fashion firmament the world over. Paquin, Worth, and Caroline Reboux, the great lady of hats in the Rue de la Paix, shared the short street between the Place Vendôme and the Place de l'Opéra with

Cartier's jewelry, Tecla and Delza's displays of perfect imitations of pearls and precious stones, and Martial & Armand's lingerie and blouse shop. Seligman and Au Vieux Paris lured collectors with ornaments and antique furniture, and Mappin and Webb with specimens of the art of gold- and silversmiths. Grunwaldt presented the magnificence of furs, Roger et Gallet, Isabey, Rigaud and Arys fragrances, creams, and powders. Jean Patou, who was creating a name for himself with his easy sportswear, invented three new scents—one for the blonde, one for the brunette, and one for the woman with auburn hair. The dark beauty had to wear Que Sais-je and not Amour-Amour, which was for her fair sister, while the woman with copper-hued tresses was permitted the most sophisticated and enticing of the trio, Adieu Sagesse. Edward Molyneux, the first Irishman to become a Parisian couturier and a creator of disciplined yet sumptuous wardrobes, imitated Coco Chanel's numbered perfume and came out with Molyneux 2, 5, and 14, while the milliner J. Suzanne Talbot had a trio of perfumes called by her initials, J, S, and T.

Patou realized that to live in the shadow of such arresting self-promoters as Poiret and Chanel was to be condemned to a slow death; so, from the moment he opened his house when he was twenty-five, he became a society lion and a perpetual gossip item. When he returned from the United States with six American models, paying them the unheard-of-salary of ten thousand francs a month, newspapers all over the world carried the story. He was excessively jealous of Coco, to the point of counting the pages of *Vogue* illustrating Chanel and comparing them to the number of pages devoted to his own collections. If Chanel's outnumbered his, he wrote furious protests to the editor, Edna Wooman Chase. Patou and Chanel would never stay in the same room. Whoever spotted the other first always left as ostentatiously as possible.

Coco kept Ernest Beaux busy in Grasse. In 1924, the perfumer invented Cuire de Russie, followed two years later by Bois des Iles. The Wertheimers' publicity department invented alluring slogans. Russian Leather was "a scent close to the heart of perfumers that only Chanel has brought to perfection"; The Wood of the Islands possessed "the call and the soul of tropical forests." Neither of the two, nor Gardenia ("the cool of a spring morning"), which followed in 1927 from the Bourjois laboratories, would ever equal the success of No. 5.

Besides Pauline de Saint-Sauveur, the aristocratic young lady who had bought nothing but Chanel hats in Deauville in 1914, several members of Russian nobility were employed by the House of Chanel. Like Grand Duke Dmitri, they were beginning to realize that, despite Lenin's death in January 1924, the Soviet Revolution would not collapse, and they would not return to any *status quo ante* anytime soon. Dmitri's sister Marie became a milliner, and although she never worked for Chanel, she created hats for New York's Bergdorf Goodman. Count Kutuzov, a friend of Dmitri who had been governor of Crimea, became Chanel's glorified doorman before joining the business staff. Baron Retern was from one of the Baltic states. He became famous when homesickness one day drove him to hail a taxi and ask the driver to drive north. They were a third of the way to the Belgian border when the cabdriver persuaded his fare to return to Rue Cambon. Then there was Princess Feodorovna, who one day tearfully told Coco how, in order to pay off a debt she owed an oil tycoon, she would have to give herself to this horrible man. When Coco asked how much she'd need to escape her fate, Feodorovna said 30,000 francs. Knowing full well that one does not loan money to Russians and that to give money in such circumstances is considered an ill omen, Coco still advanced the sum to her royal employee. A few days later Coco was invited to Feodorovna's apartment, to be greeted by a twilight of mauve intimacy, caviar on ice, vodka in a decanter, and gypsies playing balalaikas. The idea that Feodorovna had escaped the heinous clutches enchanted Coco, but the nocturnal lavishness made her ask if Feodorovna had paid the monster the 30,000 she owed him. "What do you want," stammered the princess, "I was so sad. I wanted to have a little fun first, so I kept the money."

Coco was never paid back, but a while later she saw Feodorovna with the Persian oil magnate, "a man she loved but soon left for a Czech who was even more of an ogre."

The titled émigrés lent a certain cachet to the Chanel salons. "It was the Russians who taught women it isn't degrading to work," Coco would remember, condescendingly adding, "My grand duchesses used to knit."

Coco both liked and pitied the White Russians. The only thing that was worse than having to discharge the duties of a royal prince was no longer to have to, she thought. "They say all women should have a Romanian in their lives. I think all Westerners should capitulate to the 'Slavic charm' to know what it is," she told Morand. "I was fascinated. Their 'all that's yours is mine' intoxicated me. All Slavs are distinguished, the most humble among them are never banal." For more than fifteen years, Count Kutuzov, who had come to Paris penniless with his wife and two daughters, was the backbone of her business organization.

Of greater consequence for Gabrielle's future was Vera Bate, who entered her employ in 1925. Born Sarah Gertrude Arkwright, she was a popular member of the clever, amusing, worldly set that surrounded the Prince of Wales, a circle that was not drawn from the conventional aristocracy and was setting the new society tone.

Vera's appetite for life reminded Gabrielle of her sister Antoinette, her elegance of Aunt Adrienne, and her financial problems of both. As Coco got to know her better, there were deeper parallels. Like Antoinette, Vera had married a serviceman on an impulse in 1919, an American officer named Fred Bate. Like that of Coco herself, Vera's birth was shrouded in uncertainty. Supposedly a stonemason's daughter, she was apparently the illegitimate child of Adolphus Charles, Duke of Teck, who was the brother of Queen Mary, consort of King George V, a man who renounced his German titles in 1917 and was made marquess of Cambridge.

Vera wore clothes so well that her friends often wanted to own the dresses they saw on her. It occurred to Gabrielle that if Vera wore her lines, the Chanel sales among London's smart set would increase. Society women were the new fashion dictators. They wore couture clothes and lived by the season—Deauville and Palm Springs in spring, the Riviera in summer, Scotland and Biarritz in the fall, and London and Paris in winter. Vera Bate's job was to wear nothing but Chanel and, when asked, to tell who her couturier was.

A distraction from the business empire was an invitation to do the costumes for *Le Train bleu.* Combining dance, acrobatics, pantomime, and satire, the ballet, which took its title from the new crack Paris–Riviera express, was set at a seashore resort and featured young men and women with tennis rackets in pursuit of Mediterranean pleasures.

Cocteau was trying to pull himself together after the Radiguet affair. After the publication of *Le Diable au corps*, the young writer began living with a woman he didn't love but intended to marry because he refused "to become a forty-year-old man called Madame Jean Cocteau." That was in December 1923, and Radiguet was not well. Cocteau had appealed to Coco to have her personal doctor examine the twenty-one-year-

old writer. Radiguet was diagnosed as suffering from an advanced case
of typhoid. Weakened by his excesses of alcohol and drugs, he died December 12. Cocteau ran away to the Riviera and drowned his sorrow in
an opium binge. Gabrielle paid for the funeral.

Diaghilev was in Monte Carlo, anxious to get a spring season under
way for his company and to feature his new, athletic recruit and lover
Patrick Kay, variously rechristened Patrikeyev, Anton Dolin, and Antoine
Doline. Kay, a particularly athletic Irishman, was forever doing hand-
stands and cartwheels in the wings. When Cocteau surfaced from his
opium haze—there was no drug-taking in the Ballets Russes, at least none
was condoned by Diaghilev—and he saw Kay show off his gymnastic
vigor, he came up with an idea for a beach ballet. Why not have Kay
impress a bevy of bathing beauties of both sexes with his antics on the
sands?

Diaghilev said yes. The Ballets Russes had a new rival and Diaghilev
had reason to be nervous. Under the direction of Rolf de Mare—Cocteau
called him "a rich and accomplished young Diaghilev"—the Swedish
Ballet was arousing interest in Paris. A year earlier, when Diaghilev had
declined to produce a ballet that Darius Milhaud had written to a libretto
by Paul Claudel, Mare took it on and, in addition, asked for a ballet by
Auric to a book by Cocteau. Count Etienne de Beaumont financed the
new work. The score became a collaborative effort by five of the "six"—
Auric, Milhaud, Poulenc, Taillefer, and Honegger—and the resulting *Les
Mariés de la Tour Eiffel* a hilarious smash hit.

Diaghilev realized he desperately needed to catch up. Milhaud was
writing the music for another Ballets Suédois production, *Salade*, a Neapolitan romp in the *Pulcinella* style for which Braque was doing the sets,
when Diaghilev went to see the composer and asked him to write a score
for Cocteau's beach ballet. Milhaud was fast. The day after he finished
Salade, he started on the *Train bleu* score. He finished it in twenty days.

The sculptor Henri Laurens was commissioned to do the decor. He
had never done theater sets before, but he came up with a cubistic Riviera
beach with sloping planes, lopsided bathing huts, dancing dolphins, all in
natural colors. The curtain was an enlargement of a painting Picasso
had done of two huge women, with their tunic straps loosened to reveal
their breasts, running on the beach. Picasso also did the program illustrations.

The choreography was by Bronislava Nijinska, the sister of the Ballets Russes' first star, Nijinsky, who also cast herself as the brawny Tennis Lady.

Gabrielle found herself in highly charged company. The rehearsals were fraught with tempests, intrigues, and hostilities. Cocteau fought over the staging until Nijinska was in tears. Kay wanted to incorporate a waltz for himself and the leading ballerina Lydia Sokolova, but Diaghilev was reluctant to admit that ballroom dancing could be part of a ballet.

The costume fittings were done in the relative calm of Coco's salon in Rue Cambon. Sokolova would remember trying on her pink bathing suit, which everybody thought very daring. "The question of what I was to wear on my head arose. Three women stood around me, binding my long hair with various pieces of material, until at last they decided on a dark suede. The neat little skull cap they made for me set a fashion."

Le Train bleu was the first Diaghilev production at the Théâtre des Champs Elysées since 1920. The premiere was set for June 20. The month of May turned suddenly colder, but the theater did not turn on the heat for rehearsals. The cast looked miserable and absurd shivering in their bathing costumes. Coco did not like the fawn beach pajamas Ludmilla Scholler and Ninette de Valois were to wear in a *pas de quatre* with Taddeus Slavinsky and Nicolas Zverev. With Diaghilev, Milhaud, and Laurens looking on, Coco ordered de Valois to get up on a chair. "Diaghilev seemed ill at ease as a connoisseur of bathing costumes," Sokolova would remember, "and Scholler, reminiscent in appearance of the prewar stage dancer, added to the tension by complaining that the tight-fitting brown skin bathing caps were impossible for anyone with long hair to wear."

"Shingle, Madame," snapped Chanel. "Everybody else has done it already." Shingle was of course the fashionable close-cropped women's haircut. Diaghilev hated it on ballerinas.

The dress rehearsals provoked new crises. The Chanel beachwear looked gorgeous until the cast started to dance. The costumes on the bathers, tennis players, golf champions, and pretty young things came apart at the seams and at the end of a run-through hung limp on the dancers. Coco was on her knees with threads and needle stitching costumes back on sweating bodies. Next, she ordered her workrooms to make second sets of everything.

Gabrielle was at the premiere of *Le Train bleu* with the Serts; around her were Paris's artists, patrons, aristocrats, and trendsetters. After Picasso's showstopper curtain, an absurd opening chorus featured beach gigolos and their girls in postcard poses. Nijinska entered in white tennis dress and eyeshade to a jaunty tune, followed by Kay in black hair glued to his scalp, velvet eyes, and an acrobat's jersey that made him the perfect beach Casanova, and Sokolova in her pink bathing suit. Kay—billed as Antoine Doline in the program—brought the house down with his hair-raising acrobatics. Coco's costumes were half-real, half-imaginary beachwear satirizing her clients, the tomboys with long cigarette holders hankering after emancipation.

What Coco thought of the triumph has not been consigned to posterity. She tended to be closed-mouthed, as Princess Bibesco noticed, and it wasn't only her triumphs she pretended to forget. More and more of her past was being wiped clean. Though Etienne Balsan and Léon de Laborde might pop up to ogle her models before lunch and her brother Alphonse might come to Rue Cambon when he was in Paris—he still knew how to make her laugh—they were all part of a past she was beginning to deny. She could afford to overlook her childhood and to forget the years at Royallieu, the names of the first people who helped her, the *cocottes* and actresses who bought the first hats. Her new friends saw through her. Lady Abdy would talk of Gabrielle's total devotion to the House of Chanel, Princess Bibesco would write a thinly disguised portrait of her as the queen *couturière*. Serge Lifar, the rising star of the Ballets Russes, would talk about Coco's wealth beginning to lock her into her own ivory tower, and Auric tell of her fear of being found out.

"Coco has always been impressed by people with money and titles," Abdy would write. "She, who overcame all life's barriers, was ashamed of her roots. Instead of being proud of where she came from, she tried fiercely to hide her origins. She vanquished everything except her childhood." Lifar, who became a lifelong if intermittent friend of Coco, marveled at the distance she had traveled from the orphanage. "The haunting memory of the little girl who invented a father gone to America to make his fortune, the adolescent who talked to the dead in cemeteries, never changed her fear of poverty and loneliness."

Coco would remember they all went to Misia's after the *Train bleu* premiere, but when asked "All who?" the only names that came to mind were the artists. "Like after Picasso's marriage; more or less the same people, the painters." And the musicians, Milhaud, Poulenc, Auric. It was as if deep down she rejected the glittering society that had made her rich, the society that twenty years earlier had relegated her to the demimonde. Her new friends saw it. Only artists were worth knowing.

Yet the next man in her life was the aristocrat who possessed the biggest fortune in Britain.

17

BENDOR

~~~~~~~~~~~~~~~~~~~~~~~~~~~~~~~~~~~~~~~

On August 28, 1924, readers of the London *Times* could only wonder about the ways of the very rich. The High Court, it was reported, was giving itself two weeks to decide whether to grant Violet Mary, the Duchess of Westminster, an injunction forbidding the Duke of Westminster from ejecting her and her servants from their home in Davies Street, Berkeley Square West. Surely the duchess was entitled to go to the house whenever she wished, her lawyers insisted. The duke's barrister, however, maintained that his lordship was entitled to prevent her from entering the premises. The duke's servants, the duchess's lawyer retorted, had told her maid that if her ladyship tried to enter the house she would be turned into the street. "To spare herself such an indignity," her counsel concluded, "she had refrained from going to her house." On condition that the maid be allowed to stay in the house, the court granted the two-week postponement because "highly controversial matters had been raised on the affidavits" and because the duchess had sailed for America that very morning, and the duke was also abroad.

Reporters cornered the duchess in Southampton a month later as she disembarked from the ocean liner *Homeric*. "I cannot tell you what I will do next," her ladyship told a reporter from the *Daily Express*. "Perhaps I will know when I get to London. One thing is certain, I no longer have a home. My situation is unimaginable and unfortunately I cannot help but think about it all the time."

Without naming names, a gossip item in *The Star*'s October 13 edition about "the future of a certain duke whose conjugal tousle was recently in the news," quoted reliable sources as saying "the new duchess is a beautiful and brilliant Frenchwoman who heads one of the big Parisian couture houses." Photographers caught Hugh Richard Arthur Grosvenor, the Duke of Westminster, in the company of Galloper Smith, Earl of Birkenhead, and Mademoiselle Chanel, at the annual steeplechase at Aintree near Liverpool. At the Grand National races, photographers snapped the duke and Mademoiselle alone.

In Paris, where Westminster kept a permanent suite at the Hotel Lotti, he had first been noticed at the *Train bleu* rehearsals. He was there beside Coco, watching with fascination Diaghilev, Cocteau, Picasso, and the dancers in Coco's bathing suits. The avant-garde crowd was something new for him.

Although his mother, Lady Sibell Lumley, and Winston Churchill called him Benny, his friends called him Bender or Bendor. There were several explanations for the nickname. Bendor was either the name of one of his grandfather's most prized thoroughbreds, a horse that won the 1880 Epsom Derby, or a mispronunciation of the Grosvenors' armorial crest— *azur a bend'or*, heraldic patois for a coat of arms divided in equal parts of blue and gold.

Bendor was among the very fortunate in worldly standing and wealth, a man who owned vast tracts of choice London real estate in Belgravia and Mayfair, and shot, hunted, played polo, and cruised the world aboard his own pleasure boats. The master of an enormous country house at Eaton Hall and magnificent yachts—one a converted Royal Navy destroyer, the other a four-masted schooner—he was a restless man who tired easily of people, and, as Sacheverell Sitwell would put it, was "ultimately beastly to everybody around him." The Sitwells, Sacheverell and Osbert, and his sister Edith, were often the duke's guests on Mediterranean cruises. Bendor was a capable yachtsman, though he locked himself up in his stateroom in stormy weather. Still, his guests had little to fear— his 883-ton *Cutty Sark* came with a crew of a hundred and eighty, and *The Flying Cloud* with a forty-man crew.

Since the reign of Queen Victoria, members of the royal family had dropped in unannounced at Eaton Hall, in Cheshire near Manchester, and Bendor felt obliged to keep his home on ceremonial footing at all times. To have sixty guests for a weekend was normal at Eaton Hall, where paintings of Bendor's forefathers by Gainsborough and Reynolds hung beside pictures of their horses, and canvases signed Goya and Velázquez. The duke had scandalized London in 1921 by selling Gainsborough's famous *Blue Boy* to Henry Huntington of Pasadena, California. "He hated painting, sculpture, and modern music," noted Loelia Ponsonby, the future Duchess of Westminster. "He loved jewelry for its own sake and bought with discrimination, never being taken in by a jeweler's flashy piece made of small stones in a lot of setting. He also had a great feeling for silver and would enjoy sitting in a silversmith's turning over the work of master craftsmen."

In Noël Coward's *Private Lives* the heroine says, "Whose yacht is that?" and her companion replies, in a bored voice, "The Duke of Westminster's, I expect. It always is." *The Flying Cloud*'s racy silhouette was frequently seen at Riviera ports, where, after dark, its aft deck was illuminated for extravagant parties. An invitation to cruise aboard the *Cutty Sark* or *The Flying Cloud* or to spend a summer at his Deauville residence began at the Victoria Station, where his grace's private railway car was attached to the *Orient Express* or to the boat train for the ride down to Southampton.

Coward said of the duke that he was a "floridly handsome man, who, had he lived in an earlier age, would undoubtedly have glittered with rhinestones from head to foot." To describe the dimensions of his wealth—as well as his somewhat peculiar social conscience—contemporary press reports told how, even during the summer, the central heating systems and chimneys of his various properties were kept burning. To consume coal in all seasons, he felt, was his duty toward British miners. He liked only what he called "real people." Apart from a few exceptions of his own choosing, no well-known or titled person could be real people.

"He was deeply versed in all forms of animal sports and saw into the hearts of them," his friend Winston Churchill would write of him. The two men were related by marriage—after Lord Randolph Churchill had died, Winston's mother had married Benny's first wife's brother. Churchill and the duke had met in South Africa during the Boer War and Winston enjoyed partaking of Westminster's lavish and racy lifestyle.

To watch Benny live was something that fascinated not only the Churchills, Noël Coward, and the Sitwells, but also Coco Chanel. "Let me explain who he was, because my greatest pleasure was to see him go through life," she would say twenty years later. Boredom, she soon found out, was what he feared most. "As long as you don't bore him, he is charming. He's a big hunk of a man, heavy and rugged at least on the outside. He's full of charming absurdity, and not without spite, an elephant's little vindictiveness, grudges, well planned in his mind, because he likes to tease."

He was as easily pleased as he was bored. The women in his life learned to put up with his pranks, to anticipate his sudden rages, and to deal with decisions that were impervious to argument. Still, his charm was palpable. Said Coco, "A man must be clever to keep me for ten years. Those ten years were tender and amiable years, and we've stayed friends. I loved him, or thought I loved him, which is the same thing."

If Balsan and the years at Royallieu had taught her about thoroughbreds and Dmitri had taught her about the finest pearls, she learned about afternoon teas and magnificently maintained country houses from Bendor. "Westminster is the richest man in England, perhaps in Europe—nobody knows, especially not he. I say that because unlimited wealth is not vulgar. That kind of affluence is beyond envy, and takes on almost catastrophic proportions. I'm saying this because his wealth has turned Westminster into the last product of a disappearing civilization, a paleontological curiosity whose place is in people's memories. In showing me the opulence of Eaton Hall, Lord Lonsdale said, 'When the owner is no more, what we see here will be no more.' "

Bendor's first marriage, to Constance Edwina Cornwallis-West, had produced three children, a son who had died of appendicitis at the age of four, and two daughters, Ursula and Mary, who could not inherit Eaton or the title. His current marriage to Violet Mary Nelson was childless, and Bendor was seeking a woman sophisticated enough to forgive his infidelities and fertile enough to supply him with a son, so that the bulk of his fortune would not go to William Grosvenor, a bachelor cousin he hardly knew. Most of the women he met, however, bored him to tears.

Gabrielle had met him in Monte Carlo during a 1923–24 Christmas–New Year's holiday. Coco invited Vera Bate to be her guest for a week at the Hôtel de Paris, and it was there that Vera introduced Chanel to the duke.

The Flying Cloud was moored in the harbor below and, with her habitual frankness, Vera said she had been promised a gift if she persuaded Coco to join the duke for a shipboard dinner. Transforming Vera into an English friend named Pamela, Coco told Paul Morand of the meeting, complete with dialogue.

"I'm sure I won't go," Coco told her friend.

"Please," begged "Pamela." "He wants to meet you. I've promised."

Coco agreed to a dinner the next night. But a telegram arrived from Dmitri, announcing his arrival. Coco canceled the shipboard dinner engagement. "Pamela" was present when Dmitri arrived and Coco told him she had canceled her *Flying Cloud* engagement.

"I wouldn't have minded being invited to see the yacht," said Dmitri.

The Englishwoman said she would make sure Dmitri was invited.

Two hours later, Westminster phoned and asked the grand duke to be his guest.

"You're wrong," Coco told Dmitri.

"Why?"

"I don't know. Fate shouldn't be forced."

Bendor had hired a gypsy band for the dinner under the stars, and the conversation flowed as mellow as the violins and the wine. He spoke a flavorful French; she, little English, although once they became lovers, she took lessons. Gabrielle fell into Bendor's category of real people, and he was dazzled to discover a "self-made woman," secure and intriguing.

After dinner they all went ashore to dance. Bendor was fond of gambling. *Trente-et-quarante* was his favorite game because he believed the card game gave him the best chance at laying a stake against the bank. In roulette, he often played at three or four tables at once, with casino personnel running back and forth with his stacks of chips. Coco was no mean roulette player herself.

When the evening ended, Bendor said he wanted to see her again the next day. She hesitated. He inundated her hotel suite with flowers, and, when she went back to Paris, did the same in her house in Rue Faubourg St. Honoré. His private courier brought orchids and letters from London. Flowers and baskets of fruit picked by the duke's own hand— or so the enclosed notes said—in the Eaton Hall hothouse were followed by salmon from his Scottish streams caught and dispatched by plane.

The smitten duke enlisted Vera Bate as his go-between and redoubled his ardor. By Easter, he was in Paris, ostensibly accompanying the Prince of Wales. Late one evening Joseph opened the door to see a tall man behind an enormous bouquet of flowers. "Put them down here," the butler ordered. When he was about to tip the delivery man, Bendor said he was the Duke of Westminster.

It was not the first time that Joseph didn't know what to believe. Earlier that week a young man had rung the doorbell and said that he had an appointment with Vera Bate.

"She's not in," Joseph snapped. The stranger seemed embarrassed to intrude—he said he knew the mistress of the house was busy preparing her collection, and he wouldn't dream of disturbing her—but the butler told him he might come in and wait. It was only hours later, when Vera arrived, that Joseph remembered the waiting caller. The man was no longer in the vestibule where Joseph had sat him down. The butler found the stranger in the kitchen discussing the secret of successful profiterolles with the cook. "Madame Bate has come in," Joseph interrupted. "What name shall I announce?"

"The Prince of Wales."

Pierre Galante described a night Bendor and the prince came together. Sinking into an armchair next to one of the Coromandel screens, the heir to the throne said to Coco, "Call me David."

Still, Gabrielle hesitated before Bendor's advances, and it was not calculated coyness that made her act as she did. The House of Chanel was devouring her and there was something exhilarating in being in over one's head. In a sense, her friends were more important to her now than any male conquest could be; she often saw Cocteau, Picasso, Lifar, and her new acquaintances: Christian Bérard, painter, theater decorator, homosexual, and opium addict; and Pierre Reverdy, impecunious and anguished poet and, she was sure, a clairvoyant.

She invited Bendor to a soirée with her friends and the results were disastrous. The conversation of Maurice Sachs, Cocteau, Laurens, Lifar, Bérard was too subtle, the jokes too sly, the allusions too pointed, and Jojo Sert's attractive self-mockery too quirky for the duke. Cocteau was offended by the duke's aristocratic condescension: once, when Cocteau found himself momentarily without money, Bendor suggested that he write the history of Bendor's dogs. Misia's comments on Bendor were scornful, perhaps too sarcastic, since as a result the ever-contrary Gabrielle accepted an invitation to another shipboard dinner, this time for a hundred people. *The Flying Cloud* was in Bayonne harbor, next to Biarritz. Bendor took advantage of the departure of his guests to raise anchor. He and Gabrielle were alone off the coast, with a crew of forty and an orchestra he had hired in anticipation of her surrender.

Gossip columns in Britain and America predicted Coco Chanel would become the third Duchess of Westminster. Fashion magazines gave her the lion's share of attention, and quoted her response to the duke's gifts of priceless jewels. "I couldn't wear my own real pearls without being stared at on the street, so I started the vogue of wearing false ones," she said.

Gabrielle wasn't quite sure what to think of the seignorial residence, but she learned to assume the role of mistress of Eaton Hall. From her years with the nuns in Aubazine, she carried a lifelong affection for bare stone walls and lye soap and if one thing impressed her it was the cleanliness of the manor. "What you had to admire was the flawless order of that house, its English unaffectedness. It made you forget the ugly bits. A knight in armor stuck into a corner of a staircase, that does look a little overdone—unless it has always been there. Then you see it as something that grew out of the earth, proud and straight, especially when the armor is all shiny and looks ready for action. At Eaton Hall there was one in particular, a sort of hidalgo, whose helmet especially—all it needed was the plume—caught your attention. The knight in armor became a kind of friend to me. I thought of him as being young and handsome. I said hello to him every time I went past. I used to say to myself, 'After all, what a clever piece of work that thing is. And how attractive and powerful one must feel inside.' When I was sure nobody was looking, I used to shake his hand."

Bendor called the huge Gothic Eaton Hall "St. Pancras Station." He delighted in never staying very long in any one of his houses. Besides Eaton Hall, the estate in Caithness in the Scottish highlands and the town house in London, he owned a hunting lodge in the Landes between Bordeaux and Biarritz, and a château near Deauville in Normandy, but his preference was his ships. As much as he loved sailing, Gabrielle hated the sea. She found squinting at the horizon for hours without seeing anything a crushing bore. Her fearlessness, even in the heaviest of storms, however, did much to enhance her in his esteem.

At Eaton Hall, Coco liked that no one told guests when to play tennis, when to meet at the stables, or when to have tea. Bendor was the lord of the manor. The servants feared his bullying retorts as much as his cruelty, which, once his anger blew away, he'd redeem with infinite tactfulness. He drank expensive brandy, and counted among his pranks refilling empty bottles with inferior cognac for the pleasure of seeing his friends rave and tell him they could recognize the vintage blindfolded. He kept odd animals at his estates: in Scotland, Himalayan monkeys that somehow got out one winter and joined his party of skaters on a frozen pond; in Normandy, a Brazilian guinea pig the size of a farm pig that became so fierce it was banished to a remote farm.

His sartorial eccentricities amused her. He sported spit-polished shoes with holes in the soles, and had his valet iron shoelaces every other day. To feel at ease on a dance floor he had to wear used socks, and his valet had orders to soak new socks for several days.

The duke was a brilliant shot. He loved to arrange hunts for his friends, and approved sufficiently of Coco's horsemanship to invite her to his boar hunt at Mimizan, his estate in the remote pine forests of the Landes. To the end of her life she would remember the time a discharge by one of the hunters' guns caused a tree branch to fall on her, opening a deep gash on her lower lip. Attendants lifted her to the ground, her face bloody. Bendor called off the hunt, and a veterinarian administered first aid. Sutures were needed and by night train she returned to Paris together with a maid, and a monkey and parrot she had bought for Bendor. In the sleeping compartment, ape and cockatoo began to insult each other. The monkey refused to let go of Coco's skirt and the maid couldn't get close enough to throw a towel over the enraged parrot. Coco would claim she had her first breakdown then and there.

Rumors of marriage persisted. But Bendor was in no hurry to enter matrimony for the third time, and Coco had no intention of giving up the House of Chanel for the role of Eaton Hall's châtelaine. She had even less desire to share him with a series of easy flirts and little mistresses. She had gone through that with Etienne Balsan and Boy Capel. Serge Lifar would tell of the time that Bendor brought a pretty young decorator along on a Mediterranean cruise aboard *The Flying Cloud*.

Coco was furious and the next morning *The Flying Cloud* made a landfall to disembark the young woman. Bendor, too, went ashore, and when he came back on board he had with him a gorgeous string of pearls.

"Proud and arrogant, Chanel couldn't stand being less than the one and only woman in Westminster's life," Lifar would write. "When the duke offered her the necklace, which was worth a fortune, Coco, in a gesture of superb defiance, let the pearls slide from her hand into the ocean."

If there was one thing that money and fame had given her it was freedom from being dependent on any man.

18

THE POET

~~~~~~~~~~~~~~~~~~~~~~~~~~

If Boy Capel was Gabrielle's one love and Bendor the one she could spend time with, the man who counted when rancor engulfed her old age was Pierre Reverdy. This intense poet, who sought neither fame nor recognition, was for a while her existential anchor. Always something of a recluse, Reverdy was associated with the Montmartre bohemia but never wholeheartedly a part of the avant-garde.

"Coco is crazy, she's with a koo-rey," Bendor said when he found out, pronouncing the word *curé*, for parish priest, with an inimitable long *coo* sound. Reverdy was no cleric, but in 1926 he left Gabrielle—and his wife—and retired to a Benedictine abbey in Normandy.

Was she trying to make Bendor jealous? Lady Abdy, for one, was sure the presence of the poor, taciturn poet in Rue Faubourg St. Honoré was a tit for tat for the duke's dissipated ways.

Six years younger than Chanel, Reverdy was not attractive, but he had magnificent black eyes, and spoke in a strong provincial brogue. The grandson of masons and the son of a winegrower, he was someone of her own breed, deeply marked by the soil and by his working-class upbringing. His poetry was dense, subtle, and emotional. Most people considered it difficult. Like the Montmartre scenes of his painter friend Maurice Utrillo, his verse expressed urban angst in images of lonely streets and still squares devoid of the picturesque. His spare lines evoked expectation, emotions that are about to happen but never do.

At the intersection you can hear the clock and peo-
  ple's footsteps
At the intersection, sometimes, a car is smashed up,
  only to turn up again.
The moon on the clock face
*the hands keep turning . . .**

Reverdy was married to a woman who, whenever things became too tough for them financially, took in sewing. Yet his interest in Coco was obsessive. She in turn cared desperately about him; she loved his spirituality, his mysticism, his conviction that happiness was a snare and a delusion. They argued human existence on its deepest level, he underlining its vanity, she accusing him of being unhappy on principle, of being self-indulgent. "Poetry has always been, and will always remain, the noblest outlet for a pained conscience facing a reality that is always hostile to man's divine dream of fullness, happiness, and freedom," he wrote in *Le Gant de Crin*, a collection of his most intimate thoughts and epigrams, and the book of his she liked the most. Everything she had known as a child—her father's indifference, her mother's torment and early death, her own failure to make Boy Capel want only her—should make her agree with his pessimism. Instead, she exerted herself to prove that happiness did exist.

Reverdy and Coco did not go out together. The worlds they revolved in were too different. He lived with Coco in the town house in Rue Faubourg St. Honoré, only to make sudden escapes to Montmartre. He hated himself for being unfaithful to his wife, and always returned to the woman who waited dutifully for him in their cold Montmartre flat. He believed society was organized as one vast fraud and that people would succeed only through duplicity. After an accident, friends heard him pray, "Make certain, Lord, that I die an unknown poet."

He dedicated poems to Gabrielle, wrote tender lines to her, and told her that to chase after pleasure was to chase the wind. She owned the complete works of Pierre Reverdy in first editions, had him inscribe dedications to her, and kept the books all her life.

From his native Narbonne in southern France, Reverdy had come to

Au carrefour on entend l'horloge et les pas du passant
 Au carrefour il y a parfois une voiture qui s'écrase et reparaît
 la lune sur le cadran
 les aiguilles qui tournent . . .

Paris when he was twenty-one and immediately joined a crowd of Montmartre artists and writers surrounding Max Jacob. A legendary personality and friend of Picasso and Guillaume Apollinaire, Jacob was a poet, visionary, painter, homosexual, recluse, astrologer, and humorist, who had a profound influence on a generation of young intellectuals. Born a Jew in Brittany, Jacob had converted to Catholicism the year before Reverdy met him—with Picasso acting as his godfather—after having a vision, while in the National Library, of Christ in blue and white. Jacob did much to "make" Picasso by pushing the newly arrived Spaniard toward a cubism Jacob never really liked himself but which he was the first to understand. In Jacob, Reverdy admired not only a peerless nonconformist with a boundless creative gift, but also an artist in love with perfection. Gabrielle fell for Jacob's charm when she met him in 1920. He read her palm, worked out her horoscope, suggested she launch a Christ-figure hairstyle, and asked her advice on what to wear. The spell was broken the day he told her Paul Poiret had appointed him consultant on lucky and unlucky colors, and that he was spiritual adviser to Liane de Pougy, one of the *cocottes* from the Royallieu days.

Reverdy lived in utter poverty but in the matchless company of Jacob, Picasso, Gris, Braque, and Apollinaire. He married a girl named Henriette, who was a junior cutter for a fashion house in the Place Vendóme, and sometimes posed for the artists in the neighborhood, among them Amedeo Modigliani. Reverdy found work as a newspaper proofreader. The job allowed him to set his first poems by hand and, after hours, to print a hundred copies on an old press. Henriette stitched together the bindings for the slim volume. Published with woodcuts by Gris and Laurens in 1915, *Poèmes en prose* was followed by three novels, one illustrated by Matisse. Two years later he founded the literary magazine *Nord-Sud* (named after the *métro* line linking Montmartre and Montparnasse). Misia was one of the underwriters and the enthusiastic publicist of the new publication, and Adrienne Monnier, who with Sylvia Beach was to support that unpublishable Irish expatriate James Joyce, was the first bookseller to carry it. Reverdy published Jacob and Apollinaire, Cocteau and Radiguet, and the new surrealists, André Breton and Tristan Tzara; he had Braque, Gris, Derain, and Fernand Léger illustrate the pages. Reverdy marveled at Cocteau's gifts and genius for understanding everyone who mattered, and published a piece by Cocteau, detailing the genesis of the Cocteau-Satie-Picasso collaboration on *Parade.* Like so many passionate literary magazines that sprang up toward the end of the Great War, *Nord-Sud* ceased to exist after sixteen issues.

Reverdy's austere talent was not appreciated by the clever people of the first dizzy years of peace. His publisher—and his wife's sewing—kept the couple alive while his friends from Montmartre became famous and sometimes rich. Coco suggested that he write his poems on separate sheets and, as painters do with their canvases, sign each one. "You'll be as rich as they are, if only a bit of snobbish pretense is mixed into the sauce." She would have provided the chic if he had let her, but he preferred an anonymous existence in harmony with the feelings of loneliness and strong spiritual doubt that characterized his poetry.

Coco had met Reverdy in 1920 when she was still mourning the death of Boy, and neither of them paid much attention to the other. When the relationship with Bendor was going nowhere, Coco fell for his commanding dark glance, his brilliant eloquence, his refusal to compromise, his fundamental discontent, his thirst for absolutes.

He gave her copies of his books to read, wrote notes telling her to browse through such seventeenth-century books as La Rochefoucauld's concise and biting *Maximes* and La Bruyère's satiric *Caractères*. She submitted a series of epigrams of her own for his correction. In 1938 French *Vogue* had asked her for a few quotes about her business, and she answered with a series of pithy aphorisms:

"At forty, women used to exchange youth for elegance, poise, and mysterious allure, an evolution that left them undamaged. Now they measure themselves against the very young with defenses that can only be described as ridiculous."

The purpose of fashion: "To make women look young. Then their outlook on life changes. They feel brighter and more cheerful."

On short skirts: "Women drive cars nowadays, and this you cannot do with crinoline skirts."

On educated women: "A woman's education consists of two lessons: never to leave the house without stockings, never to go out without a hat."

On fashion writers: "They should begin by going to school and learning how you cut a piece of fabric."

On the feminine psyche: "Women can give everything with a smile, and with a tear take it all back."

On love: "A botched renewal [of a relationship] is painful; reconciliation is sinister."

She wrote no aphorisms on the demands of being a couturier or the art of managing three thousand employees. For all her generosity toward artists, for which she was becoming legendary against her will—"Everybody will take me for a charity nun," she shouted at Jean Cocteau after she learned he had recited instances of her beneficence at the Boeuf sur le Toit nightclub—she was miserly when it came to her own employees. She paid for Cocteau's detoxification cures, subsidized Diaghilev's ballet, and made monthly stipends to Reverdy and Stravinsky, but compensated her models 200 francs a month,* or one-tenth of what she charged for a dress. When Madame Fred, the *chef de cabine* who had been with her since 1918, told her she would have to increase the models' salaries, Coco became huffy.

"Increase their salaries, are you out of your mind?" she answered. "They are gorgeous girls, why don't they find lovers. They should have no trouble finding rich men to support them."

Marie-Louise Deray, who had joined the house when Coco opened the Biarritz subsidiary in 1915 and was one of the *premières*, was rudely dismissed ten years later when she asked for a fifty-franc raise. She was told indirectly that Mademoiselle would not give her one franc more. She had sixty-five seamstresses under her and, with the exception of a one-hour lunch hour, worked from 9:00 A.M. until as late as 8:00 or 9:00 P.M. for 500 francs a month. When Deray left, her workers cried.

For the period, Coco's salaries were not out of line. The "rag trade"

*Equivalent to $76 in 1924 dollars, or about $460 in 1990 money.

was a labor-intensive industry of women, employing thousands of *cousettes*, as the seamstresses were called, often hired for the rush before the twice-a-year-collection showing and laid off right after. (Not until 1900 was the labor of women and children limited to a ten-hour day—men still worked twelve-hour days—and only in 1906 did a law give laborers one day off a week.)

Coco never went to the workrooms and dealt only with the *premières*. The *mannequins* were the ones who suffered her scalding tongue, hair-trigger wit, and the pricks of her pins. The models were not runway or photo models but full-time, in-house mannequins who, besides having a pretty profile and beautiful movements, usually understood the clothes they were wearing.

"Stand straight, girl," Coco would hiss through the pins in her mouth while the individual dresses were being created and re-created and the effects viewed and alterations contemplated.

Chanel was never a designer in the narrow sense of the word. Her creations were not the result of sketches turned into clothes, but elaborations on a live model, direct three-dimensional effects measured in the cut, in changes, and in the first fittings where she determined how the fabric moved on the body.

The models sagged with fatigue as the fittings went on, frequently up to six or eight hours without a break. Coco was impervious, indefatigable. "If there's no woman there's no dress," she liked to say when she finally pronounced herself satisfied.

The House made money hand over fist, but there were expenses no one in the workrooms above the chandeliered salon knew about. There were actresses that Coco dressed for free, there were grand ladies who didn't pay their bills, and clients who were given drinks, trinkets, and perfumes.

"She knew nothing about figures, but she possessed the wily foxiness of a country horse trader," her lawyer Robert Chaillet would say. "She didn't count but she loved to make money. She said, 'It's not money for money's sake that I'm interested in, but money as the symbol of success.'"

She was not the only couturier to flaunt her life-style for publicity purposes, yet she was careful with her money. Bankers tried to reign in Poiret's excessive spending and when they failed took over his house, and Jean Patou, who liked to pretend he lost heavily gambling, lost all he had made in just a few years.

Businesswomen were uncommon and tended to provoke condescending smiles. Chanel's fear of not knowing how to defend herself in the man's world of law and finance, her fear of being cheated, made her suspicious and hard as nails in any negotiation.

Coco Chanel entered her first period of great prestige and prominence, a period that lasted from the mid-1920s to the late 1930s. The 1925 exhibition of decorative arts, which gave its name to a style, saw her and her friends at the center of the excitement.

It was a memorable year for Paris. Josephine Baker and the *Revue Nègre* took the city by storm. Serge Lifar was dancing *Zéphyr et Flore* in sets by Braque; Stravinsky put on his one-act ballet, *Le Chant du rossignol*, in sets by Matisse. On Montparnasse the surrealists held their first exhibition and noisily celebrated their latest convert, Cocteau. Henri Bernstein's new play, *La Galerie des Glaces*, starring a new matinee idol named Charles Boyer, was the smash hit of the season. The centerpiece of the set was a painting owned by Bernstein—Goya's painting of the infant Don Manuel de Zuñiga, better known as *The Red Boy*.

Anticipated for a dozen years and delayed by war, L'Exposition des Arts Décoratifs et Industriels Modernes was meant to reaffirm France in the realm of taste and luxury and to give an overview of new developments in the applied arts. Pavilions from all the industrial countries straddled the Seine from the Eiffel Tower across the Esplanade des Invalides, and small boutiques displaying the creations of the carriage trade lined the Pont Alexandre III. Abstract design had replaced the exuberance of Art Nouveau, and there was not a curve in sight. The art deco style, which was called modernist and functional, included Erté on the one hand and Le Corbusier's "architectural nudism" on the other. Enormous fountains of glass played among life-sized cubist dolls, and music washed down from huge towers. Objects were in plastics and "ferro-concrete." The lamps, which had lost all their metal curves and flounced shades, were by Giacometti. Curtains hung straight and were of hand-woven fabrics designed by Dufy. Sonia Delaunay, the painter, worked with Jacques Heim, the furrier, to produce patchwork color coats that embodied the jazz age. To the horror of Coco and Patou the expo displayed their gowns together at the Palais de l'Elégance while the clothes of Worth, Callot, and Lanvin were shown beneath a glittering cascade of light aboard three river barges that Paul Poiret had commissioned and outfitted.

The expo shipwrecked Poiret. The grand priest of extravagant assertion and theatrical abandon, of the luxurious and tactile qualities of satin,
gold, and silver lamé, velvet taffeta, chiffon, faille, and moire totally missed
the art deco turn that made *easy* and *practical* the key words of fashion
seduction. Chanel understood the change. She, too, had long scarves,
whiffs of the Orient in her 1925 collection, and her models were made
up with kohl eyes, but she knew how to mold the liberated feminine body
in pliant jersey and how to make short skirts shorter. She introduced the
Chanel suit, which, with its collarless , braid-trimmed cardigan jacket with
long, tight-fitting sleeves, and its graceful skirt, would be more copied, in
all price ranges, than any other single garment designed by a couturier.
Her line also showed not-so-subtle influences of upper-class Englishness.
To her gray crepella dresses with pleated panels she added English sports
clothes—knitted suits, tweed topcoats, and jackets that were resolutely
masculine in cut.

Gloria Swanson came from Hollywood to star in the first Franco-
American coproduction, *Madame Sans Gêne*. René Hubert, a Beaux Arts
graduate, designed la Swanson's sumptuous Napoleonic-era wardrobe.
Off-screen the movie star quickly adapted the Coco Chanel silhouette. Ina
Claire was the first actress to wear Chanel clothes on screen (Edward
Steichen photographed the movie star in her Chanel outfits for *Vogue*).
Patou, Lanvin, and Vionnet followed the Chanel lead and opened sportswear shops, and *Vogue* did its first feature on her "little black dress."
Forty years before Pierre Cardin led a reluctant haute-couture industry
into ready-to-wear, the American edition of the fashion magazine predicted that Chanel's simple sheath would be universally adopted because
its convenience, perhaps even its *simplicity*, would outweigh women's fear
of being seen in the same dress. The unsigned *Vogue* editorial compared
the future of clothes to that other new mass-produced convenience, the
automobile. Did anyone refuse to buy a car because it was identical to
someone else's? On the contrary. The likeness was a guarantee of quality.
"Today, except on court occasions, who could pick out a king from a
commoner; as far, that is, as costume is concerned? or a lord from a
laborer on a holiday; or a lady of the highest rank from the ranks of near-
ladies about her, when it comes to a matter of general effect in clothes?
A person of breeding recognized another person of breeding by a thou-

sand signs: just as a connoisseur in fashion can tell the original chef d'oeuvres from the copies at a glance; but the world as a whole now looks pretty much alike to an outsider, as its civilized inhabitants prance along in the same shaped trouserings and slip-on frocks. Of course, the shapes inside these garments differ, thank goodness, and there is still an appearance and carriage called 'queenly,' a behavior known as 'princely,' and a loveliness likened to that of a 'princess in a fairytale.' But any costume that would, in everyday life, differentiate classes from masses is not to be found."

Reverdy was both captivated and repelled by the glitter of wealth and fame that surrounded Chanel. While proclaiming his hatred of all ties, he lived at Faubourg St. Honoré and accepted Coco's money. Still, he seemed to delight in embarrassing her, bursting in on guests she was entertaining or disappearing for days on end. He could not shine like Cocteau or Sem, the caricaturist who had depicted her in the arms of the polo-playing Boy Capel in 1913 and who was now a regular visitor in Rue Faubourg St. Honoré. "She loved him very much and tried to make him over in her mold," Georges Auric, the composer, would say, "but she understood that she couldn't ask Pierre Reverdy to spend evenings with Sem."

Nor was Reverdy present at the rehearsals of *Orphée*, Cocteau's new play, for which Coco again did the costumes. Cocteau's version of the Orpheus and Eurydice story was both comic and ironic—the lovers are not happy until their departure to the next world. The play depended on ingenious direction, verbal razzle-dazzle, and many props, but its reconciliation of the mythical past and the modern world was a *tour de force*.

Cocteau's stage directions said the wardrobe "should be contemporary with any production. Orpheus and Eurydice dressed for the country, as simply and inconspicuously as possible. Death is a very beautiful young woman in a bright pink evening gown and fur coat. Coiffure, dress, coat, shoes, gestures, general deportment all up to the minute." Chanel's country clothes were no less smart than her elegant evening gowns, and after the June 1926 premiere, they launched a vogue for informal dress.

Reverdy was not there for the first performance of *Orphée*. Two weeks earlier he had left Paris, fleeing Coco's high-profile living and her assortment of brilliant friends. After burning a number of manuscripts, he had moved to Solesmes, a village near Le Mans, in Normandy, to live in the shadow of the monks of the Order of St. Benedict. He would stay there, sometimes with his wife, even after he lost his faith. In his poetry, he depicted humans as essentially alone, often on their knees, seeking answers to a tragic fate through cleansing redemption. "One does not see the knees of he who prays," he wrote.

Night and blackness are the grand unifying image of his poetry, appearing again and again in titles and verses. Man constantly confronts a night that cloaks its secrets from him while at the same time provoking his appetites. With the coming of night serious life begins. After dark, people see more intensely, they think and write poems. Was there a connection between the purity and plainness of Chanel's "little black dress" and Reverdy's spare verse?

She might mingle ever more intimately in the narcissism of fashion, but she, too, had a streak of puritanism. Deep in her was a longing for simplicity, for creating a way of dressing that was lasting in its bone-simple, uncluttered, and casual elegance. "I am against fashion that doesn't last," she would tell journalists a few years later. "I cannot accept that you throw your clothes away just because it's spring. I love clothes, because, like books, I can feel them, touch them. Women want to change; they're wrong. I'm for happiness, and happiness consists of not changing."

Increasingly, Chanel became convinced that her staying power had to do with the integrity of her fashion, that taste had to do with honesty, that the aesthetic of clothes should be nothing more than the outer reflection of an inner morality, of sincere feelings. The real purpose of fashion was perhaps not to redefine the way we look so much as tell us who we are.

19

TO BE A DUCHESS, PERHAPS

Coco Chanel opened a boutique in London's Mayfair district in 1927. Her sports clothes—"that is, clothes for *watching* sports in," she tartly commented—were the strongest influence in fashion. She dressed the Duchess of York, the wife of the future King George VI, and London's leading beauties, Daisy Fellowes, Baba d'Erlanger, and Paula Gellibrand.

"Looks designed for sports graduate to country day-dressing and then arrive in town, and Chanel's country tweeds have just completed the course," British *Vogue* said. "She pins a white piqué gardenia to the neck. Her 'lingerie touches' are copied everywhere—piping, bands of contrasts, ruffles and jabots. She initiates fake jewelry, to be worn everywhere, even on the beach." Her boutique was on Davies Street, next to the Westminster residence and a few steps from Claridge's.

There was continued speculation, both in Europe and in the United States, that she would be the next Duchess of Westminster. The gossip columnists had it that the duke wished nothing more than to make her his new wife.

"He wasn't free, and nor was I," Coco would say. "I didn't want to leave the House of Chanel, which I had built all by myself and continuously reshaped." The gossip columns reported her snapping, "Everyone marries the Duke of Westminster. There are a lot of duchesses but only one Coco Chanel."

She repudiated the *mot.* "The duke would have laughed if I'd come up with a gaffe like that," she would tell Marcel Haedrich twenty years later.

In reality, the question remained implicitly open between them. The Westminsters' divorce, when it came in the fall of 1925, was messy. Since 1923, British law allowed a wife to divorce her husband on the grounds of adultery alone, without the additional offense of desertion or cruelty, but Violet's counsel charged all three. There were distasteful depositions testifying to Bendor having been caught *in flagrante delicto* at the Hôtel de Paris in Monte Carlo. The decree was pronounced against his lordship. For a while he was unwelcome at Buckingham Palace and the royal family passed up visits to Eaton Hall.

London's high society and smart set saw the coming-out party for Bendor's younger daughter, Mary, as one of those events that would flush out everybody, and perhaps mark the end of the Parisian couturier's ascendancy. Despite the divorce, Violet agreed to a longtime promise to host her stepdaughter's grand ball, and, with exquisite manners or fiendish intent, invited Coco.

The night of the ball, Coco had Bendor, his daughters, the Churchills, Count Kutuzov, and several intimate friends for dinner. When it was time to go next door to the ball, Coco excused herself; she had to change into a suitable gown. "I'll see you right away," she said.

After a while, Bendor asked Kutuzov to go and see why it took Coco so long. Kutuzov found her in bed. People were expecting her, he insisted. She told him to tell His Grace she had taken ill. In recalling the event years later, she would intimate that her absence that night had made her the queen of an evening that several dowagers had sworn would spell the end of her in London's society.

For Bendor marriage was not so much a matter of legitimizing a liaison that everybody knew about as of producing a male heir. At forty-two, Coco's childbearing years were numbered.

She consulted experts, and turned herself over to doctors and to the ministrations of women in whom she had faith. Her moods ran from surging hope to sinking despair. To increase the chances of conception, a midwife suggested what Coco would call "humiliating acrobatics" during lovemaking. Bendor showered her with letters, sometimes two letters a day, and always accompanied by flowers. She demanded modest wildflowers harvested by his own hand. He complied and hid jewels under the daisies and cornflowers. Every token of love made her believe that if worse came to worst, he would want to marry her, even if she couldn't bear him a child.

Would happiness ever be hers? She was the triumphant arbiter of fashion, the friend of dukes and dandies, a confidante of the rich and famous. But she was also a woman men loved but didn't marry, a woman for whom love turned into dross, into impossible passion. If any man could stand up to her free spirit, her success, strong convictions, independent opinions, and unswerving belief in simplicity and elegance, it was the Duke of Westminster. He was a man out of the ordinary, a man of presence, charm, and immense wealth.

Neither she nor Bendor would ever say how close they came to getting married. Coco could enumerate all the good reasons for not getting married, but her women friends were marrying. Marthe Davelli had finally wed her sugar baron; Gabrielle Dorziat had become the Countess of Zogheb while continuing her stage and screen career; and Vera Bate married Alberto Lombardi, an Italian officer and one of the best horsemen of his day. After a long liaison, Caryathis was set to marry Marcel Jouhandeau, a prolific and eccentric writer who counted André Gide, Claude Mauriac, Thornton Wilder, and Havelock Ellis among his admirers. Even Adrienne was on the verge of wedlock. Maurice de Nexon's father was dying and it seemed as if at long last Maurice would be able to make Adrienne his wife. Coco promised she would be a witness for the bride. It was not until April 29, 1930, however, that Maurice and Adrienne were married.

A friend of Gabrielle's from the Royallieu days would be the only witness attesting to Bendor's honorable intentions. Valéry Ollivier, who often visited Rue Cambon when he was in Paris, entered the Chapon Fin restaurant in Bordeaux one day and found Coco and the duke about to order lunch. He crossed over to their table to say hello. Since he was alone, Coco invited him to join them. "The conversation was lively and it seems to me that at one point the duke chided Coco for not wanting to marry him," Ollivier would recall.

The possibility of becoming Duchess of Westminster might have led Gabrielle to take action to ensure that her brothers could not embarrass her.

The idea of enterprising journalists discovering Alphonse behind his *tabac* counter and Lucien behind his shoe stall filled her with dread. Quickly and ruthlessly, she set out to choke off any embarrassment they could possibly cause her. Alphonse was the easier of the two to handle. Money had always made him do what she wanted. In exchange for his disappearing again for a decent interval, Gaby, as he still called his sister, kept buying him new cars, paying his debts, and lecturing him. She was working hard, she told him, she didn't need him to make any trouble for her. He needed her money too much not to agree to stay out of sight.

His daughters, Antoinette and Gabrielle, would remember the stories he came back to Valleraugue with. The way he described their aunt's "Hindu palace" in the Rue Faubourg St. Honoré, her manservant in morning coat, and how she laughed when Alphonse once asked her to tell the valet to bug off.

Lucien was another matter. If he was less brazen in asking his sister for handouts, it was because he thought himself, in his modest provincial way, a success. With his wife, he was to be found every market day selling shoes in the passage between Clermont-Ferrand's Rue des Gras and Rue des Chaussetiers.

Clermont-Ferrand was a town of 60,000, the industrial hub of the tire industry and a commercial center, and Lucien was a popular tradesman. Gabrielle could just see her trusting kid brother fall into the hands of the press, and Paris and London eating up the tales shoe salesman Chanel could tell about Milady's childhood.

So she wrote to him. Why didn't he retire? she asked. She had made enough money for both of them. She didn't want him to work anymore; he had been through enough. Why didn't he look for a house to buy and fix up, maybe with a big garden. He had always loved a garden. She would send whatever money he needed. His wife told him it was silly to retire. He was thirty-six years old; he liked what he was doing. Besides, a shoe manufacturer was offering him a job.

Touched by his sister's concern, however, Lucien overrode his wife's objections. He wrote back that he had his eye on a piece of land above Clermont-Ferrand.

There was one relative Chanel did introduce to Bendor, however. Perhaps because André Palasse was the orphan she and Boy Capel had once informally adopted, perhaps because he had been brought up in English prep schools, Coco had her sister Julie's son meet her lover. André had grown up to be a slim, polite, and somewhat sickly looking young man. He was married and his wife was expecting their first baby.

When a daughter was born, André named her Gabrielle, in gratitude. Coco, in turn, allowed herself to be the godmother of this grandniece. The Duke of Westminster became the godfather to "Tiny," as the girl was nicknamed in English, and until his death sent her a gift every year.

In the belief that seduction in an enchanting setting might result in pregnancy, Gabrielle bought a property in Roquebrune, high above the Mediterranean. She and Bendor first saw La Pausa, as the five-acre property was called, in December 1927. Through an olive grove, mimosa and jacaranda trees they came to the main house and its sensational view. On the left, one had a view of the coast to Menton and the Italian border, to the right one looked down on the bay and toward Monaco. Behind the house rose the sloping foothills of the Alps. The property contained two smaller guest villas, they were told; it had been developed by Sir Williamson, a well-known Riviera resident, and was currently owned by the Mayen family. Coco told the realtor she might demolish the main house and build something to her own taste. The price was 1.8 million francs.*

The "Neo-Edwardian" society, the new Americans, and even old acquaintances such as Jacques Balsan, who had once wanted Coco to marry his brother, were nearby. Daisy Fellowes at her villa Les Zoriades and Viscount Esmond Rothmere at his Cap Martin villa entertained the Prince of Wales, Lord Beaverbrook, Somerset Maugham, and the Churchills. At Cap d'Antibe, the wealthy New Yorkers Sara and Gerald Murphy were credited with making the Riviera fashionable in the summer, entertaining F. Scott and Zelda Fitzgerald, Cole and Linda Porter, Fernand Léger and his Russian wife, and Ernest Hemingway, while Consuelo and Jacques Balsan had settled in Eze, high above Monaco. A Vanderbilt by birth, Consuelo was the elder sister of the famous twins Gloria Vanderbilt and Thelma Furness. She had been the first wife of Bendor's friend Sunny Marlborough, but after divorcing the tiny duke in 1921, had married Balsan. When Winston Churchill tired of Daisy Fellowes's hospitality, he liked to stay with the Balsans. In Churchill's opinion, his best landscape

*About $2.2 million in 1990 dollars.

paintings were painted in the Balsans' garden, "all shimmering sunshine and violet shades."

Robert Streitz was a twenty-eight-year-old architect summoned for dinner aboard *The Flying Cloud* to provide suggestions for a Mediterranean villa. Within three days he was back with a series of plans.

"I demand that only the best materials be used," said the duke. Coco wanted gray-white stucco walls, a roof of the local, hand-baked red tiles, and a grand staircase. The fact that Bendor was in on the purchase and the reconstruction would lead to rumors that he bought La Pausa and handed it to Coco as a present. The deed of sale, signed in a Nice mortgage office February 9, 1929, was in her name only.

Streitz and the builder, Edgar Maggiore, set to work. Coco came from Paris once a month to inspect the progress. "She was always in the best of moods when she visited Roquebrune," Maggiore would remember. "On the site one day she slipped into a pool of mud. Instead of lamenting the loss of a dress, she laughed until the workers pulled her out." Like a Roman villa, the house was built around an inner courtyard behind a vaulted entrance. The patio was paved with 100,000 sanded bricks.

Coco's suite and the duke's private quarters occupied the right wing of the upstairs. Bendor's room was paneled and his Elizabethan bed was of massive oak. A bathroom separated his rooms from Coco's suite. Her bedroom had spare white walls and oak paneling, with a wrought-iron bed, a big blue carpet, and taffeta curtains wafting in the sea breeze. She hated central heating and in the winter had a fire in the chimney every night.

The Churchills came for a visit. Coco played piquet, the only two-person card game she knew, with Winston and made a point of always losing, for otherwise he'd be in a bad temper. Vera Bate was a bosom friend of the Churchills, Cole Porter, Somerset Maugham, and the rest of the "Anglo-Saxon" colony, and in a burst of generosity, Coco gave Vera and her new husband, Alberto Lombardi, a little house in the back of the garden.

Gabrielle wanted to be left alone until she decided to appear, and her guests enjoyed the same privilege. The left wing of the house was divided into a series of two-room apartments, allowing couples complete privacy. "La Pausa was the most comfortable, relaxing place I have ever stayed," Bettina Ballard, model and former *Vogue* editor, would write. "The house was blissfully silent in the morning. . . . Lunch was the moment of the day when the guests met in a group, and no one missed lunch—it was far too entertaining. The long dining room had a buffet at one end with hot Italian pasta, cold English roast beef, French dishes, a little of everything."

When La Pausa was finished, Chanel had spent 6 million francs,* more than three times the purchase price. No child was conceived.

Gabrielle turned forty-six that summer. She began to see herself as a prisoner of a degrading, artificial situation. Back in Paris, she picked up her old habits and old circle of friends. Even Pierre Reverdy, taking time out from the monastic existence in Solesmes, which Coco paid for, was seen at the big house in Rue Faubourg St. Honoré.

As she had done the year before, Coco gave a magnificent party at her home for the closing of the Diaghilev Ballet's 1929 Paris season. The garden was lit up, a jazz band provided the entertainment, and one of the dancers noted the caviar-filled soup tureens.

Diaghilev sat across from the hostess. Lifar was the new star of the company and that closing night at the Sarah Bernhardt Theater had danced two Stravinsky works, *Apollo* and *Renard*, and Prokofiev's *Le Fils prodique.*

"Remember this day, Seriozhka, remember it all your life," Diaghilev told Lifar. At the end of the evening, the master presented Lifar with a golden lyre pin. The young dancer immediately gave it to their hostess.

"We drank torrents of champagne," Lifar would remember. "As always, Coco began to turn on the men. She purred, and let everyone believe she could be seduced. Then, suddenly, she was gone. She disappeared at 2:00 A.M., so she wouldn't miss her beauty sleep. She let men believe everything was possible, but didn't yield anything. That was her drama. She is looking for happiness, for love. She found it once: Boy Capel, a gorgeous Englishman who had everything, money and charm. So, instead, fame and success became her revenge."

*Worth about $7.26 million in 1990 currency.

20

DEATH IN VENICE

----

66 **T**he famous Coco turned up & I took a gt fancy to her—a most capable & agreeable woman—much the strongest personality Benny has yet been up against," Winston Churchill wrote home to his wife from Bendor's hunting lodge at Mimizan in 1927. "She hunted vigorously all day, motored to Paris after dinner & is today engaged in passing and improving dresses on endless streams of mannequins. Altogether 200 models have been settled in almost 3 weeks. Some have been altered ten times. She does it with her own fingers, pinning, cutting, looping, etc. With her—Vera Bate, née Arkwright. 'Yr Chief of Staff?' 'Non' 'One of yr lieutenants?' 'Non. Elle est la. Voilà tout.' "

If Gabrielle managed to go boar hunting in Normandy with Bendor and his friends, and present twice-a-year collections that included two hundred designs, indeed if she managed both her empire and her hectic social life, it was because she had efficient and expert support. Chanel would design and adjust the prototype *toiles* on her live models, but the actual making of Chanel's fashions was easily delegated to the skilled *premières* who presided over the three thousand seamstresses. Clients were rich and exclusive, and expertly handled by the *vendeuses, habilleuses*, and *essayeuses*, leaving Chanel the essential and highly visible role of prime mover and trendsetter, in tune with the times and with society's most prominent women. She understood that proof of influence was not in being convincing but in being contagious. She was there to provide sheen and glitter, inspiration and devastating assertion.

In a role reversal that rather pleased the caustic side of Gabrielle, she and Bendor took Misia with them on a *Flying Cloud* cruise during the summer of 1929. It was eight years ago that Misia and José Sert had comforted Gabrielle after the death of Boy Capel by taking her with them on their honeymoon cruise and introducing her to Italy. Now it was Misia who needed consolation.

Jojo had divorced her and, the previous fall, married a ravishing twenty-two-year-old Russian who had charmed even the spurned Misia to the point where Misia had persuaded Coco to lower her price for the girl's wedding gown.

Roossadana Mdivani had appeared in Jojo's new studio one day when she was nineteen, a tall, slim beauty with flaxen hair and slate-gray eyes. She was doing sculpture, she said, and had come to ask if he knew where she could rent studio space. "How can someone have so much space?" she asked with an enchanting smile as she looked around the sizable Sert studio.

Always a man of grand gestures, Jojo cleared out a corner of the studio. Soon, the two of them were spending the afternoons together. "Ingenious and playful as a kitten, Roossy tumbled into Sert's bed," Misia's biographers would say, "the art lessons turned into love lessons. Before long this latest in the list of Sert's escapades became something more serious, a fact he carefully concealed from Misia." Soon he was in love as only a man of fifty can be with a girl of twenty.

He dazzled Roossy with his cruel and engrossing stories, his erudition, and the splendor of his gifts. She responded with infectious laughter and impulsive hugs. His enthusiasm for her increased when he learned she was a princess and that her family saga was worthy of one of his yarns.

Whether the Mdivanis were really noble was a question that agitated Hollywood more than avant-garde Paris after Roossy's handsome brother David married Mae Murray, the former Czech nightclub dancer and ex-Ziegfeld Follies hoofer famous for her bee-stung lips. The pursuit of European titles by movie stars was creating something of a backlash after Pola Negri and Gloria Swanson married noblemen, and the Mdivanis' status in their native Georgia was not entirely clear. Their Muslim grandfather's "château" was little more than a heap of ruins in Adzharistan, but Czar Nicholas had indeed made Zachariah Mdivani, the father of David, Sergei, Roossadana, and Alexis, the governor of Batumi.

The Bolshevik Revolution and a costly mistake by their mother (on the family's dash to the Turkish border in 1917, Madame Mdivani had inadvertently taken a trunk containing her petticoats instead of the trunk containing the family jewels) was blamed for David's need to marry a rich movie star. The Mdivanis' indigence would lead the younger sons to follow David's example and marry into American money. In 1931, when Alexis was twenty-two, he married Louise van Alen of the Astor fortune and, eighteen months later, divorced her and married Woolworth heiress Barbara Hutton. Four years later Sergei married Alexis's discarded Louise.

Misia practically adopted her young rival. Gabrielle met Roossy and admitted the young woman was captivating, but told Misia she was mad to play such a dangerous game. Misia said there were forces that drew people toward catastrophe, that her aim was to tame the calamity. She did not succeed, and when Jojo left Misia, Coco insisted that her friend come and stay with her in Rue Faubourg St. Honoré.

Both Jojo and Roossy wanted to see the dispirited Misia, but Coco refused to let them come. When Misia found out, she was furious. How dared Coco forbid their visit? She had known Jojo for eighteen years and she called Roossy a mirror of her younger self, someone who brought her fun and effervescence. Life without them would be a barren abyss. Coco backed down and after promising Misia that she would not criticize, invited Roossy to lunch.

To hang on to both Jojo and Roossy, Misia pretended their upcoming marriage was little more than a game, that since Jojo was a citizen of Catholic Spain where divorce did not exist, she would remain the real Mrs. Sert. But after the wedding, she gratefully accepted Bendor and Coco's invitation to spend the summer of 1928 with them at Eaton Hall. The gray English skies and the penumbra of the Gothic architecture left Misia melancholy. All she wanted was to be with Jojo and Roossy.

Without conviction, the newlyweds had asked Misia to join them on a cruise of the Aegean Sea, and foolishly Misia had accepted. Paul Morand ran into them in Italy and was appalled at the sight of "Sert and his two wives." Misia came to her senses when she realized that people didn't so much take her for a partner in a *ménage à trois* as the mother-in-law.

Misia was not the only friend who needed Gabrielle's sympathy. Cocteau also knew how to draw on her affectionate generosity. She let him live at Rue Faubourg St. Honoré with his new lover, Jean Desbordes, an ambitious young writer. On his good days, Cocteau contributed brilliantly to the dinner parties Coco gave, but his opium addiction gave a darker side to their relationship. She not only paid for his detoxification cures, but tried to impose some discipline on his life.

Wesson Bull, a young American who spent the summer of 1928 at the Hôtel Welcome in Villefranche, near Nice, would remember Cocteau on the telephone in the hotel lobby, pleading with someone, almost in tears.

"Later it was explained to me that he had been begging Mademoiselle Coco Chanel to allow him to go on smoking longer than had been agreed," Bull would say. "He was overdue at a *maison de santé* for a cure. And Mademoiselle Chanel had said *no!* Cocteau and Desbordes spent most of the day in their room smoking opium heavily. One always knew when, since its particular and unmistakable 'fumes' filled the corridors."

Sir Francis Rose, an English painter, would remember being asked to join Cocteau and Chanel at their lunch table. "My first impression of her," he would write forty years later, "was that she looked like a slim youth, then, when she moved, she gave me the feeling of looking at an impressionist painting of a small dark boat, on water of an indefinite colour, with bright red-and-white striped sails. Chanel had beautiful taste and bought Cocteau fine presents. She gave him a fragile archaic Greek faience mask, which she brought to the Welcome Hotel lying in a miniature wooden crate lined with a nest of sawdust. Cocteau kept it in this case forever after. She also gave him some ancient Green coins placed on cotton wool in a small white tortoiseshell, and a long, thin, and very flexible platinum snake chain on which he hung his keys and which he would twist around his neck several times before it hung heavily down to a pocket in his trousers."

The cruise aboard *The Flying Cloud* took Bendor, Coco, and Misia around Italy into the Adriatic Sea and up the Dalmatian coast to Venice. It brought headlines of a kind none of them suspected, when, off the coast of Yugoslavia, Misia received a radiogram urging her to come to Diaghilev's bedside in Venice.

Since Coco's party for the corps de ballet in June, the company had performed in Berlin and Cologne, and Diaghilev had joined his troupe for the season finale in London, telling his dancers he had excellent bookings for the fall season. During the summer recess, Diaghilev had been to Baden-Baden for the music festival, and, with Stravinsky, to Munich to meet the elder Richard Strauss. He had arrived alone at the Grand Hôtel des Bains in Venice, complaining of being unable to sleep, eat, or move. His longtime secretary, Boris Kochno, and Lifar were now with him, nursing him for what doctors called rheumatism. His temperature rose steadily and two doctors who visited him were puzzled by his condition.

After *The Flying Cloud* docked at Venice, Misia and Coco rushed to the Grand Hôtel where they found Diaghilev on his deathbed and Kochno and Lifar fighting over the master's legacy. The two women barely recognized Diaghilev, and he was struck by their appearance in his room. "They looked so young," he told Kochno after they left. "They were all in white. They were *so white!*"

To relieve Lifar, Kochno spent the night in a big armchair in Diaghilev's room. After some hours' sleep, Diaghilev was weaker and talked of going to Sicily to recuperate. Baroness Catherine d'Erlanger, the avant-garde decorator, visited in the afternoon but Diaghilev did not recognize her. He died the next morning. He was fifty-seven.

Misia gave Lifar and Kochno whatever money she had on hand to pay the hotel bill and the doctor; Coco paid for the funeral. A gondola carrying Lifar, Kochno, Misia, and Coco followed the mortuary gondola bearing Diaghilev's coffin from the Lido quay in the direction of the tiny Russian cemetery on the funeral isle of San Michele. Forty-two years later, when Stravinsky died in his home in New York, his surviving family honored his request to be buried at San Michele near Diaghilev's grave.

Three

21

CUTTING PRICES

The effects of the Wall Street stock market crash of Tuesday, October 29, 1929, the "Black Tuesday" that would haunt a generation, took a year to cross the Atlantic. The June 1930 season featured the greatest fancy-dress balls in years. Daisy Fellowes's masquerade, to which everyone was bidden to come dressed like someone everybody else knew, was the biggest party of them all, and Coco Chanel did a roaring business cutting and fitting gowns for young men-about-town who appeared as some of the best-known women in Paris.

When the recession did reach Europe, it hit the luxury trade first. In the Rue de la Paix jewelers were losing fortunes in sudden cancellations of orders, and, reported the *New Yorker*'s Janet Flanner, "little firms that live exclusively on the American trade have not sold one faked Chanel copy in a fortnight." Real Chanel couture was the most expensive in Paris, and by 1931 it was considered bad taste to even *look* rich. The women who were still wealthy wore plain dresses, furless wool coats, sweaters, and slacks. Economical and washable fabrics were popular, and Gabrielle was invited to London to help promote cotton as a fashion fabric. In her collection for the spring of 1931 she included thirty-five cotton evening dresses in piqué, lace, organdy, and net, and, to keep costs down, she began to use zippers. Her young and fresh-looking dresses with their billowing skirts were the most popular evening wear with English debutantes. Still, times were hard in France. Rich Americans were becoming an endangered species on the Riviera; the Wall Street debacle had chased most Americans back home. The devaluation of the pound sterling dislodged two-thirds of the British colony; in Nice alone, a quarter of the luxury hotels closed. Chanel cut her salon prices in half. When even that didn't bring back the crowds, she laid off workers and went to America to work for the movies.

Misia and Dmitri had been instrumental in Coco's meeting Samuel Goldwyn, the maddeningly self-centered movie mogul who, along with the rest of Hollywood, was convinced people wanted to keep their minds off the Depression. Thirteen million Americans were out of work, but Goldwyn sensed that people wanted glitzy, brassy musicals to cheer them up or gangster flicks to thrill them.

Goldwyn had to have Coco, he said—to gild the Goldwyn Touch, to dress the half-dozen pictures he made for United Artists every year, to upgrade Hollywood's fashion awareness. Hadn't he bagged the designer Erté in the mid-1920s to work for him? Hadn't Cecil B. DeMille hired her countryman Paul Iribe fifteen years before to give a sparkling *art nouveau* ambience to his epics? Wasn't Cecil Beaton at Paramount getting a Dolores del Rio and Gary Cooper layout in *Vogue*? The mercurial producer said he wanted his stars to be dressed by Chanel and no one else, onstage or off.

Coco had never met a movie producer before, and the more the blunt and wisecracking Goldwyn bubbled with enthusiasm, the more reticent she became. He was someone from the market squares of her childhood, another rube and wily cardsharp. He offered her the chance to do what no designer had ever done before—to clothe the movie stars on-screen and in their glittering private lives. She wondered whether actresses, with their notorious temperaments and insecure tastes, would agree to wear Chanel and no one else from dawn to midnight. He waxed lyrical on the fortune she'd make by turning Ina Claire and Gloria Swanson into "Chanel silhouettes." She said she loved only crime movies. He talked relentlessly of the quality of his advertising and brought up Erté, the Russian-born painter and decorator who had created Ziegfeld Follies sets on Broadway yet jumped at the chance to work in Hollywood. She said she had her business in Paris. He offered her the world's screens as her personal publicity billboard.

She hesitated. Rich Americans were already her clients.

Erté, he said, had consented without a murmur to live in Hollywood for a year. All right, he realized she could not be away from her Paris base an entire year, but if she would come to California twice a year and do the wardrobe for Gloria Swanson, Norma Talmadge, Ina Claire, and Lily Damita, he'd sign her up for a million dollars a year.

The offer took her breath away. When she still hesitated, he changed tactics. Could she agree just to visit Hollywood at his invitation and see what the pictures had to offer her?

On that, they shook hands.

Perhaps Chanel left for Hollywood to escape her unhappiness. She had spent the summer with Misia. La Pausa was Chanel's place of beauty, serenity, and comfort. The two friends were there for each other when men left them bereft. The child she could not have was a source of great pain to her. Coco had always been a woman who knew how to subdue her own passions and appetites, but Bendor's absence was keenly felt. She had wanted him all to herself, without mistresses, but she too refused to give up her life for him. For him, it was socially unacceptable that a Duchess of Westminster be active in business. For her, there was something humiliating in the way men expected a woman to be thankful for being offered a life of dependent idleness. Her resentment went all the way back to Etienne Balsan. He, too, had been unable to understand her wish to stand on her own feet.

"God knows I wanted love," she would say. "But the moment I had to choose between the man I loved and my dresses, I chose the dresses. Work has always been a kind of drug for me, even if I sometimes wonder what Chanel would have been without the men in my life.

"Men don't understand that. They tell a woman, 'I'll marry you. You can stop worrying, you won't have to work anymore.' What they mean is, 'You won't have to do anything except be there for me.' "

When Coco was in her eighties and Bendor was long since dead, she would quote Lady Sibell Lumley as having begged her to marry her son: "Darling, marry Benny. The first years are always the best." Gabrielle would remember telling Bendor, "I'll get married if I get pregnant," and would claim she meant it as a kind of blackmail, that without a child there was no reason to get married, that marriage was no guarantee two people loved each other more.

Gabrielle would have liked a clean break, especially since the press reported the Duke of Westminster was going to marry Loelia Mary Ponsonby, the daughter of the first Lord Sisonby. His wounded pride, however, insisted on seeing Coco—and being seen with her. She went along, realizing that his congenial interest in her helped her save face.

Loelia (pronounced "Leelia") was one of London's "Bright Young Things," famous for her fancy dress parties and her sardonic observations on her friends. Evelyn Waugh was one of them and in *Vile Bodies*, his new best-seller, she figures as the hostess of "masked parties, savage parties, Victorian parties, Russian parties, circus parties, parties where one had to dress as someone else, and almost naked parties in St. John's Wood." The gossip columnists chronicled a swimming-pool party she and her cousin Elizabeth Ponsonby gave where guests danced in bathing suits to a jazz band.

In the spring of 1930 when the Duke of Westminster became engaged to Miss Ponsonby, he immediately dashed to Paris to introduce his fiancée to Gabrielle, and to ask her if she thought the young woman was suitable.

While Bendor wandered restlessly around the Chanel apartment, Coco "interviewed" his twenty-eight-year-old fiancée. Loelia would recall the meeting with a measure of tart humor.

Small, dark, and simian, Coco was the personification of her own fashion. She was wearing a dark blue suit and a white blouse with very light stockings (light stockings were one of her credos). Described in this way she sounds as if she looked like a high-school girl, but actually the effect was one of extreme sophistication.

She had more or less invented costume jewelry, specializing in most attractive ropes of imitation pearls, clasped at intervals with bunches of rubies and emeralds. When I saw her she was hung with every sort of necklace and bracelet, which rattled as she moved. Her sitting room was luxurious and lavish and she sat in a large armchair, a pair of tall Coromandel screens, now to be seen in her Paris showroom, making an effective backcloth. I perched, rather at a disadvantage, on a stool at her feet, feeling that I was being looked over to see whether I was a suitable bride for her old admirer—and I very much doubted whether I, or my tweed suit, passed the test.

As she sat there at Gabrielle's feet and tried to find something to say, all she could mention was that a friend of her parents had given her a Chanel necklace as a Christmas present. Coco made her describe the jewelry and decided the necklace could not have come from her. "She would never dream of having anything like *that* on sale, and the conversation dropped with a bang."

On February 20, 1930, at a London registrar's office, Bendor married Loelia, with Winston Churchill as the best man.

There is no indication that Erté, who had lived in Paris since Poiret first hired him in 1910, warned Coco about his experiences in Hollywood. In fact, it was not Goldwyn who had brought Erté to Hollywood in 1925 but Louis B. Mayer. Hired to do the costumes for *Paris*, a preposterous story about a couturier who lives in the Louvre, the designer spent nine months waiting for the studio to make up its mind about the script. While he waited, he designed a cubist dressing room for a backstage drama called *A Little Bit of Broadway* and fought with Lillian Gish over the costumes he designed for *La Bohème*. Erté then broke his contract in a huff, went back to Europe, and, in an interview with the Paris edition of the *New York Herald*, said American movies were still in a "barbarous stage," American producers without "the slightest conception of elegance, beauty, or taste; film stars for the most part are illiterate, crotchety, unshapely, even ill-informed; scenario writers know nothing of the world outside their small narrow circle."

Coco had more ambitious ideas. It might be interesting—and lucrative—to introduce her fashion through the Goldwyn productions. The short, straight dresses of the mid-1920s were on the wane—skirt lengths were dropping to a generally accepted level of fourteen inches off the ground for daywear, twelve inches for afternoon, and ankle-length for evening. Movie theaters were dream palaces. It could be rewarding to have her new soft yet streamlined look with its intricate bias-cutting modeled by movie stars and filmed in glorious settings. Why couldn't she provide the cinema with the authority and distinction of fashion?

Leaving Countess Hélène de Leusse in charge of the boutique and taking Misia along to keep her company, Chanel left for America in late February

1931 aboard the S.S. *Europe*. On March 4, Coco and Misia arrived in New York. A nasty flu confined Coco to her hotel suite for her first ten days in the New World. On her first day journalists nevertheless besieged her suite far into the afternoon.

"It's just an invitation," she told the *New York Times*. "I will see what the pictures have to offer me and what I have to offer the pictures. I will not make one dress. I have not brought my scissors with me. Later, perhaps, when I go back to Paris, I will create and design gowns six months ahead for the actresses in Mr. Goldwyn's pictures. I will send the sketches from Paris and my fitters in Hollywood will make the gowns."

The *Times* reporter found her to be "rather bewildered at the scores of interviewers and reception committee members who crowded her suite at the Hotel Pierre" and described her as wearing long bobbed hair and "a simple red jersey gown with a short skirt of the severe kind which she first made popular in wartime France."

She fielded fashion questions by predicting long hair would be back in style, by stating that a chic woman should dress well but not eccentrically. She said flower-based perfumes were not mysterious on a woman, that men who used scents were disgusting, and that, whereas before the war fashions were set by elegant persons with experience, nowadays it was the young who set the tone.

With flu delaying her departure, the *Times* set up a second interview. Chanel spoke of her ideas about giving movies fashion authority and admitted she wasn't quite sure what she would do once she got to California. "Working for Goldwyn's pictures will be something of an evolution in technique, she points out. In her great Rue Cambon shop, she never sees her clients. Her work is impersonal. A frock is designed and that ends it for her. She seldom has an opportunity of seeing it, and even more seldom the inclination. The reverse will naturally be true with pictures. In Hollywood, she will design gowns not only for certain stars—Ina Claire, Gloria Swanson, Norma Talmadge, the leading ladies of Ronald Colman, Eddie Cantor, and other Samuel Goldwyn players—but, equally important, for certain players in roles in certain moods. It will be difficult, will it not? she asks you."

The reporter found her to be animated; "not the animation of a picture star but of a shrewd businesswoman, a woman whose business is charm in dress. She does not make speeches, nor has she any theatrical affectation or exhibition—her answers are simple, direct."

People in the fashion and film industries were laying bets on whether Coco Chanel could succeed in imposing fashion dictates on movie stars, *Collier's* revealed. If Chanel created a dress for Bebe Daniels that depended for its effect on sobriety no doubt the star herself would pin a big red rose to it. Clara Bow might pin two roses and a velvet bowtie to the same dress, just to be different. *Collier's* noted that Lillian Gish had refused to wear the clothes Erté had designed for her and that Garbo had had a run-in with Gilbert Clarke, a student of the London fashion-house owner Lady Duff Gordon. They predicted that Chanel would come up against similar difficulties. On the other hand, the high-fashion director of Bergdorf Goodman was sure Coco Chanel, and only she, would succeed. The luminaries of the screen might listen to no one else, but they would listen to her. "They are crazy over her creations," said Bergdorf Goodman's Comtesse de Forceville. "Chanel will never be short of ideas. Over the past ten, fifteen years the fashions that count have been conceived by her. It'll be a triumphant success and it will be a great plus for the cinema."

22

HOLLYWOOD

Gabrielle wrote few letters in her lifetime, and neither she nor Misia ever kept a journal. There is no record of what the two friends thought of the United States deep into its Depression, of the Hoovervilles of tar-paper shacks along the tracks and the eyes of men staring back from freight cars on sidings. The American reporters who accompanied them on their journey to Hollywood were there to report on the Goldwyn fashion coup. Their cables were all about the Chanel chic, the real champagne, and the French oo-la-la.

Before leaving New York's Grand Central Station, Coco had included Maurice Sachs in the traveling party. The young writer had popped up at the Hotel Pierre. He had been through a religious crisis and had married the daughter of an American pastor; he knew it was a mistake and begged Coco to take him with her to Hollywood. She was not usually drawn to the ornamental type of homosexual hanger-on, but Sachs was entertaining.

When they arrived at Los Angeles's Union Station after the 2,985-mile, four-day journey, Coco was greeted by the same frenzied press reception that had welcomed other celebrities Goldwyn imported.

A reception at Sam and Frances Goldwyn's home introduced Coco and Misia to Greta Garbo, Marlene Dietrich, Claudette Colbert, and Fredric March, and to the directors George Cukor and Erich von Stroheim. Stroheim was *the* Continental influence on films; he embodied the implied wickedness of European morality. In the films he wrote, directed, and starred in, he was the hand-kissing, heel-clicking cad who used and abused women. With all his Mittel-Europa panache, Stroheim kissed Coco's hand and asked, "You are . . . a seamstress, I believe?"

Coco forgave him. "Such a ham, but what a style," she would remember. Misia enjoyed all the Hollywood "royalty." And the royals pronounced themselves honored to meet the woman said—by Goldwyn's publicity chief Howard Dietz—to be "the biggest fashion brain ever known."

At another reception, Cukor introduced Coco to a young woman he had "discovered" and launched despite her lack of conventional screen glamour. Katharine Hepburn's affection for slacks and baggy sweaters and her distinct disdain for almost everyone immediately pleased Gabrielle, who saw her younger self in this bony, freckled-faced twenty-two-year-old who wanted it all and on her own terms. Coco loved the story Cukor told of Hepburn sending a friend in to say she was too ill to attend a cocktail party while Kate stood outside in full view of the assembled guests.

What the public wanted, Goldwyn said, was musicals to cheer them up. MGM had started the trend with *Broadway Melody*, and the big studios had followed with *Show Boat, The Cocoanuts, Sunny Side Up*, and *The Desert Song. Rio Rita*, the first song-and-dance film produced by RKO, grossed $2.5 million. Now United Artists was producing *Palmy Days*, and Goldwyn asked Chanel to begin designing the wardrobe for it.

The costume department was there to enhance and accentuate the different personalities of the stars. Coco saw how films were shot, met the top people in the costuming department, and learned from the best of them what "photogenic" meant and how you achieved it. She realized the camera was an engine for imposing new types and new faces—Garbo with her hollowed eye sockets and plucked eyebrows, Dietrich with her sucked-in cheeks, Joan Crawford with her bow-tie mouth.

With her staff, Coco had to come up with a wardrobe that wouldn't look outdated at the end of a film's overseas run two years later. Her assistants were Mitchell Leisen, DeMille's former costume designer, and *his* assistant, who affected French manners and went by the name Adrian. With Gabrielle, Adrian had to admit he was no Frenchman—he was born Adolph Greenburg in Naugatuck, Connecticut—but he was good. The wardrobe he had designed for Garbo's *Mata Hari* had the same accent on broad shoulders as those shown in the 1931 Paris collections at the time the film was released.

Edward Sutherland was the director of *Palmy Days*. A former actor himself, he was also the husband of the actress Louise Brooks, who Coco thought one of the loveliest visions on the screen. Busby Berkeley, who would become the master of Hollywood musical directing, was dance director.

Palmy Days was a hokey comedy-melodrama with Eddie Cantor as a bakery efficiency expert trapped in the locker room of a bakery's girl's gym. It was designed to cash in on Cantor's splash in *Whoopee* and show the Goldwyn Girls in scanty clothes. On one stage, Sutherland directed action sequences at breakneck speed while on another Berkeley concentrated on filming the high-kicking Goldwyn Girls in a rousing gym number called "Bend Down, Sister." There was little time for Coco to contribute much more than a few dresses for Charlotte Greenwood, playing the hyperactive instructor in the gym.

Beverly Hills left Coco indifferent and the ruthless studio system that made stars into salaried nonentities appalled her. "The stars are the producers' servants," she would say. "Jean Harlow wriggled her behind, looking for rich men. Garbo told me, 'Without you I wouldn't have made it, with my little hat and raincoat.' I remember her big feet. She understood that evening gowns weren't for her, that playing humble was to her advantage."

Coco was anxious to get back to her own business in Rue Cambon, and Goldwyn, who was more interested in the publicity value of the Chanel name than her actual presence in Culver City, was most accommodating. The next picture Goldwyn wanted her to design costumes for was a screen adaptation of the Broadway hit *Tonight or Never*. Gloria Swanson, who would star in it, was already in London for the premiere of her latest release, *Indiscreet.* As long as Coco designed a fabulous wardrobe, Goldwyn and United Artists chief Joseph Schenck saw no reason why the clothes couldn't be made in Rue Cambon, and Swanson induced to hop over to Paris for fittings.

Gabrielle and Misia's stay in New York on the return trip was longer and, for Coco, more productive than the stopover on the way to California. She met and charmed Carmel Snow, the editor in chief of *Harper's Bazaar*, and Margaret Case of *Vogue*. Condé Nast, the publisher of *Vogue* and a friend of Goldwyn, gave a luncheon for Coco.

She was not always on the best of terms with the elegant and fastidious publisher, who eavesdropped on his rivals, manipulated his colleagues and board, and coaxed, charmed, and tormented his employees as the sultan of chic. Nast might fire editors and writers who offended his advertisers—Dorothy Parker was sacked for calling a Florenz Ziegfeld production starring Ziegfeld's wife, Billie Burke, "a long and uneventful evening"—but *le tout New York* scrambled for invitations to his swank Park Avenue parties. Chanel did little advertising in the American *Vogue*, but for several stretches of the 1930s banned Nast's photographers from her collection shows. The reason was her irritation at seeing Schiaparelli get as much space as she in the lucrative parent publication of the Condé Nast syndicate.

What fascinated Chanel in New York in 1933, however, was not Nast's thirty-room penthouse at 1040 Park Avenue, but fashion as business. She toured the Seventh Avenue garment district and the department stores from Saks and Macy's to Bloomingdale's. The eye-opener, however, was Klein's, the discount bazaar on Union Square. Dresses that sold on Fifth Avenue for twenty dollars were priced at four dollars in this discount emporium. Without the assistance of a single saleslady, women served themselves and tried clothes on in a huge, mirrored room where signs in English, Polish, Yiddish, and Armenian said, "Don't try to steal; our detectives are everywhere." The styles were the same as in the department store couture salons; only the materials were different.

Coco was mercilessly plagiarized. Copying had always exasperated Poiret. He went as far as forbidding his clients to lend his dresses to anyone lest a too nimble-fingered seamstress get to study the secrets of his cuts. Gabrielle, on the other hand, proclaimed that knockoffs were nothing more than "spontaneous publicity." It was at Klein's that she decided that it was hopeless to try and fight it, that piracy was the flattering result of success.

When she returned from America, Gabrielle felt a need to see Bendor, and she arranged a trip to England.

Bendor was not happy. He was insanely jealous of Loelia and, as Coco and other friends noted, he drank too much. In her conversations with Paul Morand fourteen years later, Coco re-created the following dialogue:

" 'I've lost you,' he said. 'I cannot get used to the idea of living without you.'

"I answered: 'I don't love you. Don't tell me that you would want to sleep with a woman who doesn't love you.' The men with whom I've been the harshest always became the nicest.

"With me, he learned that he couldn't have everything, that to be His Grace didn't mean anything when a little Frenchwoman could say no. That was a shock to him; he lost his balance."

In England Chanel presented a fashion show inspired by what she had seen at Klein's department store in New York. The War Service Legion was desperately in need of money, and Coco persuaded her former lover to let her use his London town house for a fashion show benefit. Gertrude Lawrence, the actress whose alluring sophistication and stage partnership with Noël Coward was making her the leading beauty of the London scene, led a parade of some five hundred titled ladies, society matrons and showbusiness people who visited the show daily. "Many visitors bring their own seamstresses because this collection isn't for sale," the *Daily Mail* reported May 14, 1932. "Mademoiselle Chanel has authorized it being copied."

During the summer of 1931, Gloria Swanson came to Paris and checked into the Ritz. The London reviews of *Indiscreet* were sufficiently polite to justify carrying the celebration to France and the movie star came to Paris with Noël Coward and her director, Edmund Goulding.

Her next film, *Tonight or Never*, was to be a slice of Viennese schmaltz about a young concert singer engaged to an aging nobleman but in love with a mysterious stranger who is actually an impresario who wants to sign her to an opera contract. Goldwyn wanted to make a lavish production characteristic of a Swanson movie. No expense was to be spared.

For one week, the star came to Rue Cambon for preliminary fittings. The diminutive actress, whose screen image as the sophisticated, secure, and intriguing woman had made her the top box-office magnet of the 1920s, was every inch and every moment a star. Coco, however, thought she was a little chubby, and suggested she lose a few pounds before the final fitting. The fitting was scheduled for six weeks later. Meanwhile, she was off to Cannes, for a Mediterranean cruise aboard a yacht belonging to a British playboy.

When Swanson came back, she had gained weight.

Coco glared furiously when the star had trouble getting into the long black bias-cut gown she had been measured for six weeks earlier. Swanson said she would try with a girdle, but when she stepped before Coco again, the line where the girdle ended halfway down her thigh was clearly visible.

"Take off the girdle and lose five pounds," Coco snapped. "You have no right to fluctuate in the middle of fittings. Come back tomorrow and we'll finish the evening coat with the sable collar. Five pounds!"

Gloria Swanson was a star on the skids. On screen, the thirty-two-year-old, husky-voiced actress was still the embodiment of the intriguing woman. But her long affair with the Wall Street banker and neophyte movie financier Joseph Kennedy had led to the breakup of her third marriage. Floundering financially and emotionally, her quick tryst with the playboy Michael Farmer aboard his boat had resulted in a very unwanted pregnancy.

Already the mother of a ten-year-old daughter and an adopted son of seven, she decided to keep the baby and swore everybody in her entourage to secrecy. Michael Farmer was ardously pursuing her to marry him, but after three failed marriages, she had little faith in matrimony. All she could think of was getting through the *Tonight or Never* filming before she showed. Then she planned to go on an extended vacation, have the baby, and announce she was adopting it.

The next day, she returned to Chanel with samples of elastic straps she had been given at a doctor's office. What she wanted the House of Chanel to do, she explained, was to make her a rubberized undergarment that would eliminate the corset line and keep her slim enough for two months to get through the picture.

Coco wouldn't hear of it. "Lose five pounds."

"Maybe I can't," Swanson replied.

"Why not?"

"Reasons of health, maybe. Look, *just try it*," she pleaded. "And if it doesn't work, I'll lose five pounds."

Gabrielle was the exception to the rule that artistic temperament rarely goes hand in hand with financial acumen. Her name had stood for a fashion that repudiated the corset, but she was enough of a market hawker's daughter to shrewdly take the practical course when necessary. The in-house specialist in undergarments sewed surgical elastics into a panty girdle. It took three assistants to get Swanson into it, but the result was stunning. The actress left for Hollywood with trunks of Chanel clothes and a stack of sturdy elastic panties.

Coco followed Swanson to the Goldwyn studios. While *Tonight or Never* was shooting—neither director Mervyn Le Roy nor co-stars Ferdinand Gottschalk and Melvyn Douglas suspected their leading lady was pregnant—Chanel did the wardrobe for a witty, sophisticated screen adaptation of Zoe Akins's Broadway comedy *The Greeks Had a Word for It*. The story of three rival gold-diggers on the make, the movie benefited from inspired casting. Ina Claire played the naughty and determined gold digger—she sets out to tantalize a man by going out in a fur coat with nothing underneath—Joan Blondell was the good-humored and wise-cracking best friend, and Madge Evans the elegant and tasteful one. Goldwyn saw to it that director Lowell Sherman successfully transferred to the screen the elegant trappings that had captured New York playgoers. Chanel's eye-popping gowns and Richard Day's lavish settings were photographed by the top Goldwyn cameraman, George Barnes.

Gabrielle returned to Paris while the two pictures were in postproduction. *Tonight or Never* was Goldwyn's Christmas 1931 release. It turned out to be a disaster and to precipitate the downward spin of Swanson's career. The credits announced, "Miss Swanson's gowns designed and executed by Chanel, Paris," and reviewers dutifully noted the wardrobe. *The New Yorker* allowed itself to speculate that Chanel had left Hollywood because "they told her her dresses weren't sensational enough. She made a lady look like a lady. Hollywood wants a lady to look like two ladies." *The Greeks Had a Word for It* became a hit. "It's one of those peculiar stories, nearly always written by a woman, in which the not-too-good heroine eats her cake and has it too, and for the femme trade that formula is generally foolproof," wrote *Variety*. The trade review didn't mention the Chanel wardrobe but noted in the screen credits: "Gowns by Chanel and so advertised."

23

COMPETITION

The reasons for Chanel's return to Paris were multiple and, *The New Yorker* speculation notwithstanding, not the consequence of her wardrobe designs not being flashy enough for Hollywood. True, she found Hollywood something of a bore and in later life would dismiss it as "the Mont Saint Michel of tit and tail," but neither she nor Goldwyn had thought of her assignment as anything more than a temporary sideline. She was not about to close the House of Chanel, laying off her two thousand workers, in order to emigrate to the film capital.

In the deepening Depression, Paul Poiret closed his couture house on the Rond Point des Champs Elysées. His creditors seized everything he owned and obtained a court order giving them the right to his name. Chanel's rivals had also slashed their prices. But Gabrielle's two years as a $1-million-a-year Hollywood designer gave her a financial cushion. The sudden loss of the British and American clientele had hurt, but there were still many rich clients from South America and India. And even in the United States, after the first panic had subsided, there were people rich enough to order costly work in quantity. Chanel was convinced the best way to survive was to maintain the standards of haute couture workmanship. If anything had to give, it was the fabric. To the dismay of silk manufacturers, she began designing evening dresses in cotton.

Chanel's success in Hollywood enhanced her prestige at home. *Vogue* announced that Chanel had revolutionized Hollywood by dressing Ina Claire in the simplest of white satin pajamas. The cachet of Chanel's name became more valuable than ever. Cocteau wanted her to do the costumes for a new play, an adaptation of the Arthurian legend he called *Les Chevaliers de la Table Ronde,* and the International Guild of Diamond Merchants asked her to design real jewelry.

Perfumes and accessories were integral parts of any respectable couture house, but the franchising of designer names on everything from hosiery and eye wear to wines, rugs, and the interiors of executive jets was still decades away. Charity was still the fig leaf used to involve celebrity names in business, and the diamond merchants invited Chanel to work with real gems and to include her celebrity friends in the designing of the jewelry.

She agreed. The "artisans" she found to design baubles included Count Etienne de Beaumont, who a decade before had refused to invite her to his costume ball; Misia, who since Jojo had divorced her was living in diminished circumstances; the society hostess Lady Sibyl Colefax; and the interior decorator Elsie de Wolfe, who was said to have been responsible for making Americans antique-conscious.

The resulting artwork was exhibited at her Faubourg St. Honoré home with a press fanfare that caused the stock of De Beers, the diamond merchants, to jump twenty points on the London exchange. Private security guards were at every drawing room door as the jewels went on display among the Coromandel screens. *The New Yorker*'s Janet Flanner reviewed the event. "Mlle Chanel's mountings for the jewels are in design dominantly and delicately astronomical. Magnificent lopsided stars for earrings; as a necklace, a superb comet whose nape-encircling tail is all that attaches it to a lady's throat; bracelets that are flexible rays, crescents for hats and hair; and, as a unique set piece mounted in yellow gold, a splendid sun of yellow diamonds from a unique collection of matched stones unmatched in the world."

The Depression was deepening but with her instinct for striking when everyone else thinks the iron is cold, Coco decided real jewels were fashionable. During the booming twenties, she had made glass gewgaws "because they were devoid of arrogance in an epoch of too easy *luxe,*" *The New Yorker* quoted her as saying. Now she promoted precious stones because they had "the greatest value in the smallest volume." In the interest of economy, however, she decided to make the individual pieces convertible. All her more elaborate pieces could be taken apart: The tiaras turned into bracelets, the eardrops into brooches, the stars into buckles.

Coco Chanel at twenty-three.

Aubazine, the church and convent.

The House of Grampayre, the lingerie and hosiery shop where Gabrielle was a shop assistant.

Gabrielle and Adrienne had themselves photographed in the park in Vichy, 1906.

Royallieu.

Gabrielle Dorziat in a Chanel hat.

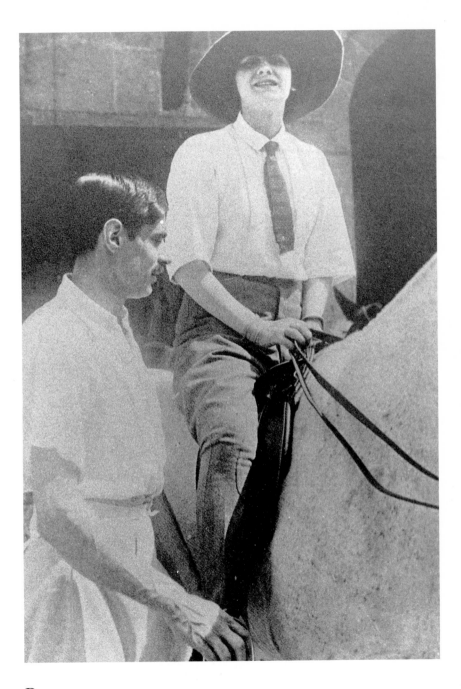

Boy Capel and Coco Chanel, 1912.

Rue Gontaud-Biron, Deauville.

Gabrielle Chanel (right) with Adrienne in front of her first boutique in Deauville.

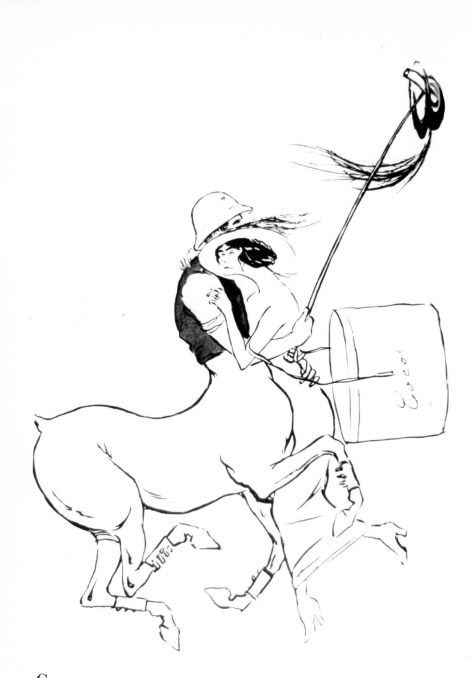

Caricature by Sem: Coco in the arms of the centaur Boy.

Misia, by Pierre Bonnard, 1908.

Diaghilev, by Picasso.

Dancers Lydia Sokolova, Leon Woizikovsky, Bronislava Nijinski, and Anton Dolin in scenes from *Le Train bleu*, wearing costumes designed by Chanel.

Jean Cocteau, 1932.

"Moi, Sert, Missia [*sic*] et Coco Chanel 1920" wrote Igor Stravinsky under this snapshot of the quartet in Venice.

Grand Duke Dmitri.

Coco, 1923.

Pierre Reverdy.

Ernest Beaux, the perfumer, who helped Chanel create her classic perfume.

Coco and Vera Bate hiking in the Alps, 1925.

Coco and Bendor at the Grand National racetrack, 1925, as rumors flew that the Duke of Westminster would soon marry Mademoiselle Chanel.

Chanel with Winston Churchill at a boar hunt, 1928.

To make sure women would still buy the artificial pearls she was famous for, she produced a few new choice aphorisms to go with the new bijou:

A woman should mix fake and real. To ask a woman to wear real jewelry only is like asking her to cover herself with real flowers instead of flowery silk prints. She'd look faded in a few hours.

I love fakes because I find such jewelry provocative, and I find it disgraceful to walk around with millions around your neck just because you're rich. The point of jewelry isn't to make a woman look rich but to adorn her; not the same thing.

Coco was going on fifty and was extremely attractive. "She was bright, dark gold-color—wide face, with a snorting nose, just like a little bull, and deep Dubonnet-red cheeks," Diana Vreeland would remember of Gabrielle in the mid-1930s.

The future editor of *Harper's Bazaar* and *Vogue* was then a woman of leisure living in London with her banker husband, Reed Vreeland. The two of them were invited to Faubourg St. Honoré. "It had an enormous garden with fountains, the most beautiful salons opening on the garden, and something like fifty-four Coromandel screens shaping these rooms into the most extraordinary *allées* of charm. There she received the *world*. It was a proper society she had around her—artists, musicians, poets—and everyone was fascinated by her. Coco Chanel became a figure in all of this—Paris society—entirely through wit and taste. Her taste was what you'd call *formidable*. She was irresistible. Absolutely."

Mary Harriman, the sister of President Roosevelt's special envoy, W. Averell Harriman, remembered Chanel as "not pretty but small and fascinating; something like the idea of the Cleopatra that Caesar loved. Her charm and her manners created beauty. She was quite different from other women of her period, far more fashionable than the fashions of the time as she had a kind of slick elegance, which later was copied by New York women, making them all slick and elegant in a businesslike way."

In her famous verbal portrait of Chanel, Colette called her friend a black bull. Other people's faces might remind us of animals with beaks, snouts, nostrils, muzzles, trunks, or manes, but "by her obstinate energy, by the way she faces you and listens, by her guarded stance, which some-times kind of blocks her face, Chanel is a black bull. Her dark hair is curled, the privilege of the bull calf. The tufts reach her eyebrows and cavort whenever she moves her head. She is said to be very rich. Luckily, she dresses without any of the infectious effluvium of gold, that indiscreet shine which exudes from feeble and sated people."

Colette caught something of Gabrielle's impulsive work method. "Chanel works with ten fingers, with her nails, the side of her hand, with her palms, pins and scissors, right on the dress, a misty white thing with long pleats, splattered with crystal drops. Sometimes she falls to her knees in front of her work and grasps it firmly, not to worship it, but to punish it a little more, to tighten the cloud of fabric across the thighs of her angel-model, smooth away fullness in the tulle. I read on her face what is so legible—two long black eyebrows that she doesn't pluck, despotic, ready to shoot up, to be lowered, quivering when the dancing tufts of hair annoy them. From the eyebrows one's attention concentrates on the mouth, but there I hesitate because at moments of concentration or irritation the center of her face seems to become cupped, drawn in, withdrawn under the eyebrows' overhang, under the black vault of her hair. Only for a moment, a kind of fierce retreat, an ephemeral immobility from which the mouth suddenly escapes—pliable lips with sad, impatient, obedient corners, punished by cutting teeth."

Yet another reason for tending to the home fires was a new rival, Elsa Schiaparelli. Coco called her "that Italian woman who makes dresses" and at first tried to ignore her, only to see Schiaparelli openings become eagerly awaited society events. Where Chanel was classic, Schiaparelli was baroque. Coco liberated and simplified, Elsa reintroduced the follies of luxury. "What I make is picked up and copied by everybody," Chanel asserted. "What I create is inimitable," Schiaparelli retorted.

The other women designers, Vionnet, Lanvin, Louise Boulanger, and the older Callot sisters, had never been a threat. This was true as well of Alix Czereskow, who went variously under the name Alix or Madame Grès. Schiaparelli was different. Her tastes might be the opposite of Chanel's, but they both appealed to the same type of women, to the crisp, neat, hard look of the mid-1930s. Gabrielle's clothes were faultlessly elegant, modern, effortless, and matchlessly chic. Schiaparelli's looked like a child's giddy vision of what a grown-up lady would wear. The styles were sober—the combination of a dress with a matching jacket—but her colors were fantastic. She married the familiar with the unexpected, the pretty with the grotesque. She would put together fuschia, purple, shocking pink, and black. "Good design," she said, "is always on a tightrope of bad taste."

Twelve years younger than Coco—and therefore all the more despised—Schiap, or Scap, as everybody called her, was of Roman nobility. She had behind her an unfortunate marriage to a Polish dreamer who took her to America, spent her dowry, and left her with a child. She began making a living in Paris by designing sweaters patterned with African art, which she persuaded Armenian refugees to knit for her.

If Coco paid the miserly going wages in the Paris rag trade, Elsa used quasi-slave labor. If Chanel never entered her workrooms, Elsa was overwhelming, full of fun, and seducing her knitters to work nights and Sundays. If anything was wrong with what they delivered, however, she was a Neapolitan fishmonger. Scap tried to sell her designs to Poiret, who turned her down, but found a financial backer in Anita Loos. The American author of *Gentlemen Prefer Blondes* got Scap a first order for forty sweaters. Scap leased rooms in the loft of a building in the Rue de la Paix, and, as Coco had done when she started in Deauville in 1912, made her debut in sports clothes. Like Coco, she had an aristocratic English connection, the brother of Lord Willingdon, the viceroy of India, who financed her Upper Grosvenor Street boutique.

Schiaparelli's creations were not for the timid. Tyrian purple was her favorite color and, renaming it "shocking pink," she created her most famous perfume. A friend of Cocteau and the young Salvador Dali, she asked for their inspiration and introduced surrealist touches to her designs. Her collections were built around themes—the circus, butterflies, music, Botticelli—and she had the manufacturers of her fabrics and accessories echo her motifs. To wear a Schiaparelli was to court fantasy, to display a sense of humor. Her clients included Greta Garbo, the mistresses of Benito Mussolini, and the Princess of Wales. Her showings in her premises in Place Vendôme, where she moved in 1935, were always well attended by high society. Schiaparelli had her showrooms remodeled by Jean-Michel Frank, the designer whose highly individual approach to decoration and furniture found admirers on both sides of the Atlantic. The new interior, Schiaparelli gleefully recorded in her autobiography *Shocking Life*, made Chanel "shudder as though she had passed a graveyard." Coco's Rue Cambon salon was the "backside" of the Ritz according to Scap, who would say, "Poor Chanel, I use the front door of the Ritz, she must use the back."

A still bigger thorn in Coco's side were the Wertheimers. Chanel No. 5 was the world's best-selling perfume—she had seen the square bottle at New York's best department stores herself—but if the royalties had made her rich, the perfume had made Pierre and Paul Wertheimer even richer. She controlled an empire that included the Rue Cambon complex, boutiques in Deauville, Biarritz, Cannes, and London, textile and jewelry factories, but not, to her grief, the perfume.

She saw her chance to get back at the brothers in 1934 when they brought out a Chanel cleansing cream. The papers incorporating Les Parfums Chanel, S.A., in 1924 were less than clear-cut. On the one hand, she had given the corporation the right to make and sell, "all the perfumes currently sold under the name Chanel, the proprietary production formulas, methods and designs copyrighted by her, as well as the exclusive right of said company to make and sell under the name Chanel, all perfumes, beauty products, soaps, etc." On the other hand, an exclusionary clause stipulated that these rights were restricted "to objects usually sold in the perfume business and limits Les Parfums Chanel's right to use the name Chanel to the sale of said articles."

Is a cleansing cream a perfume product or a beauty product? Coco had the Wertheimers served with papers forbidding the use of her name in connection with the new Chanel cream. The brothers argued that cleansing creams were one of the products usually considered part of the perfume business. And anyway, what was the difference between perfume products and beauty products? It wasn't as if they encroached on her fashion by bringing out accessories, for example.

Coco hired a young lawyer of French-American heritage with impeccable family references. Count René de Chambrun was the son of a former diplomat and the French president of First National City Bank of New York; his mother was Clara Longworth. His uncle was Nicholas Longworth, Speaker of the House, and his aunt President Theodore Roosevelt's daughter, Alice Roosevelt Longworth. René wanted to specialize in international law and had just married into politics. His wife, Josée, was the daughter of France's premier, Pierre Laval. Like Chanel, Laval was from Auvergne and, like her, he had a peasant cunning, a toughness and tenacity, and a rude manner of which he was never ashamed even after he gained great wealth and political power.

René's father, Aldebert Pineton de Chambrun, had given him a back room at the Citibank Champs Elysées headquarters saying, "Here's a desk and a telephone. Settle down." Coco Chanel was Chambrun's first client.

"Do you know Pierre Wertheimer?" she asked, looking around the spartan office.

"By name only, Mademoiselle. I'm more familiar with his famous horse, Epinard."

"Well, this Wertheimer is a crook. Are you ready to listen to my long story? Are you ready to fight?"

"I'm just starting, Mademoiselle. I've got my whole life ahead of me."

Chambrun looked into the matter and quickly realized that back in 1924 Chanel had been her own worst enemy. To make sure the Wertheimers could not encroach on her couture turf, she had signed away the perfume for 10 percent of the partnership.

In the files that Coco had her new lawyer go through—Chambrun would claim his Chanel papers would eventually exceed a ton—he discovered she had signed a power of attorney to Les Parfums Chanel in 1931. Perhaps this *assignation* could be voided. The first court fight with the Wertheimers would last five years. Chanel and her counsel would lose it.

24

IRIBE

~~~~~~~~~~~~~~~~

Gabrielle called Paul Iribe the most complicated man she had ever known. Her liaison with the multitalented artist and designer was passionate and paradoxical. He was in love with her celebrity, pretended he didn't care about her money but would have loved to see her slip from her throne, to become dependent on him. She thought of bringing him into her professional life, making him a consort of sorts. She gave him plenipotentiary powers and had him chair stormy board meetings with the Wertheimers.

"He dominated her, and that she couldn't take," Serge Lifar would say. "After a while she began to hate him as much as she loved him."

"He drained me, ruined my health," she would recall to Paul Morand.

A caricaturist before the war, Iribe had spent a dazzling and frustrating decade in Hollywood as Cecil B. De Mille's set designer. Chanel felt that she had represented for him everything he had missed out on in postwar France. "When he came back, he loved me, unconsciously, I think, out of revenge for what he had missed. I was the Paris he had not possessed, the Paris he had moped about during his years with Cecil B. De Mille in the tedious studios in California. I was something he thought was his due. He hadn't possessed me when he should have, so he took this belated revenge. Too late for both of us, but not too late for someone who wants to soothe the ghosts of what we call fixations and complexes."

Born in Angoulême of Basque parents—his real name was Paul Iribarnegaray—Iribe was exactly Gabrielle's age, a hefty man with dark hair and eyes that seemed to scorn the world. He claimed that all great nations had, at one time or another in their history, owed their greatness to the people of the western foothills of the Pyrenees. Beginning with the United States. Wasn't Christopher Columbus a Basque? And Noah? The Basques came from Asia Minor in the Bronze Age. It was the Basques, not the Moors as the *Chanson de Roland* relates, who cut the rear guard of Charlemagne's army to pieces at Roncevalles in A.D. 778.

The son of a journalist, Iribe was apprenticed to a typesetter at his father's newspaper, only to quit the job and enroll in an architecture class at the Beaux Arts. When he was seventeen, he sold his first drawings to *L'Assiette au beurre*, the most celebrated Parisian weekly, and in 1908 founded his own magazine, *Le Témoin* ("The Witness"). The turn of the century was the golden age for caricaturists and cartoonists and, apart from Sem, no one delineated current events with a sharper pen than Iribe. Iribe's drawings of feminine silhouettes caught the attention of Poiret, and the couturier asked Iribe to sit in on a fashion show and to make drawings of the models he found particularly appealing. The result was *Les Robes de Paul Poiret racontée par Paul Iribe*, an album of sensuous drawings of the couturier's most delirious creations. Poiret sent the album to all the crowned heads in Europe. *Le Témoin*, which also carried illustrations by Juan Gris and Cocteau, lasted four years. Iribe began designing furniture, fabrics, rugs, and jewels, and by 1910 he was a sought-after arbiter of interior design. Together with Cocteau, he created a new magazine in 1914. The first issue of *Le Mot* came out as the war broke out, and carried a striking posterlike drawing by Iribe of a French artilleryman facing an immense German cannon disgorging a horde of unwilling slave privates.

Iribe married Jane Diris, an actress of vaudeville and the silent screen, who died of tuberculosis in 1922. By then, he was in America and soon married to Maybelle Hogan, a New York heiress whose considerable fortune assuaged his grief over the first wife. Paramount's cofounder Jesse Lasky discovered Iribe, brought him to Hollywood and told De Mille to use the designer's talents. The first picture Iribe worked on was *The Affairs of Anatol*, a toned-down version of Arthur Schnitzler's amoral Viennese play *Anatol*. What made the picture De Mille's most sophisticated and dazzling silent comedy was Iribe's sets. Despite long wranglings during the shooting, De Mille embraced Iribe in gratitude when he saw the finished film. The art nouveau ambience created by Iribe was so intoxicating that art critics discussed *The Affairs of Anatol* in serious journals.

Manslaughter was an overwrought De Mille melodrama that became a sensation because of the gowns Iribe designed for the star, Leatrice Joy. *Changing Husbands* gave Iribe a chance to direct the divine Leatrice, while *The Ten Commandments* gave him the biggest canvas any movie designer had ever worked on.

Paramount Pictures promoted Iribe to Artistic Director with authority over the studio's designers and decorations, but he was difficult to work with. Mitchell Leisen, the De Mille assistant Coco would work with at Goldwyn Studios five years later, took a dim view of Iribe's ascension. The two became bitter enemies and their working relationship was reduced to a succession of quarrels, shouts, and slammed doors.

For *King of Kings* Iribe began to design a complete physical re-creation of Christ's era. De Mille, however, found the sets too dull, and told Iribe he was more interested in a richness of imagination than in historical accuracy. They quarreled and De Mille fired Iribe, asking Leisen to take over. Iribe never spoke to De Mille again. With Maybelle, he returned to France in 1926 and, with her money, opened a shop in Rue Faubourg St. Honoré where he custom-designed home furnishings and jewels for moneyed clients.

Colette described Iribe as "a most unusual young fellow, a Basque, chubby as a capon, with something of both the divinity student and the composing-room foreman," yet his feminine conquests were numerous. And when he found himself in financial difficulties, he thought nothing of fleecing his lady friends. When the money flowed in, he bought a Voisin automobile, a sailboat, and a house in St. Tropez near Colette's summer residence. The lengthening Depression cost him the car, yacht, and house. To survive, Maybelle managed to get him commissions to design jewels for Cartier's and for Chanel.

Coco had fun letting herself be seduced by Iribe. Self-assured and possessed of a roguish charm and a mordant wit, he challenged her to go to bed with him. He was someone for whom questions of origin didn't count—a man who, in that respect, was the opposite of Boy Capel, Dmitri, and Bendor. For over a year almost no one knew of the affair. He made no moves to divorce Maybelle, yet rumors circulated that Chanel was ready to marry him.

By the summer of 1933, Maybelle caught on to her husband's affair. Under pressure from her parents, who knew only of their son-in-law's extravagant spending, Maybelle moved out of the Iribe apartment on Avenue Rodin, and a short time later left for America with the couple's children. To be closer to Coco, Paul moved to 16 Place Vendôme.

Iribe was, in many ways, an ideal companion. It was now twenty years since Chanel had opened her first boutique in Deauville, twenty exhilarating but relentless years of running the fashion house, a textile business, and a jewelry workshop that altogether employed over 3,000 workers. To lean on a man like Iribe was tempting. He had style and wit, and he was fast on his feet. Coco even decided to ask Iribe to help her in the fight with the Wertheimers.

In the face of her lawsuits and her lawyer's subpoena of all the Parfums Chanel books, the Wertheimers tried to freeze her out as president by reorganizing the company. On September 12, 1933, Coco obtained a court order, and, giving Iribe full power of attorney, had him preside over a board meeting. With little experience in the business of Les Parfums Chanel and less knowledge of corporate law and parliamentary proceedings, Iribe refused to sign the minutes at the end of the meeting. This was enough for a majority of the members to vote him off the board.

The Wertheimers proceeded with the reorganization. Chanel herself was removed as president in 1934. The next year, Les Parfums Chanel began to cede its rights to subsidiaries and to the Wertheimers' company, Bourjois. Coco hired several executives discharged from Les Parfums Chanel, and, with ferocious vehemence, plotted new strategies to get back at Pierre Wertheimer.

Coco Chanel's power in fashion, meanwhile, was undiminished. The big news of the 1932–33 season had been her ciré satin cinema suit—photographed by Cecil Beaton for the fashion magazines—even though Schiaparelli shared the fashion limelight with her copper clamps for buttons and felt socks for hats. The 1934 look was hard and smart, and Coco scored with open-necked white shirts under artificial silk dresses, "neither musical comedy, like Schiaparelli's," commented British *Vogue*, "nor drab, like the London house Busvine, which has taken over Reville, with its heavy suits, box jackets, dark stockings and flat shoes." The big news was new elasticized fabrics that allowed a whole series of dresses to be made without fasteners, and both Chanel and Schiaparelli showed garments in the new American Lastex (later Latex) material. These stretch fabrics ranged from a crinkled, crepelike tweed in big checks to a fine ciré jersey, with the Lastex yarn being used as an integral part of the fabric design.

Iribe redecorated Coco's Faubourg St. Honoré apartment. Together they went to the opening of Cocteau's biggest stage triumph, *La Machine Infernale*, a spoof of the Oedipus legend, in which the fashion illustrator Christian Bérard made his breakthrough as a stage designer.

Together with most Parisian artists, intellectuals, and monied classes, Chanel and Iribe were on the Riviera during the summer of 1933. Colette was in St. Tropez, doing her shopping when, from behind, two hands covered her eyes and she felt a woman's body against her back. At the "Guess who?" she knew it was Misia.

They had barely exchanged greetings when Misia blurted out, "You know, she's marrying him."

"Who?"

"Iribe."

The eternal gossip knew everything. Coco was in love for the first time in her life, Misia confided.

Colette didn't like Iribe. She found his kisses fawning and his attitudes those of a man on the make. He was "slim, wrinkled, pale, and laughing with brand-new teeth. He coos like a pigeon."

To her actress friend Marguerite Moreno, Colette wrote, "I've just been told that Iribe is marrying Chanel. Aren't you horrified—for Chanel?"

25

TRAGEDY AT PLAY

Joseph Leclerc was the victim of the pending marriage. The butler, whose wife, Marie, had died in Coco's service, whose daughter had grown up in the household, was expendable. Coco wanted no comparisons, no remarks or implied reproof from the man who had known her with Boy Capel and seen her and Léon de Laborde off to the scene of his death, who had waited on Stravinsky and the Duke of Westminster, who had served Grand Duke Dmitri and opened doors for Reverdy. With the economy in depression, she explained to him, she was giving up the lease on the Rue Faubourg St. Honoré town house, moving to a *hôtel pension*, and keeping only her personal maid.

Their parting was rancorous. Joseph, however, was the perfectly faithful servant. He never spoke out against her, never sold his memoirs, and to the end of his life followed her career in the newspapers.

Chanel moved to the Ritz, where she took a two-room suite in the narrow building that housed the Rue Cambon side of the Ritz. She kept her clothes across the street in an apartment she had installed on the third floor of 31 Rue Cambon.

She concentrated her homemaking whims on La Pausa. The garden was finished, a tennis court put in, and the drawing rooms refurnished. Her entertainment was both fastidious and frugal. "I hate conventions, but one must live with habits," she said. Her dinners, served with place settings on an oak table without tablecloth, included baked potatoes, fresh chestnut puree. The cooks she hired were told in no uncertain terms to desist if she detected the merest whiff of onion. "I don't like food that talks back to you after you've eaten." Her choice of wines was classical— chilled Riesling, Chianti, or Beaujolais, and a nobler Bordeaux for the guests, but served cooler than room temperature. At the glow of her fireplace, she liked an occasional thimbleful of vodka.

Iribe persuaded Gabrielle to bankroll the rebirth of *Le Témoin*. With himself as director, editor, and cartoonist, the December 10, 1933, pre-miere issue featured articles by Colette and Jean Giraudoux, and opinions by filmmaker Abel Gance and actor Louis Jouvet.

Iribe's drawings had lost none of their bite. There was still mordant wit, startling graphics and layouts, but it was all narrowly nationalistic. The word *France* appeared in virtually every line. In cartoons he displayed Coco as the crucified Marianne of France seated under a bench of sneer-ing judges—Roosevelt, Chamberlain, Hitler, Mussolini. Flaunted on news-stands, spread out on tables, the perfectly recognizable nude Chanel was the prostrate incarnation of France.

The Depression had turned Iribe into a superpatriot and an elitist. In France, the slump was aggravated by the failure of the fumbling National Assembly to take sensible measures. Iribe shared with a large number of Frenchmen the rancor and resentment that was directed not so much against the party in office, as was the case in the United States and Britain, but, as in Germany, against the republican regime itself. In Germany, the discontent brought Adolf Hitler to power; in Paris it spawned an explosion of right-wing "leagues" whose objective was the overthrow of the Third Republic in favor of strong one-man rule, or, in the case of Charles Maur-ras's Action Française, restoration of monarchy. Iribe was no monarchist, but he found representational government ineffectual. He made no ex-cuses for his elitist views. "Taste always comes from above," he said.

Le Témoin joined the vigorous, if overheated, right-wing press that railed against Germans, Jews, and romanticism, but it was first and fore-most antiforeign. To raise circulation, Iribe used a single appeal: "*Le Témoin* speaks French. Subscribe to it."

Never a liberal—especially when it came to the pay and rights of the several thousand women who labored in her workrooms and salons— Gabrielle espoused her lover's worldview. From a stance of political in-difference, she moved toward a view of the future threatened from the

Left. Events that played themselves out below her windows in early 1934 hardened her prejudice. A demonstration by right-wing associations and politicized war veterans at the Place de la Concorde on February 6 turned into a six-hour riot as 40,000 rowdies nearly succeeded in overthrowing the government by marching on the Chamber of Deputies. Repulsed by a final barricade of police, some of the rioters headed up Avenue Gabriel toward the presidential Elysées Palace. Coco smelled the tear gas and saw booted young men in berets charging mounted police with walking sticks to which they had fastened razor blades for slashing horses' hocks. When it was all over, sixteen rioters were killed and 655 injured; one policeman was killed and 1,554 injured. It was the bloodiest encounter in the streets of Paris since the Commune of 1871. The narrow defeat of the rightist leaguers aroused the Left and further polarized the country. By summer, communists and socialists had settled their differences and formed a Popular Front to contest the 1936 elections. Dismayed, the upper classes saw France slide toward a Bolshevik revolution.

Coco's hot again, cold again relationship with Condé Nast was blowing torrid again, and a young German photographer who was embarking on a lifelong career under the sole name Horst was given the assignment to do a layout on her.

"I don't know the reason for her latest row with Condé Nast, but she invited me to lunch at the Ritz to discuss a photo session," Horst would remember. "Janet Flanner had so much liked a photograph I had done of her that she wrote me up in her "Letter from Paris" in *The New Yorker*, and *that* brought a transatlantic phone call from Mr. Nast."

At the appointed hour, the twenty-six-year-old photographer came to the Ritz and shot the layout. Before sending his pictures to New York he came back to show her his work.

"Nice photo, nice jewelry, but it's not me," she told him. To his surprise, however, she added, "Let's do it again."

The result of the second session was a photograph that became Horst's most famous portrait, a picture that fifty years later he would sell in art galleries. Struck by Chanel's profile, he photographed her in a simple black dress and her famous jewelry, reclining in a chaise lounge, looking dreamily into the distance.

"I thought she was in love with me," he would remember. "I didn't know. I was young. She took me to the Opéra and once, taking her home, I tried to kiss her. She brushed me off. 'Not that,' she said. She was extraordinarily generous toward me. She always gave me things. She had beautiful furniture that she had delivered to my place. I came to dinner with Misia."

Condé Nast sent Baron George Hoyningen-Huene, a more seasoned photographer, down to Roquebrune to do a layout on Chanel and her life-style. Hoyningen was a Russian nobleman of such towering ancestry that his father had once refused to salute Kaiser Wilhelm II because he considered the Hohenzollers upstarts. The article that accompanied the photos in British *Vogue* reported that La Pausa was "the essence of simplicity, without superfluous furniture. But what there is is the most perfect of its kind—old oak tables, chests, and cupboards, and in the airy bedrooms old Italian beds."

Chanel was not happy with the attention *Vogue* was giving Schiaparelli. On the telephone to New York, Coco had another row with Nast. As a result, the publisher decreed his magazines would carry no photos of Coco Chanel.

Coco decided to spend the entire summer of 1935 in Roquebrune. Iribe had obtained a separation from Maybelle, but he was staying in Paris during the early part of the summer. On the telephone, Coco pampered him and let him make decisions for her. She also indulged herself and brushed off tattletale warnings from her *premières* that Schiaparelli was previewing a military look with regiments of fitted suits, drummer-boy jackets and a forward "putsch" of hats. More irritating was the news that Schiaparelli was dressing Wallis Simpson. Chanel beach pajamas were everywhere on the Riviera, but for the first time in fifteen years Coco had to take notice of her competition. She would deal a death blow to "that Italian" after the holidays, she decided.

Poulenc and Lifar came for a visit. So did Horst.

It was a lovely summer, and Mussolini's invasion of Ethiopia a very distant event. The African land grab would eventually isolate Italy from much of Europe, but not Italian friends from Roquebrune, and not that summer. Luchino Visconti was one young member of Rome's "golden set" who visited. The twenty-nine-year-old Milanese nobleman and future film director found a saturnine side to his hostess. He called her "La Belle

Dame sans Merci," and would remember "her sufferings, her pleasure in hurting, her need to punish, her pride, her rigor, her sarcasm, her destructive rage, the singlemindedness of a character who goes from hot to cold, her inventive genius." To him, La Pausa was another "golden world." Coco gave lovely dinner parties but never for more than ten or twelve people. "Her gardens were special again," he would remember. "She was the first to cultivate 'poor' plants like lavender and olive trees, discard lilies, roses, and flowers of that kind. The house was decorated in beige with leather and chamois sofas, pieces of Provençal and Spanish furniture then totally out of fashion, and everything was in soft colors like a painting by Zurbarán." Visconti fell in love with Horst.

From Paris, Iribe called to announce his arrival. He would have a sleeper on the overnight express and arrive rested and ready for a tennis match in the morning. Paul Morand was inviting them on a cruise aboard his new boat—after tennis.

On Coco's tennis court the next morning, tragedy struck. Iribe was warming up when Coco joined him for a match. Halfway through the first set, she walked toward the net to tell him not to hit the ball so hard. He looked at her over the rim of his sunglasses, stumbled, and collapsed, suffering a massive coronary.

He died in a clinic in Menton without regaining consciousness. He was fifty-two.

26

POPULAR FRONT

The months after Paul Iribe's death were difficult for Gabrielle. Once again, Misia came running, offering comfort and a sympathetic ear. Coco had little to say. Again she was a woman on her own. As she had done since her childhood when calamity struck, she turned inward, swallowing her grief.

For the first time since she had started selling hats in Etienne Balsan's apartment in 1911, she let underlings run her business. On the long-distance telephone she told the staff to prepare the spring collection, for she would be staying in Roquebrune for a while. September was extraordinarily beautiful on the Riviera that year.

In October, she returned to Paris. The 1936 season was promising to be crucial. There were new male rivals—Marcel Rochas, who was credited with the first padded shoulders; and Mainbocher, a short, stocky, and relentlessly energetic American. Main Rousseau Bocher designed for Hollywood stars, and, at the recommendation of Lady Mendl, Wallis Simpson was choosing him as her designer.

That "Italian woman," however, was scoring all over. Schiaparelli had the British *Vogue* Christmas cover for 1935, and Cecil Beaton photographed Princess Karam Kapourthala, a much admired Indian beauty, wearing Schiaparelli's sari evening dresses and a cavalcade of Scap's coats and crepes in surrealist sets.

The new look for 1936 was the tunic line, pulled tight at the waist with a stiff jutting peplum, over a narrow skirt, which was often of pin pleats tight as crinkled crepe. Chanel's suits were gently fitted tweeds with open-necked white shirts; Schiaparelli's were exotic flights of fancy. Together with Salvador Dali, she created an evening dress with the skirt printed with a life-sized lobster and a few green motifs scattered on the bodice to represent parsley. To the surrealist painter's intense regret, his wish to splatter the dress with real mayonnaise was thwarted, but the gown received much publicity when Cecil Beaton photographed Mrs. Wallis Simpson wearing it.

Chanel and Schiaparelli were not only dividing the same pool of clients, they were making "schools" of fashion, and Gabrielle was now the designer for hesitant, unassertive women. Those who were reserved and feared bad taste more than anything else wore Chanel; cheeky, self-assured, and alluring women had fun with Schiaparelli's red eyelashes, black gloves with scarlet fingernails, coarse hairnets anchoring pancake hats, light blue satin pants showing under the lifted hem of a black evening dress. Scap added Lady Furness and several Hollywood stars to her list of clients, and captivated the fashion journalists at French *Vogue*, *Femina*, and the Parisian dailies who loved to report on the rivalry. "The era of the dressmaker, all bits and pieces and complicated seaming, gives place to that of the mathematician and architect," enthused *Vogue*, adding that the new mode is neither streamlined nor sentimental; "it is casual, bold, chunky and realistic; textures rough rather than smooth; colors subtly coordinated."

On Sunday, April 26, 1936, France went to the polls in heavy rain and returned—with a record 85 percent of registered voters casting their ballots—a leftist coalition. The advent of the Front Populaire was welcomed by the masses as a thrilling victory promising long-overdue social and economic reforms, and by a terrified right as bringing the country to the brink of communism. While the rich saw their fortunes and privileges threatened, workers celebrated the May 1 Labor Day. In a blaze of red banners and chants of "The International," they proclaimed the hopes and promises of a new tomorrow. The head of the coalition government was socialist Léon Blum, a man prey to self-doubts and self-criticism, and given to airing his soul-searching in public. At the opening sessions of the new Chamber, the rightist deputy François Xavier-Vallat taunted the premier for his Jewishness. The reactionary press picked up the anti-Semitic theme. "France under the Jew" was the title of the editorial in *L'Action Française* the day after Blum took office. Blum and his party had spent their entire lives in the opposition. Now, just turned sixty-four and without any cabinet experience, Blum formed a government, ready to launch the Popular Front experiment.

Because the term of the outgoing National Assembly did not lapse until the end of May, however, Blum could not constitutionally assume office until the beginning of June. Workers, so long submissive and increasingly fearful that the victory at the polls might be snatched from them, wanted the socialist administration to fulfill immediately its promises of paid vacation, extended family support, unemployment insurance, and a forty-hour work week. Without authorization from their unions or encouragement from the left-of-center parties, they launched a series of strikes that swelled to a tidal wave and threatened to wreck the Popular Front even before Blum could get to the helm. Strikes began at various airplane factories and, after May 26, spread to automobile workers. Borrowing from an American example of "sit-down" or "sit-in" strikes, workers occupied the premises, expelled the managers, or, in a few cases, locked them up. When the job action engulfed the textile industry, Gabrielle was dumbfounded. When it hit her own enterprise she took it as a personal affront. The nerve! Women on strike! What did the girls have against her? What would they *be* without her?

On the morning of Saturday, June 6, when Coco emerged from the Rue Cambon "back entrance" of the Ritz and crossed the street to go to work, she faced a scene that took her breath away. There, on the sidewalk in front of the boutique, stood a dozen of her salesladies smiling and waving to press photographers across the street. At the employees' entrance were fifty of her seamstresses in smocks. On the *porte cochère* hung the traditional strikers' collection box, handsomely decorated with ribbons, soliciting the support of passersby.

Chanel took one look, turned around, and disappeared into the Ritz.

Later in the morning a delegation of Chanel workers trooped to the Ritz. They did not use the back entrance but went around to the front on the Place Vendôme, past the doorman in his gold braid, and asked to see Mademoiselle. She sent word down that she refused to meet with any *workroom delegates*, but that she would, at her convenience, see her *workers* in her office.

René de Chambrun came to the hotel. Coco was furious; the lawyer counseled moderation. Premier Blum, who had taken office the day before, was scheduled to meet with business and labor leaders to put an end to the strikes.

Coco was being tested as never before. The House of Chanel was one of the trade's best managed in an industry where turmoil was a tradition. She had cultivated a strong team to run manufacturing and sales while she concentrated on designing collections. "The industry has a lot of prima donnas at the top who can't tolerate the development of *premières*," Chambrun would say. "Mademoiselle wasn't like that."

Chambrun persuaded her to meet her workers, but she took her time before she went down again.

When she reached the House of Chanel entrance, the workers' delegates refused to let her enter. For the second time that morning she retreated.

There was nothing to discuss, she told Chambrun. A sit-down strike on *my* dresses, she mumbled. That's an idea from your United States, a sit-down strike! Women on their behinds, it's obscene! And don't talk to me about wages. My wages are perfectly proper, and paid vacations!

She had rented a property next to the Duke of Westminster's at Mimizan and every year sent the most delicate of her apprentices to benefit from the fresh air. The more Chambrun listened the more he thought she talked like Iribe. Or like the Duke of Westminster, who burned coal unnecessarily so that miners could live.

Chambrun advised her to wait out the government's move. A Madame Renard, who had been Coco's private accountant since the time of Grand Duke Dmitri, came across the street. The workers considered her part of management and had ordered her to leave. No one was actually sitting on any dresses, she reported, but she was concerned for her boss. Paris would soon be in the hands of the rabble. By nightfall, the lawyer sent someone across the street to have a look. Most of the seamstresses had gone home, but the House of Chanel was effectively "occupied," as a notice on the door said.

Representatives of the leading employers' association and the labor leaders met Sunday afternoon at Blum's official residence, the Hôtel Matignon. The discussions, the first in French history, went on far into the night. With Blum doing most of the jawboning, the two sides reached an agreement in the early morning hours of Monday, June 8. The Matignon agreements—so named after the premier's residence in Rue de Varenne—were a series of "firsts." The workers would evacuate the factories and end their strikes in return for a policy of no reprisals, wage increases ranging from 7 to 15 percent, the right of collective bargaining, the right to unionize, a forty-hour work week, and an annual two-week paid vacation. The principle of collective bargaining existed in Germany before Hitler, in Britain and in the United States, but in France the Matignon agreements represented radical change.

Labor hailed the agreement while some of the big employers, who had urged Blum to initiate the talks, would say they had been forced to accept at the gunpoint of revolution. Union leaders had some difficulty regaining control of their rank and file, however, and four days after the agreement the strikes reached a new peak.

Gabrielle resisted the word *negotiate*, but by midweek she was doing just that. She responded to demands for implementation of the Matignon agreements by firing three hundred women. They refused to leave the premises. The tension rose on both sides. The mood among the workers was one of exhilaration. They might be working for notoriously low wages in an industry that catered to the whims and caprices of the fabulously rich, but there was change in the air. Working people were seizing the initiative. They had elected a Parliament and a government that shared their aspirations and was trying to achieve some of them.

Gabrielle, on the other hand, was mortally wounded by the occupation. Her workers were wrecking her achievement, and they had thrown her out of her own house.

Elsewhere in Paris, the walkouts were being settled. The Chanel workers wouldn't believe Coco when she offered to turn the whole business into a sort of workers' cooperative on condition she could manage it.

With her advisers she realized that if the strike wasn't settled by the end of July, there would be no hope of presenting a fall-winter collection. Schiaparelli, who had less trouble settling with her much smaller work force, was working with Salvador Dali to come up with a collection that promised to be striking. Her evening coats would include embroidered reproductions of Cocteau drawings, and her scarves and hats would be illustrated with reprints of news articles about herself. Resentment, if not envy and self-defense, demanded that Chanel swallow her pride.

She did not forgive, however. The House of Chanel was all she had left. Though she had risen from the humblest of origins, it was somehow beyond her to imagine the lives of her employees, where *they* had come from.

Decades later, she would rail against the "madness" of 1936. "People caught the thing like plague, like the Spanish flu. Even the peasants. With them it couldn't be wages, now could it? Because the land, as far as I know, doesn't pay you wages. In the southwest, the peasants went out and occupied the vineyards. You hear me? The vineyards. Don't tell me those people weren't sick in their heads! A farce with about as much sense to it as my workers having a sit-down strike on *my* dresses. A sit-down strike. Graceful, wouldn't you say? Attractive to think of women in such a position, on their behinds. I mean, what idiots those girls were!"

27

A BRAVE FACE

Coco tried to keep a brave face. Her heart was not in it, but she chose to fight her defeat with a charm offensive, to be seen, photographed, and talked about. She was bitter, exhausted, and depressed and began spending less time at the House of Chanel.

Modern management specialists have words for what ailed the House of Chanel—maturing markets and a weakened brand name. Her "line" was maturing, perhaps imperceptibly to her, along with her clientele. No fashion designer has ever stood still, or yet retained client loyalty. Coco, however, chose to believe her contributions to fashion were somehow permanent, that she was perhaps running out of luck. She consulted a fortune-teller. She was fifty-four. Was she thinking of retiring while she was on top? Did she fear the fate of Poiret if she persisted?

If the fashion press covered Schiaparelli with more zest than Chanel, it was because Scap's Place Vendôme showings were more exciting to write about than Coco's Rue Cambon affairs. Schiaparelli's "for the trade only" presentations were a sensory charge, extravagant and full of sheen and glitter. Ragna Fischer, a Danish journalist who covered the Paris fashion beat for a number of Scandinavian newspapers, would remember the Chanel shows as being "terribly sedate and a little bit dull." The celebrity clients occupied the gilt chairs while the fashion writers were huddled together at the bottom of a large mirrored staircase that Coco had had built in 1935, a staircase that became the hallmark of the House of Chanel shows. Mademoiselle always remained invisible during the presentations, sitting hidden in her favorite place between the mirrors at the top of the staircase.

"At Schiaparelli's you were rubbing shoulders with inspiration and devastating assertion," Fischer would say. "I remember especially the colors, the hysteria and tension. It was just marvelous." To go with her collection that had music as its theme, Scap orchestrated doll-sized violins, horns, and mandolins as costume jewelry. She also encouraged the wearing of bugs—grasshoppers, wasps, and dragonflies were pinned on clothing and repeated in embroidery and beading. Her unusual jewelry was wildly successful and widely copied.

Diana Vreeland would remember wearing both Schiaparelli and Chanel. "I loved the clothes I had in the thirties," she would write fifty years later. "I can remember a dress I had of Schiaparelli's that had fake bazooms—these funny little things that stuck out here. When you sat down, they sort of went . . . all I can say is that it was terribly chic. Don't ask me why, but it was. Another of my Schiaparellis that sticks in my mind was a black sheath with a long train in the form of a padded fishtail—I gave it to Gypsy Rose Lee, and she performed in it at the World's Fair—stalking the runway six times a day.

"I loved my clothes from Chanel. Everyone thinks of *suits* when they think of Chanel. That came later. If you could have seen my clothes from Chanel in the thirties—the dégagé gypsy skirts, the divine brocades, the little boleros, the roses in the hair, the paillettes nose *veils*—day and evening. And the ribbons were so pretty."

The fashion media were also discovering Cristóbal Balenciaga, a Spaniard who opened a boutique in Avenue Georges V where he showed his nonchalantly structured suits. The son of a fisherman, born near San Sebastian on the French border, Balenciaga had opened his own dressmaking establishment in San Sebastian when he was twenty and later expanded to Madrid and Barcelona. He was a perfectionist and made absolutely no concessions, in his workrooms or to his clients. Few people ever saw Balenciaga. He never appeared in his own salons, never answered letters, never gave parties or interviews, and barely allowed magazines to photograph his collections. He created parade dresses for royalty and celebrities, clothes that were beautiful but austere in spite of their richness. He had Chanel's flair for guessing next season's silhouette.

Patou's death in 1936 left Lucien Lelong as Coco's most immediate male rival. Lelong was not considered much of a creator, but women felt secure wearing his clothes, and two of his collaborators were to become top designers a decade later—Pierre Balmain and Christian Dior. Lelong was president of the new Chambre Syndicale de la Couture Parisienne that tried to be both management organization and union, and counted among its members the leading names in the industry.

Coco's friend David became king of England in January 1946. The constitutional crisis that ensued when he decided to marry Wallis Simpson moved into Gabrielle's living room nine months later, when Winston Churchill came to dine with her at the Ritz. King Edward VIII had drafted a proposed broadcast calling the British nation to rally behind him in his love for Wallis, but Prime Minister Stanley Baldwin refused to permit the use of the airwaves, while press baron Lord Beaverbrook suggested a delay in any decision. As a member of parliament, ardent royalist, and a friend of the king, Churchill also hoped a delay might sway the king to give up Wallis.

To make an evening of it, Coco asked Jean Cocteau to join Churchill and his son Randolph. The dinner was served in her suite, and Cocteau would remember Winston getting drunk and breaking out in tears. A king could not abdicate. "One doesn't put on someone else's costume," he cried. On December 10, Churchill helped David make some last-minute alterations to the abdication speech.

The Blum administration organized a new world's fair. The theme of the 1937 expo was public works and technology and not, as in 1925, the affirmation of the French luxury trade.

The show opened on May 1, Labor Day. Some of the French pavilions were not ready. The foreign exhibits were open, however, and the crowds thronged the Soviet Union's pavilion with its entrance statue of a forward-thrust couple whose hands were joined together holding aloft a hammer and sickle. The façade of the German pavilion also swept upward, toward a huge neoclassical eagle and swastika. The fair's sensation, however, was *Guernica*, Picasso's invective against war, hanging in the pavilion of the Spanish Republic.

Gabrielle used the gala opening and expo parties to court and be courted by photographers and journalists. Escorted by Christian Bérard, she arrived at the fairground wearing a dress so lightweight the press wondered what it was made of. Lightness was her new theme. She offered it as a challenge to Schiaparelli. Marlene Dietrich showed Scap's Russian furs, Joan Crawford modeled Vionnet's white taffeta gown.

Jean Renoir asked Chanel to do the French Revolution wardrobe for his film *La Marseillaise*. The filmmaker wanted her also to do the costumes for *La Grande Illusion*, but conflicting schedules delayed their next collaboration until *La Règle du jeu* in 1939. This comedy of manners must have reminded Coco of the time she spent at Royallieu and the games Etienne Balsan and his guests invented. Filmed at a château north of Moulins, *The Rules of the Game* was about a large house party, gathered for a hunt, where servants and masters begin to chase and shoot each other. The Chanel wardrobe was impeccably suited for this cruel slice of château life.

For the stage, she created the costumes for three Cocteau plays, *La Machine infernale*, *Les Chevaliers de la Table Ronde*, and a revival of *Oedipe-Roi*. Her wardrobe for the latter was booed as being heavy and outmoded.

She still supported Cocteau, paid his bills at the Hotel Castille where he lived, paid for his detoxification cures, and picked him up, literally, when rough cruising landed him in a hospital. His lover Marcel Khill beat him so savagely that he suffered cracked ribs. Like Radiguet and Desbordes before him, Khill reverted to heterosexuality, taking up with an actress. Coco was seen with Stravinsky at theater premieres, and with a new beau, Fulco della Verdura, an artist whose full Sicilian name was Fulco, Duke della Verdura, Marquess Santosfeno della Cerda. She patronized the revived Ballets Russes, now called Ballets de Monaco, under the direction of René Blum, the premier's brother. Coco's friend from *Le Train bleu* days, Serge Lifar, was the troupe's premier dancer, and she attended the reborn ballet's debut with *Seventh Symphony*, choreographed by George Balanchine in sets by Bérard. At a post-premiere midnight supper, she dined with the dancers, Dali, and Auric.

Coco showed her fall 1937–38 collection on May 5. "Sex appeal is the prime motif of the Paris collection," wrote British *Vogue*, "and sex appeal is no longer a matter of subtle appeal." Chanel showed a gold lamé evening dress and chopped jacket of pressed pleats; Schiaparelli made an evening headscarf of gold embroidery. But it was the colors that the fashion writers noted. In 1938, they reported, women would dress by color—

cardinal red, emerald green, sulphur yellow, and Schiaparelli's "shocking pink," mixed with plummy maroons and metallic gold. Hats were "quite ridiculous," *Vogue* reported, "leaning towers of grosgrain topped into hats, huge halos and cartwheels, huge brims draped with black veiling falling to the waist, and pure fantasies like Schiaparelli's wicker basket hat filled with cellophane butterflies and flowers."

Coco lashed out against the fashion magazines' overheated prose and, more privately, against homosexuals, the principal offenders in her view. Couture was not hyperbole, she said, it was a technique, a craft, a business.

In recalling the 1930s with Paul Morand ten years later, she would speak with vehemence against homosexual mentality that pervaded the industry. "When a woman is dumb she sees in him a weak person, funny to be with, and not very dangerous; when she's smart she finds him to be someone who divines her, understands and listens to her. Since all women, whether stupid or intelligent, love the flytrap of compliments and since pederasts know how to manipulate praise, or have the gall, or the malice, to toss out immoderate adoration, women are their chosen victims. Women are always ready to believe them. They speak the same language, the stinging tongue of implication, heinous gibes, and baffling hypocrisy.

"They put around women's necks garlands of compliments, necklaces of flowery flattery, with which they strangle them. And their beautiful friends are ecstatic; women no longer dress to please men but to please the pederasts, and to shock other women, because what the boys like is what is far out, outré. God, the number of young women I've seen die under the influence of 'awful queers'—death, drugs, ugliness, ruin, divorce, scandal, nothing is too much when it comes to demolish the competition and to take revenge on a woman. To triumph over her they follow her like a shadow, everywhere, except in bed. Homosexuals become stage designers, hairdressers, interior decorators, and especially couturiers. They rush into deadly eccentricity, into their own artificial netherworld.

"When I say pederasts, I mean the pederast mentality, which is even more widespread. We all know nice family men who are 'inverts,' fathers who are bent over cribs and, at coming-out balls, scour the rooms for decent husbands for their daughters. Homosexuals are the escorts of high society, the life of decadence, and as such the germs of bewitching epidemics. They are the ones who inspire hats no woman can wear, the ones who acclaim unwearable dresses, they are the canny, chatterbox commentators on stilt heels, the lethal publicists for furniture upholstered with satin. They are the only men who love makeup and red nail polish. They make up the backbiting and perceptive army for whom cynical pederasts with their beards, dirty knots of hair, gnawed fingernails, and decayed teeth are only the forerunners. They don't have the avant-garde tastes of the veterans, but they serve as links between the old guard and womanhood; they are the ones who make up the mood and the climate."

Chanel spent the summer of 1937 at Roquebrune. She sent an appropriate wedding gift to David, now the Duke of Windsor, and Wallis Simpson, who was married in a Mainbocher outfit at the Château Candé in Touraine, south of Paris, June 3, 1937. Two weeks later, Léon Blum resigned.

"I've had enough," he told William C. Bullitt, President Roosevelt's ambassador to France. "Everything I have attempted has been blocked." In a little over one year the Popular Front had run its course. The rich had never had confidence and had never stopped exporting their capital, generating billions of francs of losses for the Banque de France. Blum had been urged to regulate the export of gold and foreign exchange, as Hitler had done, but he feared such constraints on capital would destroy the faith in the economy. Also, as the first Socialist prime minister in French history, he was determined to keep his word and "to exercise power only within the framework of capitalism."

Coco fell a little bit in love with an American that summer, and when she was in her eighties would say she almost ran off with him. Harrison Williams was the kind of American she liked, a self-made man who began as a streetcar conductor in Avon, Ohio, and went on to make his fortune. Ten years her senior, Williams lived in Bayville, Long Island, and, with or without his beautiful socialite wife, spent most of the year in Palm Beach, Florida, or the Riviera.

Coco thought he was the most distinguished man she had ever met. His wife, Mona, was a friend of Ambassador Bullitt and of the Duchess of Windsor. Cecil Beaton photographed her for fashion magazines and cruised the Caribbean and Mediterranean with her and her friends.

"My wife is a fashion model, just a model," Harrison told Coco one morning. "Come with me."

"Too late, my dear," she answered.

A year earlier she might have done it, she would tell Claude Baillén, her last confidante. "He had a yacht, and isn't that the best way to start an amour? We were in his wife's house, Westminster was still alive. The only thing I regret is that I didn't leave with Williams."

The government of Camille Chautemps, a weak and ineffectual middle-of-the-road politician, was no more successful in reviving the economy than the Popular Front had been. The franc kept sliding, the economy became more depressed, while the Popular Front majority in the National Assembly split along the Socialist-Communist fault line. On March 11, 1938, when Hitler sent his troops into his native Austria, there was no government in France. Chautemps had resigned the day before over the need for executive powers to deal with the financial crisis.

Four days later, when cheering Viennese acclaimed Hitler and their country's *Anschluss* with the Third Reich, Blum had formed a government once again. In the most heartrending speech of his life, he appealed to all political factions to come together in a government of National Union. It was inconceivable, he said, that the parties of the conservative opposition, with their long tradition of patriotism, would refuse to join with the left-of-center majority to give the nation the unity it needed. Paul Reynaud, a moderate conservative, was in favor of a coalition government. When some right-wingers protested against joining a government that included Communists, Reynaud retorted, "It is not Stalin who enters Vienna today, who will menace Prague tomorrow. It is Hitler." Still, the assembled opposition rejected Blum's proposal 152 to 5. Blum's Popular Front government lasted less than a month.

Despite the political turmoil, the French upper class carried on in its usual style. The great costume ball of the summer was given by Count Etienne de Beaumont. Guests came dressed as characters from the plays and period of Pierre Racine, whose tercentenary was celebrated. Maurice de Rothschild went as the Ottoman Bajazet, wearing his mother's famous diamonds on his turban and the rare Renaissance jewels that were a part of the family's Cellini collection on his sash. Coco came as a "La Belle Dame sans Merci."

Serge Lifar escorted Coco to a fête given by U.S. ambassador Bullitt at the embassy residence. In Versailles, Lady Mendl (the former Elsie de Wolfe) gave a circus party of Gatsbyesque proportions for seven hundred guests. In aquamarines, diamonds, and a white organdy Mainbocher dress, the hostess was the ringmaster in a ring, with acrobats in satin and paillettes, with ponies and clowns. Guests danced on a dance floor built on thousands of tiny springs so that it gently heaved with the rhythms. Concealed spotlights turned the garden into a dream landscape. Coco was escorted by Armand de Gramont. She was seen talking with the Duchess of Windsor, whose wardrobe, besides her Mainbocher, Schiaparelli, and Molyneux dresses, finally included several Chanel originals. The Windsors were fully settled in their Paris home at 24 Boulevard Suchet, a four-story residence on the edge of the Bois de Boulogne.

Coco spent the rest of the summer at Roquebrune. Many of her best friends were on the Riviera—Paul and Hélène Morand, Bérard and the irrepressible Cocteau. The Duke and Duchess of Windsor were renting a British newspaper magnate's house in Cap d'Antibe. Even Loelia, the Duchess of Westminster, was there, although Bendor spent the summer aboard *The Flying Cloud.* The Churchills were no longer summering at Cap Ferrat or sailing with Bendor, however. Winston was busy campaigning for a rapid buildup of the Royal Air Force. His dire warnings of German rearmament were still ignored by the Conservative government of Neville Chamberlain, but events confirmed the accuracy of his information on Hitler's plans and progress. "He is like one of those big dolls with weights in their feet," Coco said of him. "The harder you knock them down the quicker they bob up again."

With the help of Condé Nast, Horst had emigrated to the United States and was working full-time at *Vogue* in New York. But Cecil Beaton came to visit. So did Jojo and Roossadana. The Serts were on a Mediterranean cruise and had made landing at Monaco. Coco could barely recognize Roossy. The once gorgeous girl was a specter of her former self, emaciated and wild-looking. The cruise was Jojo's idea. He didn't believe in disease, and as if to confirm the benefits of sea air, the thirty-two-year-old Roossy had gone swimming for hours. Alarmed by Roossy's permanent fever, cough, and unnatural thinness, Coco suggested the Serts see a lung specialist. X rays revealed an advanced stage of tuberculosis.

Doctors insisted Roossy be placed in a sanatorium. When she refused, Coco took charge. She was sick herself, she told Roossy, begging her to accompany her to a clinic in Prangins, Switzerland. The ruse worked. Roossy agreed to go with Coco. When they were alone in the *Train bleu* compartment, Roossy rolled up her sweater. "You see, the last gifts from Sert," she said showing deep bruises on her body. Jojo had hurt her, furious to see her leave. Roossy was hospitalized. Misia came from Paris. When she was told she could not see Roossy because the smallest upset could be fatal to the patient, she was sure it was Chanel who didn't want to let her see Roossy. On December 16, 1938, Roossy died. She was thirty-two.

In retrospect, fashion writers would attribute prescience to the Paris fashion designers of 1939 and talk of useful looks as if the designers already had war in mind. At the time, however, the fashion press called the 1939 Paris styles a hymn to innocence. "Paris, the worldly, the sophisticated— Paris, where a woman is hardly considered a passable beauty until she is thirty-five—this Paris has suddenly gone completely innocent, quaint, modest, girlish," hummed *Vogue*. "For evening your clothes will have a modest grace about them. You can choose between the provoking gypsy modesty of Chanel's bodice-and-skirt dresses, Mainbocher's peasant types, or the eighteenth-century modesty that is in every collection." Coco's fashion was a grand gesture, full of short, fitted jackets, pocketed skirts, a virtuoso feat with a red-white-and-blue wink that was more a homage to Iribe's patriotism than acknowledgment of the threat of war. Chanel was interviewed on a radio show broadcast for the first time by America's National Broadcasting Corporation (NBC) directly from Paris. Scap also appeared on the program, but the hostess, of course, interviewed them separately.

Events bigger than fashion overshadowed the collection shows. In January, General Francisco Franco's armies were in the suburbs of Barcelona and almost half a million Republican soldiers and civilians fled to the French border. A month later the government of the Spanish Republic fled into French exile, leaving its mangled armies and a starving Madrid at the mercy of the fascists. On March 13, Hitler marched into Czechoslovakia and three weeks later Mussolini invaded Albania, giving Italy a springboard for an attack on Greece. As coalition premier Edouard Daladier assumed emergency powers, France and Britain began talks with the Soviet Union on a "triple alliance" to prevent Hitler from overrunning Poland.

Coco was in Roquebrune when the news of the German-Soviet nonaggression pact changed the whole balance of power in Hitler's favor. To the consternation of London and Paris, Stalin chose the pact with Berlin, which offered him the double advantage of staying out of a war with Germany and getting back the territories in the Baltic, Poland, and Romania, which had been taken from the Soviet Union under western pressure at the end of the Great War. Léon Blum was sure the French Communist party would be torn apart, but the Daladier government suppressed *L'Humanité* and *Ce Soir* when the two communist dailies expressed lukewarm support of Stalin's realpolitik.

Coco returned to Paris to prepare the winter 1939–40 collection. Conservatives had little desire to fight fascism, which they secretly preferred to any Popular Front, and now the right was joined by millions of communists who felt betrayed by Stalin. Most Frenchmen had little confidence in the Daladier administration and many couldn't see the reason it was necessary to fight for Poland after having deserted socialist Austria and Czechoslovakia.

General mobilization in France was ordered August 26. Coco's nephew was among the million men called up. Leaving Lembeye, a mountain village in the Pyrenees north of Pau where he lived in a house Coco had bought for him and his family, André Palasse came through Paris on his way to induction. In a flush of awakened emotions, Coco demanded to see him. His health was not the best. His long years in England made him eligible for service and quick promotion in the British army, but he wanted to serve in a French unit.

Coco was home at the Ritz September 2 when, in response to Hitler's invasion of Poland, Britain and France declared war. Three weeks later, she closed the House of Chanel. Without notice, she laid off her entire staff. Only the boutique selling perfume would remain open.

28

CLOSING THE HOUSE OF CHANEL

In an industry thriving on overstatement and amplification, the closing of the premier couture house became Chanel's treason. Her workers tried to stop her. They were convinced it was her revenge for 1936, and immediately appealed to the Confédération Générale du Travail (CGT), the labor federation. The government had more pressing things to worry about. As fall—the loveliest autumn Paris had known in decades—slipped into winter, the country settled into the "phony war." After Poland's fall, German and French forces merely stood and glowered at each other across the Rhine River.

The lull on the front—and a need for home-front morale boosting—changed ministerial minds. The government wanted Chanel to stay open for prestige purposes, for the propaganda value. There would be charity balls and fashion parades, as in the First War.

Coco laughed. High fashion for the troops?

She was bitter, tired, and discouraged. In retrospect, she would have several explanations for the closing. She owed her success to the war, the other one, the Big War, she said, and she was convinced that this time would be different, that the future would not be a time for fashion. Another explanation was that on September 2, 1939, the thousands of women she employed simply vanished because they all had husbands, fathers, brothers going off to war. "In a few hours the place was empty." In talking to Marcel Haedrich twenty years later, she would say it seemed the right thing to do. "I told myself, 'You'll leave everything nice and shipshape, and do something else.' I was wrong. They never stopped selling fashion during the war."

There were rumors that she felt eclipsed by Schiaparelli. Still, one distant friend expressed his approval of her decision. From his retreat at Solesmes, Pierre Reverdy wrote to tell her he had read about the closing in a local newspaper and that the only thing to do in the circumstances was to lie low and keep quiet. "The point in life," he wrote, "is to find equilibrium in what is inherently unstable."

General Maurice Gamelin, the supreme commander, had eighty-five divisions facing an enemy, but after a perfunctory "Saar offensive," all remained quiet on the Rhine. Britain's small contingent of two divisions didn't reach the "front" until the end of September. By loudspeakers and large signs the Germans chided the frontline French about the absurdity of "dying for Danzig" and blamed the English for the whole thing. "Don't shoot. We won't if you don't." Often French troops would hoist crude signs of their own signifying their agreement. Sometimes Wehrmacht troops across the river would cheer soccer games played by Frenchmen on the riverbank.

Coco heard from her nephew, André. He was in the first line of defense. As for the rest of the family, she cut them all off. In October, she wrote to Lucien telling him the closing of the House of Chanel meant she was reduced nearly to poverty. "You cannot count on me for anything as long as circumstances stay the way they are," she wrote. She was a millionairess, but in closing her business she felt it was time to cut off the allowance to this fifty-one-year-old retiree. Touched by her purported destitution, he wrote back offering her his savings. Her message to Alphonse was similar. She was broke; Alphonse would have to stop thinking of her as his last resort.

Most Frenchmen felt there was no need for sacrifice. So long as the Germans didn't attack, why indeed shed French blood for already-lost Danzig, or Gdansk, as the Poles called the Baltic city. At night Paris was blacked out as protection against air attack. Gas masks were distributed, but the air raids never came, and life returned to near-normal. The theaters, music halls, and movie houses that had closed during the first days of the war reopened. Serge Lifar was dancing at the Opéra; Maurice Chevalier and Josephine Baker played to packed houses at the Casino de Paris. But Renoir's *La Règle du jeu,* for which Chanel designed the wardrobe, was hooted off the screen at its premiere on the Champs

Elysées in May for its portrayal of moral confusion, and banned as de-moralizing.

Molyneux presented an abbreviated mid-season collection. Instead of fifteen runway models, he had four; instead of one hundred garments, he had thirty, but Madame Gamelin, the wife of the armed forces chief, was in attendance.

Coco lost her chauffeur to the draft. With gasoline rationing and un-certain road conditions she decided to stay in Paris, but kept looking for a new chauffeur. Should things go wrong, she'd like to be able to leave.

To improve her private quarters at the Ritz, she paid the hotel to build a low flight of stairs from her two-room suite to a garret bedroom. Her new bedroom was small and narrow like a convent cell, but she liked it that way. Besides an icon that Stravinsky had once given her and a pair of statues on the mantelpiece, the only other object was Boy Capel's thick, black watch, still working and on time.

There was a sense of déjà vu about the hotel in wartime. As they had done in 1914, people who could afford it closed their houses in Auteuil and Neuilly and moved to the Ritz. They had lost their footmen to the draft, sent their children to the country, hidden the family jewels and paintings in cellars and safes, and suddenly found their big suburban residences distant and cold. Along with Cocteau, whose "rabbit hole" room Coco paid for, the immutable Ritz harbored Lady Mendl in the Imperial suite, Reginald and Daisy Fellowes in the royal suite, Schiaparelli and her daughter Gogo, Countess Minou de Montgomery, the actor Sacha Guitry, several important politicians, and many older women who wouldn't desert Paris for anything.

In February 1940 France offered itself the luxury of a government crisis. Three hundred representatives abstained when Daladier asked for a vote of confidence on the way he conducted the war. His unexpected loss of a majority brought Paul Reynaud, Daladier's energetic finance minister, to power. Reynaud agreed with his friend Colonel Charles de Gaulle that the war should be conducted more vigorously, and he had established close contacts with Britain's admiralty chief Winston Churchill, whose ideas he shared and whose energies and imagination he admired. Reynaud was thought by many to be too "Anglophile."

Suddenly in April the lull was over. After Hitler's surprise attack and occupation of Denmark and Norway, the Luftwaffe struck airfields in northern France. German armor crossed the borders of Holland and Belgium. In two days seven German panzer divisions pierced the "impenetrable" Ardennes and began rolling toward the Meuse and Sedan rivers. By May 16, the Allies had suffered their first disaster, causing panic in the high command and consternation in Paris. Three weeks later, General Erwin Rommel's armor swept across northern France to the Channel. The Luftwaffe hammered the ragged remnants of Allied armies standing at the water's edge at Dunkirk. In London, Chamberlain resigned, and Churchill, promising nothing "but blood, toil, tears, and sweat," became prime minister. Desperately, more than 300,000 men were ferried across to England from the beaches of Dunkirk.

The outskirts of Paris were bombed on June 4, and L'Exode, the flight of the civilian population ahead of the German army, began. Six days later the Reynaud government abandoned Paris and in a convoy of ministerial limousines fled south to Tours on the Loire River.

At the Ritz, Coco arranged her personal belongings in several huge trunks and had the concierge get the house painter to stencil her name on them. She paid her bill two months in advance, explaining that she was going away for a while. A hastily recruited chauffeur refused to take to the road in Coco's Rolls-Royce, and it was in the driver's own car that she headed south. Millions were fleeing homes, jobs, friends, and neighbors, all heading south spreading disorder and depleting stores. There were heavily packed limousines, buses, trucks, people on bicycles with their belongings stacked on little trailers, horse-drawn farm wagons loaded with grandparents and babies on top of piles of furniture. On June 10, Italy declared war. The next night, Italian bombers, responding to a Royal Air Force strike on Turin, carried out a series of raids on Toulon and two Riviera towns near Roquebrune. Attack planes also strafed the civilian columns of the Exodus.

The Italian bombings of the Riviera made Chanel decide against Roquebrune. Cocteau and the Aurics were in Aix-en-Provence, smoking their last reserves of opium, but Coco and her driver decided to head toward the Spanish border.

Churchill, his foreign secretary Lord Halifax, and members of his high command flew to Tours. Hastily, he was put up at the Château de Muguet, while less than a hundred miles to the north, the first German forces crossed the Seine below Paris and pressed forward along the Marne River. Going into a strategy session that night, Reynaud was gloomy, Churchill cheerful. The situation was desperate Churchill was told. He imagined

Parisians fighting block by block, house by house, a burning city collapsing on a garrison that refused to accept defeat. Coldly, a French general
told him reducing Paris to ashes would in no way affect the final outcome.
Churchill suggested that if coordinated warfare became impossible, the
French could carry on in guerrilla fashion until the Americans came into
the war. This time the eighty-four-year-old Marshal Henri Pétain objected
that by the time the United States made up its mind, guerrilla warfare
would have reduced the entire country to ashes. The alternative was no
less appalling, said the British prime minister. Over coffee and cognac,
Pétain told Churchill what he was too ashamed to tell Reynaud—France
would have to seek an armistice with Nazi Germany.

Before Churchill flew back to London, he drew Admiral Jean Darlan
aside and said, "Darlan, I hope you will never surrender the fleet." The
admiral replied, "We shall never hand it over to Germany or Italy. Orders
to scuttle will be given in the event of danger."

As Paris was declared an open city and the French army ordered to
fall back toward the Loire, Gabrielle and her chauffeur reached Pau.
Afternoon showers gave way to a sun that glittered in the steep slate roof
of the château, where, thirty years before, she had fallen in love with Boy
Capel. She continued to Lembeye and the house she had bought for
André Pallasse and his family.

It was the first time she spent more than a few hours with her god-
daughter. The ten-year-old Tiny—Bendor's nickname had stuck—was a
vivacious child with a mind of her own. A few years earlier, André had
brought her to the Ritz, where "Auntie Coco" had tossed a ball to her
and stuffed her with *éclairs* at tea. Coco had little experience dealing with
children, but Tiny preferred to be talked to like an adult.

The Reynaud government was not far away. Senators and representatives in chaotic Bordeaux were evenly split into two camps—one in favor
of the government leaving for French North Africa, the other advocating
that it remain in France. Marshal Pétain thought that not only the Battle
of France was lost, but the war itself. Britain was an island nation and
might be able to fight on, but on the Continent the Germans and their
Italian allies were triumphant from Norway to Greece. Pierre Laval
thought the only man who could negotiate an armistice with Hitler was
Pétain, the hero of Verdun. After the Germans occupied Paris on June 14
and, two days later Bordeaux, the Reynaud coalition collapsed, and
the old soldier was named premier. De Gaulle saluted his superior officer,

drove to an airfield outside Bordeaux, and flew to London. In a broadcast hastily arranged by Churchill, de Gaulle reminded his countrymen that "overseas France"—nearly half of Africa and the smattering of far-flung territories in the Caribbean and the Pacific—was not in enemy hands, that part of the navy was safe in Algerian and Moroccan ports, that whole divisions had made it across the Channel from the Dunkirk beaches, and that the British were fighting on. Pétain also went on the air. Saying the combat must cease, his broadcast sapped what little fighting fervor was left in the retreating troops.

On the eighteenth, Hitler paid his only visit to Paris, arriving at dawn. His staff car whipped through empty streets. He stood briefly on the flowing steps of the Trocadéro and looked across the Seine at the Eiffel Tower. Propaganda Chief Paul Josef Goebbels's personal representative ordered Serge Lifar to improvise a gala at the Opéra the next evening. Lifar tried to get out of it, saying he had no money in his budget for such a soirée and, besides, he was out of training. Hitler came to the Opéra early the following morning, and Lifar would boast about the hours he spent alone with the Führer. Laying a lascivious hand on the arm of the nearest young male dancer, Lifar would say, "Only two men have fondled me like this—Diaghilev and Hitler." The gala was canceled, however, because France accepted its military defeat and an armistice would be signed the following day. In the clearing in the Compiègne forest where the Allies had imposed their armistice terms to the Germans in 1918, Hitler and his generals climbed into General Foch's old *wagon-lit* on June 21, and dictated terms to a French army delegation.

Playing a refugee was not Coco's style. Everybody was trying to get home. André, she learned, was among the 300,000 French soldiers held in detention camps by the Germans and expected to be liberated and sent home in the coming weeks. She met up with Marie-Louise Bousquet, a droll and lively Parisienne whom Coco had last seen at Etienne de Beaumont's costume ball. Marie-Louise was a friend of Bérard, Cecil Beaton, and the Windsors. The duke and the duchess had fled to Spain, but the British government just didn't know what to do with them, she told Coco.

In the last week of June, Coco and Marie-Louise decided to try to make it back to Paris together. Coco had a chauffeur and a car, Bousquet knew someone who had sixty gallons of gasoline. The fuel was poured into jerry cans and whatever other containers could be found; in the summer heat, the car stank of gasoline.

They were down to their last liter of gasoline when they reached Vichy. The old spa city, where Coco had once tried to become a music-hall *gommeuse*, was the capital of the southern half of France, which Hitler had decided not to occupy. The government of Marshal Pétain and Pierre Laval was camping out in the various hotels. U.S. ambassador William Bullitt interviewed officials of the new government and, in a dispatch to President Roosevelt, wrote that "the French leaders desire to cut loose from all that France has represented during the past two generations, that their physical and moral defeat has been so absolute that they have accepted completely for France the fate of becoming a province of Nazi Germany. . . . The simple people of the country are as fine as they have ever been. The upper classes have failed completely."

"Everybody was laughing, drinking champagne," Coco would remember. "The ladies wore hats as big as this. I said, 'Interesting, it's the high season.' A man turned toward me and asked what I meant. I said, 'I mean people are pretty cheerful here.' The lady next to the gentleman calmed him down."

Marie-Louise spent the night in a folding chair in a laundry room and somebody offered Coco the bed of a gendarme who went on duty at 8:00 P.M. "A gentleman offered me his bed, on the condition that I share it with him. I managed to soften up the owner of a hotel where they knew me. They put me up in the garret where the heat was killing me. I got up every hour and went to the bathroom just to breathe."

Pétain had made Pierre Laval his minister of state and together they tried to curry favor with the dictator to have him go easy on a defeated nation. In an atmosphere of fear, defeatism, and confusion, they abolished the Republic and instituted L'Etat Français, with Pétain chief of the French State and Laval vice president.

At the same time, they did manage to frustrate the Führer in certain areas. Under the armistice terms, Vichy France was supposedly free to govern itself, but Hitler kept adding new conditions and continued to pressure Vichy to work with Germany toward Europe's New Order. By adamantly adhering to the armistice terms, Pétain refused to do the one thing Hitler wanted most—hand over the fleet. Hitler could force the issue militarily, but that would mean occupying all of France.

On July 3, Churchill preempted the issue, seizing, disabling, or destroying all French warships. In Algeria, the French fleet at Mers el-Kébir refused the British ultimatum to sink their own ships or be sunk, and the RAF bombed and torpedoed the French warships as they tried to escape the harbor. A total of 1,300 French sailors died. In Vichy, the mood was one of anger and resentment. Such British ruthlessness would have been welcome had it been executed against the Germans before the fall of France. Darlan was ready to declare war on England.

For Churchill, who announced the action in the House of Commons, it was a boost. The British people were facing the enemy alone now, and by striking mercilessly at an ex-ally, the government showed it feared nothing and would stop at nothing.

A government official managed to sell Coco a ration of gasoline. The only portable food she and Marie-Louise could find was candy and fruit pies, and with that they headed north.

In Moulins, Coco directed the driver to the outdoor market where her grandparents had once had their stall, but everything was deserted. She told the chauffeur to detour toward the mountain villages and they ended up in Bourbon-L'Archambault, a village where the Romans had first channeled the hot springs into baths. The resort was deserted. Hotel owners were distressed, every room had been booked for the season but nobody had showed up. Coco and Marie-Louise got three rooms with baths.

While Marie-Louise and the driver soaked in their tubs, Coco went for a walk. A small boy sitting on a wall caught her eye. The way he sat looked dangerous and as she approached he fell. She ran forward.

The boy didn't move. A pregnant woman came running with another child. "I'm his mother!" she shouted. Coco said no one should try to lift the boy until a doctor examined him for head injuries and fractures. He was crying. His mother also burst into tears. Coco opened her handbag and pulled out a hundred-franc note.

As soon as the boy saw the bank note, he stopped crying. Coco realized it was a con. "It's sad to say. He gave the money to his mother, who said, 'Now we can eat tonight.' "

Back at the hotel, Coco slipped into her bath. For someone who hated filth and grime, the soak was an event that would stay in her mind. "The water was black when I got up."

Marie-Louise asked what Coco had done during the afternoon.

"My dear, I gave a hundred francs to a little boy who fell off a wall and is eating tonight."

Charity toward common people was not Gabrielle's prime virtue and in retelling the story years later she would underline the extraordinary circumstances of her gesture. War made people do inexplicable things, she intimated. Was a hundred francs handed to an injured and hungry child her way of exorcising the national catastrophe, or was the sheepish gratitude and despair she read in the eyes of the boy and his mother a too-blinding mirror image of her own forlorn childhood in these hills?

29

SPATZ

~~~~~~~~~~~~~~~~

Sandbags formed zigzag obstacles at the Porte d'Orléans when Coco, Marie-Louise, and the chauffeur reached the Paris city limits at the end of August 1940. Down the Avenue du Maine nothing moved, but on Boulevard du Montparnasse they saw a few people, including girls sitting beside German officers at the terrace of La Coupole. Only German soldiers were visible in Rue de Rivoli and Place de la Concorde. A swastika flew over the Ritz. Anyone without an *Ausweiss*, a permit issued by the Germans, was barred by the sentry from entry into the hotel. Standing at the entrance to the lobby, which was filled with German officers and civilians, Chanel managed to draw the attention of the hotel manager. He came to the door, and told her she'd have to go to the Kommandantur.

"Dirty as I am?" she asked.

There would be several versions of what happened next.

In one account, no one tried to stop her as she made her way through the lobby. Her handsome apartment had been requisitioned, but the manager was able to offer her a little room on the Rue Cambon side of the hotel. She asked for no more. In another version, she told the manager to tell the high command she had arrived. After she'd gone upstairs, freshened up, and changed, she'd go and see the commandant herself. In yet another retelling, a Wehrmacht general saw her name stenciled on the trunks, and said, "If we're talking about the Mademoiselle Chanel of fashion and perfume fame, she can stay."

Whatever version we choose to believe, she got to stay at the Ritz.

She phoned Misia. Her friend, who had never left Paris and had seen the Germans march down the Rue de Rivoli from Jojo Sert's apartment balcony, was incensed that Coco would even want to live at the Ritz. Gabrielle retorted that all hotels would be occupied sooner or later.

Next, Coco went to 31 Rue Cambon. The ground-floor boutique was filled with German soldiers buying the only item on sale—Chanel No. 5. When the stock ran out, the *Fritzes* picked up the display bottles marked with the intertwined double C and paid for them. It was something to take back to the *Fräulein*, something that proved they had been in Paris.

Schiaparelli and Mainbocher had fled to America, Molyneux to London; but twelve houses managed to prepare collections for 1941 and sold their creations to recently moneyed black marketeers, German wives, and those French mistresses of Wehrmacht officers who dared to wear them.

As president of the Chambre Syndicale, Lucien Lelong successfully resisted German efforts to move the couture business, lock, stock, and barrel, to Berlin and Vienna, and in delicate negotiations, managed to keep 80 percent of the reduced work force, despite ever-increasing demands for labor for German war industries. The Occupation created an uncommon solidarity. When Madame Grès, as Alix Czereskow decided to call herself now, and Balenciaga were ordered to close for two weeks for exceeding the authorized yardage in some of their dresses, other houses joined forces to finish their collections for them.

Otto Abetz, the Reich ambassador and virtual ruler of occupied France, put the first anti-Jewish laws into effect. Pétain and Laval in Vichy went even further. Governing by decree, they stripped the citizenship from anyone who had left the country between May 10 and June 13—such as de Gaulle and his tiny band of followers—and ordered the creation of a special High Court to try ex-ministers who had "betrayed their responsibilities"—meaning Daladier and Blum. They began a review of all naturalizations and closed all public offices to anyone born of a foreign father. The Vichy decrees stipulated that no Jew could hold public office or work in the press, radio, or entertainment.

Collaborators—they liked to call themselves realists—were out in the open. Abetz, who was married to a Frenchwoman, Suzanne de Bruycker, wanted France to return to a semblance of normalcy. With the help of his Propagandastaffel he allowed newspapers to reappear, publishers to resume publishing, theaters to reopen, and the film industry to start up again. The leading authors, however, kept their distance. André Gide, André Malraux, Henry de Montherland, Colette, and others were holed up on the Côte d'Azur, mostly house-sitting villas hastily evacuated by the British owners. Serge Lifar became the director of ballet at the Opéra and, as such, greeted the top Nazis coming to Paris. Coco might catch a glimpse of Foreign Minister von Ribbentrop and his entourage at the Ritz, but Lifar entertained Reichmarschall Hermann Goering, traveling with Hitler's secretary, Gerda Daranowsky. The stories of how Lifar had entertained Hitler back in June reached London, and Free French broadcasts on the BBC now condemned him to death.

Although the "border" between German-occupied France and Vichy France was sealed, the Germans gave Lifar *Ausweisse* to travel to Vichy for interviews with the Fétain regime. After one of his trips, the dancer told Coco that President Laval wanted him to look out for her. Lifar was leaving when President Laval said, "Insofar as you have any influence in Paris, take care of the *Auvergnats*. Chanel, and all the others."

In September, the Germans began releasing most of the 300,000 prisoners of war who had been interned at the suspension of hostilities. When André Palasse was not among the liberated POWs, Coco decided to approach a German she had observed in the entourage of von Ribbentrop, a tall, blond aristocratic-looking man who spoke exquisite French and was always in civilian clothes.

The reason Hans Gunther von Dincklage spoke fluent French, he explained when she approached him, was that he had been an attaché at the German embassy in the Rue de Rivoli. Over dinner at the hotel, the distinguished Dincklage explained that he had lived in Paris as a diplomat since 1928. He was from Hannover, of Lower Saxony gentry. His mother was English. He had once played polo at Deauville. Since his divorce in 1935, he had charmed a Parisian lady, "very rich, very attractive, and not one hundred percent Aryan," he smiled over coffee and cognac. The lady had just left Paris with her husband, and Dincklage had moved into their apartment on the Rue Pergolese.

"Call me Spatz," he said. "My friends do. It's German for sparrow."

When she got to the point, he said he was not in a position to have her nephew sprung from Wehrmacht custody. He had a boyhood friend, however, who might be able to help. Why didn't she meet Captain Momm?

Theodor Momm was a cavalry captain. Hitler's war demanded raw materials and services from all occupied territories, and Rittmeister Momm's job was to mobilize the French textile industry and to assimilate its resources into the German war effort. Momm's family had been in textiles for five generations and he had grown up in Belgium, where his father had managed a dye factory. Coco warmed up to him considerably when he found a way of repatriating André Palasse. Momm ordered a small textile mill reopened in suburban St. Quentin. Next, he convinced his superiors that its proprietor was the famous Chanel, and persuaded the right authorities that Mademoiselle's nephew was the ideal person to run the plant. Julia's son was repatriated.

Spatz was a flattering companion. Coco was sure he was a good dozen years younger than she, but even at fifty-eight, she thought of herself as quite a woman still. The times were extraordinary. As she had discovered on her way back to Paris, people did inexplicable things. They became lovers.

Cocteau returned to Paris. The German occupation was proving more effective in curing his opium dependency than any of the treatments Coco had paid for over the years. With the matinee idol–actor Jean Marais, he took up residence in a tiny apartment in the west wing of the stately quadrangle of the Palais Royal, a few doors from Colette's Paris home.

The winter of 1940–41 was one of the coldest in memory. With fuel virtually nonexistent, people spent their days huddled by stoves and at night crept between icy sheets wearing every available garment. Finding food absorbed the waking hours of Parisians. Enterprising black marketeers scoured the countryside, and farmers themselves arranged to fence produce in Paris through city cousins. Food was the obsessive subject of conversations.

Coco and von Dincklage were rarely seen in fashionable restaurants. Marie-Louise Bousquet kept a black-market larder and on Thursdays gave lunches where "nice" French-speaking Germans such as Propaganda Director Gerhard Heller and Wehrmacht officer Ernst Junger showed up, sometimes with the poet Marcel Jouhandeau and Caryathis, Coco's dancer friend from before the First War. The death of Roossadana had brought Misia and Jojo back together, although on his travels to Madrid he was currently the lover of Marie-Ursel Stohrer, the wife of Hitler's ambassador to Spain. With Lifar and Cocteau, Gabrielle was a frequent guest at dinners at the Serts' in Rue de Rivoli, where Spartan meals were served by candlelight during power failures.

Jojo regaled the soirées with tales of German and British spies spying on each other in Madrid. Both the Germans and the English wore civilian clothes, spoke Spanish, and drove around in huge American cars. Each side tried to keep the balance even. If a new agent arrived in the English camp, the Germans received permission from the government to add a spy to their roster.

In May 1941, Jews were forbidden to engage in practically all businesses and professional activities. Maurice Goudeket, Colette's Jewish husband, was incarcerated at Royallieu barracks, the World War I barracks behind what had once been Etienne Balsan's property that were now converted into an internment camp. Hitler's attack on the Soviet Union a month later not only had French communists breathing easier again, it had them begin the first resistance. For the collaborators, the opening of the Eastern front allowed them to portray themselves as defenders of Western civilization against the Bolshevik hordes.

German retaliation to resistance fighting was merciless. For each member the Reichwehr killed, the Gestapo shot a number of French hostages. In Bordeaux, the ratio was fifty to one when a German major was found dead in the street. In June 1942, deportations to concentration camps began. Five months later, Hitler abrogated the armistice terms and occupied all of France.

Coco lived discreetly. Wartime living favored improvisation, the short view of things, getting by. Though the Americans had entered the war after the bombing of Pearl Harbor in December 1941, it was still unclear where it all would end. Spatz was the center of her emotional life. When people told her to be careful, she answered, "He isn't German, his mother was English."

In the intimacy of friends—Coco saw Serge Lifar almost every day, Misia and Jojo Sert, Cocteau and his lover Jean Marais twice a week—both she and Spatz proclaimed their loathing of war. For the slightly shocking effect it had on people, they spoke English to one another. They believed war was beneath contempt, vulgar and second-rate.

Coco hated the ambiguities of occupied Paris. But the need to survive made her and many of her friends reluctant to question their own acquiescence in oppression. They sought ways to soften the harshness and hide the ugliness.

Lelong, Balenciaga, Madame Grès, and the other couturiers were making the best of the circumstances, getting dispensation from fabric restrictions and showing their collections twice a year—with Suzanne Abetz in attendance. Marie-Laure de Noailles was flattered when Cocteau brought Arno Breker, Hitler's architect, to dinner. Picasso was selling his work to German officers from his studio in Rue des Grands Augustins, though the Nazis labeled him the foremost representative of "degenerate and negroid art." Louise de Vilmorin saw her novel *Lit à colonne* turned into a movie. Maurice Sachs, who could not bring himself to register as a Jew, instead flirted with the occupiers and secretly belonged to the Gestapo. Paul Morand was on the Vichy government payroll and was for a while president of the film censorship board. His wife, Hélène, who had seen the Soviet Union annex part of her native Romania in 1940, was openly pro-German and gave dinner parties where Coco again met Cocteau, Jouhandeau, Caryathis, and the ubiquitous Gerhard Heller. Theaters and movie houses were packed at every performance, although, to accommodate the curfew, performances began at eight and ended at eleven. Clandestine dancing took place in basements, and despite fines and closings, restaurants had everything that wasn't supposed to be available for sale.

During the fall of 1942, Chanel and Spatz stayed briefly at Roquebrune. While they were there, Robert Streitz, the architect of La Pausa, now a member of the local Resistance, asked Coco to intervene on behalf of Serge Voronov, a physics professor arrested by the Gestapo in Picabia's villa in Mougins. Spatz tried, though eventually Voronov would owe his freedom to someone else's intercession. Jojo Sert was luckier, or more energetic, when he came to intervene on behalf of the persecuted. Six months earlier, he had managed, through the intervention of the Spanish embassy, to have Colette's husband, Maurice Goudeket, freed from the Royallieu internment camp.

Though Chanel kept no journal of those somber years, others did. Misia, now seventy and losing her eyesight, began dictating her autobiography to a diplomat's son who was to become her last young friend. Boulos Ristelhueber was a willowy young man of delicate features, who tried to hide the astonishing pallor of his face with bizarre makeup. Boulos shared Misia's love of music and drugs, and Misia told Coco that because Boulos was not her lover, she revealed more to him than she had to any of the men with whom, as she put it, she had had "passionate bonds."

Boulos kept a wartime diary in which Chanel appeared on a number of pages:

January 5, 1941: At 6 o'clock was at Coco's. She was strumming Bach with two fingers on her piano, Misia was half asleep. . . . Sert took all three of us to dinner, prewar atmosphere, Russian orchestra, red benches, a lot of caviar. . . . Everybody talks about Jean [Cocteau] and I have a fight with Coco over him. I find it preposterous to systematically run down your friends like she does. It becomes embarrassing. I know that she actually rather likes him, but that doesn't mean that she doesn't harm her friends. I just feel I have to tell her.

January 8, 1941: Misia has me stay for dinner with Antoinette d'Harcourt and Coco Chanel. In three minutes, she improvised, despite power failure and lack of fuel, an exquisite dinner served by candlelight and with a lovely fire in the fireplace. We talked about Georges Auric and Loulou de Vilmorin; pretty neutral territory.

January 26, 1941: Arriving at Coco's, I hear the weirdest roulades. Two opera witches with flaming red hair, one at the piano, the other leaning on it, while Coco listens politely to their criticism.

"Unbelievable," Misia tells me when we get to her place.

"She's fifty-four* and seriously imagines her voice has a future!"

Cocteau began a wartime *Journal* in 1942 that would not be published until twenty years after his death but drew a singular profile of

*Chanel was actually fifty-eight at the time.

artistic Paris, and of the strange mix of Germans such as Heller who, in sometimes contradictory ways, were in charge of policing the arts. Cocteau did not go out of his way to ingratiate himself with the Germans, but when his works were in danger of being banned he did not hesitate to use his connections.

Cocteau's journal records the big gossip item of early 1942—the pending marriage of Chanel and Cocteau. Cocteau didn't know what was more horrifying, the prestige of the press or the credulity of the public— but at least his mother who in her seventies still had no knowledge of her son's sexual inclination. "It was printed everywhere: Jean Cocteau marries Mademoiselle Chanel," he wrote in March 1942. At the *Aux Ecoutes*, they went as far as to pretend they had asked me to comment, and that I hadn't denied it. I laughed, Chanel laughed, My mother, however, said, 'Why don't you admit it to me, *since it's in the papers.*' "

In 1943, Cocteau had Coco redo the costumes for a revival of *Antigone* at the Opéra. The free adaptation of the Sophocles tragedy with music by Honegger, sets by Picasso, and costumes by Chanel had disconcerted in 1924. For the revival, Honegger and his wife came to Paris from Switzerland and Picasso sat in on the rehearsals. "Chanel had spent the evening making a tiny and curious hat for Miss [Eliette] Schenneberg," Cocteau noted in his journal. "Yesterday, Mrs. Honegger comes up to her and tears it off her head. Chanel is furious. Nothing entertains me more than these little theater dramas."

For Gabrielle, the January 1943 revival of *Antigone* was a welcome respite from inactivity. She and Spatz rarely went to the restaurants where Cocteau, Lifar, Vilmorin, and other friends could be seen. Lifar, who sometimes spent an evening with her, would say that without the couture house to manage, she "returned to her first love—music and singing, accompanying herself on the piano."

She also turned her attention to the fight with the Wertheimers. Since the 1934 reorganization, she was no longer president of Les Parfums Chanel, and the court date that had been scheduled for 1940 was postponed indefinitely by the war. Still, the moment was opportune. The Germans had created a Commission in Jewish Affairs, which among other things was responsible for seizing Jewish-owned businesses and transferring them to sympathetic hands. The venerable Calmann-Lévy publishing house, publisher of *Madame Bovary*, Alexandre Dumas, and George Sand, had been confiscated because it still belonged to the Jewish descendants of founder Michel Lévy. The Occupation laws offered Chanel a chance to dissolve the partnership she had loathed for more than ten years. She was Aryan; the Wertheimers were not.

The brothers and their families had gone into hiding in southern France early in the war, and in 1940, had slipped across the border to Spain, traveling via Portugal to the United States. Raymond Bollack, a cousin of theirs who was a veteran of both wars and refused to leave France, was the caretaker administrator of both the huge Bourjois corporation and the Parfums Chanel subsidiary.

Eight years earlier, when Paul Iribe had been kicked off the company board, Coco's lawyer Chambrun had proposed they try to plant a mole on the board. She had suggested Georges Madoux, the director of sales from 1924 to 1931. In 1943 when Chanel returned to the board, she demanded that the former sales director be named chief executive officer. Madoux, she told Bollack, had been with the company at its inception; he knew the business.

Madoux was elected CEO.

But the Wertheimers' cousin was faster than she thought. Within days, Bollack found a non-Jewish aviation industrialist who was willing to front for the family. He also found a German officer ready to certify that the heap of predated documents and massive paper shuffles were *korrekt* and unassailable. When Gabrielle was ready to move, a new co-owner was in place.

Félix Amiot, a silver-haired aviation pioneer who had built the airplane propellers that had helped win the Great War, was the new co-owner. The volley of paper transfers gave the Wertheimers a 50 percent stake in Amiot's aviation company but no direct ownership of the Parfums Chanel subsidiary. Among the straw men Amiot chose to sit on the board was Robert de Nexon, none other than Adrienne's brother-in-law. The Amiot majority on the board yanked Madoux and named Nexon as the new CEO.

Once more she had lost to her eternal adversaries. Not that she was giving up; the match was merely postponed. In the meantime, No. 5 continued to be sold, by the French company in all territories occupied by the Reich, and—something she did not know yet—by the Wertheimers' independent subsidiary in the United States.

The reason Spatz never wore a uniform, Chanel biographer Charles-Roux would write thirty years later, was that he was a spy, a member of the Abwehr, the Nazi counterespionage agency. Biographer Marcel Haedrich would claim less dramatically that the handsome von Dincklage was nothing more than an administrator in his friend Theodor Momm's textile procurement service. Gabrielle herself would talk of her wartime lover without mentioning his name, but would say she had known him before the war. As for her lawyer, Chambrun would choose to remember only Momm.

Hans Gunther von Dincklage was too small a fry to be dragged up at the 1945–46 war crimes trials at Nuremberg. His long sojourn in France before the war, however, earned him a file in the Deuxième Bureau, the French counterespionage agency. The first entry in his *fichier* dated from 1937, four years after he had first visited France. Together with his wife Maximilienne von Schoenebeck, he had come to Paris in October 1933 casually looking for a job that gave him a lot of leisure time.

Soon after he arrived in Paris, Spatz became an attaché at the German embassy, and as a diplomat was welcomed in the best circles. Lesser members of the German colony would remember him as a somewhat ambiguous figure. Horst, who was spending the war in a U.S. Army uniform, thought Dincklage was a double agent, working for both the Nazis and the British. It is very likely that Gabrielle met Spatz at one of Lady Mendl or Count Gramont's parties, to which the German ambassador was invariably invited.

Whatever Spatz's mission at the embassy—whether he worked for Goebbels's propaganda section or was part of Foreign Minister Joachim von Ribbentrop's "charm commando" sent to Paris and London to improve the Third Reich's image, or whether he was merely an embassy attaché—he returned with Maximilienne to Berlin in 1935. They divorced, and a year later Spatz was back in Paris. The outbreak of the war, however, found Spatz in Switzerland. Eight months later he was once again in occupied Paris.

During the winter of 1942–43, when the German land offensive was blunted as the Wehrmacht failed to hold Stalingrad, Spatz had two fears—to be sent to the eastern front, or to find himself honored with some special mission that would compel him to plunge into the hornet's nest of upper-echelon intrigue in Berlin. In order to remain in Paris, he carried on a delicate game with his superiors in Berlin. On the one hand, he tried to show himself to be sufficiently devoid of ambition to be forgotten, and on the other, adroit enough for his presence in the French capital to be accepted without question.

It was while Gabrielle was talking with Spatz and Momm about the future and how the war would end that Chanel cut them off with an irritated gesture and said, "You Germans don't know how to handle the English! I do!"

As she spoke it occurred to her that *she* might be able to help bring an early end to the war.

30

HOW WILL IT ALL END?

~~~~~~

G abrielle turned sixty during the summer of 1943. Although the decisive battles of World War II were still a year or more away, 1943 was the turning point. The "arsenal of democracy" was at last in full production, and tanks, planes, and ships were coming off the U.S. assembly lines in increasing numbers. With Germany's defeat at Stalingrad and in North Africa, the fortunes of the German-Italian-Japanese axis appeared to be waning.

Perhaps Chanel was inspired by Jojo Sert's tales of British and German spies in Madrid or by Spatz's descriptions of the growing climate of fear in leading circles in Berlin when she decided to talk to Captain Momm. She would never say why she spoke to Momm rather than Spatz; possibly, she felt that Momm, who had arranged for the freeing of her nephew from POW camp, was better positioned to get things done.

The captain came to her drawing room at the Ritz and listened with growing stupefaction as she laid out her plan. There had to be people in the German high command who believed that Hitler's attack on the Soviet Union was a folly, she maintained, and that Japan's Pearl Harbor provocation, which drew the United States into the conflict, was a second blunder. On the other side, the war was also destroying Churchill's empire, the Great Britain of privilege and tradition she knew so well. The British prime minister was a man of courage and intelligence. There had to be moments when he, too, wondered how it would all end.

Churchill would not be surprised if she sought a meeting with him. It would be like in the old days in Roquebrune, when she and Bendor dropped in on the vacationing Churchills. Both she and Churchill hated communism. Suppose she could convince Winston to *listen*, if nothing else, to overtures of peace by members of the German high command. "Isn't it in everybody's interest to shorten the war, to save tens of thousands, perhaps hundreds of thousands of lives?"

Momm listened with increasing fascination as Chanel played herself conversing with Churchill and imagining his responses. He had promised the British people blood, toil, sweat, and tears, but that wouldn't earn him a place in history. She would say: "You must spare lives and end the war, Winston, by holding out a hand to peace you will show your strength."

"You're right, Coco," she had Winston say, as she imitated him solemnly flicking ash from his cigar. She would go to Spain, she explained to Momm. She was an acquaintance of Sir Samuel Hoare, the British ambassador to Madrid. She would contact Sir Samuel and have him relay her suggestion of Anglo-German talks, held in strictest secrecy.

Twenty years later Momm would still remember the surreal afternoon in Coco's narrow apartment, her pacing the floor, acting out the conversation she would have with Churchill. Momm would tell how in the early autumn of 1943 he went to Berlin with Coco Chanel's "peace proposal." To minimize the risks for himself—for in fanatical Nazi eyes the very suggestion of talks with the enemy would amount to treason—he decided to alert the Foreign Office. Baron Steengracht von Moyland, a secretary of state who had just taken up his duties, listened and politely ushered the cavalry officer out. This was not the sort of action anyone should pursue, Steengracht intimated.

One of the youngest SS leaders of the Abwehr, however, found Momm's proposal interesting. To Major Walter Schellenberg, the idea of sending Coco Chanel on a mission to Madrid seemed promising. At thirty-four, Schellenberg was an energetic and observant charmer. Lively, soft-spoken, and boyish, he was quite different from the bullying rigidity of most SS types. Since 1941, he had been the acting chief of foreign intelligence, a protégé of the Abwehr's top commander Admiral Wilhelm Canaris. He wore the black SS uniform with elegance and was always someone who could smooth-talk foreigners and befriend young officials in the foreign office and at the propaganda ministry. His greatest asset was the trust he inspired in Reinhard Heydrich, the chief of the SS Security Service. Even some earlier misadventures of his, including the bungled kidnapping of the Windsors in 1940, had not harmed his career.

History would contrast the craven knuckling-under of Pétain and Laval with Churchill's promise to "go on to the end" in Britain's Finest Hour. But England, too, had politicians who wondered how it all would end. In May 1940, Churchill's own foreign secretary, Lord Halifax, raised the idea of a negotiated peace at a cabinet meeting.

Churchill was firmly against a negotiated peace. He arranged for the arrest of Sir Oswald Mosley, the former Labor minister who was the leader of the small British Nazi-Fascist party, and warned his old friend Bendor not to take part in any serious appeasement efforts. The prime minister had to act with greater delicacy when it came to eminent members of the Conservative party. Churchill knew that Sir Samuel Hoare also favored negotiating with Hitler. To get him out of the corridors of power, Churchill had Hoare named ambassador to Madrid.

By 1943, negotiation with the enemy had become a common, if covert, topic at Ribbentrop's Foreign Office in Berlin. With the Russians exploiting their victory at Stalingrad while British and American armies were crushing Field Marshal Rommel's Afrika Korps, some of Hitler's commanders were trying to persuade him to consider a compromise peace.

The murderous Battle of Stalingrad had brought a peace feeler from Stalin. Admiral Wilhelm Canaris, Schellenberg's superior, felt encouraged enough by Stalin's peace overtures to persuade Ribbentrop to present a memo to the Führer. Hitler tore up the memo and threatened to execute anyone attempting to mediate on his own. There would be no negotiations, he said, until the Wehrmacht regained the initiative. He forbade Ribbentrop even to mention the matter again. "Believe me, we shall win," he said. "The blow that has fallen is a sign telling me to grow harder and harder and risk all we have. If we do, we shall win in the end."

Ribbentrop lost control of his foreign intelligence service. In March 1943, the Abwehr was absorbed into Interior Minister Heinrich Himmler's Security Service (SD). The enlarged SD added to Himmler's formidable powers. He already controlled the Gestapo, or secret police, and the political corps d'elite, and, in the Waffen SS, possessed a rival army to the Reichwehr. Ribbentrop revealed his foreboding to Fritz Hesse, his former agent in London, while the two of them walked in the snowy woods outside Hitler's headquarters in East Prussia. "All we can hope for now," said Ribbentrop, "is that at least one of our opponents will grow sensible. Surely the English must realize that it would be madness to deliver us into the hands of the Russians."

How much of this did Schellenberg know when he sat and listened to Rittmeister Momm explaining Coco Chanel's proposal? In his postwar memoirs, Schellenberg would give himself a juicy role in the subversion swirling around the Führer. Sir Stewart Graham Menzies, Churchill's cunning spymaster (who was known as "C" until decades after the war and would be fashioned by Ian Fleming into "M" and by John le Carré into "Control"), felt that Schellenberg thought that Coco Chanel could be used as a way of acquainting Churchill with what was going on inside the German government. After Stalingrad, even Himmler was receptive to Schellenberg's silky argument that any overture to the western allies was worth a try, even if it had to be done without Hitler's knowledge.

Schellenberg gave a preliminary okay to Operation *Modellhut* (hat pattern or fashion hat), as he decided to call the Chanel mission. Momm would remember that he left Berlin for Paris with assurances that if the British contacts Chanel boasted of checked out, the necessary travel documents would be issued.

Coco dampened Momm's enthusiasm the moment he came to see her. She could not travel alone, she informed him. She never had. Momm expected her to demand that Spatz accompany her. Instead, she asked for Vera Bate.

Her choice was diabolically clever. Though Vera had married an Italian cavalry officer and was living in Rome, she was British and her connections with the royal family and the nobility were as firm as her status as illegitimate daughter of the Duke of Cambridge. More important, she was much closer to Winston Churchill than was Coco. If things went wrong, Vera could save the day for them both with the Allies.

Coco was less discerning when it came to choosing which German security service should bring Vera to Paris. Coco had her old friend's Rome address. Perhaps to rehabilitate von Dincklage in his own, and her eyes, she agreed to his suggestion that his Abwehr assume responsibility for escorting Vera to Paris.

Fascist Italy was crumbling. After invading Sicily, the Americans and the British had crossed the Strait of Messina and carried the battle to mainland Italy. Like so many Italians after the fall of Mussolini, Vera's cavalry officer, Alberto Lombardi, was in hiding, ready to join the Allies. Marshal Pietro Badoglio became Mussolini's successor. German commandos, however, rescued the fallen dictator, who from a hideaway called on his followers to take up arms and "give Italy a place near the sun."

On October 23, 1943, a German officer carrying a bouquet of red roses knocked on Vera's door at 31 Via Barnaba Oriani. Colonel Lombardi was absent, he was told. The German officer explained he had come to see Signora Lombardi.

The roses were from Signorina Chanel, he explained when Vera came to the foyer. He also handed her a letter.

Vera had not heard from Coco since before the war.

Written on Chanel letterhead and dated October 17, the letter announced that Coco was opening the House of Chanel again: "I am going back to work and I want you to come and help me. Do exactly as the bearer of this message tells you. Come as soon as possible, don't forget I'm waiting for you in joy and impatience." After expressing sadness that Vera was reduced to painting screens to earn a living, the letter ended in English with, "All my love."

Vera declined. The "bearer" insisted. She remained firm; her answer was no. Three weeks later, she was arrested and transferred to the Rome prison for women.

Schellenberg became angry when, by November 1, Coco Chanel and her travel companion had not yet left Paris. Momm, who apparently knew nothing of Spatz's bungled attempt at luring Vera to Paris, was summoned to Berlin. Schellenberg's services in Rome quickly established that Vera Lombardi had been arrested by the Gestapo. When asked why, the Rome Gestapo alluded to espionage. Vera Bate was an English spy.

Schellenberg could only smile at his good fortune. An enemy spy, dragged from a prison cell, could be easily manipulated. At Schellenberg's orders, the SS chief in Rome supervised Vera's release. Without further explanation, the SS colonel told her that her friend Gabrielle Chanel was anxious to see her in Paris. Arrangements had already been made.

After spending a night at a hotel, Vera was taken to her home to pack whatever personal belongings she would need. To make her comfortable, she would be traveling with an old aristocratic friend, Eduard ("Eddie") Bismarck.

Vera didn't know what to believe. She wanted to remain in Rome. Her husband was not far away, in hiding in the Aldobrandinis; her brother was with the British army at Salerno. It could not be long before they'd be able to free her and the rest of Rome.

The next day she changed her mind. She would come with them to Paris, but she'd bring her dog Taege, a huge, intimidating mastiff. The party drove to Milan, where Momm met them and took them to an airfield.

The small plane could hold only the pilot, Momm, and Vera. She protested. Taege was separated from her, but Bismarck promised to look after the dog until the end of the war.

The flight was turbulent. Ice built up on the wings while they climbed over the Alps, forcing the pilot to land in Ulm, midway between Munich and Stuttgart. Vera was sure they had lied to her, that it was all a ruse to get her to Germany. Momm found a car and commandeered it to drive them to the railway station. After passing through Strasbourg and Nancy, Vera finally believed that they were in France.

When the train rolled into the Gare de l'Est, Momm took her directly to the Ritz and Coco's greeting arms.

Gabrielle and Vera had known each other since the end of the First War, yet when they were finally alone neither woman was honest with the other. Coco explained they were going to work together, not in Paris, but in Madrid, that they would be resurrecting Chanel in Spain. Vera immediately realized Madrid would be her escape, that as soon as they reached the Spanish capital, she'd flee to the British embassy.

Operation *Modellhut* was on.

31

OPERATION MODELLHUT

President Roosevelt and Prime Minister Churchill had met six times since the beginning of the war to discuss joint strategy, but in November 1943, a third leader, Premier Joseph Stalin, met with them in the first Big Three Meeting. As Coco Chanel and Vera Bate boarded the train for Bordeaux–Biarritz–Hendaye–Madrid, Roosevelt, Churchill, and Stalin headed for Teheran.

By blocking off all entrances, hanging up big cloth screens at the end of the street, and opening the wide iron gates, the two embassies and their grounds were converted into one big compound. For four days, the Big Three lived and worked there, dining together each night, never more than 200 yards from each other. Stalin agreed with Roosevelt's suggestion that the Reich be dismembered into five parts, while Churchill, agreeing in principle, cautioned that a searching examination of historical and economic facts should be considered.

It is hard to know what Coco thought of her mission as she and Vera crossed into Spain on their German *Ausweisse*, but certainly her motive was not to help the Germans. She could be terribly French and jingoistic, echoing Paul Iribe's elitist nationalism in her sarcastic remarks about foreigners, but her conviction of England's rightful superiority made her crave their appreciation. She might have a German lover, but throughout her life she had displayed a vehement sympathy for all things British. It was Boy Capel who had pulled her out of the narrow circle of demimondaines, loved her, and helped her begin her career. It was his compatriots at the polo grounds in Deauville who had offered her respect, who had inspired her first triumphs. Her period of professional prominence had coincided, in part, with her years with the Duke of Westminster. Together they had built the house of Roquebrune where Churchill came to play cards. It was in her suite that Churchill had cried his heart out over the taint his king's decision to marry Wallis Simpson had put on the British monarchy. Old Winston would no doubt be glad to see her again.

In Madrid, she and Vera checked into the Ritz Hotel. Generalísimo Francisco Franco's capital—and the hotel—had the feel of Biarritz during the First War. Here, aristocratic refugees, Argentine gigolos, and spies all mingled, watching each other. As Jojo had told her, both the German and the British agents wore civilian clothes and spoke Spanish. What was new was the swelling number of British and American spies. Apparently, the Franco government sensed the fortunes of war were shifting toward the Allied side because it no longer contrived to keep the spies' balance of power equal. It is not known whether the Allied *apparat* signaled Coco and Vera's arrival to the appropriate authorities, but in Berlin, Schellenberg was immediately informed.

After the war, Coco would remain discreet about the entire affair. Relying on post-war interviews with Vera and Momm, biographer Edmonde Charles-Roux would claim that Coco left the hotel immediately for the British embassy. Providentially alone, Vera waited only a few minutes before setting off in the same direction. In this version, Gabrielle got to see Sir Hoare while a few minutes later Vera was whisked into the office of the on-duty intelligence agent.

Chanel, Charles-Roux would write, told Ambassador Hoare of her wish to see her old friend Winston, indeed of his wish to see her. Without so much as mentioning the presence of Vera in Madrid, she relayed Schellenberg's message that the highest German command was ready and willing to enter secret talks with the western Allies.

Down the hall, Vera told the intelligence officer the story of her arrest by the SS in Rome, her transfer via plane and train to Paris, all so she could help her old friend Chanel reopen her fashion house in Madrid. She denounced Coco as a German agent. The Charles-Roux version allowed for a dramatic confrontation, when, after their respective meetings, Coco and Vera ran into each other on the embassy stairs. Both stared, transfixed, Charles-Roux would write: "It seems to have been Gabrielle who first recovered her aplomb. She is alleged to have said, 'Well, this is a fine thing! Are we going to stand here forever staring at each other like a couple of cats?' "

British intelligence archives, declassified in 1985, offered a different account. According to the archives, it was not Rittmeister Momm but a certain Colonel Schiebe who first alerted Schellenberg to the idea of using Chanel to get in touch with Churchill. After Schellenberg's capture at the end of the war, he told his British interrogators that he had had Chanel brought to Berlin and that she arrived with a certain Dincklage, an "honorable correspondent" of the old Abwehr. At the meeting, Chanel proposed "that a certain Frau Lombardi, a former British subject of good family then married to an Italian, should be released from internment in Italy and sent to Madrid as an intermediary." Far from keeping Vera in the dark, Schellenberg told his interrogators, Coco had her friend in on the scheme, agreeing to go to the embassy alone, carrying a letter from Chanel. The reason Operation *Modellhut* failed was that Vera had "denounced all and sundry, including Madame Chanel, as German agents to the British authorities."

Ambassador Hoare apparently told Chanel and Bate-Lombardi to wait in Madrid while he sought instructions from London. Coco and Vera stayed at the Ritz and were given as a contact a young man who, although English, never gave any other name than Ramón. News spread that Churchill would be coming through Madrid on his way back from the Big Three summit. There were also reports that the prime minister was ill.

The flight plans of the world leaders were kept secret, but Churchill had left Teheran December 2 for Cairo and was now just across the Mediterranean at General Eisenhower's headquarters. Rumors of Churchill being at death's door became so widespread that a bulletin was issued from Downing Street on December 16 to inform the British people that the prime minister had had a quiet night and that "a certain improvement was observed." The official version was that the sixty-nine-year-old Churchill had caught a bad cold while in Cairo. In reality, he was out with pneumonia at Eisenhower's seaside headquarters in Tunisia. Doctors feared pleurisy and when Churchill's heart began showing signs of strain, his wife and a medical team were flown in.

All Hoare could tell—or would tell—Coco was that Churchill could see no one. Chanel bowed to that. Her ego could accept that Churchill's grave illness prevented him from seeing her.

She told Vera she was going back to Paris. Vera said she was staying in Spain. On the eve of Gabrielle's departure Vera left the hotel, finding refuge with an Italian diplomat and his wife, and, later, with "Ramón." In December, she received a letter from Coco, four hurried pages written in pencil:

Dear Vera,

In spite of the frontiers everything travels quickly. I know of your betrayals! You will gain nothing from them, except having hurt me deeply.

I did everything in my power to render your stay less painful. Patience, money, etc. But I could not become rabid on the Italian subject, or, on the German subject, hear or say low things which I leave to the retarded. To scorn your enemy is to debase yourself.

My English friends cannot blame me, at any rate, or find the least wrong in what I have done.

That is enough for me.

I have seen M. I said nothing that could make trouble for you. If you want to go back to Rome, forty-eight hours after you reach Paris you'll be there with your real friends!

Your indifference on the subject of my business in Spain makes it unnecessary for me to talk about it! But I have good news and hope for success.

I have a most pleasant memory of your friend "Ramon" although his help in business matters seems negligible.

I will also tell you that I did not leave Spain under orders—I have given a lot of them in my life and not taken any yet. But my visa was up. S.* was afraid I might have problems.

I hope with my whole heart that you find your happiness again.

But I am surprised to see that the years have not taught you to be more trusting and less ungrateful. Times as cruel and sad as these should be able to work that sort of miracle.

Coco

Coco went to Berlin to meet Schellenberg. When exactly is unclear. The last days of 1943 and January 1944 have been mentioned as possible dates, but British intelligence would place the meeting in April 1944,

*We do not know who M. and S. are, but Momm and Schellenberg are good assumptions.

practically on the eve of Germany's collapse. It is not known what she intended to accomplish, how long she stayed in Berlin, and what she told Schellenberg. His debriefing before the Nuremberg Trial would reveal only that the meeting took place during an air raid.

In February 1944, Chanel became involved in efforts to save Max Jacob from deportation to Germany's death camps. From the Saint-Benoît-sur-Loire monastery where he was living, the poet, visionary, and painter who had once read Chanel's palm wrote to Cocteau on February 2, asking if he and Chanel could intervene on behalf of his imprisoned sister: "I'd like to write to Chanel. Maybe you can go and see her. Together, you two can save my sister." Three weeks later, the Gestapo arrested Jacob at Saint Benoît and transferred him to the Drancy political camp northeast of Paris. Gabrielle brought Sert into the rescue effort. He used his influence through the Spanish embassy, while Cocteau met with Georges Prade, a newspaper publisher who was an acquaintance of Otto Abetz. On the twenty-eighth, Cocteau noted in his *Journal*, "Prade telephoned to tell me we may succeed." Sealed trains filled with deportees left Drancy for German concentration camps every night; Jacob's brother, sister, and brother-in-law were among those exterminated in the camps. But the sixty-eight-year-old Max was hospitalized at the Drancy infirmary with pneumonia. On March 14, Prade obtained a release order, but Jacob died the next evening before the order could be executed.

On June 6, 1944, the Allies landed at dawn on a 120-kilometer stretch of the Normandy coast. Parisians anticipated the Allies' imminent arrival, but the battle proved fierce. It took the Allies three weeks to capture Cherbourg. On June 26, de Gaulle landed to establish a new government on French soil. By early July, the Americans were on the outskirts of Chartres, fifty-six miles southwest of Paris.

Resistance leaders were in agreement on one point: Paris should liberate itself. When German troops moved down Boulevard St. Michel on the afternoon of August 18, passersby whispered, "They're pulling out." But the Germans were still arresting and deporting people and the swastika was still flying over the Sénat in the Luxembourg Garden. The next day, the Préfecture de Police was liberated. The City Hall, the Gare de Lyon and the majority of public buildings were in the hands of the insurgents. But a week later, the Germans were still there.

Spatz wanted Coco to come with him and the retreating German army. He planned for them to disappear in the growing confusion of the collapsing Reich; they would then head for Switzerland. Coco refused. She had never been a coward. She could face the music. She had nothing to fear.

On August 17, Wehrmacht trucks were ready to evacuate the top French collaborators. Serge Lifar sought refuge at 31 Rue Cambon after he heard rumors that the Germans were "inviting" him to accompany them in their retreat. Some 20,000 Militia members and French fascists piled into the trucks and military trains only to find themselves caught up in the retreat eastward, exposed to Allied bombing raids and Free French sabotage. Maurice Sachs was one of a handful of intellectuals who fled France, only to die in an air raid in Hamburg. In Vichy, Pétain, claiming he was a prisoner, was driven away under armed guard; along with Laval and the remnants of the Vichy government, he was taken to the former Hohenzollern castle of Sigmaringen on the Danube near Stuttgart. The fiction of a French government-in-exile fighting de Gaulle and his foreign paymasters was maintained until the end of the war.

Together with her manservant and her maid, Coco and Lifar witnessed the last German tank rumble down Rue de Rivoli, heard the last street fights between retreating Germans and the Forces Françaises de l'Intérieur (FFI), and saw firefighters hoist French flags at the Opéra. Across Rue Cambon, they heard the "Internationale" being sung in Russian in the Justice Ministry, the first building to be occupied by Russian partisans.

On August 26, Coco and Lifar were on Jojo and Misia's balcony on the Rue de Rivoli to see the end of de Gaulle's triumphant march from the Arc de Triomphe to City Hall. Jojo and Misia were together as if the Roossadana episode had never happened, and fifty people were invited to watch the parade and partake in a luncheon of ham, sausage, and fruits that Jojo had imported from Spain. Lifar and Count Etienne de Beaumont were there, anxious about their high-visibility roles with the Germans; they hoped Jojo could perform a reverse miracle and shield them from the summary justice of the FFI as his Spanish nationality, money, and influence had shielded others from the Germans during the Occupation.

Preceded by tanks, police, and FFI troops, who, with arms linked, stretched from one side of the Champs Elysées to the other, General de Gaulle walked down to the Place de la Concorde, watched by millions.

It was below the Serts' balcony that sniper shots rang out as de Gaulle got into a car for the ride down Rue de Rivoli to the Hôtel de Ville. The Serts' guests dove under tables, but Jojo stayed on his balcony. It was a false and brief alarm, and Misia, Coco, and the rest of the guests joined him to watch de Gaulle drive by.

Two weeks later Coco Chanel was arrested.

32

EXILE

~~~~~~~~~~~~~~~~~~~~~~~~~~~~

Two youths wearing FFI armbands, and revolvers stuck in their belts, appeared at the Ritz early one morning in September 1944, knocked upon Mademoiselle Chanel's door, and asked her to come with them.

On whose orders? she asked.

"Le Comité d'Epuration."

The *épuration*, the purges that were a mixture of popular wrath and private settling of scores, was in full swing, and a noted collaborationist—"collabo" in the current slang—could expect the worst humiliations. Suspects were imprisoned for months without trial, women who had consorted with Germans had their heads shaved in public, property was summarily seized, careers terminated on hearsay. Yesterday's collaborators were often today's superpatriots, making wholesale denunciations to escape their own punishment. De Gaulle was appalled by the unleashed fury of the populace, but his fragile coalition government let the vengeance run its course.

Germaine, Chanel's maid, burst into tears. For a moment, Coco stared down the two young men. Without a word, she picked up her gloves and handbag and walked past them out in the hallway. She wanted to get out before they started ransacking the room, because Serge Lifar was hiding in a closet. The Russian dancer was no longer bragging about Hitler's caresses, and instead was prepared to swear the reason he had sought out the Führer's intimacy was to be able to murder him. "Only fate stayed my hand," he would say in the autobiography Boulos Ristelhueber was writing for him.

"Coco behaved like a queen, like Marie Antoinette being led to the scaffold," Lifar would remember. "She left with the two Frenchmen who came to arrest her with her head high."

The detention lasted three hours. When she was shown a photograph of von Dincklage and asked if she knew him, she answered, according to biographer Marcel Haedrich, "Of course. I've known him for twenty years." To her interrogator's question, "Where is he?" she answered, "He's a German. I suppose he's in Germany. When he came to say good-bye—because he's a gentleman he came to say good-bye—he told me he was going to Germany."

The way Cecil Beaton heard it, when Coco was asked if it were true that she had consorted with a German, she replied, "Really, sir, a woman of my age cannot be expected to look at his passport if she has a chance of a lover." Pierre Galante, who had spent the war years as a secret agent for the American OSS, would speculate that Chanel was accused of sleeping with a German, and that her defense was to compare herself with the rest of the fashion industry. She, at least, had closed her house at the outbreak of the war, whereas the others, Lelong, Madame Grès, Balenciaga, had never skipped a beat. Hadn't Lelong presented two collections a year and hadn't his assistant Pierre Balmain dressed the wife of Otto Abetz? Not to talk about the Wertheimers' trusted Félix Amiot. Hadn't his Société d'Emboutissage et de Constructions Mécaniques supplied airplane propellors to the Luftwaffe?

Coco would never speak of the three hours of questioning, and would nourish an intense hatred of de Gaulle. If anyone dared bring up the subject, she would lash out at the Resistance movement. A quarter century later, she would describe the Occupation years in words and inflections of the period with no hint of self-justification. She felt no need to burnish her image. She had done nothing wrong. Who had any right to judge her? To whom was she answerable?

Self-pity was not her style.

"They made me laugh," she would say of the Free French, and then she would point out the ease with which she obtained British and American visas in 1945 and 1946 as if to prove she was clear of all suspicion. "I was the first to go to London. First I had detoured via Switzerland to pick up some money because I didn't have any left."

Visas to the United States were scrutinized, but she bragged about how easy it was for her. "I saw the [American] consul, and said to him,

'Monsieur, I need my passport by tomorrow.' He asked me to fill out a questionnaire. I said, 'Monsieur, you know more about me than I do.' He said, 'At least you've got to give us your fingerprints.' The whole thing lasted one minute.'"

British Foreign Office files inadvertently declassified in 1972 would give a different explanation for her quick release. If she was free after only three hours it was because she was in possession of secrets the British did not want revealed.

Winston Churchill was coming to Paris for the commemoration of the November 11 armistice. Together with de Gaulle, the prime minister was scheduled to drive to the Arc de Triomphe, lay a wreath at the tomb of the Unknown Soldier, and walk down the Champs Elysées. De Gaulle would be pressing for a share for France in the imminent occupation of Germany, and wanted no skeletons coming out of any closets.

What did Coco know that could embarrass Churchill? That he had violated his own Trade with the Enemy act, and, since 1940, had paid the Germans to protect the Duke of Windsor's property. The Windsors were still lingering in Bermuda, but their apartment on Boulevard Suchet had never been touched. The Germans had paid the rent at the château at Cap d'Antibes, and thoughtfully laced its lawns with land mines to protect it still further. As Charles Higham would say of Chanel in *The Duchess of Windsor*, "Had she been forced to stand trial with the threat of execution as an employee of an enemy government, she could easily have exposed as Nazi collaborators the Windsors, and dozens of others highly placed in society. Despite the hatred of the Windsors at Buckingham Palace, the royal family would not willingly tolerate an exposé of a family member."

If the FFI never found out about Operation *Modellhut*, the Chanel mission to Madrid was generally known among British intelligence agents. Stationed in Paris after the Liberation, Malcolm Muggeridge was one member of the M16 who marveled at the way Coco escaped the purges, "By one of those majestically simple strokes which made Napoleon so successful a general, she just put an announcement in the window of her emporium that scent was free for GIs, who thereupon queued up to get the bottles of Chanel No. 5, and would have been outraged if the French police had touched a hair of her head. Having thus gained a breathing space, she proceeded to look for help *à gauche et à droite*, and not in vain thereby managing to avoid making even a token appearance among the gilded company—Maurice Chevalier, Jean Cocteau, Sacha Guitry, and other worthies—on a collaborationist charge."

Lifar "surrendered" to the purge committee a few days later, though lurid headlines had placed him in South America or described him as a millionaire bathing in champagne in Monte Carlo. Lifar was sentenced to a one-year suspension from the Opéra. The *épuration* dealt more harshly with Paul Morand, who had been the Vichy government's consul general in Bern, Switzerland. In absentia, the writer-diplomat was stripped of his civil-servant status, and his author's royalties frozen. He did not dare return to France.

Though summary judgments, including executions of Vichy officials, were meted out in liberated cities and towns all over France, the war was not yet over. Nazi Germany still held half of France. In mid-October, the rains started and, it seemed, never stopped, and the closer the Allies drove the enemy toward his own border the harder became his resolve. In December, the Battle of the Bulge began in eastern Belgium; it was Hitler's carefully conceived offensive to avert defeat. Two hundred thousand Germans attacked through the snow with all they had, and it was not until mid-January 1945 that the Battle of the Bulge was won by the American forces, and the push to the Rhine resumed.

Where was Spatz in all this? Coco cared enough for him to try to save him from the ruins of the collapsing Germany. She had done it for her nephew with the Germans, why couldn't she do it for her lover with the Allies? It was a long shot but a glimmer of an opportunity presented itself in the form of Hans Schillinger, a young G.I. on furlough, who asked for her at the Ritz and, once she came down to meet him, told her he came with greetings from Horst.

"How many Germans are you in the U.S. Army?" she asked, amused, when Schillinger told her Horst was alive and well and spending the war at Fort Belvoir in the Blue Ridge Mountains photographing servicemen for army magazines. It was a long story. On the eve of the war, Horst had managed to get Schillinger to America. When Schillinger enrolled he was assigned to General Patton's Third Army. "If you get to Paris," Horst had told him, "give my love to Coco."

The young German-American was on his way back to the front. Before he left, Coco stuffed his duffel bag with bottles of No. 5—exchangeable for almost anything at any black market. She was sure that once the war was over, his fluency in German would make him valuable to Allied headquarters. Perhaps he would be assigned to interpreter duty at inter-rogations of enemy officers or prisoners of war. If ever he ran across someone named Hans Gunther von Dincklage, she told him, he should write her a postcard. Very simple: Coco Chanel, The Ritz, Paris.

The Nazi high command was getting desperate. In February 1945, Schellenberg tried again to make a separate peace with the West. He arranged for Himmler to meet with Sweden's Count Folke Bernadotte, who came to Berlin to seek the release of Norwegian and Danish concentration-camp prisoners into the custody of the Swedish Red Cross. Himmler was unwilling to commit himself.

Churchill, Roosevelt, and Stalin were meeting in Yalta, and, although Schellenberg could not know it, they discussed what should be done if some group in Germany, in Stalin's words, "declared that they had over-thrown Hitler." In such a case, Churchill thought, the Big Three should immediately consult each other and, if "such people were worth dealing with, the terms of surrender should be laid before them; if not, the war would be continued and the whole country occupied by strict military government."

On April 23, 1945, the day Roosevelt died, Himmler and Schellenberg came to Lübeck in northern Germany for another meeting with Bernadotte. By now, Himmler was ready to capitulate on the western front but not in the east. Bernadotte said he did not believe Britain and the United States would agree to a separate peace, but on condition that Norway and Denmark be included in the surrender, he agreed to forward the proposal to the Swedish foreign ministry.

Bernadotte set off for Stockholm, and Himmler began to think of the government he would form and to discuss with Schellenberg the new Party of National Union that would replace the Nazi Party. The Soviet and U.S. armies were about to link up on the Elbe River, when Bernadotte returned with the news that the Allies refused to consider a separate peace and insisted on unconditional surrender. The news that Himmler sought a separate peace was reported on British and American broadcasts on April 27. Hitler heard the news in his Berlin bunker. That Himmler, in whose loyalty he had placed unlimited faith, should betray him served to crystallize the decision to commit suicide three days later.

German forces surrendered piecemeal. The Third Reich outlasted its founder by one week.

During the first weeks of peace, the Wertheimers came back from America. They found the Bourjois Corporation, the stock they had left with Félix Amiot, and the Neuilly headquarters intact. Félix Amiot returned his shares to the Wertheimers, who in turn made sure the Allies would not hear of his airplane procurement for the Germans.

Pierre Wertheimer came to see Coco. It was his turn to exult, but instead he told her he had deposited her royalties in her Swiss bank account.

What royalties?

He and his brother had slaved away in America. Their first break had been meeting Arnold van Ameringen, the president of International Flavors and Fragrances. (Ameringen's girlfriend, who had only recently changed her name from Estelle Lauter to Estée Lauder, was aggressively pushing a skin cream she had invented.) With Ameringen's help, they poured every dollar they had and every dollar they could borrow into a factory in Hoboken, New Jersey. Wall Street was complicated. They had sold their shares in Les Parfums Chanel to a new corporation called Chanel, Inc., and they had managed to start production of Chanel No. 5. It was out of the question to get the ingredients from Grasse, but who would know the difference? They had borrowed another million dollars to pay for a publicity campaign and had seen No. 5 conquer the wartime market. Today, you could find No. 5 in every armed forces PX store from Manila to Frankfurt, from Anchorage to Miami.

When he told her the royalties deposited in Zurich amounted to $15,000,* she knew the Wertheimers must have made millions. She had been had again.

"I want revenge," she told René de Chambrun.

For someone who only months before stood accused of being a collaborator, this was not the moment. Her lawyer, who had spent the war years in the United States with his American relatives, suggested she lie low for a while, that she spent some time in Geneva or Lausanne. "Not exactly exile when one is French," he smiled.

*About $60,000 in 1990 currency.

In 1920, Coco had been the incarnation of the postwar woman plunging into a flaming new decade. Now she was the name behind an adulterated perfume, a prewar fashion designer without a fashion house in a postwar era of diminished perspectives. The settling of scores created its own contradictions. Paul Morand became a nonperson while Marie-Louise Bousquet, the friend Coco had returned to Paris with in 1940 and who had given lunches on her "Thursdays" for "nice Germans," became the Parisian editor of *Harper's Bazaar*.

Coco told Chambrun she would leave, but she still wanted to get back at the Wertheimers. The lawyer explained there was little she could do except sue. Les Parfums Chanel was now a subsidiary of Chanel, Inc., the company the Wertheimers had set up in America.

"But I own ten percent of Les Parfums Chanel," she said. "Why can't I pull out entirely, withdraw my assets, my No. 5 formula?"

"You can't do that," Chambrun said, "but you can sue for damages."

As the son-in-law of Pierre Laval, who was executed for treason in October 1945, Chambrun had his own reasons for keeping a low profile, and when Coco pressed him to sue, he arranged for the President of the Bar, Maître Chresteil, to join him on the case. The senior attorney advised Chanel that she could indeed sue for damages, and, once she obtained a judgment, perhaps petition a court for the restitution of her assets, but he told her she would do better to settle the case. The Wertheimers were not without counterarguments. Yes, they had started with her 1924 formula, but they had also poured a lot of money into les Parfums Chanel and turned it into a worldwide business.

"Tell me," she asked Chambrun and Chresteil, "can I do what I want with a still in my own place?"

"Absolutely," said Chambrun.

"And what I make, I can give to your wife as a gift?"

"There's no law against that."

A few days later she was back in Chambrun's office. She had thought it all over, she said. From her handbag she came up with several small bottles and lined them up on his desk.

"Not for you," she told Chambrun. "Give them to Josée and ask her what she thinks."

She wouldn't say how and who had produced the perfume samples for her. Josée de Chambrun, however, found the scents to be ravishing.

Coco had found a small Swiss perfumer who made a few hundred sample bottles for her. The perfumes were reminiscent of the originals and to underscore the likeness, she merely added "Mademoiselle" to the labels—Mademoiselle Chanel No. 5, and, in new versions of Ernest Beaux's 1924 and 1926 inventions, Mademoiselle Chanel Cuir de Russie and Mademoiselle Chanel Bois des Iles.

Chambrun confirmed she had the right to give these samples to her friends. The samples were sent to Samuel Goldwyn in Hollywood, to Bernard Gimbel and Neiman Marcus. In 1946, she began selling the scents in her boutique. Chambrun was convinced that the contract with Les Parfums Chanel did not prevent her from doing that. The Wertheimers, however, went to court alleging counterfeiting and, with a court order, descended on Rue Cambon and seized the lot.

Gabrielle told her lawyers she was being robbed in her own house. Chambrun and Chresteil again suggested an out-of-court settlement. She wouldn't hear of it and told them to begin the lawsuit. Then she left for Lausanne.

More than a chance to produce a line of competitive perfumes to provoke the Wertheimers drew her to Switzerland. A postcard from Hans Schillinger, addressed to Coco Chanel, The Ritz, Paris, told her Spatz was alive in Hamburg. Spatz had been in a POW camp, but Schillinger had gotten him out. "I cannot tell you how Schillinger did it but I can tell you why," Horst would say more than forty years later. "He did it because Coco Chanel had been friendly to him, and in a way to please me. I had told him about her, how she had given me a second chance to shoot the famous profile picture of her. I was nobody in 1936, but she didn't dismiss me. She invited me back and said, 'Let's do it again.' "

It was out of the question to get Spatz to France, but it was possible to slip him into Switzerland. In the beginning, Coco and Spatz lived quietly, but after a while, they were seen in Lausanne. Coco had Swiss lawyers, one each in Geneva, Lausanne, and Zurich, and she and Spatz socialized with them and with a Dr. Théo de Preux and two other physicians. Those who knew Spatz would remember him as an aging playboy, destitute but still a man of striking bearing and exquisite manners.

Lausanne was the residence of all kinds of exiles, including several deposed monarchs. At the Beau Rivages Hotel on the lakefront, Coco exchanged greetings with the ex-queen of Spain and dined with Princess Marie-José of Italy. Coco's life assumed a circular monotony as she wandered between Paris, Roquebrune, and Lausanne. She liked the dour Swiss, she said, their knack for staying out of wars, their serious work ethic and respect for money, so different from the French, always embroiled in partisan passions and vindictive rancor.

Coco brought her nephew and grandniece to Switzerland as well. André Palasse had never recovered from the POW camps and suffered from tuberculosis; Coco thought the Swiss air would do him good. Apart from Adrienne, André and his daughter were the last family members she acknowledged. Adrienne was living as the *châtelaine* of the Nexon château, family-minded as ever, making her residence a vacation home for some of her nephews and nieces. Gabrielle's brothers, whom she had last seen before the war, were now dead. Lucien had died of a heart attack in 1941 and Alphonse died shortly after the war. Alphonse's son Yvan died, leaving several orphans that his sisters, Gabrielle and Antoinette, brought up. Coco chose to ignore them all.

Coco and Spatz stayed in hotels in St. Moritz, Klosters, and Davos in the German-speaking Alps. Paul and Hélène Morand were nearby and during the long winter of 1945–46, author and *couturière* spent long hours together, she talking, summing up her life, he taking notes. "I found her listless, at loose ends for the first time, ready to fly off the handle," he would write. "Melancholy showed in her still sparkling eyes, under the curves of eyebrows accented with grease pencil into dark-glazed arches; volcanoes from Auvergne that Paris wrongly believed were extinguished."

News reports told of the sixty-eight-year-old Duke of Westminster divorcing Loelia and, still in pursuit of a son, marrying Anne Sullivan, a brigadier general's only daughter. Chanel said she had no regrets. "It's probably not just by chance that I'm alone. I was born a Leo, astrologers know what that means. It would be very hard for a man to live with me, unless he's terribly strong. And if he's stronger than I, I'm the one who can't live with him. . . . I'm neither smart nor stupid, but I don't think I'm a run-of-the-mill person. I've been in business without being a businesswoman, I've loved without being a woman made only for love. The two men I've loved, I think, will remember me, on earth or in heaven, because men always remember a woman who caused them concern and uneasiness. I've done my best, in regard to people and to life, without precepts, but with a taste for justice."

While she was living in Switzerland, Chambrun and Chresteil started legal action against Les Parfums Chanel both in French and American courts in 1947, the same year that Paul Wertheimer died and Pierre bought out his brother's heirs. In France, her suit charged Les Parfums Chanel had produced merchandise of an inferior quality, and demanded that the company be ordered to cease all manufacturing and selling and that sole ownership and rights to products, formulas, and manufacturing be restored to her. American laws were more protective of minority stockholders than were French statutes. In her American complaint, she accused the American subsidiary of fiduciary abuse, and the Wertheimers of producing counterfeit perfume.

Coco and Spatz moved to Villars-sur-Ollon, a winter resort near Lausanne. Somebody snapped a picture of them in the snow, she a thin little lady in overcoat and boots, folding a kerchief as if to put it on her head, he in a felt hat set cockily on his tall head and smiling at the camera.

33

YEARS OF
OBLIVION

~~~~~~~~~~~~~~~~~~~~~~~~~~~~~~~~~~~~~

Attorneys for Pierre Wertheimer asked René de Chambrun for a conference.

"What does she *want?*" Wertheimer exploded when he and his lawyers met with Chambrun and Chresteil.

Chambrun smelled victory and began improvising a settlement. She might have been satisfied with 10 percent of French sales before the war. Now, she wanted 2 percent of all perfume sales worldwide, he said, and she wanted to be able to make her perfume in Switzerland.

The negotiations went on until late at night, with Chambrun calling Coco at the Beau Rivage Hotel, Lausanne's lakefront hotel. This time, the Wertheimers sued for peace. The new agreement stipulated first that Chanel had the right to produce and sell "Mademoiselle Chanel" as long as she didn't attach the numeral 5 to it; second, that the wartime royalty settlement of the contraband No. 5 would be increased to $180,000, £20,000 and 5 million francs*; and, finally, that starting in 1947, Coco would receive 2 percent royalties of all Chanel products, worldwide, approximately $60,000, or $360,000 in 1990 currency, a year.

In a cover story on the Chanel empire forty-two years later, *Forbes* would add an intriguing footnote. If Pierre Wertheimer settled in 1947,

---

*The total settlement in period dollars was $326,000—$180,000 plus $96,000 (£20,000 at $4.80 to the pound) plus $50,000 (5 million francs at 100 francs to the dollar)— approximately $2 million in 1990 currency.

the American business magazine said, it was because he was afraid "a legal fight might illuminate Chanel's wartime activities and wreck her image—and his business." It was as if he and Coco were locked in a Faustian pact.

After the settlement was signed, Gabrielle shared a bottle of champagne with Josée and René de Chambrun as they relaxed in her suite at the Ritz in Paris. She was pleased, she told the lawyer; she had made a lot of money—spent a lot, too. Thanks to him, she said, putting her legs up on the coffee table, she would never have to work again. She used to keep her business papers in the coffee-table drawer. "I won't need this anymore," she said, pushing the table toward Josée. "I'll let you have it."

Pierre Wertheimer came to Lausanne to seal the peace. His brother was dead, and his thirty-seven-year-old son, Jacques, was no great businessman, he complained. Coco thought the younger Wertheimer was a sad sack and called him "Bonjour Tristesse." In a moment of candor, Pierre once agreed with her that his son was not the most cheerful of companions.

She was rich but fading from fashion consciousness. Only women with long memories recalled the last Chanels, the velvet suits buttoned with jewels, the gold lamé evening dresses, and the pleated, chopped jackets of 1938–39. Not that a definitive postwar look had evolved. Hems were lower, heels higher, waists nipped in, but there was an air of indecision.

On February 12, 1947, Christian Dior exploded on the fashion scene and with one collection put an end to the war and its drab aftermath. The models who swept into the salon of the pristine new headquarters at 30 Avenue Montaigne looked totally different from the women in the audience. With yards of fabrics in their skirts, the models spun up the aisle to the sound of rustling petticoats.

In one swish of newly discovered stiffened nylon, the fifty-year-old Dior swept away thirteen uninterrupted years of the square-shouldered, military, Schiaparelli-inspired look. The dressmaking techniques were immensely complicated, some Victorian, some newly evolved. The skirt burst into pleats, sometimes stitched over the hips or blossoming out under the stiff curved peplum of the jacket. The hems rustled around twelve inches from the floor; the models wore the sheerest of nylon stockings and the highest of pointed shoes.

Carmel Snow, accompanied by Marie-Louise Bousquet, occupied the reserved seats for *Harper's Bazaar*. Helen Gordon-Lazareff, editor of the new *Elle* magazine, sat between Ernestine Carter of the London *Sunday Times* and Eugenia Sheppard of the *New York Herald Tribune*, while a few chairs away *Vogue*'s gilded chair was occupied by the French edition's formidable Michel de Brunhoff.

A strike paralyzed the Parisian newspapers the next day, so the foreign press were the first to trumpet the triumph of what was immediately called the "New Look." Dior restored, in one afternoon, world confidence in Paris as fashion leader.

Coco read about it in the Swiss newspapers. She read about Dior and his staff working eighteen-hour days to accommodate I. Magnin, Bergdorf Goodman, and the first famous customers, the Duchess of Windsor and Eva Perón. Both curious and furious, she returned to Paris, and caught Christian Bérard, who illustrated the New Look in *Vogue*, as he entered the Ritz and accused him of helping to promote the ruin of French couture.

"Stop pretending you're it," he snapped back, furious.

There was more to Dior's success than clever publicity. The elegant women of Paris were shaking off the wartime traumas. Balenciaga, Lelong, Fath, and Rochas unveiled collections that were far more sumptuous than their prewar presentations. "Women had been deprived of everything for five years so they threw themselves on fashion like hungry beasts," Marquise Emmita de la Falaise would recall.

Gabrielle returned to Lausanne, but she remained in touch with friends in France. Pierre Reverdy sent her a copy of his new anthology of poems, *Main d'oeuvre*, inscribing her copy: "Here, dearest Coco, in my own hand, the best that I've made of myself."

Charles Chaplin became her neighbor, a refugee from Hollywood's witchhunt. Exile was bitter for him. He and Coco had the same lawyer in Lausanne, and when they met, she asked him how he had discovered his Little Tramp costume.

"Little by little," he answered, "in music halls, among ragpickers."

To her question of why he had given up making movies, he answered, "I can't play an *old* tramp."

Spatz slipped out of her life around 1950, though she may have continued to support him. Coco traveled, spent more time in France, in Roquebrune, in Paris, but kept returning to Lausanne. There she enjoyed the company of Marguerite Nametalla van Zuylen, a lively and provocative Egyptian with sparkling eyes and mischievous laughter who was married to Baron Egmont van Zuylen, a Belgian diplomat. She found new Swiss friends, a Dr. Félix Vallotton and his wife, whom she invited to vacation at La Pausa. The doctor would remember Chanel and Maggy van Zuylen singing turn-of-the-century music hall numbers together; his wife would recall that Coco never mentioned fashion and couture.

Despite her failing eyesight, Misia came to Switzerland. Jojo Sert had died in 1945, and Misia made trips to Lausanne to visit Coco and to buy the cocaine she could no longer live without. Luchino Visconti also came to visit. He was becoming a leader in Italian cinema, and was thinking of doing Shakespeare's *As You Like It* as a fantasy fairytale. Coco told him to make Salvador Dali his collaborator.

In September 1950, when Misia returned to Paris from one of her visits with Gabrielle, she took to her bed. Alerted by friends, Coco returned to Paris to be with her seventy-eight-year-old friend at the time of her death. When Misia died, Gabrielle did something she had never done for anyone. She had the body carried to Jojo Sert's big canopied bed, and made everyone leave the room. She dressed her friend in white, combed her hair, made her up, and adorned her with jewels. When she opened the doors an hour later, the assembled mourners saw Misia elegant one last time.

Paul Claudel, the grand old man of French letters, came to pay his respects, and thought Misia looked astonishingly young. He noted in his *Journal*, "Jean Cocteau, whose hands I had to admire, was there; Chanel, thin like a skeleton." Gabrielle's gesture found its way into Evelyn Waugh's comic-macabre novel *The Loved One* via Princess Dolly Radziwill, who described in detail to her friends how Chanel cleaned Misia's nails, "but perhaps put a bit too much makeup on her."

Gaston Bonheur became Coco's first would-be biographer. He was invited to stay with her at Roquebrune during the summer of 1950, but soon gave up. At Cocteau's suggestion, André Fraigneau became the next author-journalist to try. Cocteau was sure she would be a pithy memorialist, and in 1951 she and Fraigneau began a series of interviews that were quickly abandoned.

She told her friends she wanted to avoid the pitfalls of old age, espe-

cially the self-centeredness that she believed accelerated the aging process
in women. She could afford young admirers, but maintained that the lure
of younger men was charming only as long as a woman knew how to
resist it.

Many of her former lovers and old friends were gone. Grand Duke
Dmitri had died of tuberculosis during the war in Davos, near St. Moritz,
at the age of fifty. For a while in the 1930s he had been a champagne
salesman in Palm Beach, Florida. Christian Bérard died in 1949; in 1953
Etienne Balsan was killed, like Boy Capel, in an automobile accident.
Bendor also died in 1953, suddenly, of coronary thrombosis, leaving behind Anne, the fourth Duchess of Westminster, but no male heir. Coco
went to see Colette on her deathbed in 1954. In Rome, Vera Bate passed
away, an embarrassing witness of things past.

At the same time another discomfiting witness reappeared. A voice
on a long-distance telephone in June 1951 said he was Walter Schellenberg. He was just out of prison, he said.

At the collapse of the Third Reich, Himmler's crafty deputy had escaped to Sweden. With the help of Count Bernadotte, he had drawn up
a memorandum stressing his efforts to wrest a negotiated peace from the
Allies, so that when he was extradited to stand trial as a war criminal he
had a basis of defense. His trial lasted fifteen months, and of the twenty-
one war criminals tried at Nuremberg, his seven-year prison conviction
in April 1949 was the lightest penalty the court inflicted.

Under an assumed name, Schellenberg and his wife were now taking
refuge in Switzerland. Private diaries by intimates who had witnessed
Hitler's end were all the rage, and Schellenberg decided to publish his
memoirs. Alan Bullock, a British broadcaster and Nuremberg Trial
specialist who had already edited Ribbentrop's memoirs, was going to
help him.

Literary agents were encouraging. Schellenberg and Bullock talked to
them all. Hitler's former secret police chief made no mystery of anything,
and made no effort to hide his true identity. To Coco, however, he suggested she might not want to see her story in his memoirs.

After finishing a rough draft of his memoirs, Schellenberg died in Italy
in 1952 at the age of forty-two. Coco paid a large sum of money to his
widow in Düsseldorf. When *The Labyrinth* came out, the Schellenberg
memoir made no mention of Chanel.

Gabrielle went to the United States in the spring of 1953. It was her first trip since the Goldwyn days. Les Parfums Chanel asked her to approve the remodeling of the new and expanded New York offices, and she threw herself into the project with enthusiasm. Something to do.

She had a panel of Coromandel screens brought over, and insisted on beige carpets, honey-beige straw-cloth walls, blond-beige woods—walnut, pearwood—and rosy-beige leather on old French chairs. African bronzes and paintings by Henri Rousseau and Auguste Renoir completed the decor.

She spent three months in New York as the houseguest of Egmont and Maggy van Zuylen, and weekends on Long Island, at the Harrison Williams estate or at Horst's more modest beach house. Harrison Williams, Coco's admirer who had asked her to sail away with him in 1939, had died, and Mona, his society wife, was now married to Eddie Bismarck, who on Gestapo orders had donned an SS uniform to escort Vera Bate from Rome to Milan in 1943.

Coco and Maggy inspired each other to hilarity and sarcasm. Maggy's daughter, Marie-Hélène, had recently married Guy de Rothschild and the mother of the bride told the funniest asides on the *beau monde* at the wedding—"'a marriage of fire and water" she said of her spirited daughter and the head of the French branch of the illustrious family.

It was from the sidelines that Chanel witnessed the major change in French fashion—the postwar emergence of men as top designers. Between 1920 and 1940, the most influential couture houses had been in the hands of women. Besides Chanel, Lanvin, Vionnet, and Schiaparelli, Nina Ricci and Alix Czereskow—first as Alix, then as Madame Grès—successfully directed their own houses. Now fashion design belonged increasingly to men.

Lucien Lelong, Marcel Rochas, Jean Patou, Edward Molyneux, Mainbocher, and Cristobal Balenciaga had all opened their houses before the war, but Young Turks were beginning to nip even at the heels of Dior. Hubert James Marcel Taffin de Givenchy followed Pierre Balmain and Pierre Cardin in opening small couture studios.

The men were different. They worked on paper, sketching their ideas rather than molding them on dummies or models. Their designs were often more daring than those of the women designers, probably because they did not have to wear what they created. For the male designers, practical considerations were secondary to striking effects. "Designing is a sublimation of the urge to put on women's clothes," said Jacques Lenoir, the elegant owner of the Chlöe ready-to-wear label. "They neither love nor hate women. They are rarely in love, especially the most successful among them, like Freud, who stopped making love at forty-one when he became totally caught up in his work."

The success of the New Look exerted tremendous pressures on Dior and French fashion. Over the next three years, the Parisian couturiers took the look into exaggerated, geometric shapes, boldly asymmetric and stylized directions. For 1948–49, Dior produced his *envol* line, superimposing an angle of fullness upon an arrow-thin sheath. A year later, Balenciaga created blown-out taffeta pumpkin evening dresses, and Fath came out with a lemon-yellow tent coat. The "trumpet skirt," which flared out below a narrow point, turned full-length evening dresses into fishtail sheaths.

Commercially, it all amounted to a high-wire act. If the principal designers differed too much in their "lines"—Dior's *envol* was followed by the princess line, the tulip line, the I and H line—there was confusion and alarm among the buyers. If they did not change enough from the line of the previous season, buyers complained they were not given a decisive lead. Answering its own rhetorical question: Where has the waist gone? British *Vogue* answered, "Anywhere but where you expect it."

Rumors that Coco Chanel was planning to reopen her couture house cropped up in 1950, the year Schiaparelli threw in the towel and closed *her* house. The idea seemed preposterous. Apart from the perennial perfume, Chanel was history. Two years later, the rumors surfaced again. Newspapers wrote of a February 1954 launch; some speculated that the House of Chanel would reopen as a ready-to-wear boutique, others said it would present the most extravagant couture collection ever seen.

It was Maggy's daughter, Marie-Hélène de Rothschild, who would get the credit for persuading Coco to go for it. Because Pierre Wertheimer thought she was an old lady who should just live off her fortune, the perfume company got to pay for it.

Four

34

COMEBACK

At seventy, Gabrielle was a spare, taut figure, hung with jewels. Her broad, shrewd face was marked by her wide mouth, furrowed chin, angular jaw, and determinedly penciled eyebrows. Except for the enormous glasses that sometimes hid her widely spaced eyes, she looked much as she had in 1939 when she closed the House of Chanel. Her powerful, broad-knuckled hands, her strong fingers without nail polish still revealed her common sense and stubbornness. Her voice had grown deeper but she still spoke a continuous monologue in her familiar muted tone.

Marie-Hélène de Rothschild had bought an extravagant ball gown for the most important party of 1953.

"What a horror!" Coco exclaimed when the young baroness showed the strapless evening dress cutting across her front. Nothing was uglier, Coco felt, than boned and corseted bodices.

Marie-Hélène, a woman a third Chanel's age, bought clothes with impulsive boldness; Coco was convinced Marie-Hélène had inherited her excesses from her mother. On the spot, Coco improvised a substitute gown, a dress cut from one huge curtain of crimson taffeta.

The day after the fête, Marie-Hélène told Coco that everybody had asked who her designer was. "That's what made her decide to go for a comeback," Marie-Hélène would claim twenty years later.

A ball gown fashioned from a scarlet curtain was only half the challenge. The other half came from Pierre Wertheimer, if unwittingly.

Wertheimer came to Ouchy on Lausanne's lakefront during the summer of 1953 to see Coco at the Hôtel Beau Rivage. He had decided he should tell her the bad news to her face. Fashion magazines might be quoting Marilyn Monroe's famous line that all she wore to bed was Chanel No. 5, but the fact remained that sales were slipping for the first time in thirty years.

He was relieved when Coco took the news calmly.

During a stroll along the lakefront before his return to Paris, she suggested they launch a new Chanel fragrance.

He didn't think it was a good idea. Perfumes and cosmetics were a bruisingly competitive business. The life span of name scents was getting shorter every year and the made-in-Paris labels no longer meant automatic leadership. Fortunately, the Americans were not asking for a new Chanel fragrance. The No. 5 income was still more than substantial, he said.

To his surprise, she didn't insist. He returned to Paris thinking she had finally mellowed, that at seventy she was accepting her golden sunset.

A few days later, she was back at the Ritz.

Fifteen years of inactivity had quelled all desire for leisure living. She sold the villa at Roquebrune. The buyer was Emery Reves, Winston Churchill's literary agent. There is a measure of irony in the fact that the British statesman she had tried so arduously to meet in Madrid in the middle of World War II would spend long periods of his old age at La Pausa, and would write several volumes of his memoirs of the war at the house.

Coco was back in town to start up again, to reopen the couture house.

She sensed the time was right. She believed in the overwhelming appeal of her classic line, refined again and again but never fundamentally changed. She believed in an unmistakable *look* that was flattering, easy to wear, and timeless. A dress should not be a disguise. If a fashion wasn't taken up and worn by everybody, it was not a fashion, but an eccentricity, a fancy dress.

Fundamental changes were revolutionizing the industry. From the basic silk, wool, and cotton available when Chanel started before World War I, dozens of alternatives—grease-resistant, permanently pleated, glazed, shrink-proof, waterproof, washable—were coming on the market.

Nylon transformed the wardrobe, and acetate, Orlon, rayon, and the other drip-dry synthetic fibers allowed women to put on clean clothes every day, something once thought to be an eccentricity of the Empress Josephine.

She wanted to be at the front of the revolution. The new fabrics and the new system of mass production that ready-to-wear represented quickened the entire fashion tempo, and made for *courants d'air*, for wind currents that not only carried the message out from the designers' studios, but whipped influences back from an increasingly fashion-conscious mass market. Coco had always believed that any fashion that wasn't adapted by a majority of women was a flop. To see herself copied in the street was the greatest compliment.

One day in September, Robert Chaillet, the head of the Bourjois legal department, got a telephone call from René de Chambrun.

"I've got a good one for you. She's starting up again. I think you should tell the boss."

Pierre Wertheimer was more than interested. A revived Chanel image in couture would boost sales of the Chanel perfumes, just as an embarrassing flop would hurt. More important, Mademoiselle was the sole owner of Chanel Couture, meaning she could franchise her name on anything and everything from nylon stockings to bath towels, thereby cheapening the prestige of Parfums Chanel.

And the prestige value of Chanel No. 5 was priceless. Diana Vreeland, the new editor of the American *Vogue*, praised it in words no copywriter could imitate: "Chanel No. 5, to me, is still the ideal scent for a woman. She can wear it anywhere, anytime, and everybody—husbands, beaus, taxi drivers—*everybody* loves it. *No one* has gone beyond Chanel No. 5."

Coco was not waiting for Les Parfums Chanel to bankroll the startup. She had Marie-Louise Bousquet query her boss at *Harper's Bazaar* in New York about a direct sale of Chanel originals to Seventh Avenue ready-to-wear. On September 24, 1953, Carmel Snow wired back:

KNOW FIRSTCLASS READYTOWEAR MANUFACTURER
INTERESTED IN REPRODUCING YOUR LINE STOP
MARIE-LOUISE IS VAGUE REGARDING DETAILS STOP
WHEN WILL YOUR COLLECTION BE READY STOP
ARE YOU COMING TO NEW YORK WITH COLLECTION

STOP DO YOU DELIVER FABRICS STOP WILL BE HAPPY
TO HELP YOU.

Six days later, the Chambrun office drew up Coco's reply:

September 30, 1953

Mrs. Carmel Snow
Harper's Bazaar
572 Madison Avenue
New York City

Dear Carmel,

I received your cable and confirm my answer.

During the summer I got the idea that it would be fun to go
back to work, because work is all my life. No doubt I already told
you that one day sooner or later I'd resume my métier, which
consists of creating a new style adapted to a new life-style and that
I was waiting for the opportune moment. That moment has come.

The current climate in Paris in which more and more women
are shown collections they cannot afford is pushing me to do something completely different.

One of my primary goals is to have an American manufacturer
produce a ready-to-wear line on a royalty basis. I feel that this would
arouse considerable interest throughout the world.

My first collection will be ready November 1, and I believe it
would be prudent for me not to try anything further until I have an
offer from the first-class manufacturer you mention. Perhaps it would
be best if he flew to Paris. Nothing of course would make me hap-
pier than to see you also. For the moment, I don't plan to show my
own collection in America, but I don't say no. That could come a
little later,

As ever,
Gabrielle Chanel

Coco and her lawyer carefully leaked the implication of American
ready-to-wear back to the Wertheimers. As a result, Pierre Wertheimer

decided he could not afford *not* to help bankroll the Chanel revival. Les Parfums Chanel would pay half the cost of the collection, he agreed. It could be charged to the perfume publicity budget. To sign the accord, Coco and Chambrun drove out to the Wertheimer residence on Avenue de Neuilly. Pierre Wertheimer greeted them and led them upstairs.

Coco was seated at the end of the table next to Richard de Nexon, Adrienne's brother-in-law, who was still the chief executive officer of Les Parfums Chanel. When the time came to talk figures, Nexon politely leaned toward Mademoiselle and asked how much they were talking about.

"Anything over fifteen million* would be an exaggeration," she said. A year later, she and the perfume company would lose six times that amount.

Coco plunged into the work with gusto. She sold the adjoining buildings, while airing out 31 Rue Cambon and making it ready for work. The ground-floor boutique, which had never closed but sold only perfume, was renovated. Most of the salesgirls had not known the House of Chanel in the pre-1939 years. They greeted Mademoiselle with smiles and told her they were happy that they were no longer to be the lone guardians of a temple. Taking a cue from them, she told journalists she was re-opening a fashion house, not a museum. The faded mirrors in the second-floor grand salon were replaced and two upstairs workrooms made ready. Several former employees were located, including Madame Lucie, who had opened her own boutique in Rue Royale. Madame Lucie closed her shop and found herself close to tears when she saw the workrooms again.

Although she continued to sleep at the Ritz, Coco began to live in the building again. Her third-floor apartment was repainted, and she had her meals and received her friends there. Again she moved among her treasures, the Coromandel screens, the mirrors above the fireplace, sculpted blackamoors, bronze deer, and a fourth-century B.C. Aphrodite. Next to the Venus stood the statue of a wild boar, a meteorite that had fallen in China thousands of years before. And there were objects in mother-of-pearl, ebony, ivory, gold, and crystal, and a wall of rare books. The scent of tuberoses was everywhere.

---

*Fifteen million francs equaled $36,000 in 1954 money or $300,000 in 1990 currency.

To mark her second coming, she gave Dior and other couturiers a caustic going-over in a series of snappy interviews. In the "exclusive" interviews she gave to everyone, she claimed she had told Dior, "I adore you, but you dress women like armchairs." When asked what her collections would look like, she snapped, "How do I know? I keep changing until the last moment."

She wrestled with each costume. With the wall-to-wall mirrors as her sole reference, she pulled apart and pinned together again, shortening, lengthening, denuding, touching up, all to pare down to the function and logic of the body.

Her hands flew over the model's body, the seams, the fabric, folding layers of fabric like a handkerchief here, puffing out there. "I don't want to see the hips," she'd say. "Look at the behind. The fabric clings, scoots up." In the mirror the model smiled to herself.

She didn't "create," she liked to repeat. "Couture isn't an art, it's a business." She was oblivious to fatigue and distractions as she sent the model off to put her hair up in a chignon. "You've got a pretty face and a pretty brow, why hide it?"

After six, seven hours, the models, young and energetic, sagged with fatigue, while Mademoiselle worked on, seemingly indestructible. The next models in their white smocks waited on gilded chairs for their turn at a fitting.

Marie-Hélène helped her find models. Coco wanted well-bred, elegant society girls. The face didn't matter as much as the figure, the carriage, the ability to walk exquisitely. Marie-Hélène found a nineteen-year-old namesake, Marie-Hélène Arnaud. When Gabrielle showed an affectionate interest in the big-eyed, broad-faced Arnaud, the girl was rumored to be Coco's grand-niece, the elder of André Palasse's two daughters by a Dutch woman. No one established this as a fact, and the fashion press reported Arnaud to be the daughter of a Banque Rothschild director.

Vogue sent Cecil Beaton over. The celebrity photographer—and of late, Hollywood costume and set designer—was surprised at being allowed to snap pictures of the work in progress. Most couturiers swore their personnel to secrecy and banned publication of collection photographs until department-store buyers had time to reproduce authorized copies from *toiles*, but Chanel was supremely confident that quality would prevail—that the real Chanel suit would be instantly recognizable from all "knockoffs."

Beaton told an incongruous story of a young woman who was aggressively pursuing him. It was someone Coco knew, someone who could have been her daughter, he winked.

"June's mad about me," he said.

When Coco's curiosity was sufficiently piqued, he told her that June Osborn, the widow of the pianist Franz Osborn, was none other than Boy Capel's daughter. The girl born to Diana Capel, later Countess of Westmoreland, a few months after Boy's death in 1920, was very much an aristocrat, insouciant and witty, and the mother of a school-age son.

Coco checked out the story with Lady Abdy. It was all very true. Apparently, the thirty-three-year-old June even knew that Beaton was sixteen years her senior and a homosexual.

The 130-model collection would not be ready for November 1, nor for December 1, nor January 1. As always, Coco decided to show on a fifth, her lucky number, and the premiere was set for February 5, 1954. On the eve of the collection opening, she had the girls parade in front of her while she was lying flat on her stomach to see if the hems were right. She ordered boxes of flowers, ribbons, and buttons, to be added if necessary. But instead of adding, she more often took away details already there.

The 2:00 P.M. show was the hottest ticket in Paris and the refurbished grand salon filled to capacity half an hour early. A heady mix of Beautiful People, buyers, press, and photographers crammed into the room. Louise de Vilmorin was there with her sister, Mapie de Toulouse-Lautrec. Boris Kochno was seen with Sophie Litvak, Luchino Visconti with Annie Girardot. Carmel Snow sat next to Philippe de Crosset, whose father Francis had been in love with Coco in her Royallieu days. Condé Nast publishing had its American, British, and French *Vogue* editors in place. Lucien François, the fashion "oracle" from *Combat*, headed the Parisian press. Hélène Terzieff was there with her team from *Elle*, the successful new French fashion monthly. The London newspapers had their own contingent of writers. There were few young faces in the audience.

The first model skipped down the runway to still the small talk and focus the attention. Mademoiselle was nowhere to be seen, perched as always at the top of the mirrored staircase where she could gauge the precise modulations of applause with infallible precision. A photographer caught her on top of the stairs, in her white chemise, black silk vest, and severe skirt, mutely looking down. The mannequins, with bows at the back of their heads, came out six steps apart until there were often seven or eight of them at once, each reflected in the mirrored walls until the room overflowed with feminine allure. The tall models walked slowly, the small rounded ones walked faster.

The presentation was quaint. Buyers, journalists, and fashion devotees had grown used to the zip of Dior's shows, where models came out moving quickly, outfitted with handbags, gloves, and even umbrellas. Here, the audience saw the models enter, pose, pause for an editor in the front row to feel the fabric, pose again, turn slowly—all the while carrying a numbered card in one hand.

Knowing glances were exchanged. Where was the news? The advance publicity had made everybody expect anything but unchanged simplicity. The presentation ended in icy silence. There was a sudden rush for the doors as if everybody was anxious not to be late for another appointment. A few friends wanted to go upstairs. Coco met them on the stairs. She was a winner, someone said. The congratulations sounded like condolences. She muttered something of an explanation. Young people no longer knew who she was.

Callers were told, "Mademoiselle is exhausted." Madame Lucie stayed all evening. To her, Mademoiselle allowed herself to wonder whether she had not lost her touch.

The next day's reviews were devastating. *Le Combat*'s François led off under the headline: "Chez Coco Chanel à Fouilly-Les-Oies en 1930" (roughly, "In the Sticks with 1930 Coco Chanel"): "From the first dress we knew that the Chanel style belonged to the past. Dresses tucked in at the waist, balloon sleeves, round décolleté conjured up little more than a furtive memory of a period that is difficult to situate, 1929–30, no doubt. Chanel makes herself so much at home in a legend idealized by memories that we forget her fashion was already mortally wounded in 1938. But there are no 1938 dresses here, only ghosts of 1930!" *Le Figaro* wrote, "It was touching. You had a feeling you were back in 1925."

The London press was no better. The *Daily Express* headlined the Chanel revival: "A Fiasco—Audience Gasped!" and said it was too soon to try to recapture the prewar era. A more temperate London critic called it a collection for mothers ("Mums"). Simone Baron of *France-Soir*, the biggest afternoon paper, managed to catch Coco for her reaction. "What can I tell you? People no longer know what elegance is. When I work, I think of the women I try to dress, not the couture house. How can anyone get it so wrong? Once I helped liberate women, I'll do it again."

When Pierre Wertheimer went to see Coco in Rue Cambon, he found her in dark glasses, working on her next collection. She admitted she felt exhausted, that she was disappointed. He stayed until she was ready to close up and walked her across to the Ritz.

"You know I want to go on, go on and win," she told him.

"You're right," he said. "You're right to go on."

Chaillet, the Wertheimer lawyer, thought she took the defeat with dignity. "She claimed women were too smart to stay away," Chaillet would remember. "She behaved as if it was everybody else who was wrong, or under the sway of the 'little queers,' as she called Dior and the other male designers. Without bitterness, she said neither she nor those who helped her were responsible. The journalists were responsible."

It was only in retrospect that Wertheimer's resolution to continue to back her would be seen as a brilliant business decision. At the time, several members of the Parfums Chanel board were dead set against it. Chanel was seventy-one. It was folly to believe she could be resuscitated, that her fashion could be relevant again.

Wertheimer, a man who had had many mistresses in his day, was used to paying women's personal expenses. Coco, in fact, could never make up her mind whether she wanted Pierre to treat her as a business-person or as a woman, with the result that he treated her with the listless forbearance a lover exhibits toward a mistress who has outstayed her welcome. Still, he was also afraid of her, and during the decade following her comeback would phone a mole at Rue Cambon to gauge Coco's mood. If her mood was good, he'd call and take her to lunch. A heavy meal, wine, spirits, and a good cigar and Pierre was liable to nod off, something that greatly irritated her. "Pierre, are you listening?" she'd ask, startling him.

Wertheimer overruled their objections and renegotiated the contract with Gabrielle. Coco obtained from Wertheimer an agreement stipulating that the perfume company would pay the entire cost of Rue Cambon, that Les Parfums Chanel would pick up her personal expenses and what-ever French taxes she would be assessed. In return, the corporation reas-serted its ownership of the name Chanel as it applied to perfumes. The paragraph in the 1947 settlement that gave her the right to produce and sell Mademoiselle Chanel perfume as long as she didn't attach the numeral 5 to it was scrapped, as was her prerogative to consider Switzerland her private domain for the making and selling of new scents.

With all the concessions she had torn from him in renegotiating the contract, Wertheimer wanted a kiss from her for the press photographers, and invited her on a cruise aboard his new yacht. She refused. When his colt Lavandin won the Epsom Derby, she was sure he would be insufferable. Indeed, he couldn't wait to share his good fortune, and the moment he was back in Paris dashed upstairs to her apartment, followed at a more leisurely pace by Chambrun. To catch his breath, he let himself collapse into an armchair.

Pretending not to have heard about his turf victory, she said, "You don't look too good, Pierre."

He got up and opened his arms. "Aren't you going to kiss me?" he beamed.

Parisian newspapers carried a United Press International news photo showing the top-hatted Wertheimer walking his horse to the winner's circle, but Coco pretended not to know anything about his triumph.

"Don't you know I've won the Derby?"

With a crooked smile, she said, "And you didn't call me?"

Three weeks later, *Life* magazine led the American raves. In an introduction to a four-page spread, the picture weekly wrote that Chanel, "the name behind the most famous perfume in the world," had lost none of her prewar skills. "Her styles hark back to her best of the thirties—lace evening dresses that have plenty of elegant dash and easy-fitting suits that are refreshing after the 'poured-on' look of some styles—and also feature such innovations as nylon."

The March issue of the French *Vogue* followed. Marie-Hélène Arnaud in a navy-blue jersey suit with squared shoulders, tucked crisp white blouse with a bow tie, sailor hat tipped to the back of the head, and her hands in the skirt pockets, was on the cover.

35

UNMISTAKABLE INFLUENCE

Less concerned with fashion history than the Parisian fashion press, women found the pared-down Chanel silhouette young and easygoing in ways that were more truly modern than Dior's careful sophistication and Balenciaga's sculptural formality. After six years of cinched-in waists and clothes so constructed they could stand up by themselves, elegance that allowed freedom of movement somehow *was* new. Bettina Ballard, the French *Vogue* editor who put Marie-Hélène Arnaud on the cover, was sure the Chanel look would appeal overwhelmingly and directly to the public. Chanel was unmistakably Chanel and wearing her clothes gave women security. To be smart-looking was more desirable than being too done-up; the look was safe, hence flattering.

Ballard's successor at French *Vogue*, Francine Crescent, would remember Ballard's explanation for choosing the Chanel outfit. Ballard had possessed before the war an ensemble almost identical to the one on the cover, and she wanted to own such an outfit again. "Bettina was sure that if other women saw these clothes, they, too, would want them," Crescent recalled.

Karl Lagerfeld was one apprentice designer who also thought Chanel got it right. Recently arrived from his native Hamburg, the seventeen-year-old Lagerfeld was one of a class of students from the Chambre Syndicale design school who saw the new Chanel clothes. "You had a feeling you were seeing something prehistoric, but I loved this look that harked back to a prewar world I hadn't known but found more intoxicating than any current fashion," he would remember twenty-five years later. "Chanel was so alive and intuitive, and she found the right compromise between her style and the 1950s look."

The reception of the second Chanel collection in the fall of 1954 was still only lukewarm, but it divided the Paris couture in two camps. Dior, Givenchy, Balmain, and Fath—now carried on by Jacques Fath's widow, Geneviève—designed clothes with body and shape of their own, clothes that were popular with shops for their "hanger appeal." Chanel headed the second camp, whose clothes, made of soft fabrics such as jersey and silk tweed, generally took their shape from the wearer. Balenciaga's day clothes, Patou and Lanvin belonged to this group. A year later, fashion began catching up with Coco. Taking a deeper, second look at the revolution she had wrought, *Vogue* said that with the exception of Fath, the entire Paris couture was "permeated with the easy, underdone sort of clothes that were the basis of Chanelism at its height."

"Other couturiers have interpreted Chanel in today's versions," the fashion magazine wrote in the spring of 1954. "Chanel herself followed her 1939 ideas so closely that the public, whipped into a frenzy of expectation by the extraordinary advance publicity, gasped in surprise at the unchanged simplicity, and many of them gasped in disappointment. They came expecting the same sort of fashion miracle which Chanel had performed in 1919 when she introduced her 'nothing of a dress' into a world of elaborate, overdone clothes. In 1954, the fashion world looked for another surprise—and the surprise was that none appeared. But if the simplicity of her line was not new, was suited perhaps more for meticulous private clients than for astonishing the multitudes, its influence is unmistakable. Whether this collection was simply a 'beau geste' on Chanel's part, or a return to her career, it was—and is—the excitement of the Paris Collections."

With the rest of the Rothschilds following Marie-Hélène to Chanel's door, Coco's clients again constituted a litany of best-dressed women of the decade. Grace Kelly, Lauren Bacall, Ingrid Bergman, Elizabeth Taylor, and Rita Hayworth followed Marlene Dietrich to 31 Rue Cambon.

Dietrich's measurements from 1933 were still on file and the *vendeuse* tactfully insisted they had not changed a centimeter.

Dietrich was called "the most beautiful grandmother in show business." She launched a second career in Las Vegas, bellowing out throaty songs dressed in a slinky, near-transparent silk dress.

With Lady Abdy, 1929.

Chanel, 1929.

Photo portrait of Chanel by Cecil Beaton, 1937.

With actress Ina Claire, 1931.

Gloria Swanson in
Chanel wardrobe for
Night or Never, 1931.

Paul Iribe.

Coco in Venice, 1936.

Chanel at fifty, by George Hoynigen-Huene.

Chanel, 1936.

René de Chambrun, Chanel's attorney, with his fiancée, Josée Laval, 1935.

Striking Chanel personnel at the Rue Cambon employee entrance, showing their traditional strikers' collection box, 1936.

Chanel at fifty-five.

Between Salvador Dali and Christian Bérard in
Monte Carlo, 1938.

Swiss exile, 1949—Coco and Spatz.

Coco in her apartment in Rue Cambon, 1954.

With Maggy van Zuylen
on Long Island,
New York, 1953.

Pierre Wertheimer
leading his colt Lanvin
after winning the 1956
Derby at Epsom Downs,
England.

Chanel on the eve of the 1954 comeback.

Kate as Coco—
Katharine Hepburn on
Broadway, 1969.

With Romy
Schneider, actress.

Chanel at work.

Chanel at Chantilly racetrack with her trainer
François Mathet, 1964.

Gabrielle Chanel's grave in Lausanne.

"Why did you start up again?" Marlene asked Coco after a fitting.

"Because I was bored to death."

"You too?"

For Les Parfums Chanel, Chanel Couture was becoming a financial black hole. The Chanel look was popular but couture was no longer as profitable as it had been. In fact, couture was totally unsuited for the instant obsolescence of throwaway fashion and much of the new taste in fashion consciousness. The money was in mass-manufactured ready-to-wear and accessories, and the renewed popularity of Chanel couture did not cause sales of No. 5 to pick up immediately.

Coco hated to be accountable to "the gentlemen in Neuilly," as she called Wertheimer and his perfume executives, and in the spring of 1954, she summoned Wertheimer to come and see her. She suggested they renegotiate, and, when he agreed, she immediately tried to gain leverage by wondering aloud what would happen if she sold the couture house to a foreigner. She wouldn't want that, of course, but she was old. She could die at any time. Wertheimer was sure she didn't believe a word of it, but he got the point. It would not be in his interest to see Chanel couture sold to new owners who might have their own ideas about exploiting the logo.

On May 24, 1954, he bought her out.

In return for underwriting the fashion house 100 percent, Les Parfums Chanel acquired the couture house, her real estate holdings in the Rue Cambon buildings, her interests in textile mills, everything that bore the name Chanel, including Chanel Publishing, dormant since Paul Iribe's death. The price was never made public, but under the new contract she kept her perfume royalties, including portions of the income from Pour Monsieur, the first Chanel scent for men, which the Wertheimers were putting into production. The royalties would revert to Les Parfums Chanel, however, after her death. She kept sole control of her collections and her choice of collaborators. "We paid everything," Les Parfums Chanel lawyer Chaillet would say, "the Ritz, her secretaries, servants, everything including her telephone bills and postage stamps."

Adrienne died in 1955, leaving Maurice de Nexon a grieving widower. Apart from André Palasse, Adrienne had been the only member of the family Coco cared for. Her other relatives she had turned her back on. One day shortly after the reopening of the couture salon, Coco's nieces, Gabrielle and Antoinette Chanel, came to 31 Rue Cambon. Alphonse's two daughters were in their late twenties. They happened to be in Paris, up from Valleraugue, and just wanted to say hello, perhaps see their aunt, or at least her famous dresses. They were told Mademoiselle was not in, and that they needed an invitation to look at dresses.

They inquired when their aunt might be in. They had not come to ask for anything, they insisted. No one had any idea when Mademoiselle would be in.

Coco refused to see her two nieces, yet she stayed in contact with André Palasse's daughter after he died. When this grandniece married and had a son, Coco asked them to visit her at the Ritz. Gabrielle La-brunie would remember Coco suddenly asking her seven-year-old son if he was working hard in school.

"How do you spell *rhinoceros?*" she asked.

When the boy hesitated, she changed the subject. The next day she sent the boy a beautiful album on animals, with the picture of a rhino circled in red.

Now that she had reached an agreement with the Wertheimers, Coco Chanel needed to fight *someone* and picked the Chambre Syndicale de la Couture Parisienne, the trade association started by Lucien Lelong. To-gether with the Chambre Syndicale du Prêt à Porter, the ready-to-wear sister organization, the Chambre Syndicale de la Couture Parisienne was both management and union. Collection schedules and accreditation were coordinated by the Chambre, but the trade association's most important task was to ride herd on piracy. The first French law specifically protect-ing fashion creations was passed in 1920, giving couture designs almost the same protection as literature, films, and patented inventions.

Knocking off clothes had been a problem as far back as the eighteenth century when Versailles courtesans tried to bribe Marie Antoinette's dress-maker to reveal details of the queen's latest gown before she wore it for the first time. Despite the screening of buyers, press, and private clients, stealing designs had grown into a fine art since the 1930s. When cameras were banned from shows, teams of two or three sketch artists worked separately on specific portions of a silhouette—one concentrating on the sleeves, the other on necklines, the third on the skirt treatment. After the show, they assembled the total look.

Chanel felt that even to try to protect fashion ideas was hopeless. She claimed she had caught industrial spies going through her trash cans in Rue Cambon looking for swatches that would tell them what fabrics and colors she was working with. She liked to tell of the time one of her employees had discovered a street hawker selling fake Chanels off the back of a truck at an outdoor street market. At 50 francs apiece, Coco said, ecstatic, the dresses sold like hotcakes.

Her decision to disregard Chambre rules on "for the trade only" showings and to allow photographers to snap pictures of her designs brought her into a head-on collision with Raymond Barbas, the Chambre president.

Barbas defended the rules. They were intended to give members of the press equal access, and to make sure buyers who paid hard currencies for couture models were not being knocked off before they could get the new fashions into their stores.

Coco didn't agree. "Come to my place and steal all the ideas you can," she told the press. "Fashion isn't made to be canned. Fashion in cans becomes quickly obsolete." She held aloft a letter from a little seamstress somewhere in France who said she couldn't afford to buy a Chanel model, and asked to be allowed to have a peek at her collections once in a while.

The controversy heated up. Gabrielle claimed counterfeiting was the flattering ransom of success. Couturiers, who lived and breathed publicity, were hypocrites when they demanded press embargoes. Draping himself in the French flag, Barbas retorted that knockoffs added up to lost hard currency. If anybody was hurt by the Chambre edicts, she retorted, it was little French seamstresses. In anger she fired off her letter of resignation:

Mr. President,

Allow me to submit a resignation you wish to receive, but which, out of a tactfulness I can only thank you for, you hesitate to demand.

This way the conflict that opposes me and the Chambre is settled.

(signed) Chanel

Givenchy and Balenciaga followed her lead and allowed photo coverage of their collections. Quietly, the Chambre dropped its press embargo rules.

Chanel's chief competitor, Dior, was overworked and feeling beleaguered. The buildup of expectations since 1947 created tremendous pressures, and Dior, who had already had two heart attacks, kept gaining weight and some days looked more like a seventy-year-old than a man in his early fifties. He had no financial or domestic worries, but he had to "deliver." The House of Dior was incorporated in five countries, franchised in five others, and Dior himself was sent on endless overseas publicity tours. His assistant was a shy young man from North Africa named Yves Saint Laurent.

The reception of Dior's 1956–57 winter collection was only polite. The spotlight that season focused instead on Pierre Cardin, who had set himself up in business in 1949 and whose first client had been none other than Christian Dior. Dior had ordered a lion's costume for what turned out to be the last costume ball of Count Etienne de Beaumont.

To decide whether Saint Laurent was a true creator or merely a young man who had been lucky, Dior asked him to design the spring 1958 collection on his own. Dior never got to judge the collection. In October 1957, while visiting the Montecatini spa in Italy, Dior died of a heart attack.

Dior management decided it was too late to call in an experienced designer and that the twenty-year-old Yves would have to take over.

Coco was in Dallas, Texas, at the time, the guest of Stanley Neiman-Marcus, to receive a fashion award "for being the most influential designer in the last fifty years." *Elle* magazine was an ardent champion of her style and message, and in a preview of the trip put Coco and her Texas-born model Suzy Parker on the cover. *The New Yorker* caught up with her at the Waldorf Astoria on her way back to Paris and found her to be "sensationally good-looking, with dark-brown eyes, a brilliant smile, and the unquenchable vitality of a twenty-year-old, and when, giving us a firm handshake, she said, 'I'm très, très fatiguée,' it was with the assurance of a woman who knows she can afford to say it." When asked why she had been in retirement so long, she bristled. Giving the magazine an example of her flavorful English, she told her interviewer that in her heart she had never really retired. "During the war, nobody thought any more of making beautiful clothes," she said, "and after the war I watched the couturiers, the young men, to see what they were doing. I traveled. I enjoyed my country place in Switzerland. But I was bored not having anything real to do. Always, I observed the new clothes. At last, quietly, calmly, with great determination, I began working on *une belle collection*. When I showed it in Paris, I had many critics. They said that I was old-fashioned, that I was no longer of the age. Always I was smiling inside my head, and I thought, I will show them. In America, there was great enthusiasm. In France, I had to fight. But I did not mind. I love very much to battle. Now, in France, they are trying to adapt my ideas." Fashion, she said, was always of its time. "It's not something standing alone."

Diana Vreeland invited her to dinner. Coco agreed only after being assured that she wouldn't have to talk, that it would be an intimate dinner for her and her date and Diana and Reed Vreeland. Yet when she came to dinner, she never stopped talking, and midway through the dinner, she asked if Helena Rubinstein could join them afterwards. Wertheimer had talked about Rubinstein, about her walking on her hands around a room because she had been brought up in the circus. When Rubinstein arrived, she and Coco retired to Reed Vreeland's study. "The two of them stayed in there the rest of the evening talking about God knows what," Diana would write. "I went in from time to time to check up on them. They never sat down. They stood—like men—and talked for hours. I'd never been in the presence of such strength of personality. Both of them. Neither of them was a real beauty. They both came from nothing. They both were so much richer than most of the men we talk about today being rich. They'd done it all. Of course, there'd been men in their lives who had helped them, but they earned every cent they made. You ask if they were happy. This is not a characteristic of a European. To be contented— that's for the cows. But I think that they *were*, at least when they were in power, at the wheel, and when they were running everything. And they did."

Three months after Gabrielle returned to Paris, headlines proclaimed that Yves Saint Laurent had saved the country, that the great Dior tradition had been saved. Eugenia Sheppard wrote that the January 30, 1958, show "was the best Dior collection I've ever seen," and the following Sunday, *France Dimanche* told the world that on the fateful day, a Dior saleswoman had given birth to a 3.2-kilo baby boy and promptly named him Yves.

The backbone of Saint Laurent's first solo collection for Dior was the trapeze line, a simple black silk and wool dress flaring from narrow shoulders to a short, wide hemline. Hemlines were a crucial matter during the fifties. No woman could forget that, with one collection, Dior had made her entire wardrobe obsolete, and by the late 1950s, women were rather defensive about a too-abrupt hoisting and lowering of hems; so much so that the Paris houses allegedly had a tacit understanding not to change the length of their hems by more than two inches per season.

The psychological winner of the 1958 season was Mademoiselle Chanel, as she was increasingly called. By keeping hemlines more or less where they had always been, hovering below the knee, and by offering an easy-to-wear, recognizable head-to-toe look that did not date after six months, her clothes were a shrewd alternative. Her cardigan suits with chain-weighted jacket hems, beautiful linings, and real pockets to hold cigarettes and keys gave the woman who wore her clothes a lot of self-confidence.

Saint Laurent's trapeze line was a hit—the House of Dior sold more than half as much as all the other Paris houses combined in 1958—but as if to confirm Chanel's unswerving belief in simplicity, the wonderboy's follow-up was a dud. Under pressure to come up with an encore, Saint Laurent unveiled a winter 1958–59 collection that dropped hemlines to three inches below the knee. The confidence invested in the now twenty-two-year-old designer was swept away by the outcry of the press. *Vogue* presented his collection with the kindest words: "When a new line is greeted with cries of indignation, it's a healthy sign. . . . It means that the fashion world is alive and kicking." The seventy-five-year-old Coco knew how to hurt. "Saint Laurent has excellent taste. The more he copies me, the better taste he displays."

The fashion press caught up with her. Only four years after her re-entry, she was called the major fashion influence in the world. "If fashion has taken a turn to the woman, no one can deny that much of the impetus for that turn stems from Coco Chanel—the fierce, wise, wonderful, and completely self-believing Chanel," wrote *Vogue* in March 1959. "It is not that other Paris collections are like Chanel's. They are not. But the heady idea that a woman should be more important than her clothes, and that it takes superb design to keep her looking that way—this idea, which has been for almost forty years the fuel for the Chanel engine, has now permeated the fashion world."

Chanel's 1959 line was not much different from her clothes of other years, and, as usual, the refinements were in the details. Her jersey suits and blazer jackets were copied down the line, and she was responsible for the popularity of men's shirts, jeweled cuff links, gold chains and medallions, gilt and pearl earrings, Breton sailor hats, and sling-back shoes with contrasting toe caps. Women copied her model's hairstyles, brushing out their hair instead of flattening it to the head and cutting bangs across the forehead.

Coco cared little about the myths that swirled around her. "What do I care what people write about me? Each year they will invent a new story. I will never sue." Over the years, she added, with somewhat pixyish glee, to the tangle of dates, places, and names. At other times, she brushed questions aside. Remembering was a waste of time.

Thomas Quinn Curtiss, who covered the Paris cultural scene for the *New York Herald Tribune*, thought her story was a twentieth-century version of the life of Madame du Barry. Like the last and loveliest of the mistresses of King Louis XV, Coco was educated in a convent, became a shop assistant and the mistress of a man who made a fortune as a war contractor. Marie Jeanne Bécu married her arms dealer, the Gascon nobleman Jean du Barry, but Coco matched the famous adventuress in her prodigality as a patron of artists and men of letters. "Coco always had lunch at the same table on the terrace of the Ritz, surrounded by her entourage," Curtiss would remember.

She could be huffy. When *The New Yorker* interviewer had complimented her clothes and asked about the cuff links on her crisp white chemise, she had snapped, "Stravinsky gave them to me thirty years ago. Why? Out of admiration. The admiration I had for him, what do you think?"

A woman's age meant nothing, she maintained. "You can be gorgeous at twenty, charming at forty, and irresistible for the rest of your life." She also said that the face a twenty-year-old woman had was the one that Nature gave her, that life modeled a thirty-year-old woman's face, but that at fifty, a woman had the face she deserved. In private, she put her maxim a bit more crudely: "At thirty a woman must choose between her face and her ass."

As if to remind her of her own mortality, Paul Reverdy died in the Benedictine monastery in Solesmes in June 1960.

They were the same age. They had known each other since they were in their forties. They had gone their separate ways but their past had been sealed in a lasting friendship, and he had sent her a copy of each new edition of his work. But he had left stern instructions with his wife and the fathers at Solesmes that no one should be notified, and Gabrielle read about his death in the newspapers. When asked to comment, she said his death was the hardest to bear.

A year later, Bertha Capel died. Financially, she never had cause to regret her hastily arranged marriage to Herman Michelham. She had lived a life of leisure and rarely seen the slightly retarded Herman. Once when both happened to dine at the same Riviera hotel, Herman thought he dimly recognized the lady a few tables away. As he rose, he quietly asked his steward who she was.

'But Milord," the footman whispered, "it's Milady."

Herman, it was reported, hurried away.

In the revolutionary 1960s, Coco Chanel sprang no surprises, only refinements on what was her classic look—the short, straight, collarless jacket, the slightly flaring skirt, and hems that never budged from mid-knee. She ridiculed the "mini" and the "maxi," and was ridiculed in turn by André Courrèges, the former Balenciaga assistant who made history with his space-age skirts above the knee, vivid colors, and "moonbeam" accessories. "I'm the Ferrari, Chanel the old Rolls, still in working order but inert," said Courrèges, whose company—a sign of the times—was 50 percent owned by the cosmetics company L'Oréal.

She was working for women, she retorted, not teenagers. "I hate the old little girls," she said of women over thirty wearing miniskirts. She faulted the taste of the clothes-conscious Jacqueline Kennedy. "She's got horrible taste and she's responsible for spreading it all over America," she said in 1967 of Jacqueline Kennedy. She was criticizing the white Courrèges dress that the president's widow had worn to the dedication of a monument to John F. Kennedy in Runnymede, England.

The selective memory Gabrielle employed made her forget that Mrs. Kennedy had worn a Chanel suit for her visit to Dallas on November 22, 1963. Its raspberry wool was stained with her husband's blood.

Claude Pompidou, the wife of de Gaulle's successor, wore Chanel. President Pompidou invited Coco to dinner at the Elysée Palace, where she told Claude Pompidou that as First Lady she could no longer wear red.

When Cocteau died in 1963, Coco called up Serge Lifar and told him to come with her to the funeral. Afterward, they had a sumptuous champagne dinner at the Ritz. With a radiant smile, she said, "Jean is gone!" lifting her glass for a toast to the survivors. Later, she had only sarcastic remarks to make. "Jean, a poet? You make me laugh. The true poets were Supervielle and Reverdy. When I think that no one mentions Reverdy anymore. Cocteau never discovered anything. Give me one of his books and in no time I'll find the lines he stole from others."

She had never lost faith in Reverdy. To rescue him from the oblivion into which he had fallen, she petitioned President Pompidou to have Reverdy inserted into school poetry anthologies. Reverdy, she claimed, inspired her belief in a fourth dimension, in an afterlife, in the idea that nothing ever disappeared.

36

YOUTHQUAKES

~~~~~~

She turned eighty July 19, 1963, and chose to forget her birthday. Photographed for British *Vogue* wearing one of her boaters, her scissors hanging from a ribbon around her neck, her fingers held firmly together in spite of severe arthritis, she was going "from strength to strength," according to the magazine.

Diana Vreeland would remember being fitted by her in the mid-1960s. "She was extraordinary. The *alertness* of the woman! The charm! You would have fallen in love with her. She was mesmerizing, strange, alarming, witty." About Chanel's collection, the *Vogue* editor would write: "These postwar suits of Chanel were designed God knows *when*, but the tailoring, the line, the shoulders, the underarms, the *jupe*—never too short, never making a fool of a woman when she sits down—is even today the right thing to wear."

Perhaps the strongest tribute to her prominence was the fact that women of wealth who took pride in exclusivity of design did not mind being seen in the same clothes as working girls. Both groups wanted, and were willing to pay for, in varying degrees, the Chanel look. The well-known names, who could afford to pay her prices—about $1,000 in 1960s money for a suit—often added knockoffs to the original Chanels in their wardrobe.

By 1968, the payroll at the couture house was up to four hundred employees. Figures were hard to come by in the notoriously secretive French fashion trade, but by the time Chanel was in her late eighties,

Time estimated her fashion empire, including the perfume, to bring in over $160 million a year.

Chanel ruled her salon like a royal court. She was increasingly temperamental, willful, and, at times, vitriolic. Young models sometimes compared her to an insect, complete with stingers. Her parakeet voice never stopped speaking her mind. People jostled for favors, almost fearing success, and braced for reversals. Marie-Hélène Arnaud was only the first of many models she took an affection to—and afterward heard herself rumored a lesbian.

"You must be crazy," Coco snapped. "An old garlic clove like me. Where do people get those ideas from?" She would claim one of her collaborators threw herself at her, convinced Mademoiselle had always had a taste for women. "*Finita la commedia,* neither women nor men anymore," Coco said she answered. She said she didn't like women, that in life's game women were cheats. "Women never interest me. I can't be their friends (they don't know what friendship is). Besides, in France, the odds are against friendship. Women don't know what the word *honor* means."

Rumors of her lesbianism persisted. "It was sort of a known thing," Thelma Sweetinburgh, the *Women's Wear Daily* longtime Paris correspondent, would say. Hollywood's titillating pop novelist Jacqueline Susann insisted Coco made sexual advances to her, and based, not a female character, but the second husband of her *Valley of the Dolls* heroine on various bisexual designers, among them Chanel.

"Yes, my girls are pretty, and that's why they do this job. If they had any brains, they'd stop doing it." That she loved to be surrounded by beautiful young women added to the lesbian gossip. Many in the fashion industry presumed that she was gay, at least in her later years. With knowing winks, some would say they knew So-and-So who had been Mademoiselle's lover. Such informants would shy away from giving the name of the woman on whom Chanel had pressed her ardor, or they would retreat to generalities.

Horst would deny she was a lesbian. "Not those kind of exercises," she laughingly told him once. Horst recalled, "It was not physical with her. Suzy Parker went around mumbling, but the reason she lost her job at Chanel's was that she got pregnant and married her lover without telling Coco."

Chanel's work method, her need to touch and feel a woman's body might explain the Sapphic inferences. At other houses, a dress emerged from sketches and was stitched together when the fittings began. At Chanel's the dress was fashioned on the mannequin, according to the model's reflexes, her movements. Coco worked on her body, used scissors and needles on her until a dress was a symbiosis of body and fabric.

She would pin up a dress as many as twenty times to get it right. Armholes were her bane—and the engineering secret of her jackets. "The armhole was never high enough, and she'd reset a sleeve six times," Jackie Rogers, a Boston-born mannequin, would recall. "The high armhole gave the jacket the cleaner, closer fit she wanted."

"A sketch, that's not a body," she said. "Here, we don't sell slips of paper. For a dress to be pretty, the woman who's wearing it must look as if she were nude underneath."

Her models were young Parisian society women and international beauties. Countess Mimi d'Arcangues and Princess Odile de Croy joined Marie-Hélène Arnaud; Nichole Franchomme and Paule Rizzo followed Suzy Parker. They would remember her flair, scalding tongue, ineffable charm, and capacity for work, and most of all her running monologues during fittings. With her hair-trigger wit, she dispensed unsolicited advice ("There is a time for work, and a time for love. That leaves no other time," was a much-quoted adage), and when she told fragments of her own story made herself look good in all situations. To hear her tell it, there was nothing in her era she had missed.

The idea of writing it all down made Coco renew her acquaintance with Louise de Vilmorin. Where journalists like Gaston Bonheur and André Fraigneau had failed, surely the elegant and witty novelist would succeed. Chanel admired Vilmorin's ease and clarity, combined with an astringent irony. Max Ophuls had recently filmed her novella *Madame de . . .* with Danielle Darrieux in the title role, Charles Boyer as her husband, and Vittorio de Sica as her lover. It was a story of love beginning in narcissistic flirtation and ending in desperation.

The sixty-year-old Vilmorin's social life was hectic. She was having an autumnal love affair with André Malraux, who as the Minister for Cultural Affairs sent the Louvre treasures on globe-trotting tours, had Chagall paint the Opéra ceiling, and asked Coco to decorate a suite of rooms at the Louvre for an exhibition of forty masterpieces from the museum reserves. But Vilmorin was not writing anything at the moment, and she agreed to come to the Ritz for a series of interviews destined to lead to the published Chanel memoirs, urbane and clever, sophisticated and *sans* moralizing pretensions.

Instead, the collaboration turned into a head-on clash of highly charged egos. "Talk to me about *me*," Louise quipped. Vilmorin was driven to despair by Chanel's lies about her childhood and early years; Coco resented the author's borrowing money from her. Louise persuaded Coco to read *Victorian Duke*, a biography of Bendor's colorful grandfather. "To understand what Bendor was *not*, you have to know what his grandfather had been," Louise told Coco. When Vilmorin gave up, Chanel used Louise's words to recommend *Victorian Duke* to the succeeding would-be biographers.

They remained friends. Vilmorin sent Coco a copy of *La Lettre dans un taxi*, her new book, and a week later announced her forthcoming visit. Coco told her she had been unable to get past the first ten pages. Louise got angry. To soothe her, Gabrielle said, "My dear, you know very well I'm illiterate."

Pierre Wertheimer died in 1965, leaving the huge enterprise adrift. His son Jacques became head of the corporate Chanel. Coco called him "the kid," although he was fifty-five. Jacques Wertheimer had spent most of his adult life at his racing stables, and was practically without business experience.

He and the family trustees thought Coco's preference for the vivacious Marie-Hélène Arnaud could translate into an eventual succession. Arnaud's father was hired away from the Rothschild Bank and named a director of Chanel, S.A. The idea backfired. By paying too much attention to Marie-Hélène, corporate headquarters committed lèse-majesté. Coco fired her.

Margot McIntyre, a Seattle-born model who worked first for Madame Grès and then as a free-lance model during the early 1960s, would remember that Chanel preferred socially prominent girls because clothes seemed to matter to them. In talks with friends, however, Coco said the young bluebloods came to work for her because they were bored. "Their mothers and grandmothers had other ways of amusing themselves," she said. "Aristocratic men didn't work; they were available for infatuations and passions like the heroes in a Bernstein play. These girls phone each other. 'And suppose we became models at Chanel. We'd find other girlfriends, and we'd get to wear fabulous clothes!' So they come for one collection, they stay, and they still don't have anybody to fall in love with."

She didn't mind if her models borrowed clothes to go out in. "I like when the dresses don't sleep here, when they're out and around."

The period of patrician models was followed by a German era. Coco liked tall, hard-boned, and earthy German girls because they knew how to walk. American models came next—elusive and brought up with care, but asking too many questions, she thought.

"We never worked in the morning," McIntyre would remember. "Mademoiselle rarely arrived before noon, and everybody knew the moment she entered the building." Once *la pose* began—the period when the individual dresses are created and re-created—no one left the salon without a very good excuse. Mademoiselle was a terror, commanding, ridiculing, pinching and watching, standing up, sitting down, on her knees, on all fours.

"You're already tired?" she'd goad after several hours. "A Chanel suit is made for a woman who moves. Now walk!" Coco's friend Serge Lifar called her tireless adjustments, her last-minute adding of accessories and pruning of excesses, the "final notes" of her collections, and—to underline her creative labors of giving birth to new fashions—her "cesarean."

When she was asked how old she was, she either said she was a hundred or, "That depends on the day you ask." She took vitamins by the handful, claiming that without them she'd wake up in the middle of the night with cramps. Because of her arthritis, she sometimes jabbed needles into her own hand by mistake. Sucking on a bloodied thumb, she would wonder why she continued. "There are days I want to drop everything," she said in 1969. "French people couldn't care less. The Americans, however, would realize that closing the House of Chanel would be a loss. I work more and more. Sometimes, I realize I'm ridiculous in being so demanding.

"Elegance is not a matter of slipping into a new dress. You're elegant because you're elegant, a new dress has nothing to do with it. You can be elegant in a skirt and a jersey. Each couture house used to have its own style. I've developed mine; I can't get out of it. I can't get myself into clothes that I haven't made myself, just as I can't make anything I can't wear myself. I always ask myself the same question: Can I wear this? I don't have to ask anymore; it's an instinct now."

She created Delphine Seyrig's wardrobe for Alain Resnais's avant-garde film *Last Year in Marienbad* in 1962. The big media stars, from Juliette Greco to Anouk Aimée, Romy Schneider, and Françoise Sagan, were her clients, and, in the case of Jeanne Moreau, a friend. The camaraderie with Moreau lasted until the actress started living with Pierre Cardin. "I used to get all my clothes from Chanel," Moreau said in 1966, "but one day I went to see Cardin's collection and I fell in love with everything. Then I met Cardin. Since then he has designed for me my personal clothes and those for my films."

Coco never ceased her verbal barrage against the miniskirt—and against her confrères. Balmain might be excused, she said, because "Someone has to dress the women in the boondocks." She called Paco Rabanne, who designed using such materials as aluminum and plastics, "the metallurgist." She hated Cardin for being the king of franchising, lending his designing ways, or at least his logo, to just about every wearable, digestible, drinkable, and disposable product. She was at a theater premiere when, during the intermission, someone introduced them.

"What a nice boy, really," Coco said afterward. "As for what he does, he will be the end of fashion."

Balenciaga, who was only twelve years younger than she, was the exception, the couturier she professed to admire. In the early 1960s, he came to dinner in Rue Cambon. They had long, involved discussions, and even if she didn't agree she respected his opinions.

"Cristóbal, let's get married," Coco said to Balenciaga one night, according to *Le Figaro*'s fashion editor Augustin Dabadie.

When his face registered shock and surprise, she said she was joking, of course, although the idea of telling the press they were getting married would be fun.

They went out together, lunched in St. Cloud. She told him of an upcoming press reception. She wanted him to come, but he told her he loathed the press.

He would recall her confidences and the fear of loneliness he felt behind her quips and complaints. "She said, 'This is my last collection.' I said, 'You say that at every collection.' She said, 'What will I do if I no longer work? I'd be bored to death. I've bought a house in Lausanne, not on the lake, which is hideous with swans that smell. Up in the hills at Lac de Sauvablin, something small. You can't live in a house that demands more than two servants.' "

Instead of staying in her house, she fell in love with the Lausanne-Palace. She liked to sit in the lobby of the hotel in one of the deep wing chairs where she imagined no one could see her and watch the rich female clientele. "It's when you see other people's bad taste that you learn discrimination," she told Antoine Livio, a journalist who came to luncheon one day in 1964 with Serge Lifar.

It was Lifar's sixtieth birthday. Before he and Livio arrived at the hotel, the dancer told his young companion the history of his difficult relationship with Mademoiselle, how much not only he but the Ballets Russes owed her. Lifar told Livio to make sure Mademoiselle didn't discover he was a reporter. When they were introduced, she delighted in seeing the young man squirm when he had to admit he was neither dancer nor choreographer, designer nor photographer. She gave up and instead made a few nasty remarks about Cocteau.

"You can't have lunch with him," she said as they sat down. "You eat; he keeps talking. The meal is over in no time. He talks, eats next to nothing, and stays slim as chicken wire."

Her sense of humor was mocking and caustic, Livio would remember. "She had the eyes of an eagle. She didn't miss anything." She didn't like the way the women dressed, whether they were foreigners or the wives of Lausanne doctors and industrialists. "What they need is simplicity, maybe because they want to make sure we don't think they are short of money. What they are lacking is class." She preferred the company of men, she said, "because their appearance is more restful to the eye."

Her friendship with Balenciaga blew hot and cold. They shared long, exquisite dinners where each took credit for lifting the other's morale out of funk and depression. They were both smarting under the defiant strength, allure, and power of youth. The media talked about nothing else, it seemed, than the exalted beauty and genius of the young.

Youth made fashion as much a matter of mood as of style. London was becoming the most inventive fashion leader, Carnaby Street the household word, and America's ubiquitous blue jeans the uniform of the young of the world, including France. Designers were spilling out of art and trade schools, bursting with new ideas. By 1967, England's Mary Quant exported 30,000 dresses to France alone, and in three years, Barbara Hulanicki's Biba boutiques were a multinational success.

Haughtily, Balenciaga held on to tradition; Chanel said to make clothes that were timeless was neither heresy nor a contradiction in terms. Yet they both felt exhausted, and when she gossiped about his gloomy outlook their friendship ended. "When we said goodnight we were more friends than ever, or so I thought," Balenciaga told Dabadie. "Two days later I read in the newspaper how she had dined with Balenciaga, that the poor Cristóbal was so tired she couldn't understand how he'd be able to present his collection.

"I was furious. Three times she phoned me. I had somebody tell her I was not available. I never saw her again. I'm sorry and I think she was sorry, too."

Still, there was some truth in what Chanel cattily told the press, for Balenciaga found the revolutionary sixties were making haute couture into an anachronism. Women wanted to look like their daughters, and ready-to-wear manufacturers no longer trusted the couture lead. Younger, more resilient firms such as Dior, Courrèges, Ungaro, and Yves Saint Laurent followed Cardin's lead and opened ready-to-wear boutiques in major cities all over the world. In 1968, Balenciaga quietly closed his house.

Despite the challenge of Cardin and Saint Laurent, Chanel had the stars as her clients, from Sophia Loren to Catherine Deneuve and Elizabeth Taylor. Anouk Aimée modeled for her. Mamie Van Doren found her pale and autocratic. "She wore cascades of pearls and chains to accent the stark black of her suit and the bright white of her silk blouse," the actress would remember of a 1964 visit to 31 Rue Cambon. "Her dark eyes piercingly evaluated the black feathered dress on me. There was a faintly roguish glint in her eyes as she swept me up and down. Finally she said, 'Ahh.' "

Chanel seemed ageless. She was a character, almost an institution. In 1966, she allowed reporters to ask a few questions about her life. Thinking back on her long existence, what would be her advice to women?

"I will surprise you perhaps, but all things told, I think that if a woman wants to be happy, it's best for her to follow conventional morality," she said. "Otherwise, she will need courage of heroic proportions, and at the end she pays the terrible price of loneliness. There's nothing worse for a woman. Solitude can help a man find himself; it destroys a woman."

She talked about sex, and said she liked the story of the Mexican paisano who tied his woman to a tree with his poncho, slung one of her legs over a branch, and made love to her standing up. "It's a matter of presentation. You aren't slumped on a bed. A woman shouldn't submit. Sex is a function."

When asked why she had never married, she said the reason was no doubt her work. "The two men I loved never understood. They were rich, and never realized that a woman, even a rich woman, wants to do things. I would never be able to abandon the House of Chanel. It was my child. I made it, out of nothing. When it comes to men, I've never wanted to weigh more than a feather on their shoulder."

Or let a man weigh you down?

"To flee boredom makes you gain weight. Few people know that, but I've never been happy. Except when I was seventeen or eighteen and got to experience happy moments. And anyway, do you know anybody who has been totally happy?"

The feminist revolution left her baffled. The quest for equality with men seemed to make women accept everything. She was appalled that young models shacked up with men and often supported them. "The men are pathetic. Women no longer know what it is to be loved. They are more interested in the crease in the boys' pants than in the boys or in themselves. I wouldn't have any of the boys polish my shoes.

"The men aren't even capable of doing something crazy for a woman. Women are heading toward catastrophe. Work, always work, run, avoid having children because that puts you at a disadvantage, run after money while pretending to do better than the men. Soon, society will want women to do everything because they are stronger than men. The Chinese know that, the Russians, too. They've sent a woman into space. A woman can withstand everything. Imagine a man trying to give birth; he wouldn't survive it. A man is wasted if he has a head cold. Today, it's the man who's the queen bee."

The news media loved to collect her monologues, her *mots*, even if they often failed to notice the irony of her advice—her telling women to grab what she herself had never gotten from men.

On February 13, 1967, she submitted to yet another press conference. The newspeople drank her champagne while she sat on her suede sofa, dressed in one of her sand-colored suits. If she talked too much, she said, "it's because I'm terrified of having to listen to others. If I die one day, I know the reason is boredom."

What did she think of fashion?

"Fashion is reduced to a question of hem lengths," she began. "Haute couture is finished because it's in the hands of men who don't like women and can only think of ridiculing women.

"After forty, women used to exchange youth for poise and allure, an evolution that left them undamaged. Nowadays, they compete with young girls using weapons that are absurd. All they haven't tried yet is the pigtail and the school satchel.

"Men dress like women, women like men, and no one is happy with what he or she has. I know what I'm talking about. I have three hundred women working with me. Boredom is practically institutionalized. Before the war nobody had ever heard of Freudian fixations or depression syndromes. What can I tell you? We were romantic. Maybe it's silly but to fall in love is a lot more fun."

The only fashion that had meaning was the fashion "that goes down in the street." A fashion that stayed in drawing rooms had no more relevance than the offerings at a costume ball.

Of educated women, she said, "A woman's education consists of two lessons—never to leave the house without stockings, never to go out without a hat."

Fashion writers: "They should begin by going to school and learn how to cut a piece of fabric."

The movies: "Nonstop talk, nowadays."

Loneliness: "It's awful."

Friends: "Always trying to get money out of you."

Physicians: "They start by kissing your hand."

Her workers: "They steal from me."

Her models: "You think it's funny to kneel in front of girls. They don't even smell nice."

Lovers: "Jump out of the window if you're the object of a man's passion. Don't dream about grand passions. That's not love. Love is warmth, tenderness, affection. There are so many ways of loving, of being loved."

Nureyev: "When you've known Nijinsky, you don't want to see Nureyev."

And Nijinsky? "Besides his big leap in Le Spectre de la rose, what's there to talk about?"

37

COCO OR KATE

~~~~~~

When people were not out for her money, they were out for her story. Frederick Brisson was a Broadway producer who in 1962 trooped to 31 Rue Cambon in the hope of selling her on the idea of turning her life story into a multimedia package, musical and movie.

"It's been a dream of mine since forever," he told her, assuring her Paramount Pictures was providing the financing.

"And who will play me?" she asked suspiciously.

"Hepburn."

Coco thought he meant Audrey Hepburn, and that it would be a story of her youth and her romance with Boy Capel.

"Not Audrey Hepburn," the producer corrected. "Katharine Hepburn."

"She's too old to play me. Why, she must be close to sixty!"

It was not the first time Hollywood had been after the Coco Chanel story. Between 1936 and 1940, Metro Goldwyn Mayer had made offers to her, which she had declined. It was her 1954 comeback that prompted Brisson's wife, Rosalind Russell, to urge her husband to approach Chanel.

"I don't understand you," she told him, "why don't *you* go after the story of Chanel? Here's a woman who's seventy-four or seventy-five years old, and instead of sitting in the shade with her cat, she's finding new worlds to conquer."

Brisson could be persuasive. He had induced Ignacy Paderewsky to appear at a piano in *Moonlight Serenade*, the only film the pianist, composer, and statesman ever made, and had convinced Harold Pinter to let him stage *The Caretaker* on Broadway. He and lyricist-writer Alan Jay Lerner had been seeking backing for the musical Chanel biography since the early 1960s. Coco had no idea who Lerner was until the producer told her Lerner had written *My Fair Lady*.

"Awful—I mean the clothes, the sets," she sneered.

"Cecil Beaton."

"You should see what the real Ascot looks like."

Originally, Brisson wanted his wife to play Coco on stage and screen. They had done it before, he producing and she starring in successive Broadway and film productions of *Never Wave at a WAC*, *The Girl Rush*, *Pajama Game*, and *Five Finger Exercise*. By the time Coco seemed willing to listen to Brisson's entreaties, however, acute arthritis had sidelined Rosalind and she could no longer be considered for the title role.

The Danish-born Brisson spoke excellent French and wooed Chanel every time he came to Paris. Roz, as his wife was called, came along and remembered Coco talking up a storm at her dinner parties. "She made powerful and expressive gestures. I remember that a bracelet flew off her arm and she went right on talking, and the butler reached down, picked up the bracelet in a napkin, and Chanel held out her arm, while continuing to speak, and the butler put the bracelet back on."

Roz didn't think Chanel was beautiful, yet she never introduced Coco to a man who wasn't overwhelmed by her. Coco was fussy about whom she was willing to meet, but gentlemen friends of the Brissons were always welcome. When the Brissons and such a male companion left the 31 Rue Cambon apartment after a dinner party, Roz would just wait. Invariably, "the man would say, 'Gee, I'd have loved to have had an affair with her.'"

Pierre Wertheimer was still alive when Brisson thought he had charmed Coco into letting him buy the rights to her story. Someone warned him, however, that he had better check with this Wertheimer.

Freddie wasn't worried. "Nobody owns Chanel but Chanel."

Still, he found it prudent to look into the corporate Chanel. Indeed, it seemed this Wertheimer owned the rights to everything that spelled Chanel. When underlings told Brisson the CEO had no intention of seeing him, he decided to lay siege to Wertheimer.

Wertheimer was to be found at the Neuilly headquarters between 3:00 and 4:00 P.M. only. Except for lunch at Maxim's, he spent the rest of the day at his stables, reputed to be bigger than the Aga Khan's. When Brisson finally managed to get an appointment and was whisked into Wertheimer's office, the Bourjois boss told him, "There's no reason for you to sit down. You won't be here long enough. There's no way I'm going to let you do Chanel's story, so I'm sorry if I've led you up the garden path."

When Coco heard of this she was incensed. She commandeered Wertheimer to Rue Cambon, and told him it was tit for tat. If she didn't own the rights to her own life, she would *quit.* That's right, there would be no next collection. Wertheimer gave in shortly before he died. He would not interfere, or sue, or make trouble. Brisson could go ahead with the show, as long as he, Wertheimer, was not portrayed in the musical.

The musical would be called *Coco*. André Previn was signed to write the score. Brisson brought Lerner to Paris to help him persuade Gabrielle to agree to it all. She had her journalist friend Hervé Mille over the night Brisson and Lerner came to dinner. The way Lerner saw it, this was the story of a woman who sacrifices everything for her independence and who, once she attains it, realizes loneliness is the price she has to pay.

"That's the theme for a tragedy," Mille said.

"All right then," said the lyricist, "it will be a *musical tragedy.*"

Gabrielle thought it should be the story of her youthful years. Brisson and Lerner left promising the musical would encompass the 1920s and 30s. By the spring of 1966, however, Coco was still not persuaded she should have her life "musicalized." To make her say yes, Brisson brought Lerner and Previn to Paris. In her salon in Rue Cambon, Lerner sang several of his songs, accompanied by Previn on the piano.

Chanel was noncommittal, but thought the musical should open with her father bent over her crib, cooing at her, and nicknaming her Coco. Her grandmother would enter, agree to the pet name, and, over the crib, foretell a life of glory, wealth, but also of solitude, for the newborn girl.

The arithmetic of a big-scale Broadway musical demanded a star. Katharine Hepburn couldn't sing, but in 1967 when she agreed to star, Gabrielle said yes, and the production went into high gear. The budget was close to $900,000, which made it the most expensive show in Broadway history, wholly capitalized by the $2.75 million Paramount Pictures paid for the film rights.

To make *Coco* a Katharine Hepburn showcase, the youthful years were dropped and rewrites turned the musical into the story of the seventy-year-old Chanel trying for a comeback. Through a series of flashbacks using filmed sequences on mirrored screens, Coco's past love affairs would be recalled. She would develop motherly feelings for one of her young models and become a meddlesome participant in a flimsy triangle involving herself, the model, and the girl's lover. A venomous designer who "has gone way past homosexuality" would give her a setback or two, but he would never threaten her triumphant comeback.

Coco wanted to design the clothes herself. Brisson, however, insisted on Cecil Beaton being used to create the theatrical version of her fashions. Lerner and Beaton had worked together before. It was only on the condition that Beaton do the sets and costumes that Lerner had agreed to write the score for the stage and screen adaptation of Colette's *Gigi*, which was based on the real-life love affair of Coco's old friend Marthe Davelli and the sugar tycoon Constant Say.

Beaton was hot. He had just finished the costumes for another Alan Lerner musical, *On a Clear Day*, and Paramount wanted him for *Nicholas and Alexandra*, but he came to Paris for several meetings with Coco. In February 1967, he wrote in his diary, "Chanel is slowly going mad in a rather interesting way." In June 1969 when he spent five grueling hours with her, he found she started the day slowly, "but by 3:00 P.M. she was galvanized and can be the great personality she was."

Beaton designed two basic sets, Gabrielle's apartment and the mirrored salon below, connected with her no less famous mirrored staircase. Built on a giant turntable that rose, split, revolved, and descended in whole or in part, the salon decor allowed for a rousing fashion show finale with mirrors and platforms turning in different directions.

Before the show went into rehearsal in the early fall of 1969, Hepburn flew to Paris. She was terrified at the prospect of being inspected by the legendary woman she was incarnating. "Here I was, supposed to be meeting this great figure of fashion—and look at me! I've worn the same coat for forty years!"

Dressed in her best trousers and jacket, Hepburn marched into the Ritz and watched as Chanel appraised her from head to toe. Coco smiled and put the actress at ease. Hepburn was taken by Coco's wit and style, and, after leaving the apartment and realizing she had forgotten something, returned to find Coco stretched out for a nap. "Now I *knew* I could play her," Hepburn said. "She's a human being!"

Gabrielle promised she would come to New York for the premiere.

Obsessively, she dedicated her waking hours to the couture house. She hated Sundays when she couldn't cross Rue Cambon and work herself into a stupor on collection preparations. Away from the feverish activity she was nothing more than a very old woman. Few people telephoned her, and when Hervé Mille came for a visit and told her the latest Paris gossip, she said she wasn't interested. She resented happily married couples. Lilou Grumbach, her press secretary, had to be available for lunches, to escort Coco back to the Ritz at night, even to sit in the salon until Mademoiselle fell asleep. Coco was annoyed, however, when Lilou so much as mentioned her husband, Philippe Grumbach, an editor at the weekly magazine *L'Express*. She was offended by the presence of old people at the Ritz, but on television watched the state funerals for Winston Churchill in 1965, and Charles de Gaulle in 1970.

On most Sundays, Coco ordered the chauffeur to bring her Cadillac to the front entrance, and after lunch, had him drive her to the Père Lachaise cemetery. As she had done as a child, she walked among the tombstones and talked to the dead. None of the people who had mattered in her life were buried at the Père Lachaise, but they were all gone— Julia, Antoinette, Boy Capel, Misia, Bendor, Dmitri, Iribe, Reverdy, Adrienne, Cocteau.

There were Sundays when she asked her new friend Claude Baillén to come along. The young woman was a distraction for Chanel, and for Baillén, a psychiatrist herself and also the daughter of a well-known psychiatrist, Coco was an endless fascination. "She was so passionate, so captivating, that I instinctively grasped and held on to the effluvium of her perfume, and those deeper fragrances that emanated from her unchanging adolescence," Baillén would say.

Baillén knew how to make Chanel talk about her youth. On their cemetery excursions Coco told about her childhood and about Julia. By now even Antoinette disappeared from Coco's monologues, because Julia was the only sibling she admitted to have existed. She spoke of the "aunts" and the rituals of weekly baths: "You bathed in your chemise; it was a sin to watch one's body."

"My aunts taught me cleanliness, consistency, honesty, and, first and foremost, to speak without an accent, for which I'm eternally grateful."

The racetracks were another way of fleshing out empty Sundays. Chanel bought a filly named Romantica, and went to the races at Auteuil, Vincennes, and Longchamp. She didn't go to the weighing-in, but to the paddocks to smell the grass. Journalists and photographers caught her at the 1964 Prix de Diane race on the arm of her trainer, Georges Mathet. After Romantica failed to win the race, Coco said she would retire her filly to become a brood mare. "I have my horses born, I don't buy them," she told the press. She found it unbecoming of stable owners to have their foals named by their stable boys. "Chanteuse de Charme! How can you give an animal such a vulgar name."

When her stallion Romanesque won a race in St. Cloud, she came to the enclosure. Romanesque was spent, and her stable hands were rubbing him with camphoric. "The boys are nice; he loves to be rubbed. Horses are nicer than people."

A new man came into her life. François Mironnet was hired as her manservant and imperceptibly became her caretaker, guardian, confidant, apprentice, and, on lonely evenings, her companion. He was a married man a third her age who inspired confidence, always called her Mademoiselle, and knew his place. He was from Cabourg, near the Deauville of her youth, and what she liked was the country boy in him, his unaffected round face, his humor, and his omelettes. When they were alone, she told him to take off his butler's vest and sit down with her. She spoiled him, gave him the keys to her strong box, took him with her to the racetracks, sent him to Switzerland to lose weight, gave him money to buy a car and an apartment. She never saw his wife but wanted to meet his mother.

Television fleshed out empty evenings, and endless nights when she tried to stay awake long enough not to succumb to sleepwalking. One morning she was seen hurrying down the hotel corridor, her expression wild and lost, but impeccably neat in her nightgown. Hotel personnel managed to guide her back to her room without awakening her. Lilou Grumbach and François, the butler, played cards in the salon while Coco tried to fall asleep in her tiny bedroom. Their presence reassured her but also prevented her from falling asleep. On the butler's nights off and when Grumbach was not available, Jeanne Céline, Coco's personal maid, was assigned by the hotel to wait until she dropped off and then lock her into her suite.

Chanel said her sleepwalking had to do with her childhood. "When I was little it happened all the time," she told Baillén, "when I'm like that people have to tie me up." To Haedrich, she said her father used to bring her back to bed without waking her up. Jeanne Céline watched her once sleepwalk to the bathroom, where she tried to break a comb and then turned the water on. "When I'm sick, all I can think of is washing myself." She believed good and bad microbes were in mortal combat in her body.

Baillén returned from a short trip to find Chanel in bed at the Ritz, in pain and despondent. Coco told her she had suffered a fall in the street. She had gone to a clinic in Rue Violet near the Eiffel Tower, but found the place so dirty she had left without seeing a doctor. Baillén called a physician. Coco was taken to a hospital where X rays showed her to have three broken ribs. The examining doctor had her strip to the waist. She did as she was told but later said that sitting there naked in front of the physician made her want to slap him.

Suffering from insomnia, Chanel injected herself with Sedol. She lost weight. Rings fell off her fingers. She wanted to move out of the Ritz because room service had brought up fresh asparagus with a veal cutlet ("The asparagus will smell up the room all day!" she complained). She stayed, but became increasingly difficult when it came to food odors. When she went down for dinner at the Espadon, the Ritz "grill room," the maitre d' went through strategic contortions to make sure several empty tables separated hers from those of other diners. "To eat with the smell of other people's food, what a horror!" she said repeatedly.

She let another young woman court her. Frances Patiky Stein was a fashion editor for *Glamour* magazine who was given entry at Rue Cambon and who came away with a deep admiration for the way Coco presented herself. "She was an old woman then, but every move she made was so seductive, so female," Stein would remember. "She was constantly touching herself, her jewels, using her pockets as a gesture. She understood that in clothes you need the barest lines, the simplest, to carry accessories. She was completely modern."

In New York, *Coco* went into rehearsals for a December 27, 1969, premiere. The principal numbers of the musical were "The World Belongs to the Young," "On the Corner of the Rue Cambon," "Coco," "Ohrbach's, Bloomingdale's, Best, and Saks" and "Always Mademoiselle."

The show's publicists made the musical sound irresistible. "Both Chanel and Hepburn are stubborn charmers, wily craftsmen, wise in their work, and, fortunately, they know it," wrote *Vogue* a month before the scheduled premiere. In private, Beaton was far from optimistic and, in a letter to his secretary, wrote that the book was "lousy," the music old-fashioned: "K.H.'s singing voice is really pitiful and I can't think the show will get anything but appalling notices."

Gabrielle had a sequined dress made for her appearance at the Broadway premiere, but as her departure date approached, she became increasingly anxious. She wouldn't fly. She'd sail, aboard one of the British *Queens*. A week before she was scheduled to leave she suffered a ministroke. Her right arm was paralyzed. She could think of no worse humiliation. However gnarled and arthritic her hands might be, her life's work was in them.

Journalists laid siege. She was transported to the American Hospital in Neuilly. She woke up in the afternoon to find a Catholic priest at her bedside.

"Too soon," she snapped.

38

ONE HUNDRED, FOREVER

The Mark Hellinger Theater premiere of *Coco* was greeted by one favorable and eight lukewarm reviews. According to the critics, Lerner's story was simple to the point of disappearance, his dialogue only occasionally witty; Previn's score was tuneless, Michael Benthhall's direction had no color or drive. But most of the critics cheered Katharine Hepburn. Under the headline, *"Coco*: About Coco—or Kate," *The New York Times*'s Walter Kerr said the evening was about a phenomenon named Katharine Hepburn. "Not that the events dramatized, or undramatized if you want to know the truth, have anything to do with Miss Hepburn's past history. Her own life cannot have been so lifeless. But each time the actress comes down the staircase—she comes down it scowling, comes down it serene, comes down it like a cavalry attack, comes down it drunk—she is coming down it to be Hepburn, to be present before all of us, to stand with her feet apart and her hands in her pockets and her chin tilted high as the balcony's eye because that is the image we have of her as she wants to assure us that it is, absolutely, real. It is."

When it came to Beaton's designs, the *Times*'s Marylin Bender was merciless: "Beaton's Chanels are as much like Chanel's Chanels as a jar of gefilte fish on a supermarket shelf is to *quenelle de brochet* at Grand Véfour. There's a circus-pink sequin Chanel, worn by Noëlle, the model, that must have been copied line for line on Division Street."

Hepburn's blithe spirit and her voice ("a neat mixture of faith, love, and laryngitis, unforgettable, unbelievable, and delightful," wrote the *New York Post*'s Clive Barnes) carried the musical through to September 1970. Danielle Darrieux took over the role on Broadway, but the miracle didn't strike twice. Hepburn was ready to take the musical to London, and only a lack of a theater that met with her approval prevented a London run.

Three months of therapy restored the use of Gabrielle's right hand. The American Hospital was so expensive, Chanel complained, she hadn't dared to eat there. Worse, a nurse assigned to night duty snored so loudly she kept Coco awake. When Chanel returned to the Ritz, Céline was on vacation, and the replacement maid assigned to her was an "old lady."

Gabrielle returned to her work, her right hand wrapped in a black spandex brace. Her workers and models pretended not to see the brace. Serge Lifar came to see her and mentioned a therapist in Sweden he knew. She ordered him to bring the man to Paris immediately. That Lifar, at seventy, exercised two hours a day impressed her. To strengthen her hand, Coco thought she'd take up guitar playing. Her friend Baillén sent a certified masseuse, but Coco refused to see her. "Once you let people like that near you, you're really slipping. A woman who jabs a nail into your big toe and asks, 'You feel that?' Thank God, I feel."

She grew increasingly suspicious. Baillén was present one day when the receptionist called up to announce the arrival of a lawyer who had an appointment.

"He's a spy," Coco said before the attorney entered. "He'll do anything for Les Parfums Chanel, a foot in each camp. One day, I'm going to tell him, 'Monsieur, you are a scoundrel. I know, because so am I.'"

Chanel hired a new lawyer, Robert Badinter. She told François, the butler, that she was replacing René de Chambrun with this young attorney, because she felt Chambrun had not advised her very well over the years. Badinter, who in the 1980s would become the Mitterrand administration's justice minister, got on well with Chanel. Chanel told him plainly that she had no objection to his being Jewish. He was a calming influence, alleviating whatever riled her; he made sure she was happy.

Chanel was both very distant and very close to Badinter, and on a number of occasions told him intimate details of her life. She also discussed with him her wish to turn her fortune into an endowment for young artistic talents, but ultimately nothing came of the idea.

The question of succession preoccupied her. To her male friends—Lifar, and the senior fashion journalists Marcel Haedrich and Hervé Mille—she talked of her need for someone to help her run her "empire," someone to lean on. When they mentioned Jacques Wertheimer, she winced.

"I don't have a man in the house," she sighed.

At home, she relied more and more on her butler, François Mironnet. She taught him the rudiments of jewelry making and told Haedrich one day, "François is taking care of the jewelry business, and, thanks to him, we've got increased sales."

François made a copy of a necklace that the Duke of Westminster had once given Gabrielle. When François showed it to her, she gave him the original rubies. It was quite a gesture.

She was touched when he said that if she became incapacitated, he wouldn't allow anyone to carry her off to some asylum, that he would take her to live with his parents in Cabourg. She asked him to take off his white gloves and sit down to dinner with her. She took him to the races. She brought him along when she flew to Amsterdam aboard the Rothschilds' private jet for the funeral of her friend Maggy van Zuylen.

She lent François money to buy a car, though she knew he would probably never pay her back. He had the key to her hotel safe. He never stepped out of his butler's role, never tried to isolate her from Baillén, Mille, and Haedrich who came to visit. They couldn't figure him out. They saw him prosper, but his honest face and simple manners disarmed them. Besides, who were they to object? Coco was so happy to have him.

Television came to interview her. Jacques Chazot, a former ballet dancer turned TV personality, wanted to do a series on famous women. At a reception where Coco was present, he mentioned his plan. She wanted to know who he had in mind. He said Maria Callas, Grace of Monaco, Marlene Dietrich, and Françoise Sagan, and casually asked if she would like to be one of his female personalities. To his surprise, she said yes. To his greater surprise, she agreed he wouldn't have to submit questions in advance and that, if at all possible, they would do it in one session. Half of the hour-long show would be Chazot's interview with her, the other half a filmed presentation of her newest collection. The filming would be done in her apartment in Rue Cambon with a minimal crew—

two cameramen, a sound engineer, no one else. She and Chazot talked nonstop for twenty-five minutes. When he was ready to yell "Cut!" she said, "Well, if they aren't happy with this, what do they want?"

Chazot decided to leave in her last sentence.

The August 1969 TV audience heard her rapid-fire talk and repartee. When Chazot said she had started the feminine revolution by having women cut their hair, she snapped, "I cut *my* hair, which isn't the same thing. . . . They cut their hair because they saw that I looked attractive. *I* was the one who changed, not fashion. I'm the one who was fashionable." For someone who had always thought of herself as independent of men, she repeated thrice that a woman who was not loved was a nobody: "Whatever her age—young, old, mother, mistress, whatever you want, a woman who is not loved is a woman lost." Was she thinking of herself when she added, "She can die and it means absolutely nothing."

She spoke of Yves Saint Laurent as her heir apparent. Fashion was not an art, she repeated, but a trade that demanded discipline. She hated the Mao suits that were fashionable and lashed out against miniskirts. "Do you think that a woman looks any younger because she shows her knees and her thighs? It's gaudy and it's indecent; two things I hate."

If she kept on working, it was because she was afraid of being bored. "If I wasn't working I'd be playing cards like three-quarters of women. What do you think—I'm not crazy."

The TV special resulted in a stream of letters from viewers, most of them agreeing with what Chanel had said. One letter was from a woman who said she had been a trainee in 1909 and remembered Antoinette Chanel doing hats while singing her scales, and Coco making her bring pastry from Fauchon's and money from the bank ("In a linen bag, how imprudent!") while walking her white dog.

Gabrielle Labrunie—Tiny, as the Duke of Westminster had called her— was the only member of the extended family that Coco stayed in contact with. Coco had taken her grandniece with her to America in 1946, and their relationship was cordial. It was to her butler François and Lilou Grumbach, however, that Chanel gave instructions on what to do if she should die.

"You put me in the back of the car, between the two of you," she told the butler and the longtime assistant. "If anybody at the border asks

you anything, you tell them, 'This is Mademoiselle Chanel. Pay no attention. She's senile.' And you two, don't be silly. I'll be with you—in another dimension." To Alfred Hier, her Zurich lawyer, she said that once
she was dead she wanted no publicity surrounding her name. "I'm longing for peace," she told him. "I hope you'll leave me alone once I'm
dead."

Since the war, she had lived a number of years in Switzerland. In
1965, she bought a cemetery plot for herself in Lausanne. She had no
direct heirs, and upon her death the corporate Chanel would become the
property of the Wertheimers. Still, she could not accept the idea that her
personal fortune would disappear into the coffers of the French Treasury.
Hier told her Liechtenstein was even better than Switzerland when it came
to tax shelters.

A Liechtenstein foundation called Coga, for Coco-Gabrielle, was set
up in Vaduz, the vineyard-girded village capital that was the legal do-
micile of over 50,000 holding companies, trusts, and foundations, most
of these elusive corporate shells with no other visible assets in Liechtenstein than letterheads in the drawers of some local lawyers.

Her will was three lines long:

This is my last will and testament.
I establish as my sole and universal heir the Coga Foundation,
Vaduz.

Lausanne,

Signed October 11, 1965,

Gabrielle Chanel

If she was thinking of a successor, she was not looking among her
cultivated, upper-crust models, as Jacques Wertheimer had imagined, nor
among her staff, but among the competitors and journalists she claimed
to loathe. She tried to lure Pierre Bergé, Saint Laurent's business partner
and intimate, away from the young designer. The cocky Bergé was turning
YSL into a money tree, and quickly turned down the offer of a subservient
role to the Wertheimer interests. Marcel Haedrich had become the editor-
in-chief of *Marie-Claire*, the leading French women's magazine, and a
fashion commentator at Europe No. 1, France's premier radio station. In
1970, Coco asked Haedrich to become the codirector of the House. Sensing that what she needed was someone to be at her disposal, not someone

with whom she would share decisions and responsibilities, he turned her down.

She turned eighty-seven that summer and soldiered on. Next to the Bastille Day fireworks, *Ladies' Home Journal* fashion editor Anne Chamberlin wrote, the weeks preceding the Chanel collection presentations were one of the great pyrotechnic spectacles of Paris, witnessed by a privileged few.

"Mademoiselle takes up her station on one of the gold ballroom chairs in the big showroom, with a pair of scissors hanging from a rope around her neck and a box of straight pins on the chair beside her, asks to see the first dress, and the fun begins," Chamberlin wrote. "She suffers from rheumatism and arthritis. Yet she still literally attacks each fitting with her bare hands, clawing and pushing at the fabric, jamming in pins, tearing out seams, sending seamstresses off in tears behind the fitting screens, where they get revenge by jabbing pins into the models."

Journalists told her that Cecil Beaton wanted her to contribute a dress to a planned Museum of Costume. To urge rich and famous women to contribute originals, Beaton told a horror story of how he approached a Chicago millionaire, whose deceased mother and wife had been famously fashionable, only to learn the widower had burned all their clothes. Coco was not moved by the story of the widower making a bonfire of unopened boxes of Balenciagas, Poirets, Vionnets, a Fortuny, and a mass of Chanels. Said she of Beaton, "All he really wants is to give it to some woman."

The reporters insisted that it was all serious.

"He flunked the *Coco* wardrobe. Everybody says so."

Chanel worked on her spring 1971 collection, to be presented to 300 buyers and members of the press on August 5, 1970. Clothes were becoming pure decoration, and if there was a theme for the new decade it was that there was no theme, no one trend or style. Fashion was becoming repertoire. Clothes were tweedy, ethnic, pop, Hollywood, classic, glamorous, executive, and nostalgic. Saint Laurent put spotted shirts with tile-patterned kilts, adding a patchwork-knitted vest. The new Japanese influence was seen in the tucked and quilted white cottons from Kenzo Takada and Kansai Yamamoto's Kabuki theater satins. Chlöe's Karl Lagerfeld had tap dancers in silk gym knickers.

Chanel stuck to the classic and scored again. Paris, London, Rome, and, more reluctantly, New York, had voted for the "maxi," or ankle length. Stores were intimidated. Many of them wanted to compromise between high fashion and sales and settled for just-below-the-knee hems. Not since Dior's New Look had the world been so caught up in fashion. Cover stories, talk shows, and dinner conversations were devoted to the maxi and consumer revolts against what Gloria Steinem called those "Germanic, stick-and-carrot urgings" to fall in line. Ready-to-wear manufacturers lost millions betting on the maxi. A poll by New York's *Women's Wear Daily* showed women preferred Chanel, and her mid-calf length, although some observers thought her hemlines were a fraction shorter than usual, a typical Chanel gesture of nonconformity.

Gabrielle cut out the *Women's Wear Daily* article and carried it in her purse. "Why don't *they* say that in France?" she asked.

Forever thriving on confrontations, she picked a new fight with Jacques Wertheimer and the lawyers. She wanted to launch a new Chanel perfume, and she was also looking into a fragrance for men. "Nothing oriental—musks and incense are feminine scents," she told Chaillet. "You see, a perfume has to be like a slap in the face. Nobody wants to wait three hours to decide whether it smells. It has to be full-bodied, and what makes a perfume muscular and sturdy is what costs a lot of money."

Nobody in the perfume industry wanted a rival to No. 5. She threatened to produce and market the new scent herself. Jacques Wertheimer gave in.

The new perfume was launched in December 1970. For a while Gabrielle had wanted to call it Coco like the musical, but Robert Chaillet, the Wertheimer lawyer, dissuaded her.

"It doesn't sound like much," he told her. "It sounds like communist, *mon coco*, rococo, cocaine."

She agreed to name it after her birthday, the nineteenth. As she had done almost fifty years earlier with No. 5, she went around spraying Chanel No. 19 on friends and clients, and asking for their verdict. An approving smile made her day. If women remained politely silent, she was ready to phone the Bourjois production manager and cancel the whole thing. The new perfume was not easy to make. The principal ingredient was floral extracts from roses, and real estate speculation on the Riviera was swallowing up the hillsides above Nice. Where farmers sold 2,000 metric tons of jasmine the year Coco and Ernest Beaux invented No. 5, the production in Grasse was now down to less than 300,000 kilos. New suppliers were found in Tunisia and Egypt, but Jacques Polge, the new chief perfumer at Les Parfums Chanel, lamented the lack of "personality" of imported flowers. "It's like wine, it's the soil that counts."

The new perfume made its debut at a news conference. Gabrielle told reporters she had been wearing it herself for weeks, that the perfume had provoked a passerby outside the Ritz to stop her. She had been ready to give the man a whack with her umbrella, but the American—she recognized the accent—just wanted to know what perfume she was wearing so he could buy some for two women friends. "To be stopped in the street by a man isn't bad at my age," she added.

She spoke with her one good hand, a fakir's bony limb slashing the space in front of her. Her lipstick, reflected in the purple of her chemise, was almost indecently red.

When asked how old she was, she snapped, "A hundred, forever."

Forever was reduced to a few weeks.

39
DEATH ON A SUNDAY

She spent January 1, 1971, alone at the Ritz. When Claude Baillén telephoned to wish her a Happy New Year, Coco told her how much she hated the holidays, extra-long this year since New Year's Day was a Friday and everything was closed until Monday the fourth. She hated the half-empty hotel, the skeleton staff, the forlorn Christmas tree in the grill room, and especially, the idea she couldn't go to work.

"Midnight mass at Christmas, New Year's Eve, 'Auld Lang Syne,' just the words make my teeth stand on edge," she rattled on. "And it dislocates everything, business. You've got to be able to say, Screw it all, because if you don't what a disillusion, what a shit thing. . . . Tomorrow, you'll find me working in Rue Cambon."

She spent the day reading in her room, but by Saturday couldn't take it any longer. She phoned a *première* named Manon, a woman who had started with her as a trainee and was still in her employ, and persuaded her to come to work. The fall collection show was set for February 5, and the two women spent Saturday going over the dresses.

Despite her feverish need to work, to be busy, she was terribly fragile. A burst of wind, it seemed, could make her topple over. No one dared contradict her, yet under her defensive armor, her vulnerability began to show.

"All things told, you're the one who got it right," she told her grandniece Gabrielle Labrunie. You've got a husband, children. I've got nothing. I'm alone with my millions."

Baillén came to see her Sunday. The young psychiatrist found Coco at her mirror, applying face cream and combing her hair, and saying she would go to work for as little as two clients. Jeanne Céline, the maid, held up her favorite suit, but Coco said she would keep it for the collection show, and slipped into a dress.

After a long lunch, Chanel invited Baillén to come for a drive. The chauffeur took them up the Champs Elysées, through the Bois to the Longchamp racetrack. The pale wintry sun was setting when they drove back, prompting her to say that she hated a setting sun, that she should have brought her sunglasses.

That evening, Gabrielle didn't feel well. Céline had to help her to bed and to administer a sedative. By Monday morning, however, Coco was back at work. She was busy all week and on Friday afternoon she had someone bring a transistor radio to the grand salon so that while she worked she could hear a Marcel Haedrich broadcast on her triumphant revenge on the maxi length.

Sunday afternoon, she invited Baillén to join her for another ride in the chauffeured Cadillac. When Baillén left her at the Ritz entrance, Coco said, "Tomorrow, I'll be working." François, the butler, and Lilou Grumbach were not there to play cards until she fell asleep, but for a change Gabrielle felt terribly tired. She stretched out on her bed without taking her clothes off. Céline managed to take her shoes off. Coco watched television for a while, then told the maid to turn the lights out.

"She slept a little," Céline would say. "After a while she got up, looked at the room-service menu and said, 'I'll have something to eat here.'"

Suddenly, Coco cried out, "I can't breathe! Céline, open the window."

Céline rushed to the bedroom and found Mademoiselle holding the syringe she always kept within reach. Coco no longer had the strength to break the vial. Celine took the needle and hoisted up Coco's dress.

"They're killing me," Coco stammered. Her face was bathed in tears.

Céline got the needle into Chanel's thigh, and called the hotel's physician but because it was a Sunday night he was not immediately available.

Gabrielle was lucid to the very end. Her last words were, "You see, this is how you die."

Céline closed her eyes.

AFTERLIFE

ome twenty years after her death, the timeless appeal of Gabrielle
Bonheur Chanel reigns supreme. The Chanel look is everywhere, can-
onized and copied with more fervor than ever before. Fashionable without
being forward, the Chanel suit achieved new currency and appropriate-
ness, a look that was rich, refined and, above all, dressed. Women's
clothing based on gentlemanly elements, suits with jackets that fit like
sweaters, masses of bogus jewelry replacing the demure real stuff, little
black dresses, crisp white shirts, gold buttons, pleated skirts, navy jackets,
quilted bags, and the black-tipped sling-back shoes are staples in the
wardrobes of professional women.

In eclipse at those times when fashion favored eccentricity and exaggeration and in demand during periods of self-doubt and quests for cer-
tainties, Chanel's fashion is once more called eternally modern. Coco
Chanel, who died on a Sunday—the only day, her friends said, that could
kill her—was a force and a legend in her time. She ruled for long periods
over almost six decades. Posthumously, her reign is stretching to cover
the century. Chanel No. 1.

There is a measure of irony in the fact that the career woman's Chanel
look, with its implied efficiency and certain perfection, was invented by
someone who was outspoken and independent and lived fearlessly among
artists, intellectuals, and aristocrats. But fashion is never reasonable. The
annals of fashion are not a chronicle of common sense, but the history of
power-consciousness and, yes, of beauty. Novelty is both imitation and

opposition. Chanel showed that innovations can be basic, that the casual can be elegant, that to be modern is not so much to measure oneself against current obsessions as to measure against past excellence.

Charm, Chanel believed, is a gift, a form of grace; and clothes are a disguise intended to project an image of ourselves, to show ourselves in precisely the way we want to be seen. Our choice of clothes allows others to understand many facets of our character, psyche, beliefs, and attitudes toward life. It is within a given code of conventions that individuals are daring and innovative. Their best ideas have a tendency to be adopted by others and to end up becoming the next set of conventions.

Coco Chanel had influence before she had money. She was the Pied Piper who led women away from complicated, uncomfortable clothes to a simple, uncluttered, and casual look that is still synonymous with her name.

The Ritz insisted on a quick removal of the body. Gabrielle Labrunie, the grandniece, enforced Chanel's wish that no one be allowed to see her dead. François and Grumbach did not get to prop up the dead Chanel between them in the back of the Cadillac for a quick getaway to Switzerland, but they did follow the coffin to Coco's final resting place in Lausanne.

The January 14, 1971, memorial service at the Madeleine Church, a few hundred yards from Rue Cambon, was a somewhat sparsely attended state funeral. The casket was covered with mostly white flowers, roses, gardenias, orchids, and red roses from Luchino Visconti and from the Chambre Syndicale de la Haute Couture. Most of the confrères she had so often mocked were there, including Balmain, Balenciaga, Saint Laurent—Cardin did not show up. They shared the pews with Antoinette Bernstein, who had first entered the Gabrielle Chanel boutique in Deauville with her mother in 1912, with Serge Lifar, Salvador Dali, Lady Abdy, Jeanne Moreau, several Rothschilds, and all the Chanel models.

Chanel was quietly buried in Lausanne's main cemetery under a simple marble stone with five—her lucky number—lion heads to commemorate her zodiac sign. The show of her last collection—moved forward to January 25 from the traditional February 5 date—turned into an emotional review of the work of someone whose absence at the top of the mirrored staircase was keenly felt. First Lady Claude Pompidou presided over the show, which began with a pale tweed suit, followed by soft dresses, tailored suits, tunics, two-piece woolens, pleated skirts, and, finally, the three white evening dresses that traditionally ended a Chanel collection. The models wore their hair pulled back in a knot topped with a black bow that journalists believed was a discreet gesture of mourning. At the end, the applause was protracted. "The audience remained seated in the stifling closeness, glancing covertly toward her famous staircase, as if, by their clapping, they could summon that ageless figure to take a bow," wrote the *New York Times*.

Both buyers and journalists wanted to know what would happen to the House of Chanel. It would continue, it was announced. Gaston Berthelot, a former Dior designer, would take over as chief designer. The Wertheimers owned it all, but continued to obscure their control.

The question of Chanel's wealth stirred passion and speculation. In its January 25 issue, *Time* estimated that at the time of Coco's death the fashion empire brought in over $160 million a year, but no one came close to guessing the enormity of the fortune. Gabrielle's fear and loneliness during the last years had made her want to possess people, to buy their company if not their affection, and more than one friend trooped to Robert Badinter's law office with tales of Mademoiselle's alleged promises.

There were no direct heirs—the closest was grandniece Labrunie—and it seemed François Mironnet was the one who inherited everything. The manservant would tell how he was called into Badinter's office and how the attorney sat him down and said, "François, you've inherited Mademoiselle." The will supporting this claim, however, was never found—Mironnet would maintain it disappeared under mysterious circumstances.

The fortune was in Liechtenstein, administered by Alfred Hier and his Zurich law firm, and on February 17, 1971, a Lausanne circuit judge confirmed the validity of the 1965 last will and testament, which left everything to the Coga tax shelter. In that will Chanel directed her executors to apportion money to certain people who had been in her service as well as to help the needy and, as she had once told Badinter, to endow gifted young artists. The details were so vague, however, that a conscientious lawyer could either give it all away in a week or, with the exception of the bequests to former employees specifically mentioned, never release any money on the grounds that no one was truly worthy of the late couturier's munificence.

In addition to the traditional secrecy of Swiss banking, the discretion Chanel supposedly had demanded of her lawyers allowed them to evade any and all questions regarding the Coga Foundation. "Mademoiselle loved Switzerland because our country offered her security, because Switzerland reassured her," said Matthias Auer, a partner in the law firm handling her estate. Held in trust by Allgemeine Treuhandunternehmen, in Vaduz, Liechtenstein, and administered by Auer and Alfred Hier in Glaros, the notorious tax haven outside Zurich, Coga escaped the glare of any publicity, and as Auer would piously say, "It was Mademoiselle's wish that she be left in peace after her death. I'm here to respect her wish."

Still, how much?

Mironnet brought suit but settled out of court. "Mademoiselle's fortune was ninety-eight billion francs," Mironnet would say nineteen years later.* "All the money is left in Swiss banks in general, and in the Union Bank of Switzerland (UBS) in particular." The Wertheimers claim, however, that Chanel's banker was Credit Suisse and the estate totaled a more modest $30 million, or nearly $90 million in 1990 currency.

For the fashion exhibition that Cecil Beaton organized at London's Victoria and Albert Museum in 1971, an Englishwoman donated a dress specially made for her by Coco Chanel for the 1919 Peace Conference. Coco's personal wardrobe and jewelry were sold at Christie's for $137,000 seven years later. A museum in Oslo bought a suit for $4,500 and the Smithsonian Institution in Washington, D.C., paid $800 for a handbag.

The industry wondered how long the Rue Cambon workrooms could carry on without "the iron hand of Mademoiselle." Without Chanel and without direction from Wertheimer, Chanel, Inc., drifted during the early 1970s until it was little more than its fragrance line and the boutique in Rue Cambon. In 1974, Alain Wertheimer, Pierre's twenty-five-year-old grandson, who had never met Gabrielle, moved to take over. The elderly trustees overseeing the family's holdings sided with the younger Wertheimer.

Gabrielle might have loved to be copied, but Alain Wertheimer zealously guarded the Chanel name, refusing licensing deals and suing anybody caught counterfeiting the label. In 1977, he expanded the Chanel fashion into ready-to-wear. He retained Philippe Guyborget to design the line, and, in 1980, chose Catherine d'Alessio to run the fashion opera-

---

*At 6.5 francs to the 1971 dollar, the equivalent of $1.5 billion, or, in 1990 currency, about $4.5 billion.

tions. To create excitement in the couture ready-to-wear lines, d'Alessio hired Karl Lagerfeld away from Chlöe.

Claude Baillén wrote a slim Chanel biography, an intuitive evocation of her friend and her world. The title more than the book was adapted to the screen and in 1980 became the movie *Chanel Solitaire*. George Kaczender directed Marie-France Pisier of *Cousin, Cousine* fame in the title role. The film promised gorgeous people, money, jewelry, castles, caviar, champagne, and love, but lacked that one essential quality— glamour. *Chanel Solitaire* told the story of the early years, with Timothy Dalton as Boy Capel, Rutger Hauer as Etienne Balsan, and Brigitte Fossey as Adrienne. The most conspicuously flashy figure in the cast was Karen Black's Emilienne d'Alençon. Kaczender shot the exteriors at Royallieu, which had been acquired by the town of Compiègne and turned into a park.

Pouring money and resources into the Chanel image that his family now owned exclusively, Alain Wertheimer filed suit against the movie, claiming "trademark infringement, unfair competition, invasion of common law right to publicity, common law misappropriation, trademark dilution, and injury to business reputation" involving the use of Chanel in the title. A Paris judge dismissed all the claims, calling the court action frivolous. Critics, however, also dismissed *Chanel Solitaire*. They called it handsome, disappointing, and old-fashioned, and chided Pisier in the title role for doing little to enliven the film. "Kaczender's film pays little attention to its heroine's unconventional side," said the *New York Times*. "She may say things like, 'I'd rather be respected than respectable,' but her behavior lacks the audacity of her proclamations."

Chanel employed its own perfumers, its own craftsmen and jewelry designers. To keep the image exclusive, Wertheimer hired a Washington law firm to help remove Chanel No. 5 from American discount drugstores without violating federal equality-of-business-opportunity laws. He hired Carole Bouquet, a high-cheekboned actress, for an expensive "share the fantasy" advertising campaign. D'Alessio was removed from the fashion operations after a clash with Lagerfeld, who by the mid-1980s was one of the hottest Paris designers. Arie Kopelman, an American advertising executive, replaced d'Alessio in 1981 when Alain Wertheimer moved his base of operations to New York.

Espousing the takeover ethics of the late 1980s, Chanel, Inc., expanded into areas beyond fashion. One can only wonder what Coco would have thought of Chanel, Inc.'s acquisition in 1989 of Holland & Holland, a British manufacturer of high-quality guns. Though some observers were convinced that Alain Wertheimer's affection for stylish hunting rifles lay behind the acquisition, Wertheimer maintained that Holland & Holland was acquired to allow the company to branch into the flourishing market for masculine accessories and toiletries while keeping the Chanel name associated exclusively with feminine fashions. When *Forbes* magazine did a cover story on "The Man behind Chanel" in 1989, Alain Wertheimer alternately threatened lawsuits and warned he would take the story to another business publication. He refused to discuss the relationship between his grandfather and Chanel or the current value of the business. *Forbes* estimated that the Chanel empire "is easily worth over $1 billion." Hers was the fame; theirs the wealth.

Except for one silly season in 1988, Lagerfeld aggressively and brilliantly revitalized the classic Chanel, keeping the trademark trims, piled-on pearls, and toe-capped pumps looking youthful and up-to-date.

By the end of the decade anything at any price in the Chanel mode rang cash registers worldwide, and not only for Chanel, Inc. In Paris and Rome, designers as diverse as Christian Lacroix, Saint Laurent, Cardin, and Franco Moschino paid tribute, each in his way, to Chanel, while in New York, Anne Klein, Oscar de la Renta, Calvin Klein, and Carolyne Roehm came out with navy blazers and fluid pants—the kind Coco might have worn at Roquebrune in 1925—navy or cream-colored silk cardigans, gold-buttoned sailor pants, contrasting piping on trim little dresses. Lagerfeld had to admit that the Chanel formula was "an open secret," a fashion that to all intents and purposes was generic, in the public domain.

On the theory that what only a small minority of women can afford is the real thing, Wertheimer raised the prices to the industry's highest—$180-an-ounce perfume, haute couture originals that started at $11,000, blouses that started at $500, classic CC handbags at $960, ballerina slippers for $225, and multiple strands of fake pearls for $360, all showcased in Chanel boutiques around the world. "No one believes us, but I have had to limit the number of bags we sell; three to a customer," said Molly Carrara, manager of the Chanel boutique in San Francisco's Maiden

Lane, in 1989. When the House of Chanel hired Lagerfeld to design both its haute couture and ready-to-wear, there were nineteen boutiques; by 1990 there were over forty. We can only guess what Coco herself would have thought of blouses printed with No. 5 perfume bottles or drop earrings in the shape of tiny gold quilted pocketbooks. Not everybody applauded the sight gags and overkill, the tarty sex appeal. Adolfo, the designer, would say that Lagerfeld's updating may have made the Chanel style newsworthy, but the true Chanel style was ageless. By the end of the decade, *The New Yorker*'s Holly Brubach wrote that where Coco's motifs alluded to a world beyond fashion, Lagerfeld's Chanel style referred primarily to itself. "Although solipsism may be in keeping with the times, it's absolutely contrary to what Chanel herself stood for."

But Lagerfeld honed himself. By the time he presented the 1989–90 Chanel haute couture at the Théâtre des Champs Elysées to the tune of Stravinsky's *The Rite of Spring*, the collection was full of fitted jackets, pleated mid-calf skirts, and spare strands of pearls, less aggressive and more graceful, more Gabrielle Bonheur Chanel. His winter 1989–90 collection, a transmutation of the basic elements of Gabrielle's style, was called his best.

The Coromandel screens still adorn the Chanel offices on West 57th Street, but the woman who had fallen in love with the screens in 1910 was someone who had influence before she had money, someone who more than once broke the rules and stopped the parade, someone who insistently challenged her own success and other people's assumptions. Historians of fashion divide designers into the purists, the entertainers, the extravagants, and the realists. If Schiaparelli is classified as an entertainer, Vionnet as an architect, and Saint Laurent among the extravagant, Chanel belongs, with Patou and Madame Grès, among the designers who insisted on a purity of style. However, there was nothing dogmatic about her purism. She refused the arrogance of wealth and taught the rich to blend the real with the fake. From the time she rode bareback on Etienne Balsan's thoroughbreds in Compiègne forest, she knew that nothing ages a woman more than what makes her look rich, what is florid, puckered up. From beyond the grave, her name is enough to define a pair of shoes, a hat, a pocketbook, a suit, a perfume. It conveys prestige, quality, taste, and unmistakable style. It is a sign of excellence, of fulfilled sensibilities for women who want to be in fashion without screaming fashion.

Her life is darker than her legend. The modern career woman who has adopted her style as well-bred and safe is almost a caricature of Chanel the woman who lived free and unconstrained, and loved a man too ambitious to marry her. She was an orphan who feared rejection and fled poverty. As a child and as an old woman, she talked to the dead in cemeteries and had to be tied to her bed so she wouldn't run away in her sleep. She reached the top and suggested the Broadway version of her life should begin with her father bent over her crib, and her grandmother predicting exactly what she got—riches, fame, and solitude.

She was someone who resolved to invent herself. She owed her first success to her wits and pretty face and to successive lovers with culture, influence, and money. After the death of Boy Capel, love eluded her. Despite rapturous encounters, love too often turned into dust. "Cut off my head, and I look like a thirteen-year-old," she said. Coco Chanel was a woman with a scathing tongue, who was always that fierce little thirteen-year-old of sudden fury, sly grins, and a desperate need to be loved.

In her, the elements of contention were more diverse than in most people. The conflicts were waged with more exuberance and desperation, but also more éclat, revealing the striking contradictions, but also the promises, of her experience. Her burning goal as a young woman was to escape penury and humiliation. Her work was her escape, her triumph, and she never let go of it. She made things that possessed plainness, intelligence, and austerity, and carried a whiff of purity, of the "aunts'" lye soap and homespun sheets, and the confident flair of Boy Capel on the polo grounds.

As her friend Colette said of her, "It is in the secret of her work that we must find this thoughtful conqueror."

Notes on Sources

Scores of hours of interviews with those who knew Gabrielle Chanel, including her longtime lawyer René de Chambrun, her Swiss attorneys, Yves Saint Laurent, Karl Lagerfeld, Sophie de Vilmorin, Horst, François Mironnet, and many others are the primary sources of this book, as are earlier French books on Chanel and articles in the fashion press. Translations from the French are by the author. Full source citations are given in the bibliography. Documentation supporting certain portions of the narrative are cited below.

1. A FAMILY TO DISAVOW (1883–1894)

The details of Coco Chanel's (CC's) ancestry, birth, and early childhood are based upon the author's research in Paris, Issoire, Courpière, and Vichy and, selectively, on CC's remarks to several biographers. The author met CC's longtime lawyer René de Chambrun, attorney Léon Lévine, Sophie de Vilmorin. Vilmorin told the author of CC's varied reactions to reading Louise de Vilmorin's notes for her life story. Marcel Haedrich, *Coco Chanel*, p. 31, quotes CC's "I, who never told the truth to my priest?" after Claude Delay-Baillén suggested Chanel see the psychiatrist Jean Delay. The selective memory CC employed made her add yearly to the maze of dates, places, and names. In writing her *New York Times* obituary, Jan. 11, 1971, Enid Nemy reports CC's age was never proven, but that it is generally accepted she was born Aug. 19, 1883. From Jean Croquez, the successor to the Courpière notary who drew up the marital contract for Albert Chanel and Jeanne Devolle, the author obtained confirmation of the birth registration, testifying to the birth of Gabrielle Chasnel at 1600 hours, Aug. 19, 1883, at the hospice in Saumur. Pierre Galante, *Les Années Chanel*, frontispiece, establishes the documentation for the birth and marriage of CC's grandparents, parents, sisters, brothers, and herself, Edmonde Charles-Roux, *Chanel*, p. 7, the family origins in Ponteils. Paul Morand's 1946 question-and-answer sessions with CC, reproduced in Paul Morand, *L'Allure de Chanel*, pp. 18–27, and CC's late-life talks with Baillén, in *Chanel Solitaire*, pp. 17–21, detail her early years. Haedrich, p. 25, recites CC's anecdote of her birth in Saumur, her telling of a half brother. André-Louis Dubois told the author how CC said she was born in a train compartment. CC confides her memory of playing in churchyards to Morand, p. 17.

2. ORPHANS, FOUNDLINGS, AND ILLEGITIMATES
(1894–1900)

Various interviewers of CC have reported her reticence in speaking of her early adolescence; some have detailed her slips of the tongue when talking of her "aunts." Haedrich, p. 267, reports her saying her aunts agreed to bring her up, not to love her, and that she was not an easy child. Morand, p. 18, recites her story of how her father took her to the aunts, and, p. 23, quotes her, "I've been ungrateful toward the odious aunts." Descriptions of Aubazine, Etienne d'Aubazine, and the history of the medieval cloister and irreverent popular saying are noted in *Le Guide Michelin*. CC's years at Aubazine are detailed in several retellings, notably in Charles-Roux, *Chanel*, pp. 40–44, who reports CC's aversion to hearing her mother called "Poor Jeanne," and CC's "You *can* die more than once in your life." Baillén, p. 191, reports the grandfather's annual five-franc gift; Charles-Roux, *Chanel*, p. 47, how Louise Costier inspired the girls. Haedrich, p. 35, tells the story of the mauve dress a local seamstress made for CC when she was sixteen; Baillén, p. 196, relates the prostitute's dress sent from the father in America. Haedrich, p. 35, details CC's adolescent preference for novels of Pierre Decourcelle.

3.   COCO (1900–1904)

Late in life, CC reminisced about the Auvergne adolescence on a number of occasions. She confided to Baillén that "no one can live with low horizons." The 1893 edition of *Petit Larousse* depicts Moulins's primary industries as being cabinetmaking, millinery, and the vinegar trade. The lyrics of "Les Cuirassiers de Reichshoffen" are by H. Nazet and Villemer; music by Francis Chassaigne. Pierre-Olivier Walzer, *Littérature française: Le 20è siècle.* Vol. 1: *(1896–1920)*, describes turn-of-the-century popular entertainment. The author interviewed Vichy hôtelier H. D. Venis on the spa in 1900, and found period material in Moulins. Charles-Roux, *Chanel*, p. 56, reports the Desboutins' preference for girls recommended by nuns. Morand, p. 26, recalls CC's memories of her aunts' grazing grounds for army horses. Charles-Roux, *Chanel*, p. 64, tells of the lieutenants in the tailor shop. The "Qui qu'a vu Coco" lyrics are by Baumaine and Blondelet, the music by Ed Deransart.

4.   BALSAN (1904–1907)

The prominence of the Balsan family has remained, and the author interviewed nephew François Balsan. The author shares Haedrich's speculation, p. 48, that a botched abortion might have been behind CC's inability to conceive. CC made few references to her reproductive organs, but did talk of being "narrow" and of having female organs that were like a very young girl's. *Who's Who in France* 1961–62 and 1972 profile the Balsan family. Galante, pp. 26–27, and Haedrich, p. 42, detail Etienne Balsan's youth and military service. Descriptions of Maud Mazuel are based on period photographs. The Chanel girls' friendship with Maud Mazuel is documented in family photos and in Haedrich, p. 46, and Charles-Roux, *Chanel*, pp. 80–84.

5.   GOLD DIGGERS AND CLAUDINES (1907–1910)

At the time CC came to Royallieu, Etienne Balsan had the reputation of being a rich young man trying to make a mark. Emilienne d'Alençon was a notorious *croqueuse de diamants* and her story appears in a number of accounts, including the fiction of Marcel Proust. Galante, p. 32, cites King Leopold II telling Emilienne, "I am going grouse hunting in Scotland. . . ." CC had the highest regard for Emilienne and spoke respectfully of her sense of humor and cleanliness. Descriptions of the 1905–10 turf world and racecourses are delineated in Elisabeth de Gramont, *Mémoires*, vol. 2, *Les Marronniers en fleurs*, pp. 176–78. Charles-Roux, *Chanel*, p. 93, quotes Etienne on his surprise at seeing CC stay in bed until noon, and CC's definition of how a woman must ride astride a horse. The quote "I didn't know anything," by which CC explained her provincial credulity, and her asking Etienne, "You find her pretty?" when they passed a ravishing lady at the races were told Haedrich, p. 56, as well as her reaction to society women. Colette, *Prisons et paradis*, pp. 159–63, contains her portrait of CC. Galante, p. 34, quotes Valéry Ollivier's appraisal of young CC at Royallieu. Gramont, p. 168, enumerates the "Mondays at St-Cloud, Tuesdays at Enghien etc." week of the world of the races. Both Charles-Roux, *Chanel*, p. 66, and Haedrich, p. 57, report Balsan family stories of Etienne's liaison with CC, and her taking her meals at "the office"; Haedrich, p. 56, her reaction to "ravishing duplicity." Gabrielle Dorziat's long career in theater and films is summarized in *Dictionnaire du Cinéma*, p. 135.

6. ROYALLIEU (1907–1912)

CC's recollections of Balsan were published in *Marie-Claire*, Oct. 7, 1958. Haedrich, p. 55, quotes CC on Jacques Balsan's proposition that she marry Etienne. Jacques Chazot in a 1969 ORTF-TV broadcast has CC tell of her first trip in an automobile. Charles-Roux, *Chanel*, p. 144, reports on Lucien Chanel's discovery of his father, Albert, in Quimper in 1909; Galante, p. 34, Etienne Balsan's response to CC's wondering about her future. CC told a number of interviewers of her desire to escape the kept-woman status at Royallieu and how her talent for millinery led her to selling hats in a haphazard fashion in Etienne's pied-à-terre in Paris. Charles-Roux, *Chanel*, p. 110, and Galante, p. 34, detail CC's conversations with Etienne regarding her future and his decision to let her use his Boulevard Malesherbes bachelor apartment.

7. BOY CAPEL (1910–1911)

The dialogue of CC and Arthur Capel's riding in the Pau forest is based on Louise de Vilmorin's conversations with CC, and was related to the author by Vilmorin's sister, Sophie de Vilmorin. CC told the story of how she met Arthur Capel, her "You are leaving?" to a number of writers. Morand, p. 32, and Baillén, p. 20, report her following Capel to the Pau railway station. The *Who's Who in Great Britain*, 1922, lists Herman Alfred Stern, the second Baron of Michelham, as having married in 1919 Bertha Isabella Susanna Flora, daughter of the late Arthur Joseph Capel. CC told Morand, p. 34, that Boy was "my brother, my father, my whole family," and reported how, after Etienne's return from Argentina, Boy and she went to see Balsan. Haedrich, p. 64, and Galante, p. 40, detail the two men's gentlemanly talk; Haedrich, p. 64, suggests CC's transfer from Balsan to Capel was a "gentlemanly" affair, and, p. 67, that they might have shared her. Baillén, p. 21, tells how, once Etienne had lost her, he discovered he loved her. Frances Kennett, *Coco*, p. 26, tells of the ring Balsan gave CC. Morand, p. 36, reports her reaction to women wishing Boy would drop her, their dialogue about her looks.

8. RUE CAMBON (1911–1912)

Galante, p. 43, reports on the *fonds de commerce* that Boy Capel bought for CC at 21 Rue Cambon, and in her *Mémoires*, vol. 4, *Chimie sociale*, p. 237, Gramont relates how Boy felt he needed to occupy Coco. Morand, p. 41, reports CC's anger at finding out it was Boy's bank credit that allowed her to stay in business, Baillén, p. 24, quotes CC's "I was convinced I was making money." Morand, p. 41, tells how CC ordered her assistant not to spend money without her authorization, how CC hated to have to deal with clients and was aware that to be too available shattered some of her allure. Both Charles-Roux, *Chanel*, p. 111, and Galante, p. 44, quote Lucienne Rebaté, the first professional milliner to join CC. Charles-Roux places the expert's arrival at the time Chanel was still in Etienne's apartment; Galante, more logically, in early 1912. Baillén, p. 26, details CC and Boy's adoption of André Palasse, and the child's exclamations when seeing coal barges on the Seine. Morand, pp. 50–51, quotes CC on her and Capel's social life, and his loving her in the setting she had created for them. CC told a number of journalists about the origins of her affection for Coromandel screens, and the Bernsteins' reaction to her first interior decorating. CC told on several occasions of her attending the May 13, 1913, premiere of Stravinsky's *The Rite of Spring.* Haedrich, p. 89, tells of CC's enchantment at seeing the Ballets Russes.

9. FIRST SUCCESS (1913–1914)

The opening of the Gabrielle Chanel boutique in Deauville's Rue Gontaut-Biron during the summer of 1913 is detailed in literature issued by the House of Chanel Services de Presse, and by Charles-Roux. Haedrich, p. 119, tells of Capel reading from the Bhagavad Gita to CC, and, p. 121, of CC's disappointment when *France Soir* publisher Pierre Lazareff could not arrange a meeting with Oppenheimer. Baillén, p. 29, quotes her, "Nothing dies . . ." Galante, p. 45, quotes Antoinette Bernstein on her first meeting CC in her Deauville boutique. Yvonne Deslandres told the author the history of late-nineteenth-century fashions and Madame Paquin; Georgina Howell, *In Vogue,* p. 10, traces the rise of Jeanne Lanvin and Madeleine Vionnet. CC repeated her expression, "One did not talk to one's tradespeople when I started" on a number of occasions, including her "Maximes et sentences" in French *Vogue,* Sept. 1938. In the overview of fashion, Carole Rennolds Milbank, *Couture: The Great Designers,* stresses the internationalism of CC's personal style and her awareness of the need to be at the right spot at the right time as the basis for her fame, and Catherine Ormen in *Chanel: Ouverture pour la mode à Marseille* discusses CC's choice of fabrics. Her own description of her debut is related in Morand, p. 45. Haedrich, p. 72, quotes CC on her first sales, and, p. 68, her "I was sure that he loved me."

10. WAR (1914–1916)

The pre–World War I career of Paul Poiret, including his run-in with Baroness Diane de Rothschild, is detailed by Poiret, *En Habillant l'époque,* and Palmer White, *Poiret le magnifique.* Elisabeth de Gramont, vol. 2, p. 190, tells how with the outbreak of war the summer satins disappeared from the Deauville wardrobes. CC told Morand of "selling slim-ness" and Yvonnes Deslandres and Florence Muller, *Histoire de la mode*, of her innovative use of jersey. Galante, p. 54, relates Capel taking CC to the National Assembly. Baillén, p. 292, and Haedrich, p. 35, report CC's meeting Decourcelle at the golf course in Biarritz. Galante, p. 49, quotes Marie-Louise Deray on the opening of CC's Biarritz store and CC's work methods, countenance with her staff, and life-style in 1915. Des-landres and Muller, p. 202, describe CC and her use of jersey for quint-essential make-do wartime creations. Charles-Roux, *Chanel*, p. 152, describes CC's efforts to have her sister and aunt help oversee the ex-panding House of Chanel. Galante, pp. 52–53, quotes Deray's "We did lovely things."

II.   *MISIA AND DISTRACTIONS (1917–1918)*

CC remained a friend and, especially early on, a great admirer of Misia Edwards-Sert, and both women spoke often and eloquently of each other, of their friendship, of José Sert, Misia's lover and soon-to-be hus-band, of Sergei Diaghilev and Igor Stravinsky. Their meeting at actress Cécile Sorel's dinner in May 1917 is documented by Misia Sert, *Misia par Misia*, pp. 140–41; Arthur Gold and Robert Fizdale, *Misia*, pp. 239–40; and Morand, p. 63. Gold and Fizdale, pp. 197–202, include a chap-ter on CC that Sert, apparently at CC's request, suppressed from her autobiography. George Painter, *Proust: The Later Years*, p. 162, quotes Degas, "How very Spanish . . ." Dominique Desanti, *La Femme au temps des Années Folles*, p. 203, quotes Valentine Gross on Misia. The author paraphrases Gold and Fizdale in describing Sert's awakening Misia to sexual pleasures. Morand, p. 67, quotes Coco's retelling of Adrienne's re-action to meeting Misia. Arthur Capel's *Reflections on Victory and a Project for the Federation of Governments* was reviewed in the *Times Literary Supplement*, May 10, 1917. Clemenceau's rise to premier of France in 1917 is detailed in Philippe Erlanger, *Clemenceau*, p. 481. Paul Morand, *Journal d'un attaché d'ambassade 1916–17*, p. 228, tells of Stravinsky being commissioned to write a new Russian national anthem. Haedrich, p. 90, describes CC's reaction to seeing *Parade*, and quotes her "It was too new," and her reaction to meeting Picasso. Gramont, vol. 4, p. 190, observes upper-class women at frontline hospitals and canteens.

12.   SPURNED (1919)

Gramont, vol. 4, p. 181, tells of "noble and well-mannered ladies." The author described Diana Lister Wyndham from family photographs. In Morand, *L'Allure de Chanel*, pp. 33–34, CC tells of her feelings for Capel; *Who's Who in Great Britain*, 1918, lists the Ribblesdale and Wyndham genealogies. Galante, p. 61, reports Antoinette Bernstein's reaction to Capel's marriage decision, "Boy was a very captivating man. . . ." Charles-Roux, *Chanel*, p. 169, details CC's choice of the Quai de Tokio apartment. Manuel Burrus, *Paul Morand: Voyageur du 20e siècle*, p. 59, tells how Morand found CC to be "very alone. . . ." The Bertha Capel marriage to Herman Stern, the son of Lord and Lady Michelham, and Boy Capel's involvement in the hastily arranged marriage are covered at length in Colin Simpson, *Artful Partners*, pp. 173–76. The postwar craze for fast automobiles is described in Burrus, p. 89. The London *Times* published details of the Arthur Capel & Co. law case, Dec. 13, 1918, and Capel's being appointed CBE, Jan. 9, 1919. Charles-Roux, *Chanel*, pp. 178–79, details the death of Capel. Capel's obituary was published in the *Times*, Dec. 24, 1919, a notice of funeral arrangements, Dec. 29, 1919.

13.   GRIEF (1920–1921)

Morand, *L'Allure de Chanel*, pp. 54–55, quotes CC on her grief at Boy Capel's death. Charles-Roux, *Chanel*, p. 184, tells of her ordering butler Joseph Leclerc to drape her bedroom in black. The London *Times* published Capel's last will and testament Feb. 10, 1920. Miscalculating by a year, Charles-Roux, *Chanel*, p. 153, would hint that the bride was two months pregnant when in fact the Capels' only child, June, was born in early 1920, not early 1919. Hugo Vickers, *Cecil Beaton*, p. 427, tells how Diana later became Countess of Westmoreland. Gold and Fizdale quote from Misia's unpublished Chanel chapter on the Serts' and CC's appearance at the Ferdinand Blumenthals' fancy dress ball and CC's exclusion from the Etienne de Beaumont party. Misia Sert, *Misia par Misia*, p. 202, describes the Beaumonts. Standard music encyclopedias, including Grove, *Dictionary of Music and Musicians*, vol. 18, tell of Stravinsky bringing his family from Switzerland to Brittany in the summer of 1920, and in September of CC placing her home in the Paris suburb of Garches at his disposal. Haedrich, p. 85, tells of CC and Marthe Davelli at Biarritz, and Dorziat, Davelli, and CC as the center of attraction; Charles-Roux, *Chanel*, p. 199, quotes Davelli's suggestion that CC can have Grand Duke Dmitri as her lover. Galante, p. 81, quotes Marie Laurencin's observations on CC's silky manners. CC's joining Misia and Jojo Sert on their Italian honeymoon is related in several biographies, including Gold and Fizdale, p. 161, and Richard Buckle, *Diaghilev*, p. 366. Buckle, p. 324, tells the cruel joke that Grand Duchess Maria Pavlovna would be sure to arrive penniless and would have to be put up. Morand, *L'Allure de Chanel*, p. 67, quotes CC's comments on Sert as traveling companion and tour guide. Gold and Fizdale, p. 277, Buckle, p. 368, Haedrich, p. 93, and Boris Kochno, *Diaghilev and the Ballets Russes*, p. 178, cite different figures in their accounts of CC's gift to Diaghilev to underwrite *The Rite of Spring* revival, but 300,000 francs is mentioned most often. References to CC meeting Gerald Tyrwhitt in London are in Stravinsky, *Selected Correspondence*, vol. 2, p. 155.

14.   STRAVINSKY (1920–1922)

Misia's unpublished Chanel chapter and CC's conversations with Morand detail the Chanel-Stravinsky affair. Morand, *L'Allure de Chanel*, p. 121, tells of Misia picking up the scent of the tryst. The author relied on a number of sources for the overview of CC's impact on the 1920s, including interviews with Deslandres, Yves Saint Laurent, Karl Lagerfeld, and Thomas Quinn Curtiss. Deslandres and Muller, Howell, Desanti, and Nemy place CC's breakthrough in the 1920s in the historical context of fashion evolution. Boni de Castellane's quip, "Women no longer exist; all that's left are the boys created by Chanel," is quoted in *Vogue*, Dec. 1969. Galante, p. 75, and Desanti, p. 23, note *La Garçonne* influence. Maurice Sachs, *La Décade de l'illusion*, pp. 134–35, contains the portrait of CC. Morand, *L'Allure de Chanel*, p. 123, quotes CC on the Serts as self-proclaimed guardians of her virtue and their confronting Stravinsky. Vera Stravinsky and Robert Craft, *Stravinsky in Pictures and Documents*, pp. 235–37, detail the biographical background of Vera de Bosset's meeting with the composer. Morand, *L'Allure de Chanel*, p. 115, quotes CC's "I've squandered millions . . . ," and, p. 124, her dinner conversation with Grand Duke Dmitri. Gold and Fizdale, p. 280, report Misia's cable to Stravinsky and Diaghilev's wire to CC. Charles-Roux, *Chanel*, p. 204, describes the 1922 CC-Dmitri idyll at Arcachon. Vera Stravinsky and Craft, p. 210, call CC's affair with Igor Stravinsky "the bragging of her late-in-life memory," while Gold and Fizdale, p. 230, quote the composer's 1933 letter to Misia. Czar Nicholas in a letter to his mother, quoted by Robert K. Massie, *Nicholas and Alexandra*, tells of his fears that other members of the imperial family might follow Grand Duke Paul's example. CC repeated her fashion maxims on a number of occasions, including, "Fashion is not something that exists in dresses only. . . ." Desanti, p. 64, delineates Cocteau's fights with CC during *Antigone* rehearsals. Desanti, p. 311, reports CC's *mot* about women and fashion. Morand, *L'Allure de Chanel*, pp. 75–76, quotes CC's sarcasm about "the darlings," and her "To earn a living in the feminine trade. . . ."

15. GLITTER AND NO. 5 (1922–1923)

CC's move to Faubourg St. Honoré and her munificence toward gifted artistic friends are detailed in Morand, *L'Allure de Chanel*, p. 98, Charles-Roux, *Chanel*, p. 210, Galante, p. 105, Sachs, p. 133, and Rose Fortassier, *Les Ecrivains français et la mode*, p. 208. Kennett, p. 45, quotes CC's "Those Grand Dukes. . . ." Princess Marthe de Bibesco, *Noblesse de Robe*, pp. 195–205, describes CC's ascendancy. Charlotte Gere, *Marie Laurencin*, p. 24, quotes Laurencin's "Unlike certain salons . . ." Morand, *L'Allure de Chanel*, p. 102, describes CC's 1922 Christmas party, CC's comments on less-than-honest society people, pp. 86–90, her friendship with Laure de Chevigné, and, p. 127, CC's giving dresses to a select number of Parisian women. Henri Raczymow, *Maurice Sachs*, pp. 110–11, Francis Steegmuller, *Cocteau*, pp. 274–76, and R. M. Albères, *Histoire du Roman moderne*, pp. 88 and 327, detail Raymond Radiguet's literary rise and relationship with Cocteau. The author relied on literature furnished by Chanel Information and the Syndicat d'Initiative de Grasse for the Chanel No. 5 genesis and the career of Ernest Beaux. Galante, p. 83, suggests Colette introduced CC to the perfumer and, p. 80, quotes CC on her desire for a synthetic scent, her finding Beaux and his test tubes mesmerizing. Baillén, pp. 59–60, tells of CC and Beaux inventing No. 5. Chanel Information, *Chanel*, chronicles the principal dates of CC's perfume inventions. Gold and Fizdale, pp.244–45, cite Misia's claim to have suggested a perfume to CC. Galante, p. 90, quotes CC on her publicity strategy for launching her new perfume, and, pp. 166–67, Théophile Bader's reaction to her suggestion that his Galeries Lafayette carry her perfume, and his introducing her to Pierre and Paul Wertheimer.

16.   THE WERTHEIMERS (1923–1924)

Galante, p. 168, cites CC's meeting and initial agreement with the Wertheimers, and, p. 165, her epithets of Pierre Wertheimer. For an appreciation of the Wertheimer family, the author relied on interviews with Alain Wertheimer and attorneys René de Chambrun and Léon Lévine. The *Forbes* cover story, "The Man Behind Chanel: Alain Wertheimer," appeared Apr. 3, 1989. The conservator of the City of Grasse Musée International de la Parfumerie furnished the author with details of Ernest Beaux's other perfumes for CC. Morand, *L'Allure de Chanel*, p. 78, reports on CC's aristocratic employees and Feodorovna's story. Kennett, p. 50, quotes CC on the grand duchesses. Raczymow, p. 112, and Steegmuller, *Cocteau*, tell of Cocteau's drug abuse. Buckle, p. 399, details the pressures Diaghilev was under to match the success of the Swedish Ballet; pp. 432–43, *Le Train bleu* inception, rehearsals, and CC's decision to make second sets of the costumes. Lydia Sokolova, *Dancing for Diaghilev*, p. 222, recalls CC's bathing suit and improvised skullcap for the ballerina. Ninette de Valois, *Invitation to the Ballet*, pp. 48–49, quotes CC's "Shingle, Madame." Galante, p. 111, quotes Lady Abdy on CC. Serge Lifar details his lifelong affection for CC in *Ma Vie*, p. 156. Charles-Roux, *Chanel*, p. 235, tells of CC remembering only the artists present at Misia's post-premiere party.

17.   BENDOR (1924–1925)

Loelia, the third Duchess of Westminster and later Lady Lindsay of Dowhill, quotes the newspaper accounts of the end of the duke's marriage to Violet Mary Nelson in her memoirs, *Grace and Favour*. Winston Churchill's tribute to the Duke of Westminster was published in the *Manchester Guardian*, July 22, 1953. Morand, *L'Allure de Chanel*, p. 154, quotes CC on life at Eaton Hall, and, p. 149, tells of her meeting the Duke through Vera Bate during the 1923–24 Christmas–New Year's holiday.

Colin Simpson, *Artful Partners*, p. 206, relates the Duveens' sale of Westminster's *Blue Boy*. Noël Coward wrote of the duke's florid handsomeness in a foreword to Loelia's *Grace and Favour*. Morand, *L'Allure de Chanel*, pp. 150–51, quotes CC's "Let me explain who he was. . . ." Loelia relates the duke's gambling habits and affection for odd animals. Rumors of the Duke of Westminster's marrying CC were widespread. Press speculation in London reached a climax in July 1926 when the P & A Photo Agency reported, "Mme Chanel's name is again linked with the Duke of Westminster." Charles-Roux, *Chanel*, p. 250, tells of Westminster's courtship and CC's meeting with Edward, Prince of Wales; and Galante, p. 119, the prince's "Call me David." Cocteau writes in his *Journal 1942–45*, p. 404, of Westminster suggesting the poet write the history of the duke's dogs. Charles-Roux, *Chanel*, p. 253, quotes CC's wish to shake the hand of the knight in armor at Eaton Hall. Baillén, p. 48, reports CC's story of her boar-hunt accident and return to Paris with monkey and parrot. Galante, p. 117, relates Lifar's comments on sailing with Westminster and CC when she spurned the duke's jewels and threw them overboard.

18.   THE POET (1925–1927)

The author relied on Gérard Bocholier, *Pierre Reverdy*, for the bibliographic notes on the poet and for quotes from his poems. The poem "L'Homme et la nuit" appeared in Reverdy, *Sources du vent: Poèmes* (Geneva: Editions des Trois Collines, 1929). Both Charles-Roux, *Chanel*, p. 261, and Haedrich, p. 116, quote Westminster's comment on Reverdy. Galante, p. 147, cites Lady Abdy's hypothesis that CC made Reverdy her lover in order to make Westminster jealous. The lines from Reverdy's poem are from *Sources du Vent*. Haedrich, p. 117, relates CC's suggestion to Reverdy to write his poems on separate sheets and, like painters, to sign each, and, p. 116, CC's submitting her maxims to Reverdy. Under the heading "Maximes et Sentences," French *Vogue* published CC's aphorisms in its Sept. 1938 issue. CC's "Increase their salaries, are you out of your mind?" was recounted in the *New York Times*'s CC obituary, Jan. 11, 1971. CC's generosity toward artists was as legendary as her parsimony when it came to her own employees. The author interviewed former client Marquise Emmita de la Falaise and model Margot McIntyre-

Greenberg. Galante, p. 93, describes the dismissal of Marie-Louise Deray in 1925, and, pp. 100–101, attorney Robert Chaillet's comment on her financial acumen. Anne Chamberlin in *Ladies' Home Journal*, Oct. 1963, quotes CC's "Stand straight, girl." CC repeated her oft-quoted "If there's no woman there's no dress" to TV interviewer Jacques Chazot in the ORTF broadcast, 1969. *Vogue*, May 1, 1926, published Edward Steichen's photographs of Ina Claire in CC outfits. The "Democracy in Dress" editorial on the future of dressmaking appeared in *Vogue*, Nov. 1, 1925. Galante, p. 108, cites Georges Auric on CC's love for Reverdy. Haedrich, p. 173, quotes CC's "I'm against fashion that doesn't last. . . ."

19.   TO BE A DUCHESS, PERHAPS (1927–1929)

CC's comments on her sports clothes at the opening of her London boutique are quoted by Howell, *In Vogue*, p. 86. Haedrich, p. 106, details CC's repudiation of her much-quoted *mot* that there are a lot of duchesses of Westminster but only one CC. Galante, p. 125, and Baillén, p. 44, detail Mary Westminster's coming-out party and CC's strategy for avoiding the ball. Charles-Roux, *Chanel*, p. 255, Galante, p. 130, and Haedrich, p. 106, report on CC's inability to conceive, Charles-Roux on CC's "humiliating acrobatics." Galante, p. 128, reports Ollivier's running into CC and Westminster in the Bordeaux restaurant and the duke's apparent chiding of CC for not wanting to marry him. Charles-Roux, *Chanel*, p. 256, cites Alphonse's daughters on his visits to Faubourg St. Honoré, and CC writing to Lucien to offer him money to retire. Baillén, p. 52, and Galante, p. 127, relate Westminster's involvement in the remodeling of La Pausa, and, p. 134, Robert Streitz on CC visiting the work site. Martin Gilbert, *Winston S. Churchill*, part III, cites Churchill's Jan. 4, 1922, letter to Clementine Churchill on the Balsans' garden. Bettina Ballard, *In My Fashion*, describes La Pausa. Lifar, p. 93, tells of CC's party after the 1929 *Fils Prodigue* premiere.

20.   DEATH IN VENICE (1929)

Churchill's letter is quoted in Kennett, p. 71. The Adriatic cruise of Bendor, CC, and Misia during the summer of 1929 and the background of the Mdivani family are covered in biographies of CC, Misia, and Diaghilev. Gold and Fizdale, p. 302, describe the beginning of the Jojo-Roossy affair; Gloria Swanson, *Swanson on Swanson*, p. 278, on Hollywood's reservations when it came to the authenticity of the Mdivanis nobility; and Morand in *Venise: Souvenirs*, p. 78, tells of his embarrass-ment at seeing the Serts and Roossadana Mdivani. Steegmuller, *Cocteau*, tells of Cocteau's opium problems and, p. 389, quotes Wesson Bull on the poet pleading with CC for more time with the drug. Sir Francis Rose reminisced about CC in *Vogue*, Dec. 1969. Lifar, pp. 97–100, relates his presence during the last days of Diaghilev's life; Haedrich, p. 96, and Buckle, p. 539, cite the rivalries of Lifar and Kochno, of Diaghilev finding CC and Misia looking so young and so white.

21. CUTTING PRICES (1930–1931)

Martin Battersby, *The Decorative Thirties*, pp. 39–41, discusses the impact of the Depression on the decorative arts. Janet Flanner reported on the impact of the widening Depression on the Paris luxury trade in *The New Yorker*, reprinted in *Paris Was Yesterday: 1925–1939. Collier's*, Apr. 1931, reported Samuel Goldwyn's meeting with CC. His offering her $1 million to come to Hollywood received wide period publicity, including the *New York Times*, Mar. 13, 1931. Charles Spencer, *Erté*, pp. 12–14, covers Erté's early Hollywood years. Haedrich, p. 106, quotes CC's "God knows I wanted love." Baillén, p. 46, quotes Westminster's mother asking CC to marry Bendor. Loelia, p. 159, tells of her being presented to CC in Paris as Westminster's fiancée. Erté's comment on illiterate film stars appeared in the *New York Herald*, Dec. 16, 1925. The *New York Times*, Mar. 5, 1931, covered CC's arrival and quotes her "It's just an invitation. . . ." The *Times*'s interview with CC appeared Mar. 15, 1931. Galante, p. 184, quotes Comtesse de Forceville on CC's chances in Hollywood.

22. HOLLYWOOD (1931–1932)

The author interviewed William Wyler and Jesse Lasky, Jr., on Gold-wyn, his studio and productions in the early 1930s. CC's reception is mentioned in Raczymow, p. 186, and Arthur Marx, *Goldwyn*, p. 176. Galante, p. 189, replicates Erich von Stroheim's "You are a seamstress." Publicity handouts by the Howard Dietz office described CC as "the biggest fashion brain." Baillén, p. 105, quotes CC saying, "The stars are the producers' servants." *Variety* reviewed *Palmy Days*, Sept. 29, 1931, and *Tonight or Never*, Dec. 22, 1931. Galante, p. 192, tells of CC's impressions of the Klein's discount emporium. Morand, *L'Allure de Chanel*, p. 158, quotes CC's remark on Westminster, "With me he learned. . . ." Swanson, p. 429, re-created her dialogue with CC during the *Tonight or Never* wardrobe fittings. The Dec. 22, 1931, issue of *The New Yorker* speculated that Chanel had left Hollywood because her dresses were not sensational enough. *Variety* reviewed *The Greeks Had a Word for It*, Feb. 9, 1932.

23.   COMPETITION (1932–1933)

Morand, *L'Allure de Chanel*, p. 145, quotes CC calling Hollywood the "Mont Saint Michel of tit and tail." *Vogue*, May 1, 1936, published the Steichen photo of Ina Claire in a CC gown and said CC revolutionized Hollywood glamour by dressing the actress in white satin pajamas. CC repeated on a number of occasions, notably in a Jacques Chazot 1969 television interview, that wearing real jewels is "provocative." Flanner's review of CC's jewel display and CC's *mots* on precious stones and fakes appeared in *The New Yorker*, Dec. 14, 1932. Diana Vreeland, *D.V.*, describes CC, p. 130; Mary Harriman's memories of CC in the 1930s are quoted in *Vogue*, Dec. 1969. Colette's portrait of CC appears in *Prisons et paradis*, pp. 161–62. Elsa Schiaparelli, in *Shocking Life*, p. 33, says, "Good design is always on a tightrope. . . ." Yves Saint Laurent quoted to the author Schiaparelli's *mot* about CC having to use the "back door" to the Ritz. Photographer Horst P. Horst repeated CC's most-quoted line that Schiaparelli is "that Italian woman who makes dresses." Galante, p. 124, quotes CC's assertion that everything she fashioned was copied and Elsa Schiaparelli's retort, "What I create is inimitable." René de Chambrun told the author of how he met CC and became her lawyer.

24. IRIBE (1933–1935)

Paul Iribe's background, Hollywood years, and triumphs in Paris as advertising designer, cartoonist, editor, decorator, and editor are detailed in a number of 1930s memoirs, including those of Misia Sert, Serge Lifar, and Jean Giraudoux, as well as in Raymond Bachollet, Daniel Bordet, and Anne-Claude Lelieur, *Iribe*. Galante, p. 161, quotes Lifar's "He dominated her, and that she couldn't take. . . ." Palmer White, *Poiret le magnifique*, p. 104, details Iribe's work for Poiret. Colette, *Lettres à Marguerite Moreno*, p. 122, contains her description of him as "a Basque, chubby as a capon." Morand, *L'Allure de Chanel*, p. 103, quotes CC on Iribe's criticism of her life-style. Bachollet, Bordet, and Lelieur, p. 203, detail Iribe and CC's excursions and the onset of his ill-health. Pierre-Olivier Walzer, *Littérature française: Le 20è siècle*, Vol. 1: *(1896–1920)*, p. 112, classifies *Le Témoin* among the "presse d'opinion" and Iribe among the leading caricaturists. British *Vogue* comments on CC's 1934 look quoted in Howell, p. 137. Colette's letter dated Mar. 15, 1933, and published in *Lettres à Marguerite Moreno*, p. 232, mentions her apprehension at hearing of CC's plans to marry Iribe.

25. TRAGEDY AT PLAY (1935–1936)

Charles-Roux, *Chanel*, p. 292, cites CC's reasons for dismissing Joseph Leclerc, her butler since 1918. Baillén, pp. 14–15, reports CC's eating habits and "I don't like food that talks back to you. . . ." Horst told the author of his meetings with CC. Howell, p. 116, repeats British *Vogue*'s description of La Pausa. Gaia Servadio, *Luchino Visconti*, p. 50, quotes Visconti calling CC "La Belle Dame sans Merci." Bachollet, Bordet, and Lelieur, p. 210, and Baillén, p. 53, tell of Iribe's 1935 collapse and death on CC's tennis court.

26. POPULAR FRONT (1935–1936)

Vogue, Mar. 15, 1936, covered the Paris couture and Chanel-Schiaparelli rivalry. Battersby, pp. 210–11, details the Schiaparelli fashion. William L. Shirer, *The Collapse of the Third Republic*, pp. 268–312, delineates the Popular Front election victory, the investiture of Léon Blum's socialist coalition and reform program. Keystone Press Agency photos show the June 6, 1936, Chanel strikers in front of 31 Rue Cambon. Chambrun told the author of his counseling CC during the strike against the House of Chanel, and his observation about industry prima donnas. Battersby, p. 210, tells of the Schiaparelli-Dali collaboration. Charles-Roux, *Chanel*, p. 299, quotes CC's bitterness against her workers and resentment against the "madness" of 1936.

27.   *A BRAVE FACE* (1937–1939)

Ragna Fischer told the author of the differences between the Chanel and Schiaparelli collection shows. Vreeland, pp. 95–96, describes wearing both Schiaparelli and Chanel. In an Apr. 17, 1942, entry in his *Journal 1942-45*, Cocteau notes how he reminded CC of her dinner at the Ritz in late 1936 at which Winston Churchill got drunk and lamented Edward VIII's decision to marry Wallis Simpson. British *Vogue* reviewed the 1937–38 Paris collections and sex appeal theme in its Aug. 1938 issue. Steegmuller, p. 428, reports Cocteau's love affair with Marcel Khill and CC's continued support of the poet. Morand, *L'Allure de Chanel*, pp. 110–11, cites CC's denunciation of homosexuals in the fashion trade. Shirer, pp. 307–9, details Léon Blum's desire to exercise power within the framework of capitalism. Baillén, p. 54, tells of CC's missed affair with Harrison Williams. The costume balls were covered by the fashion press. Photos by Roger Schall of CC with Stravinsky, Bérard, and Dali appeared in *Vogue*, May 15, 1938. Lifar, p. 156, mentions his escorting CC to Ambassador William Bullitt's fête; Charles Higham, *The Duchess of Windsor*, p. 262, and Howell, p. 117, describe the Lady Mendl Versailles party. *Le Figaro*'s Augustin Dabadie told the author of CC's pro-Churchill sentiments and her comparing the British leader to "one of those big dolls. . . ." Gold and Fizdale, p. 334, detail the illness of Roossy Sert and CC's persuading her to go to Switzerland for treatment. Baillén, p. 160, quotes CC on the origin of the bruises Roossy shows CC on the train. *Vogue*, Mar. 1, 1939, reviewed the Paris collections under the headline: "Out of the Paris Openings a New Breath of Life—the Air of Innocence."

28.   CLOSING THE HOUSE OF CHANEL (1939–1940)

Haedrich, p. 127, cites CC on her disappearing personnel Sept. 2, 1939. Reverdy's letter approving her decision to close the house is published in *En Vrac—Notes*, p. 32. Charles-Roux, *Chanel*, p. 307, quotes from CC's Oct. 1939 letter to Lucien and in a footnote notes that the letter, as all the remittances to the brothers, was addressed from 160 Boulevard Malesherbes, the apartment she had kept since Balsan gave it to her to open her first millinery shop. *Vogue*, Jan. 1, 1940, published a "Life in Paris Now" article by the Duchesse d'Ayen, mentioning CC's remodeling of her Ritz Hotel suite. Shirer, p. 785, tells of Churchill's Loire meeting with the Reynaud administration, and the prime minister's aside to Darlan. Lifar, pp. 225–28, describes Hitler's June 1940 visit to the Paris Opéra; Gold and Fizdale, p. 357, cite Lifar's telling how he was fondled by Hitler. Bullitt's dispatches from Vichy to Roosevelt and Secretary of State Cordell Hull are quoted in Orville Bullitt, *For the President, Personal and Secret*, pp. 481–87. Haedrich, pp. 128–29, quotes CC on L'Exode, her and Marie-Louise Bousquet's return to Paris via Vichy, and, pp. 130–31, CC's giving money to a supposedly injured boy in Bourbon-L'Archambault.

29.   SPATZ (1940–1943)

CC described the German occupation of the Ritz and her own return to Paris at the end of Aug. 1940 on several occasions. Haedrich, p. 129, quotes her on her need to clean up before seeing the *Kommandantur*, Charles-Roux, *Chanel*, p. 319, on German soldiers buying No. 5 at 31 Rue Cambon, and Lifar, p. 230, of the Free French condemning him to death on London Radio, and, p. 242, how in Vichy Pierre Laval told him to look after Chanel. Haedrich, pp. 137–38, delineates Hans von Dincklage's background, including his involvement with a Parisian lady not 100 percent Aryan, and quotes CC's "He isn't German, his mother was English." Haedrich, p. 139, and Charles-Roux, *Chanel*, pp. 324–27, recount the career of Rittmeister Theodor Momm and his intervention on behalf of André Palasse. Gerhard Heller, *Un Allemand à Paris, 1940–1944*, p. 62, records Marie-Louise Bousquet's "Thursdays." Gold and Fizdale, pp. 340 and 359, detail Sert's wartime record and his knowledge of rival spy nests in neutral Madrid, and quote from Boulos Ristelhueber's unpublished "Journal." Haedrich, p. 138, tells of Dincklage and CC speaking English together. Galante, p. 212, reports Dincklage and CC's efforts on behalf of Serge Voronov. Jean Cocteau's entire *Journal, 1942–45* chronicles Parisian attitudes during the Occupation. Cocteau mentions CC a dozen times, including the Mar. 1942 rumors that they would get married. Galante, pp. 213–14, and Charles-Roux, *Chanel,* p. 320, relate CC's efforts to seat Georges Madoux on the Parfums Chanel board, and Raymond Bollack's countermoves and imposition of Félix Amiot. Charles-Roux, *Chanel,* p. 314, terms Dincklage an Abwehr spy; Haedrich, p. 137, assumes Spatz was little more than an administrator. Galante, p. 210, cites the Deuxième Bureau file on Dincklage.

30.   HOW WILL IT ALL END? (1943)

The author relied on interviews with René Chambrun and recently declassified British M-16 archives, reported both by Anthony Cave Brown in *"C": The Secret Life of Sir Stewart Menzies* and to the author by Charles Higham, for reconstruction of the details of CC's 1943 "peace mission." Chambrun quoted from a letter received after the war from Momm on her outlining of the plan. Charles-Roux, *Chanel,* p. 326, cites CC's imaginary conversation with Winston Churchill and Momm's mission to Berlin. Foreign Secretary Lord Halifax told a May 26, 1940, War Cabinet meeting the issue now was "not so much . . . a question of imposing a complete defeat upon Germany, but of safeguarding the independence of our own Empire and if possible that of France." Higham, p. 274, relates Churchill's reservations regarding Sir Samuel Hoare's peace initiatives; John Toland, *Adolf Hitler,* p. 853, quotes the Führer's "We shall win in the end," and Ribbentrop's expressing the hope to Fritz Hesse that the British would not deliver Germany into the hands of the Russians. Walter Schellenberg gave himself a determining role in the subversion swirling around Hitler in *The Labyrinth.* Brown, pp. 565–66, tells of Sir Steward Menzies's theory that Schellenberg's use of CC was a way of making Churchill aware of the intrigue inside the German goverment. Charles-Roux, *Chanel,* p. 332, cites CC's letter to Vera Bate and the details of Bate's transfer to Paris.

31. *OPERATION MODELLHUT* (1943)

The historic 1943 Teheran conference and Churchill's subsequent illness are described in *Keep on Dancing*, Sarah Churchill's memoirs of her wartime trip there with her father, and in Martin Gilbert, *Winston S. Churchill*, part VII, p. 1178. The description of Madrid during the war derives in part from José Sert's eyewitness accounts as reported by Gold and Fizdale, p. 341, and Lifar, p. 330. Charles-Roux's narrative, *Chanel*, pp. 339–40, of CC and Vera Bate-Lombardi's approach to Ambassador Samuel Hoare is contradicted by Brown, p. 566, who quotes Schellenberg in his Nuremberg trial interrogations as saying the reason Operation *Modellhut* fell apart was that Bate-Lombardi told everybody CC was a German spy. CC's letter to Vera is reproduced in Charles-Roux, *Chanel*, pp. 342–43. British archives and Nuremberg Trial debriefing of Walter Schellenberg established CC's presence in Berlin during the winter of 1943–44. Cocteau's *Journal*, pp. 481–87, tells of the efforts to save Max Jacob. Lifar, p. 340, tells of the fears of collaborators and his seeking refuge at 31 Rue Cambon. David Pryce-Jones, *Paris in the Third Reich*, tells of the last days of the German Occupation; Gold and Fizdale, p. 351, of José Sert's Liberation party and who attended; Lifar, p. 341, of his hiding from the Free French in Chanel's apartment. Raymond Aron, *Memoires*, p. 270, tells of de Gaulle's motorcade along Rue de Rivoli.

32. *EXILE* (1944–1946)

CC's reticence in talking about her 1944 arrest allowed biographers a certain latitude. Charles-Roux, *Chanel*, p. 345, describes the arrival of the FFI at the Ritz, Haedrich, p. 139, establishes part of the interrogation dialogue, and Lifar, p. 98, describes her queenly demeanor. Cecil Beaton, *Memoirs of the 40s*, p. 20, has CC's reply, "Really, sir, a woman of my age. . . ." Galante, p. 217, contrasts CC's wartime conduct with that of anything-goes couturiers Lelong, Grès, and Balenciaga. CC's dislike of de Gaulle is well documented in her 1960s press conferences. "They made me laugh" and references to the ease with which she obtained British and U.S. visas are cited in Haedrich, p. 142. Details of the payments made to the Germans for the upkeep of the Duke and Duchess of Windsor's French properties during the Occupation are given in Higham, pp. 318–

19, and, p. 358, speculation of what would have happened to CC had she been forced to stand trial. Malcolm Muggeridge, *The Infernal Grove*, p. 242, tells of meeting CC; Lifar, pp. 348–49, describes how Jojo Sert pretended not to know him and his own arrest, and Manuel Burrus, *Paul Morand*, pp. 148–59, Morand's legal difficulties. Details of Schellenberg's peace overtures appear in Alan Bullock, *Hitler: A Study in Tyranny*; Schellenberg's surrender in Sweden at war's end appears in Count Folke Bernadotte, *The Curtain Falls*, p. 332. Bullock quotes from Nuremberg Documents, Reitsch 3734-PS, on Hitler's unlimited faith in Himmler and the Führer's reaction to Himmler's negotiations. The author's conversations with René de Chambrun and Léon Lévine, and Lee Israel, *Estée Lauder*, p. 27, detail the Wertheimers' American success. Galante, p. 225, reports the Wertheimers' settlement offer, CC's rejection, and cites CC's wish to pull out entirely from Les Parfums Chanel and Chambrun's suggestion of a lawsuit. Haedrich, p. 149, reports CC's 1946 sales in her own boutique of her Swiss-made Mademoiselle Chanel No. 5, the Wertheimers' alleging counterfeit perfume, and seizure at 31 Rue Cambon. Galante, p. 226, quotes Chambrun on CC shipping samples to Samuel Goldwyn, Bernard Gimbel, and Neiman Marcus. CC's nephew André Palasse and family's coming to Switzerland is described in Galante, p. 221. In his introduction to *L'Allure de Chanel*, p. 8, Morand tells of his and CC's exile in Switzerland and quotes her "I have no regrets."

33.   YEARS OF OBLIVION (1947–1954)

Chambrun and *Forbes*, Apr. 3, 1989, concur on the terms of the 1947 out-of-court settlement. Galante, p. 226, quotes Wertheimer's and his lawyers' "But what does she want?" Chambrun told the author of the champagne celebration at the Ritz and of Pierre Wertheimer sealing the peace by coming to Lausanne. Saint Laurent told the author of Christian Dior's Feb. 12, 1947, New Look triumph. Galante, p. 232, reports CC's reaction at meeting Christian Bérard and his retort. Emmita de la Falaise told the author of women throwing themselves on clothes "like hungry beasts." Thomas Quinn Curtiss told the author of CC's meeting Charles Chaplin and questioning him on his career; Baillén, p. 130, quotes CC's asking Chaplin how he discovered the Little Tramp. Horst told the author of CC's affection for travel and advice about tips to Maggy van Zuylen, and, during her trip to New York her visit to his Long Island weekend home. Servadio, p. 223, mentions Luchino Visconti's visits with CC. Gold and Fizdale, pp. 360–63, delineate Misia's last years. Paul Claudel notes his paying respect to Misia Sert on Oct. 15, 1950, in his *Journal*, vol. II, p. 750. Dolly Radziwill's description is quoted in Harold Acton, *Nancy Mitford: A Memoir*, p. 147. Fortassier, p. 209, mentions Andrée Fraigneau's attempt at collaboration on CC's memoirs. The author obtained details of the liberated Schellenberg's blackmail of CC from Munich filmmaker Peter Gehrig. Jacques Lenoir told the author the Freudian explanation for the prominence of male designers. *Vogue*, Aug. 1953, reports CC's overseeing the redecoration of Les Parfums Chanel New York offices; Beaton, p. 45, Mona Williams's marriage to Eddie Bismarck. Howell, p. 227, quotes British *Vogue*'s "Where has the waist gone?"

34.   COMEBACK (1953–1954)

Guy de Rothschild, *The Whims of Fortune*, and Haedrich, p. 157, tell of Rothschild's whirlwind courtship of Hélène van Zuylen and CC's remodeling of the new bride's ball gown. Galante, p. 239, details Pierre Wertheimer's 1953 visit with CC in Lausanne and, pp. 239–40, her wish to launch a new perfume. CC's fashion thinking and reasons for reopening the House of Chanel were outlined in a series of fashion press interviews, including a lengthy feature in U.S. *Vogue*, Jan. 1954. Clementine Churchill's *Memoirs*, p. 608, mentions CC's selling of Roquebrune to Churchill literary agent Emery Reves and Sir Winston's staying at the Riviera house. The author's interviews with Yves Saint Laurent and Howell, *In Vogue*, pp. 208–9, are the basis for descriptions of changes in the fashion industry in the mid-1950s. Both Galante, p. 242, and Haedrich, p. 164, reproduce Carmel Snow's wire to CC, and, with slight variations, French translations of CC's reply. Chambrun told the author of the contractual agreements with Wertheimer. Galante, p. 244, quotes CC's, "Anything over fifteen million would be an exaggeration." Details of couturiers' work methods come from the author's interviews with Yvonne Deslandres and Saint Laurent. Both Baillén, p. 76, and Haedrich, p. 221, quote CC's

"Couture isn't art, it's a business." The *Vogue*, Feb. 15, 1954, issue described her new 31 Rue Cambon quarters. *Le Figaro, Elle, Paris-Match, New York Herald-Tribune*, and *France-Soir* published "exclusive" CC interviews in Nov. and Dec. 1953. Hugo Vickers, *Cecil Beaton*, p. 552, tells of Beaton's observing and photographing CC and her collection, and June Capel Osborn's flirtation with him. The Paris fashion press reported the winter 1953–54 details in the House of Chanel relaunch. The Paris and London daily press describe in great detail the Feb. 5, 1954, collection presentation, and the reaction to the CC comeback. *France-Soir* published CC's reaction in its Feb. 7, 1954, issue. Karl Lagerfeld and Saint Laurent provided the author with details of presentation differences; Galante, p. 255, quotes Chaillet on CC's reaction, her feeling that her clients were too smart to stay away. Both Charles-Roux, *Chanel*, p. 367, and Galante, p. 254, report Wertheimer's visit to CC; Chambrun and Robert Badinter the details of the renegotiated contract; Alain Wertheimer, his grandfather's relationship with CC; *Life* published its review in the Mar. 1, 1954, issue.

35. UNMISTAKABLE INFLUENCE (1954–1958)

The overview and sense of history of the CC comeback rely on the author's interviews with Francine Crescent and Colette Gros. Saint Laurent told the author of his years with Dior, the division of designers into two camps, and the economics behind the ready-to-wear success. *Vogue*, Mar. 1, 1954, analyzed the surprise strength of Chanel. Galante, p. 250, recounts the Marlene Dietrich anecdote, and Badinter on the Wertheimers' decision to buy CC out. Charles-Roux, *Chanel*, p. 308, details the visit of the Valleraugue nieces; Galante, p. 323, the relationship between CC and Gabrielle Labrunie. Augustin Labadie provided the author with the details of CC's fight with the Chambre Syndicale, and Saint Laurent the circumstances of Dior's death and his own takeover of the House of Dior. The *Elle* cover with CC and Suzy Parker was published in Sept. 1957. *The New Yorker*, Sept. 28, 1957, published its interview with CC. Vreeland, pp. 132–33, tells of her dinner party and CC speaking with Helena Rubinstein. Eugenia Sheppard's review of the Jan. 20, 1958, show appeared in the *New York Herald Tribune* Jan. 31, *France Dimanche*'s item on a baby boy names Yves Feb. 1. *Vogue*, Sept. 1958, politely reviewed Saint Laurent's 1958–59 collection for Dior. Saint Laurent told the author of CC's much-quoted line about his excellent taste in copying her. *Vogue*, Mar. 15, 1959, analyzed "Chanel Power" and the notion of wearers being more important than the clothes. Howell, p. 246, cites British *Vogue*'s assessment of CC's importance four years after her comeback. Thomas Quinn Curtiss told the author of CC's luncheon habits at the Ritz. Chanel Information published a summary of CC's maxims. Charles-Roux, *Chanel*, p. 370, reports the details of Reverdy's will and death. The author's interviews with Saint Laurent, André Courrèges, Karl Lagerfeld, France de Dieuleveult, Crescent, and Deslandres form the basis of the overview of the 1960s fashion and CC's position in it. Haedrich, p. 138, quotes CC's cruder maxim on a thirty-year-old woman's choice. CC's comments on the First Lady's wearing CC in Dallas in 1953 were recounted in the *New York Times*'s CC obituary, Jan. 11, 1971. Lifar reports CC's attitude toward the death of Jean Cocteau; her sarcastic remarks on the poet were told to Baillén, p. 144, and CC's reverence for Reverdy by Charles-Roux, *Chanel*, p. 214.

36. YOUTHQUAKES (1960–1968)

Diana Vreeland reports the eighty-year-old CC's vitality in *D.V.*, pp. 128–29. The *Time*, Jan. 25, 1971, obituary estimated CC's income. The basis for speculation about CC's lesbian tendencies and her work methods with models are the author's interviews with former *Women's Wear Daily* Paris correspondent Thelma Sweetinburgh, former models Margot McIntyre-Greenberg, Jackie Rogers, Colette Gros, and Claude Leusse. Haedrich, p. 182, quotes CC's objections to rumors of her being a lesbian, "You must be crazy. . . ." Morand, *L'Allure de Chanel*, p. 130, quotes CC's dislike of women, and Barbara Seaman, *Lovely Me*, pp. 244 and 293, tells of Jacqueline Susann's reaction to CC's alleged sexual overtures to her. André Malraux and Sophie de Vilmorin told the author of Louise de Vilmorin's work on a CC biography. The book Vilmorin suggested to CC was Gervas Huxley, *Victorian Duke*. Haedrich, p. 209, quotes CC's answer to Vilmorin, "My dear, you know I'm illiterate." *Forbes*, Apr. 3, 1989, cover story on Alain Wertheimer recounted the Wertheimer family story since the 1965 death of Pierre Wertheimer. McIntyre-Greenberg told the author of working as a free-lance model in Paris in the 1960s.

Haedrich, p. 181, quotes CC on boring young aristocratic women becoming models. Galante, p. 284, describes CC goading her models after long working hours. CC told Jacques Chazot's television audience, "There are days when I want to drop everything. . . ," and defined her sense of elegance. Baillén, p. 76, reports CC's approval of models wearing her clothes from her collection off-hours, and on CC's arthritis and regimen. Haedrich, p. 185, reports CC's preference for German models. Jeanne Moreau told *Cosmopolitan*, July 1966, of deserting Chanel fashion for Pierre Cardin. Saint Laurent and Deslandres told the author of CC's comments on fellow designers; Galante, p. 272, on her comments on Pierre Cardin and Pierre Balmain. Dabadie told the author of the CC–Cristóbal Balenciaga relationship; Galante, p. 275, Balenciaga's anger at CC, "I was furious." Antoine Livio wrote to the author about Serge Lifar's sixtieth birthday luncheon with CC in 1960. Saint Laurent and Courrèges told of Balenciaga's distaste for the 1960s fashion. Mamie van Doren, *Playing the Field*, pp. 197–98, describes CC in 1964. CC's observations on modern women and men, marriage, social mores, and fashion are her pre-collection press conferences, Feb. 5, 1966, and Feb. 13, 1967. CC's comments at her Feb. 13, 1967, press conference are verbatim.

37.   COCO OR KATE (1968)

Frederick Brisson told the author the details of his approach to and negotiations with CC and Wertheimer over the rights to her life story and the Broadway *Coco* production; supplemented by Vickers, *Cecil Beaton*, p. 539, Rosalind Russell and Chris Chase, *Life Is a Banquet*, pp. 226–28, and Anne Edwards, *A Remarkable Woman: A Biography of Katharine Hepburn*, pp. 361–65. Hervé Mille told the author of his reaction to Lerner's synopsizing of CC's life, "That's the theme of a tragedy," and of CC's suggestion that the musical open with her father bending over her crib. Vickers, p. 539, quotes Beaton's diary, Feb. 3, 1967, "Chanel is slowly going mad," and Beaton's letter to Diana Vreeland, June 30, 1969, saying that "by 3:00 P.M., she was galvanized." Russell and Chase, p. 227, tell of Hepburn's meeting with CC and CC's remark about the actress's age; and James Spada, *Hepburn: Her Life in Pictures*, p. 172, Hepburn's "Now I *knew* I could play her." Haedrich, p. 223, and Baillén, p. 175, remark on CC's growing solitude and her hating Sundays, and Baillén, p. 179, CC's remarks on horses. Christian Marquant, Lilou

Grumbach's brother, told the author of CC's relations with her press secretary and her resentment of happy couples. In her foreword to *Chanel solitaire*, p. 7, Baillén writes she found CC "so passionate, so captivating." Sophie de Vilmorin told the author of CC's last years, CC's idle and difficult Sundays. Baillén, p. 164, and Haedrich, p. 205, quote CC on her childhood sleepwalking. Baillén, p. 169, tells of CC's threats to move out of the Ritz because of odors, her fall in the street, and "horror" of smelling other people's food. Frances Patiky Stein told the author of seeing CC in the late 1960s. *Vogue*, Dec. 1969, headlined its pre-premiere *Coco* comment: "Chanel and Hepburn, Les Grandes Mam'zelles, stars of 'Coco.' " Beaton wrote of his criticism of *Coco* and his premonitions of "appalling notices" in a Nov. 1969 letter to secretary Eileen Hose. The Parisian press reported CC's mini-stroke and inability to attend the Broadway premiere of *Coco*.

38. ONE HUNDRED, FOREVER (1968–1970)

The *New York Times* and the *New York Post* reviewed *Coco* on Dec. 28, 1969. Baillén, p. 171, records CC's complaints about medical costs at the American Hospital in Neuilly; p. 172, Lifar's suggestion of Swedish therapy; and, p. 140, tells of the lawyer's visit and CC's "He's a spy. . . ." Butler François Mironnet told the author of CC's relationship with Badinter and of his own importance in CC's life during her last years. TV producer Jacques Trebouta gave the author the details of the 1969 television taping. Haedrich, p. 231, reports CC's instructions to Lilou Grumbach and Mironnet to take her to Lausanne for burial when she died. The author relied on interviews with Matthias Auer and Alfred Hier, contemporary trustees of the Coga Foundation, for the details of CC's setting up of her Swiss and Liechtenstein tax shelters, and text of her 1965 will. Pierre Bergé told the author of CC's overtures to him to take over her company. Haedrich, p. 223, notes CC's offer to her to "codirect" her empire. *Ladies' Home Journal* carried Anne Chamberlin's reportage, Oct. 1963. Baillén, p. 144, reports CC's retort when Beaton tried to get Chanels for the Victoria and Albert Museum exhibition. The author details the *Women's Wear Daily* maxi-versus-mini controversy in *Yves Saint Laurent*, pp. 180–81. *L'Express* magazine of June 16, 1989, cites Jacques Polge on No. 19 ingredients and cutbacks in flower cultivation; the *International Herald Tribune*, the launch of the Chanel No. 19 perfume.

39. *DEATH ON A SUNDAY* (1971)

Mironnet told the author of CC's last week. Baillén, p. 208, quotes CC's loathing of Christmas and New Year's. Galante, p. 325, quotes CC's reflection to her grandniece, "All things told. . . ." The Parisian press and United Press International quoted Jeanne Céline on CC's last hours, her last words, and on Jan. 10, 1971, her death at the Ritz Hotel.

AFTERLIFE (1971–1990)

Saint Laurent described the Jan. 11, 1971, funeral in the Madeleine Church. The *New York Times*, Feb. 8, 1971, covered the posthumous collection presentation, and reported that people wondered how long the workrooms could carry on "without the iron hand of Mademoiselle." The author interviewed Matthias Auer in Zurich in 1988. Mironnet told the author of being named heir to the CC fortune and of the disappearance of CC's alleged last will and testament. Howell, p. 306, mentions Beaton's Victoria and Albert Museum show. Chanel, Inc.'s acquisition of Holland & Holland was announced in the *New York Times*, July 11, 1989. *Forbes*'s April 3, 1989, cover story details Alain Wertheimer's taking over the direction of Chanel, Inc. and the reorganization of the firm. *Variety*, *Hollywood Reporter* reviewed *Chanel solitaire*, the movie, Oct. 7, 1981; *Los Angeles Times*, Oct. 16, 1981. The *New York Times* and *Chicago Tribune* reported the hiring of Carole Bouquet as Chanel No. 5's, "new woman." *The New Yorker*, Feb. 29, 1989, published Holly Brubach's CC reassessment; *Forbes*, Apr. 3, 1989, the Chanel, Inc. marketing strategies and price ranges. The *San Francisco Chronicle*, July 12, 1989, reported on "a Chanel-crazed world" and three-to-a-customer rationing of Chanel handbags. The *New York Times*, July 26, 1989, quoted Ellin Salzman of Saks Fifth Avenue as calling Lagerfeld's winter 1989–90 collection "probably the best Chanel Karl has ever done."

Bibliography

It would not be practical to list all the books consulted in the preparation of this biography. Here, however, is a list of the particularly useful books, the ones from which extracts are quoted and a few rarer ones.

Acton, Harold. *Nancy Mitford: A Memoir.* New York: Harper & Row, 1975.
Albères, R. M. *Histoire du roman moderne.* Paris: Albin Michel, 1962.
Alençon, Emilienne. *Sous le Masque.* Paris: E. Sansot, 1918.
Aron, Raymond. *Mémoires.* Paris: Julliard, 1983.

Bachollet, Raymond, Daniel Bordet, and Anne-Claude Lelieur. *Iribe.* Paris: Denoel, 1982.
Baillén, Claude. *Chanel solitaire.* Paris: Gallimard, 1971. New York: Quadrangle, 1974, English translation by Barbara Bray.
Ballard, Bettina, *In My Fashion.* London, 1960.
Battersby, Martin. *The Decorative Thirties.* New York: Whitney Library of Design, 1988.
Beaton, Cecil. *Memoirs of the 40s.* New York: McGraw-Hill, 1972.
Bernadotte, Count Folke. *The Curtain Falls.* New York: Harper, 1945.
Bibesco, Princess Marthe de. *Noblesse de robes.* Paris: Grasset, 1928.
Bocholier, Gérard. *Pierre Reverdy: Le Phare obscur.* Seyssel, France: Editions du Champ Vallon, 1984.

Brown, Anthony Cave. *"C": The Secret Life of Sir Stewart Menzies.* New York: Macmillan, 1987.

Brown, Frederick. *An Impersonation of Angels: A Biography of Jean Cocteau.* New York: Viking Press, 1968.

Buckle, Richard. *Diaghilev.* New York: Atheneum, 1984.

Bullitt, Orville. *For the President, Personal and Secret.* Boston: Houghton Mifflin, 1972.

Bullock, Alan. *Hitler: A Study in Tyranny.* New York: Harper & Row, 1962.

Burrus, Manual. *Paul Morand: Voyageur du 20e siècle.* Paris: Librarie Seguier, 1986.

Capel, Arthur. *Reflections on Victory and a Project for the Federation of Governments.* London: Werner Laurie, 1917.

Carey, Gary. *Katharine Hepburn: A Hollywood Yankee.* New York: St. Martin's Press, 1983.

Chalon, Jean. *Florence et Louise les magnifiques: Florence Jay-Gould et Louise de Vilmorin.* Monaco: Le Rocher, 1987.

Chanel: Ouverture Pour la mode à Marseille. Texts by Germain Viatte, Edmonde Charles-Roux, Catherine Ormen, Claudette Joannis, and Karl Lagerfeld. Marseille: Musée de Marseille, 1989.

Charles-Roux, Edmonde. *Chanel.* Translated by Nancy Amphoux. New York: Alfred A. Knopf, 1975.

——. *Le Temps Chanel.* Paris: Editions du Chêne, 1979.

Churchill, Sarah. *Keep on Dancing.* New York: Coward, McCann & Geoghegan, 1981.

Claudel, Paul. *Journal.* Vol. II. Paris: Gallimard, 1969.

Cocteau, Jean. *Journal, 1942–45.* Paris: Gallimard, 1989.

Colette. *Lettres à Hélène Picard: Lettres é Marguerite Moreno.* Paris: Flammarion, 1988.

——. *Prisons et paradis.* Paris: J. Ferenczi & Fils, 1932.

Craft, Robert. *Stravinsky: Chronicle of a Friendship.* New York: Alfred A. Knopf, 1972.

Decaux, Alain. *Les Heures brillantes de la Côte d'Azur.* Paris: Librairie Académique Perrin, 1964.

Delaunay, Sonia. *Nous irons jusqu'au soleil.* Paris: Robert Laffont, 1978.

Desanti, Dominique. *La Femme au temps des Années Folles*. Paris: Stock/ Laurence Pernoud, 1984.

Deslandres, Yvonnes, and Florence Muller. *Histoire de la mode*. Paris: Flammarion, 1978.

Dictionnaire du Cinéma. Paris: Seghers, 1962.

Edwards, Anne. *A Remarkable Woman: A Biography of Katharine Hepburn*. New York: William Morrow, 1985.

Erlanger, Philippe. *Clemenceau*. Paris: Grasset/Paris-Match, 1968.

Flanner, Janet. *Darlinghissima: Letters to a Friend*. Edited by Natalia Danesi Murray. New York: Random House, 1985.

———. *Paris Was Yesterday: 1925–1939*. Edited by Irving Drutman. New York: Viking Press, 1972.

Fortassier, Rose. *Les Ecrivains français et la mode*. Paris: Presses Universitaires de France, 1988.

Galante, Pierre. *Les Années Chanel*. Paris: Mercure de France/Paris-Match, 1972.

Gere, Charlotte. *Marie Laurencin*. London: Academy Editions, 1977.

Gilbert, Martin. *Winston S. Churchill: Road to Victory, 1941–45*. Boston: Houghton Mifflin, 1986.

Gold, Arthur, and Robert Fizdale. *Misia: The Life of Misia Sert*. Paris: Gallimard, 1981. English edition, New York: Alfred A. Knopf, 1979.

Goudeket, Maurice. *Close to Colette*. New York: Farrar, Straus and Cudahy, 1957.

Gramont, Elisabeth de. *Mémoires*. Volume 2: *Les Marronniers en fleurs*. Volume 4: *Chimie sociale*. Paris: Grasset, 1929 and 1934.

Haedrich, Marcel. *Coco Chanel*. Paris: Pierre Belfond, 1987.

Hartwig, Julia. *Apollinaire*. Paris: Mercure de France, 1972.

Heller, Gerhard. *Un Allemand à Paris, 1940–1944*. Paris: Editions du Seuil, 1981.

Higham, Charles. *The Duchess of Windsor*. New York: McGraw-Hill, 1988.

Howell, Georgina. *In Vogue*. New York: Schocken Books, 1976.

Huxley, Gervas. *Victorian Duke*. London: Oxford University Press, 1940.

Israel, Lee. *Estée Lauder: Beyond the Magic.* New York: Macmillan, 1985.

Kennett, Frances. *Coco: The Life and Loves of Gabrielle Chanel.* London: Victor Gollancz, 1989.

Kochno, Boris. *Diaghilev and the Ballets Russes.* New York: Harper & Row, 1970.

Leymarie, Jean. *Chanel.* Geneva: Skira, 1987.

Lifar, Serge. *Ma Vie.* Paris: Julliard, 1965.

Madsen, Axel. *Gloria and Joe: The Star-Crossed Love Affair of Gloria Swanson and Joe Kennedy.* New York: Arbor House/ William Morrow, 1988.

———. *Yves Saint Laurent.* New York: Delacorte Press, 1979.

Marx, Arthur. *Goldwyn: A Biography of the Man Behind the Myth.* New York: Norton, 1976.

Massie, Robert K. *Nicholas and Alexandra: An Intimate Account of the Last of the Romanovs and the Fall of Imperial Russia.* New York: Atheneum, 1967.

Milbank, Caroline Rennolds. *Couture: The Great Designers.* New York: Stewart, Tabori & Chang, 1988.

Morand, Paul. *L'Allure de Chanel.* Paris: Hermann, 1976.

———. *Journal d'un attaché d'ambassade, 1916–17.* Paris: La Table Ronde, 1948.

———. *Venise: Souvenirs.* Paris: Gallimard, 1971.

Muggeridge, Malcolm. *The Infernal Grove: Chronicles of Wasted Time.* New York: William Morrow, 1974.

Ormen, Catherine. *Chanel: Ouverture pour la mode à Marseille.* Marseille: Musée de Marseille, 1989.

Painter, George D. *Proust: The Later Years.* Boston: Little Brown & Co., 1959 and 1965.

Pearson, John. *The Sitwells: A Family's Biography.* New York: Harcourt Brace Jovanovich, 1978.

Poiret, Paul. *En Habillant l'époque.* Paris: Grasset, 1930.

Pryce-Jones, David. *Paris in the Third Reich.* New York: Henry Holt, 1981.

Raczymow, Henri. *Maurice Sachs*. Paris: Gallimard, 1988.

Reverdy, Pierre. *En Vrac—Notes*. Monaco: Editions du Rocher, 1956.

———. *Main d'oeuvre*. Paris: Mercure de France, 1949.

Rothschild, Guy de. *The Whims of Fortune: The Memoirs*. New York: Random House, 1985.

Russell, Rosalind, and Chris Chase. *Life Is a Banquet*. New York: Random House, 1977.

Sachs, Maurice. *La Décade de l'illusion*. Paris: Gallimard, 1950.

Seaman, Barbara. *Lovely Me: The Jacqueline Susann Story*. New York: Morrow, 1987.

Sert, Misia. *Misia par Misia*. Paris: Gallimard, 1952.

Servadio, Gaia. *Luchino Visconti: A Biography*. New York: Franklin Watts, 1983.

Schellenberg, Walter. *The Labyrinth*. Introduction by Alan Bullock. Translated by Louis Hagen. New York: Harper, 1957.

Schiaparelli, Elsa. *Shocking Life*. New York: E. P. Dutton, 1954.

Shirer, William L. *The Collapse of the Third Republic: An Inquiry into the Fall of France in 1940*. New York: Simon & Schuster, 1969.

Simpson, Colin. *Artful Partners: Bernard Berenson and Joseph Duveen*. New York: Macmillan, 1986.

Soames, Mary. *Clementine Churchill: The Biography of a Marriage*. Boston: Houghton Mifflin, 1979.

Sokolova, Lydia. *Dancing for Diaghilev*. Edited by Richard Buckle. London: Murray, 1960.

Spada, James. *Hepburn: Her Life in Pictures*. Garden City, N.Y.: Doubleday, 1984.

Spencer, Charles. *Erté*. New York: Potter, 1970.

Stassinopoulos-Huffington, Arianna. *Picasso: Creator and Destroyer*. New York: Simon & Schuster, 1988.

Steegmuller, Francis. *Cocteau: A Biography*. Boston: Atlantic Monthly Press/Little Brown, 1970.

Steele, Valerie, *Paris Fashion: A Cultural History*. New York: Oxford University Press, 1988.

Stravinsky, Igor. *Selected Correspondence*. New York: Alfred A. Knopf, 1984.

Stravinsky, Vera, and Robert Craft. *Stravinsky in Pictures and Documents*. New York: Simon & Schuster, 1978.

Swanson, Gloria. *Swanson on Swanson.* New York: Random House, 1980.

Toland, John. *Adolf Hitler.* Garden City, N.Y.: Doubleday, 1976.

Touzot, Jean. *Jean Cocteau.* Paris: La Manufacture, 1989.

Valois, Ninette de. *Invitation to the Ballet.* London: John Lane/Bodley Head, 1937.

van Doren, Mamie. *Playing the Field.* New York: G. P. Putnam, 1987.

Vickers, Hugo. *Cecil Beaton.* Boston: Little, Brown, 1985.

Vreeland, Diana. *D.V.* New York: Alfred A. Knopf, 1984.

Walzer, Pierre-Olivier. *Littérature française: Le 20è siècle.* Vol. 1: *(1896–1920).* Paris: Arthaud, 1975.

Waugh, Evelyn. *The Letters of Evelyn Waugh.* Edited by Mark Amory. New Haven, Conn.: Ticknor & Fields, 1980.

Westminster, Loelia, Duchess of. *Grace and Favour.* London: Weidenfield & Nicholson, 1961.

White, Palmer. *Poiret le magnifique.* Paris: Payot, 1986.

Index